Inventing Prosperity

Inventing Prosperity

Science, Technology, and the Future of American Innovation

ASHISH ARORA
SHARON BELENZON
ANDREA PATACCONI
JUNGKYU SUH

OXFORD
UNIVERSITY PRESS

OXFORD
UNIVERSITY PRESS

Oxford University Press is a department of the University of Oxford.
It furthers the University's objective of excellence in research, scholarship,
and education by publishing worldwide. Oxford is a registered trademark of
Oxford University Press in the UK and in certain other countries.

Published in the United States of America by Oxford University Press
198 Madison Avenue, New York, NY 10016, United States of America.

CIP data is on file at the Library of Congress.

ISBN 9780197826393

DOI: 10.1093/9780197826393.001.0001

Printed by Sheridan Books, Inc., United States of America

The manufacturer's authorized representative in the EU for product safety is
Oxford University Press España S.A. of Parque Empresarial San Fernando de Henares,
Avenida de Castilla, 2 – 28830 Madrid (www.oup.es/en or product.safety@oup.com).
OUP España S.A. also acts as importer into Spain of products made by the manufacturer.

FSC www.fsc.org MIX Paper | Supporting responsible forestry FSC® C008955

Contents

Preface

This book grew out of a series of questions we have explored over the past decade and a half about how innovation in America is organised. It began when we documented a marked withdrawal from science by large American corporations in the 1980s. The private value attributable to internal scientific research declined, even as the contribution of science to inventions increased. Companies continued to value the "golden eggs" of science but became increasingly unwilling to invest in the "golden goose" itself. In other studies, we documented that when other companies use the science a firm produces, the originating firm's ability to capture returns on its investment shrinks, often leading it to scale back future research.

These findings led us to ask what caused this retreat from industrial research and what that retreat meant for the broader innovation ecosystem. The modern innovation ecosystem gathered much of its strength in the twentieth century from the systematic application of science to technology, often inside corporate laboratories that integrated multiple disciplines at the scale required to solve major technical problems. As these labs withered, the division of innovative labour between universities, startups, and large firms became more pronounced. However, the combination of universities and startups was not always an adequate substitute for corporate labs, particularly in many deep-tech sectors. We came to realise that large firms often anchored the science-based innovation system.

This recognition shaped the next step in our intellectual journey. To understand why companies withdrew from science, we needed to understand why they invested in it in the first place. Our historical research showed that in the early twentieth century, some firms built internal scientific capabilities because invention itself was becoming increasingly dependent on science, but the knowledge they needed was not available from universities. Firms at the forefront of industries such as chemicals, electricity, and telecommunications had to advance scientific knowledge while simultaneously applying it to their inventions.

We then tackled the issue of why corporations continued to expand their scientific investment even as universities became much stronger following World War II. We found that most of the firms that operated industrial research labs after the war did so to absorb scientific breakthroughs produced by universities rather than push the scientific frontier themselves. What changed in the 1980s was a set of institutional and economic reforms that encouraged universities to further develop their discoveries and package them for licensing or commercialisation by startups. This shift created a market for technology that allowed firms to benefit from publicly funded university research without having to maintain expensive in-house scientific teams. For firms whose primary investment in science had been to absorb knowledge produced mainly by universities, the business case for maintaining those capabilities weakened sharply. Indeed, our research showed that corporations withdrew from research in response to the entry of universities into downstream commercialisation. This pattern is consistent with the results of our initial study, which showed that corporate withdrawal from science was privately optimal for firms (as measured by stock market evaluations of firms' scientific capabilities).

As we were carrying out our work on corporate science, new evidence began to accumulate on the nature of science itself. Several studies suggested that scientific research was becoming more incremental and perhaps less important for driving economic growth and productivity. Our research led us to a different conclusion. We did not find that the fundamental importance of science had diminished, nor that the quality of the science being produced had declined. Rather, what had changed was the anchor that once connected science to technology. The translational layer of science had shifted away from large firms that had historically integrated scientific advances into technological breakthroughs and toward startups as the primary vehicle for translation.

Importantly, not all sectors can flourish when translation occurs only through startups. Some fields require scale, capital intensity, long development cycles, and integration across complex supply chains, which are conditions that are often challenging for startups to meet on their own. Understanding this shift and charting ways to rebuild the institutional scaffolding that connects science to innovation are the central tasks of this book.

Thanks and Acknowledgements

We owe a heavy debt to our co-authors whose ideas, data, and critiques shaped the arguments that follow. We are especially grateful to Wes Cohen, whose scholarship helped open our research agenda. We are also thankful our PhD students Larisa Cioaca, Colleen Cunningham, Jay Nagar, Ziv Netserel, Luis Rios, Lia Sheer, Dror Shvadron, and Hansen Zhang and to the many research assistants who built datasets, coded patents, read archives, and pressure-tested early drafts. Colleagues across universities and agencies shared their time and knowledge. We are also indebted to Dan Gross, Matt Marx, Petra Moser, and Yishay Yafeh, whose data were instrumental to our analyses. Many managers and engineers opened their labs and plants, and many public servants explained programs with clarity. Although any remaining errors are ours, much of the insight is theirs. We thank all of them for helping us understand how American innovation works in practice and how it can work better in the years ahead.

Ashish Arora: This book is dedicated to S.S., with whom all things are possible.

Sharon Belenzon: To my parents, who taught me the importance of purpose. To Mark Schankerman, whose guidance shaped the questions I ask. To my wife, LB, whose support has been my foundation and my greatest blessing. To our children, HB, IB, and NB, may they see an innovation system equal to the challenges of their generation.

Andrea Patacconi: To my family. First and foremost, to my mother MTC (yes, I am Italian). To my wife, AS, and my children, LP and AP, for their love, patience, and unwavering support.

Jungkyu Suh: To E.Y.S. and T.H., and to the memory of H.C.

1

Inventing Prosperity

Science-based innovation has transformed modern life so profoundly that its importance is easy to overlook. Electricity, antibiotics, semiconductors, and digital networks are now taken for granted, yet each began as a fragile idea, shaped through the interplay of scientific inquiry and industrial application. Science and technology advance together, each extending the reach of the other. As Nathan Rosenberg once observed, the effort to improve production generates technical challenges that stimulate new scientific research. Discoveries in science in turn open pathways to new applications. The result is a process of mutual reinforcement in which the boundary between discovery and use is often indistinct. In practice, we treat them as inseparable, captured in the familiar shorthand of "science and technology" or "R&D."

However, there is growing concern that the bond between science and technology is weakening. Evidence of slowing productivity growth has led some to argue that the era of rapid technological advance is ending. Critics contend that scientific research has become too incremental and detached from practical needs, no longer delivering the transformative ideas that once drove productivity and economic prosperity.

We disagree. Private returns to R&D have grown as markets have expanded and global competition has intensified, and science now contributes more, not less, to innovation. The difficulty lies elsewhere. In many technology fields, the translation of new scientific knowledge into commercial products has become harder. This bottleneck is not inevitable. Rather, it reflects changes in the architecture of the U.S. innovation ecosystem, which defines the pathways ideas must follow and the obstacles they must overcome as they travel from the laboratory to the marketplace.

In the decades following World War II, corporate labs of large American corporations nursed ideas from petri dish to production line. They integrated basic research, applied science, and product development under one roof. This model facilitated coordinated transitions from discovery to application. Today's landscape, by contrast, is a decentralised and diverse mosaic—a structure known as "division of innovative labour" (DOIL, for short). America's innovation relay now passes the baton from universities (basic science) to startups (proof of concept) and finally to large firms (mass production). DOIL delivers efficiency and variety, but in some sectors it can leave a gap in translational research—the work that turns a discovery into something a factory can build, regulators can certify, and customers can trust and enjoy. As corporate labs withered during the 1980s and 1990s, startups filled the gap. They prospered in information technology and life sciences but often struggled in advanced materials and clean energy, where tight coordination between market needs, technical development, and scientific research is critical. This created a significant gap in the innovation ecosystem.

This book charts America's journey from the rise of unified corporate research labs to today's fragmented, startup-centric innovation system. The core problem, we argue, is the missing layer of translational research: the organisations and institutions that turn promising ideas into products that can be manufactured at scale. Rebuilding that layer requires a new relationship with the heirs to the old industrial labs and stronger institutions supporting DOIL. More funding for basic science is valuable, but it will not by itself close the gap. Without a bridge between discovery and production, many university breakthroughs will stall and lose value. Restoring the translational layer is the most direct way to turn scientific strength into sustained growth and renewed prosperity.

This chapter proceeds in three steps. We begin by addressing the claim that science has exhausted its potential and no longer drives technology, showing why this view is mistaken. We then examine how the locus of translational research has shifted over the past several decades. Finally, we develop the book's central argument: DOIL benefits some sectors while disadvantaging others. Specialisation improves efficiency but also magnifies coordination costs. Because these effects differ across industries, the shift from integrated corporate labs to a fragmented system has produced uneven outcomes, strengthening some parts of the American economy while undermining others. We close by outlining policies to rebalance the innovation ecosystem.

Have the low-hanging fruits of science been picked?

Robert Gordon documents the remarkable productivity growth of the U.S. economy from the late-nineteenth to mid-twentieth century.[1] Using data from the United States, he shows that real GDP per hour (labour productivity) grew substantially in the middle of the twentieth century, from 1.79 per cent per year between 1870 and 1920 to 2.82 per cent per year between 1920 and 1970. However, in the most recent period (1970–2014), productivity grew by a modest 1.62 per cent per year. Gordon concludes that productivity rose between 1920 and 1970 largely because of significant technological progress, but more recently, technological advances have been much less potent in spurring growth. The slowdown is especially notable given the sustained expansion of scientific input (measured in terms of research dollars spent) and output (measured by academic articles published) from American academia, as shown in Figure 1.1.

One interpretation is that the low-hanging fruits of science have already been picked, perhaps because, as Ben Jones has argued in a widely cited paper, new generations of researchers have to assimilate ever-growing amounts of already discovered knowledge before they can create new knowledge of their own.[2] Because of this "burden of knowledge," researchers must specialise narrowly, splintering the mighty river of knowledge into tiny streams, with ever-diminishing impact.

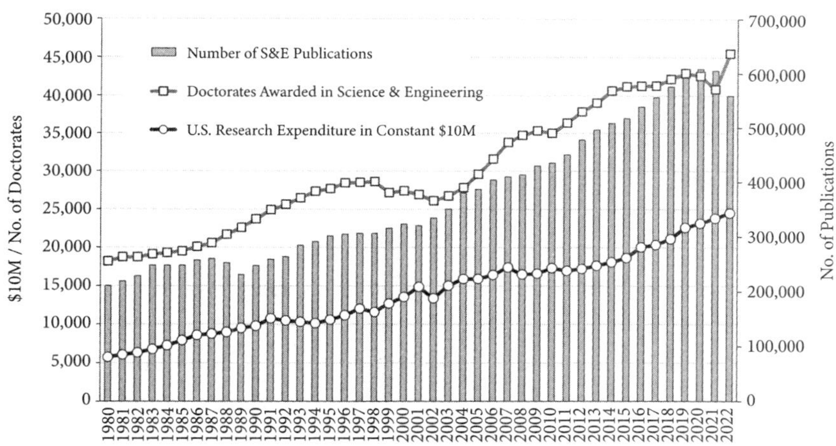

Figure 1.1 U.S. Scientific Investment and Output (1980–2021)

Notes: "Number of S&E Publications" is sourced from the Clarivate Web of Science and includes all scientific articles in the Science Citation Index-Expanded (SCI-EXPANDED) with a U.S. author. "Doctorates Awarded in Science & Engineering" are calculated from the National Science Foundation's Survey of Earned Doctorates and excludes degrees in the social sciences. U.S. Research Expenditure figures are calculated from the *National Patterns of R&D Resources: 2021–22 Data Update, NSF 24-318* report from the National Science Foundation and adds basic and applied research expenditure. Dollar values are denominated in constant 2017 dollars.

The burden of knowledge hypothesis is complemented by the incrementalism hypothesis. A recent study by Park, Leahey, and Funk argues that scientific and technological advances are increasingly incremental, representing minor improvements rather than breakthroughs. They calculate a "disruptiveness" index that measures how different a paper is from its predecessors relative to how similar subsequent papers are to it.[3] Park and coauthors find that, over time, papers have become less disruptive in every field of science and technology. Using a similar approach, they also find that patents have become less disruptive.

Another explanation for stagnant productivity, despite rising scientific output, is that science has become a less potent driver of technological progress. Nick Bloom and coauthors present evidence suggesting that the relationship between investments in research and productivity has weakened. For instance, maintaining exponential growth in semiconductor performance (a benchmark set by "Moore's Law")[4] in 2014 required around 18 times the number of researchers it used to take in 1971.[5] In the life sciences, the number of researchers has increased by 6 per cent annually, while the research productivity measured by the discovery of new molecular entities per number of researchers has decreased by 3.5 per cent per year. Although growth rates for yields per acre for corn, soybeans, cotton, and wheat have averaged around 1.5 per cent, the number of researchers in the agricultural sector has grown by a factor of between 3 (wheat) and 25 (soybeans), a decline in research productivity of about 4 to 6 per cent per year.

We are sceptical of claims of scientific irrelevance or a scientific slowdown. Claims of a broad-based slowdown in scientific progress rest on mixed evidence, and they ring hollow in light of breakthroughs in gene editing, artificial intelligence, and quantum computing. True, the number of discoveries per research dollar may have fallen in some sectors, but in others there is no such trend. For instance, a recent paper finds no evidence of falling productivity in wheat.[6] Using detailed data on the creation and adoption of new wheat varieties in the United States over the past century in each of sixteen wheat producing U.S. states, Alston and Pardey find that the number of new varieties introduced divided by the stock of R&D devoted to wheat research did not decline between 1970 and 2018. If anything, it has tended to increase since 1990.

Furthermore, the steep rise in private-sector R&D shows that firms anticipate higher, not lower, payoffs from new technology. Diminishing returns, in other words, reflect the sheer scale of current investment: companies are pouring in more money because innovation has become more valuable. In a market economy, capital flows away from activities that no longer pay, just as miners abandon a played-out seam unless the remaining ore is worth more than ever.[7]

In the United States, R&D as a share of GDP for the first time exceeded 3 per cent in 2019, surpassing its levels during the height of the space race of 2.8 per cent in 1964.[8] Figure 1.2 plots data from the National Science Foundation (NSF). Since the 1980s, U.S. total expenditure on scientific research has risen around fourfold in real terms, while corporate research expenditures have risen five times.[9] In fact, research as a share of GDP increased by 45.5 per cent during this period (from 0.79 per cent in 1980 to 1.15 per cent in 2020), with privately funded research increasing even faster. The business share of research has also risen from 36 per cent to 46 per cent of the national total over the four decades since 1980. Moreover, patent citations to science have jumped threefold since 1980 (from 4 per cent to 13 per cent in 2020), casting doubt on the notion that scientific knowledge is less useful for inventive activity than before.

Continued investment in R&D does not, by itself, reveal the character of the discoveries it funds. Has the average breakthrough grown more

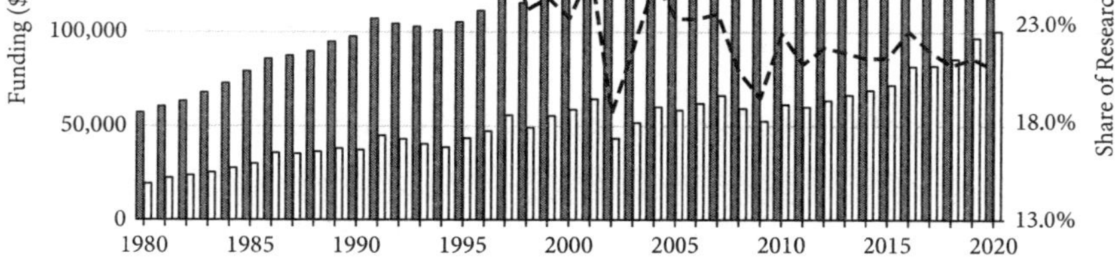

Figure 1.2 Trends in Basic and Applied Research Expenditures in the U.S. (1980–2021)

Notes: Bar graph for "Total U.S. Research Funding" plots the expenditure on applied and basic research by U.S. academia, businesses, non-profit organisations, and federally funded research and development centers (FFRDCs). "Research Funded and Performed by Business" plots the subset of this expenditure that was funded and performed by U.S. businesses. The dashed line divides dollars expended by businesses on research (applied and basic) by their expenditures on research and development. All dollar figures are deflated to 2017. Data is sourced from the National Center for Science and Engineering Statistics.[10]

incremental? Possibly so. But technological progress hinges on deploying the best ideas, not the average one. What matters is whether the most disruptive scientific papers and patents have become less disruptive over time. Here, the answer is clear: Park, Leahey, and Funk's own analysis shows that, although the *share* of "disruptive" papers and patents has decreased, their absolute numbers have not declined; as the authors themselves note, "there is little change in the number of highly disruptive papers and patents."[11] A recent replication study by Holst, Algaba, Tori, Wenmackers, and Ginis also demonstrates that the tendency towards greater incrementalism depends on how one deals with outliers, underscoring the challenge of tracking systematic changes in the significance of ideas over time.[12] Furthermore, a more recent study by An Zeng, Shlomo Havlin, and colleagues notes that not all disruptive papers are influential.[13] Many are themselves disrupted by future papers. It is the persistently disruptive papers that propel science. Highly cited works, including those that have won the Nobel Prize, consistently show persistent disruption. The data show that the number of these persistently disruptive papers has not declined. If anything, papers in recent years are more likely to show persistent disruption. Another study finds that disruptive patents have increased, not declined.[14] The analysis by Park and colleagues also suffers from measurement problems as citations to patents published before 1976 are omitted from the data. As a result, patents issued in, say, 1980 are deemed to be more disruptive than an otherwise identical patents issued in 2020, which mechanically causes patents to appear less disruptive over time. After adjusting for these factors and changes in U.S. patent law that allow for citations to patent applications in addition to patent grants, and updating the analysis to 2016, Macher and colleagues find that the number of highly disruptive patents has *increased* since 1980, particularly since 2008.

The history of science also cautions us to beware of claiming the completeness of current scientific knowledge. In 1878, Max Planck's mentor advised him against studying theoretical physics, calling it a nearly mature field, approaching a degree of completion as geometry had centuries ago.[15] Two decades on, no less a scientist than Albert A. Michelson, renowned for his precise measurements of the speed of light, also fell into this trap when in 1894, during the dedication of the Ryerson Physical Laboratory at the University of Chicago, he said: "The more important fundamental laws and facts of physical science have all been discovered, and these are now so firmly established that the possibility of their ever being supplanted in consequence of new discoveries is exceedingly remote."[16] However, this mistaken belief was soon refuted by a series of revolutionary discoveries that transformed our understanding of the universe, including Einstein's theory of relativity and the development of quantum mechanics. The spate of breakthroughs, ranging from mRNA vaccines to generative AI and quantum computing, serves as a salutary reminder that one must be extremely careful about claiming that scientific and technological advances have slowed.

Nor is the burden of knowledge a new one. Indeed, the growth of science itself reduces this burden. Science, as an endeavour to generalise from particular observations, also opens more efficient ways to reach the frontier. As Peter Medawar, a Nobel laureate in biology, put it:

> The ballast of factual information, so far from being just about to sink us, is growing daily less. The factual burden of a science varies inversely with its degree of maturity. As a science advances, particular facts are comprehended within, and therefore in a sense annihilated by, general statements of steadily increasing explanatory power and compass — whereupon the facts need no longer be known explicitly, that is, spelled out and kept in mind. In all sciences we are being progressively relieved of the burden of singular instances, the tyranny of the particular. We need no longer record the fall of every apple.[17]

Although ever more is known, not all of it needs to be stored in individual human brains, nor applied through human bone and sinew. Humans have created ever more sophisticated tools to help. Some of the ballast of factual information, as it were, is now embodied in tools and software, whence it can be readily accessed, manipulated, and analysed. In a 2018 study, Florenta Teodoris showed that the release of the open-source version of Microsoft Kinect, an advanced motion-sensing technology, meant that academic robotics projects were less likely to feature computer-vision specialists; much of their knowledge was now embedded in Kinect.[18] The growing applications of machine learning to scientific discovery bear witness to the claim that the ballast of factual information is not a crushing burden. Vast amounts of data and information can be readily stored, assimilated, and summarised. Machine learning methods can make connections across discoveries in seemingly unconnected fields.[19] Human intuition and creativity can be substantially augmented.

Nor is the growing specialisation of researchers in itself a sign of danger. Narrow specialisation is a natural response to the growing number of researchers: each researcher must specialise to contribute something different from the many others working in the area, not merely to save on having to assimilate accumulated knowledge. In other words, specialisation is a way of reducing duplication. Duplicate discovery has little social value. Both Newton and Leibnitz independently developed differential calculus, but science and society would care little if only one of them had done so. Narrow specialisation has the virtue of reducing the likelihood of such duplication. What is known may have grown by leaps and bounds, but it seems an unlikely reason for the apparently disappointing returns to societal investment in scientific research.

In short, the evidence does not support a general slowdown in scientific or technological progress, nor the claim that science has become less useful to invention. Business spending on R&D continues to rise, signalling that firms still expect strong payoffs from new ideas. Where they spend, however, has changed. Over the past four decades, the corporate research budget has shifted away from basic inquiry (the "R") towards downstream development (the "D"). As incumbents grow larger and yet concentrate on fewer product lines, they direct funds toward incremental refinements of existing offerings instead of exploring new avenues. These efforts may raise profits, but they add little to economy-wide productivity. They also leave incumbents less able and willing to recognise, absorb, and translate valuable discoveries into market-ready products and processes. The burden, therefore, shifts to startups, which in many sectors are potentially less efficient at this task.

Trends in international trade and economic integration help explain some of the shift in corporate R&D. Since the 1980s, falling tariffs and booming foreign demand have expanded markets for American firms even as competition has intensified. Empirical research by Chan Kim shows that as markets expand and rivalry intensifies, firms become both larger and more narrowly specialised.[20] James Bessen and colleagues reach a similar conclusion: rivalry for those larger markets raises the private returns to R&D but also shortens the life of each payoff, as competitors imitate or leapfrog one another.[21] Faster obsolescence, in turn, pushes companies toward narrower, quick-hit projects over long-horizon research. The result is the same compositional drift we observe in the data: more "D," less "R" in corporate R&D.

A key consequence of this shift is that universities and startups are now expected to supply the next breakthroughs. Yet in many sectors, these organisations struggle to turn academic discoveries into marketable products. Neither has filled the gap left by the research once conducted in industrial labs. (Chapter 4 discusses these voids in greater detail.)

This discussion leads to the book's central argument: the deepening of DOIL in the United States, marked by corporate withdrawal from scientific research, creates uneven benefits and costs across sectors, producing clear winners and losers. The problem is not a shortage of important scientific discoveries or an inevitable drift toward incremental work. Rather, in several sectors, it is the widening gap between discovery and production, reflected in the slowdown of translating scientific advances into technologies that generate economic value. The challenge, in short, is not too little science but too little translation.

Indeed, a growing body of evidence points to a slowdown in translating scientific advances into practical applications. Figure 1.3 plots the share of high-quality scientific papers (i.e., papers in the top decile in terms of being

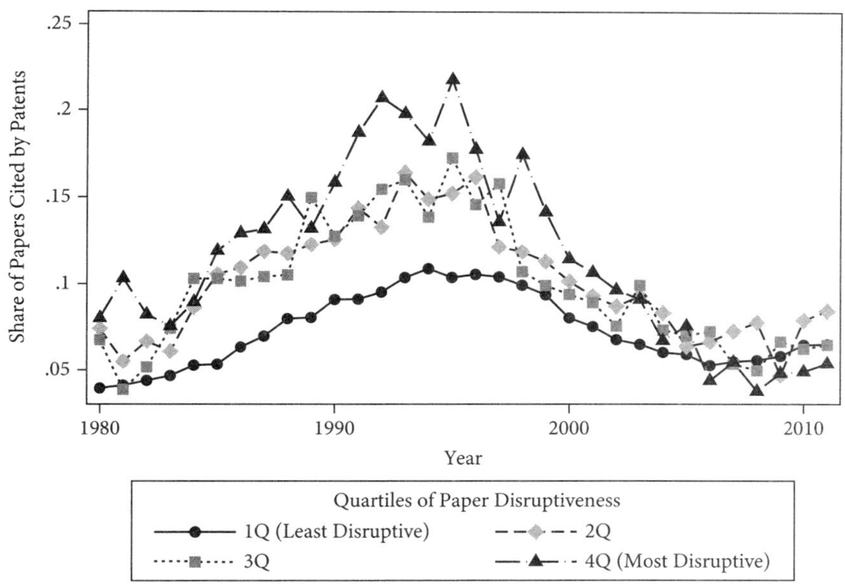

Figure 1.3 Share of High-Quality Papers Cited by Patents, by Scientific Disruption Quartiles (1980–2011)

Notes: The binned scatterplots show the share of papers cited by patents within five years of paper publication, separated by quartiles of the papers' disruptiveness indices (CD-5) from Holst, Algaba, Tori, Wenmackers, and Ginis (2024).[22] Sample is limited to papers that are in the top 10 per cent of forward paper citations for their field and year and with nonnegative CD-5 scores. Patent citations to papers are sourced from the *Reliance on Science* dataset of Marx & Fuegi (2020) throughout this book.[23]

cited by other papers) being cited by a patent, by varying degrees of Park and coauthors' Consolidation-Disruption (CD) measure.[24] Throughout the sample period, we find that the most disruptive papers tend to be cited more often by patents, with those in the top (fourth) quartile (with 12 per cent of papers cited by patents) 60 per cent more likely to be cited than those in the first quartile (7 per cent cited by patents). However, the probability of a high-quality disruptive paper (within the top quartile of CD scores) being cited by a patent has dropped substantially since the mid-1990s. At its peak in the early 1990s (1990–1995), 19 per cent of disruptive papers were cited by patents, while in the 2010s, they dropped down to 6 per cent. In contrast, the least disruptive papers (in the bottom quartile) show a patent citation rate of 7 per cent in the 2010s as well. Scientific papers are less likely to be used in patents, especially if they are novel.

Translational research: the nexus between science and application

Understanding why the widening gap between discovery and production matters requires a closer look at translational research, the stage that links scientific discovery with commercially viable technologies. Far from being a routine adaptation of laboratory results for industrial use, translational work often demands solving unforeseen scientific and technical problems, and in doing so, it can reveal deeper insights into the natural world.

To appreciate what translational research involves, consider how information technology (IT) made its way from academic prototype to economic productivity. In his paper, *The Dynamo and the Computer*, Paul David examined why the IT revolution took so long to register in productivity statistics—an instance of the so-called productivity paradox.[25] He noted that even major leaps in technology can fail to yield immediate economic benefits because they require improvements in the initial discovery, complementary innovations, and organisational overhauls to use the new technology. Electrification also faced delays. Early factories clung to the group-drive system rather than adopting more efficient individual electric motors, and supporting tools such as better transformers and AC-to-DC converters also took years to mature. It also took time to redesign products that could more fully benefit from the improved precision made possible by electric motors. And some of the benefits — quieter, cleaner factories that were less susceptible to fire and accidents — were less likely to show up in productivity statistics.

Nathan Rosenberg underscored the importance of bridging this gap between early-stage discovery and practical implementation. Quoting Alfred North Whitehead, Rosenberg writes:

> It may be useful here to recall Alfred North Whitehead's oft-quoted saying that *The greatest invention of the nineteenth century was in the method of invention.* ... The sentence just quoted from Whitehead's book, *Science and the Modern World*, is well known, his subsequent observation is not, but deserves to be. *It is a mistake to think that the bare scientific idea is the required invention only to be picked up and used. An intense period of imaginative design lies between. One element in the new method is just the discovery of how to set about bridging the gap between the scientific ideas, and the ultimate product. It is a process of a disciplined attack upon one difficulty after another.*[26]

This disciplined attack on commercialisation obstacles is evident in a range of breakthroughs. The Haber-Bosch process, aimed at converting atmospheric nitrogen into nitrogen fertilizer, was restricted in scale because Fritz Haber employed osmium, a rare metal, as a catalyst. It required ongoing research by Carl Bosch and Alwin Mittasch to formulate a more accessible catalyst comprising iron, aluminium, and potassium, enabling nitrogen fertilizers to effectively prevent widespread hunger.

Similarly, antibiotics would not have become lifesaving wonders had researchers not conquered the large-scale production issues that followed Alexander Fleming's 1928 discovery of penicillin's antibacterial properties. In 1941, scientists at the United States Department of Agriculture's Northern Laboratory in Illinois made three advances that transformed a scientific discovery into a drug that saved countless lives. Instead of shallow trays, they adapted a submerged fermentation process used by Pfizer for gluconic acid, adopted corn steep liquor as a nutrient medium, and discovered a more effective strain of Penicillium. These steps increased the output rates more than a hundredfold.[27] A stark reminder of the consequences of this translational research is that in World War I, more than one in six soldiers with bacterial pneumonia died; in World War II, only one in a hundred died.

Solid-state electronics and laser communications tell a similar tale. Early lasers were bulky, prone to overheating, and short-lived. It took refinements in crystal growth processes at MIT Lincoln Labs, Texas Instruments, and RCA Labs to create compact, reliable diode lasers. Even then, high-speed optical communication awaited Corning Glass Works' development of low-loss optical fibre, building on Charles Kao's insight that ultra-pure glass was essential for long-range light transmission. Kao's work, which later garnered a Nobel Prize, not only solved a practical barrier but also expanded the frontier of our understanding of light and materials.

These efforts were not just "mere engineering" or "mere development." They involved creativity and scientific inquiry of the highest calibre. Louis Pasteur harnessed microbiology to develop vaccines and revolutionise fermentation, simultaneously addressing urgent public-health concerns and redefining core aspects of biology.[28] Irving Langmuir's quest to improve light bulbs at General Electric required investigating adsorption from tungsten filaments, contributing to our understanding of surface chemistry.

Translational research often blurs the boundary between "basic" and "applied." Practical challenges can demand new theoretical perspectives, and the process of adapting discoveries for large-scale use can unearth unexplored scientific territory. Yet, translational research sits awkwardly between pure science, which typically resides in universities focused on fundamental understanding, and practical application, where commercial considerations are essential. As the American innovation system has become more specialised, the responsibility for moving discoveries from the lab to the factory floor has at times fallen through the cracks.

Passing the baton: who translates science

Corporate labs once played a pivotal role in translating scientific discovery into market-ready technologies. Many of America's largest firms operated centralised research laboratories—General Electric Research Labs (GERL), AT&T Bell Labs, DuPont Central Research, IBM's Watson labs, and Xerox PARC, among others—that combined fundamental science with practical engineering. The entire innovation "supply chain," from research down to product development, was housed within the boundaries of one firm. For instance, nylon was invented by Wallace Carothers's team at DuPont's Experimental Station. DuPont engineers developed the chemical process for producing nylon, and DuPont also produced and sold nylon fibre.

Corporate research labs rose around the interwar period when large integrated firms in the electrical and chemical industries reached the technological frontier. Industrial research aimed to understand more deeply the phenomena, materials, and instruments relevant to the sponsoring firm. (Chapter 8 explores the rise of corporate research in America.) As university research in polymer chemistry, photochemistry, and radio engineering was inadequate, firms such as AT&T, General Electric, Kodak, and DuPont started hiring American professors (initially trained in Europe) and PhDs. The number of firms operating research labs rose almost eightfold (from 526 to 4,145) between 1920 and 1960.[29] While many firms operated labs for routine troubleshooting and applied work, a handful produced cutting-edge scientific research. Clinton Davisson, a physicist at AT&T, for example, explored ways to control electron emissions from metallic grids used in vacuum tubes. His examination of the patterns of emission from the surface of single crystals of nickel led to the discovery of electron diffraction and the wave properties of electrons, for which he was awarded the Nobel Prize in 1937.[30]

World War II galvanised the federal government to develop American research capabilities, in both corporations and universities (discussed further in Chapters 9 and 10). The Cold War that followed continued this trend. Industrial research, designed to understand the fundamental mechanisms behind practical problems, contributed to science itself. Claude Shannon's fundamental research laid the basis for information theory. It was applied in the development of algorithms for data compression, cryptography, and error correction, without which modern computers, mobile telephony, and the internet would likely not have been possible.

The hegemony of corporate research laboratories lasted through most of the Cold War. Thereafter, however, these corporate labs scaled back their investments in long-term research, shifting much of the translational burden onto universities, startups, and smaller specialised institutes. Starting in the 1980s, firms gradually closed (DuPont's Experimental Station), spun off (PARC from Xerox, Bell Labs from AT&T), or redirected (IBM) basic research functions, ceding their place to universities.

Multiple data sources point to this pattern. Figure 1.2, using NSF data, shows that the share of basic and applied research in business R&D expenditures dropped from a high of 31 per cent in 1986 to 21 per cent in 2020. Mezzanotti and Simcoe, using confidential census data, confirm that even as business R&D has increased, the share of research in business R&D has indeed fallen since the turn of the century.[31] Our prior work also shows that scientific publications per dollar of sales revenue by U.S. public firms fell by half between 1980 and 2015, signalling a decline in "intramural" scientific research at firms.[32] Consistent with this finding, Rafel Corredoira and his colleagues show that universities and private firms have grown in importance as sources of breakthroughs.[33] Between 1985 and 2009, universities had more than their share of novel patents (patents using new terms not found in earlier patents), rising from 1.8 to 4.2 per cent, while VC-backed firms increased their share of highly cited patents tenfold, from 0.5 to 5.3 per cent. Corredoira et al. also find that foreign firms have become more important sources of breakthroughs.

This scaling back of industrial research has left gaps, which universities and startups have struggled to fill. Academic engagement with market-oriented innovation is not new: agricultural extension services and national labs in the United States, as well as Britain's technology centres, Australia's CSIR labs, and Germany's Fraunhofer Institutes, have long helped move scientific insights out of the lab and into commercial products. Yet, translation works best when it is close to application. University medical centres do well, in part, because the generation, translation, application, and health-care delivery are combined. But whereas health care is delivered by universities and teaching hospitals, universities are not natural places for finding industrial applications of scientific discoveries, let alone translating them. Corporate labs are a more natural place in many instances.

The promises and pitfalls of a division of innovative labour

The decline of industrial research and the rise of venture-backed startups reflect the division of innovative labour in the American innovation ecosystem. We conceptualise America's innovation system as a "tripod." Universities drive basic research, and big firms excel at large-scale commercialisation. Startups often bridge the gap, transforming lab breakthroughs into technologies ready for mass adoption. When they do so successfully, this division of labour delivers impressive results. Yet, it also carries clear risks: when research and commercialisation lie in separate hands, knowledge transfer becomes more complex, and incentives may become misaligned.

DOIL involves a trade-off between gains from specialisation and challenges of coordinating startups (exploring commercial applications of inventions) and large firms (responsible for introducing them to the market). Effective investment requires value-sharing agreements before translational research begins; yet matching the startup with the right partner is often difficult at the outset. Uncertainty about the most promising commercial applications and the prospects of the required improvements in the technology may require extensive coordination, which is harder to accomplish when two or more organisations are involved. In contrast, vertically integrated firms manage coordination challenges more effectively, especially because returns on complementary investments are less of a concern when all parties sit under one roof. We explore these issues in Chapter 4.

mRNA vaccines as a division of innovative labour success story

The rapid creation of mRNA vaccines demonstrates the power of DOIL. This success story was made possible by harnessing expertise from multiple actors. Universities provided foundational knowledge about mRNA, much of which was publicly available; biotech startups developed proprietary delivery systems; incumbent pharmaceutical firms and contract manufacturers scaled up production; and logistics specialists managed worldwide distribution. The government guaranteed demand for vaccines.

Decades of mRNA research, funded mainly by governments, laid the foundation. University research had shown that many viruses, including the one responsible for the COVID-19 pandemic, use a spike protein to bind to cells in the body. Instead of using dead or attenuated viruses, vaccine designers could now use mRNA to instruct the body's own cells to produce the spike protein. The immune system of the vaccinated individuals would then produce antibodies against this spike protein, enabling it to combat the virus if the individual were to become infected.

However, there were two significant challenges in the application of the science of mRNA. First, injecting mRNA into the bloodstream caused an immune response from the body, which would also destroy the mRNA before it could get the body to produce the spike protein. Katalin Karikó and Drew Weissman, 2023 Nobel Prize winners in medicine, addressed this problem. Karikó discovered a way to minimise immune detection and subsequent degradation of synthetic mRNA by incorporating pseudouridine instead of uridine, a nucleic acid that is a constituent of mRNA. Weissman validated that this modified mRNA could efficiently produce the intended proteins without undesired immune reactions. Their 2005 paper showcased the potential of modified mRNA to safely and effectively produce proteins without triggering inflammation.[34]

The second challenge was that mRNA molecules are fragile and easily degraded. Lipid nanoparticles (LNPs) provided a solution by encapsulating mRNA and protecting it from premature breakdown. The LNP technology was developed by startups such as Acuitas, Arbutus Biopharma, and Genevant, which licensed it to Moderna and BioNTech.

Large firms were important partners. BioNTech and Pfizer combined expertise to stabilise mRNA within LNP and ensure effective cellular delivery. BioNTech, skilled in mRNA technologies and LNP stabilisation, innovated ultra-cold storage conditions (–70°C) to preserve the vaccine. Pfizer leveraged its extensive experience in large-scale clinical trials, regulatory navigation, and global manufacturing and distribution. Moderna also managed to scale rapidly by leveraging strategic partnerships with Lonza for production and McKesson for distribution.

Governments did their part as well. The National Institutes of Health (NIH) identified the SARS-CoV-2 spike protein as a crucial vaccine target. The World Health Organisation (WHO) was instrumental in coordinating global research efforts. The U.S. government's Operation Warp Speed (OWS) further accelerated vaccine development, manufacturing, and distribution by guaranteeing demand for the vaccines.

Extensive global clinical trials, involving simultaneous collaboration between countries, were crucial. Contract Research organisations (CROs), such as IQVIA, PPD, and Covance, managed trials, from site selection and patient enrolment to data collection. Data analytics firms, such as Medidata and Veeva Systems, offered cloud-based platforms that streamlined the collection, storage, and real-time analysis of clinical data. The logistics companies DHL and FedEx offered fleets of temperature-controlled trucks and planes and storage facilities to deliver the vaccines. They also used real-time tracking systems, ensuring that each vaccine dose was maintained at the required temperature as it reached its destination. The storage challenges also prompted the development of specialised packaging solutions. For example, Pfizer's thermal shippers maintained the necessary cold temperatures using dry ice and innovative insulation, ensuring the vaccines remained viable during transit.

Much like Adam Smith's eighteenth-century pin factory, specialised entities along the vaccine development chain coordinated effectively through the market for technology—institutional arrangements that allow ideas, patents, and other intellectual assets to be licensed, sold, or otherwise transferred between parties. Robust intellectual property (IP) rights not only shield innovators from imitators and opportunistic partners but also enable the transfer and diffusion of knowledge. This reflects the broader "grand bargain": society grants inventors temporary monopoly rights in exchange for disclosure that facilitates wider use. Without an efficient market for technology, specialised entities that lack the commercialisation capabilities to profit from their inventions would be reluctant to participate. This would not only slow knowledge diffusion but also discourage highly capable research organisations from contributing, ultimately stalling innovation.

Several important lessons emerge about the power of a specialised innovation ecosystem. For specialisation to be effective, entities must be able to contract with each other at low cost. In a capitalist system, these contractual interactions occur through markets and, in the context of innovation, through the market for technology. In order for the market for technology to function well, patents and other forms of intellectual property protection must be effective. Here, patents serve a dual purpose. First, they protect early inventors from being expropriated by subsequent entrants. Second, they facilitate the dissemination of knowledge within the innovation ecosystem. Patents are the essential lubricant that enables the market for technology to operate smoothly. Without them, trade in technology would stall and specialised entities would be reluctant to participate, halting knowledge diffusion and ultimately causing innovation to stagnate.

A final takeaway from this case is that large firms did not significantly contribute to the early development of mRNA science, unlike in many other examples we will discuss in later chapters of this book. Instead, large firms concentrated on scaling and commercialising various technological solutions developed by startups, which, in turn, heavily relied on university research. In this example, therefore, science-based startups became the primary locus of translational research, playing a critical role in transforming mRNA university breakthroughs into vaccine shots.

Coordination frictions in a specialised innovation ecosystem

The mRNA case points to a broader trend: over time, companies have increasingly relied on startups and universities to "package" scientific discoveries into practical, usable forms. Established firms now account for less than a quarter of the licenses granted by U.S. universities, while startups and small firms handle the majority.[35] Specialisation in the innovation process raises efficiency, and yet it also widens the gap between discovery and production.

Publishing scientific findings does not ensure that firms can incorporate them into R&D. Firms must first invest in their own scientific capability and then fund translational work that will map discoveries to commercial use.[36] Recent evidence shows that university papers, even in fields aligned with corporate invention, do not affect firm R&D. Scientific knowledge produced by universities affects corporate R&D only when it is embodied in university patents or in graduates who carry it into industry.[37]

In a DOIL system, universities discover while firms commercialise. Moving science to market requires a clear view of potential uses and technical hurdles. Because universities and their spinouts often lack this view, fragmented systems may underinvest in translation. In integrated systems, large firms also invest in research; their scientists work with product, manufacturing, and sales teams and know how to bring ideas to market.

Uncertainty shapes DOIL by deterring startups from innovating: they may struggle to secure a partner for commercialisation or may anticipate preemption by a larger firm. Early contracts could mitigate these risks, but when applications are unclear and translation has yet to materialise, identifying the right stakeholders remains a formidable challenge. Not surprisingly, ventures seeking to apply cutting-edge science to economic production often struggle to raise capital. Their difficulty in attracting investors is less a cause than a symptom of a deeper problem. In many cases, the commercial application of a discovery and the trajectory of technology development are interdependent. As translation proceeds, new information may shift the target application and necessitate further R&D. This process is especially difficult when multiple specialised organisations must coordinate. We discuss these issues in detail in Chapter 3.

Finally, when established firms retreat from research and focus on incremental innovations, startups lose potential partners. Because they depend on incumbents for complementary downstream investments, startups then have fewer incentives to pursue transformative innovations. To be efficient, therefore, a division of innovative labour must remain incomplete: some incumbents must continue to invest in research, or the innovation ecosystem as a whole will weaken.

Looking ahead: Outline of the book

America's innovation system is at a crossroads. Some observers question whether the pipeline of scientific breakthroughs is drying up, but the evidence we present suggests that such pessimism is misplaced. The uneven pace of progress across sectors is best explained by the increasingly specialised division of innovative labour. In fields such as mRNA-based vaccines, this ecosystem has delivered rapid and transformative gains. But in many deep-tech sectors, innovation has lagged because the technologically sophisticated incumbent, the firm capable of translating science into large-scale commercial application, is missing. This book traces how and why the translational layer of science has shifted away from large firms toward startups, examines the consequences for sectors where this shift is problematic, and explores how the institutional scaffolding that connects science to technology can be rebuilt. Addressing the imbalance caused by the loss of corporate research will require targeted policy interventions to support innovation in areas where market forces alone fall short.

We propose a two-pronged strategy. First, policymakers should support companies that undertake substantial, long-term investments in scientific research and its translation into commercial applications. Such firms often possess significant market power, drawing legitimate antitrust scrutiny. Yet not all large firms are alike. Some, like Alphabet, deliver considerable social value by bridging the critical gap between fundamental science and practical innovation, a gap that startups or universities often struggle to fill. A rigid or formulaic approach to antitrust enforcement risks inadvertently undermining precisely the kinds of translational research needed for sustained technological progress. Instead, regulators should distinguish between companies whose dominance stems from genuine scientific innovation and those whose primary advantage is scale.

Yet, even with policy adjustments, the division of labour in the innovation ecosystem is here to stay. Hence, our second recommendation focuses on strengthening the institutions underpinning the specialised innovation ecosystem, particularly in deep-tech sectors. Policymakers should ensure university research continues to thrive while also facilitating its translation into scalable, economically valuable technologies. In some sectors, the government may also have to reclaim its role as the "buyer of first resort," providing early-stage demand for innovative technologies that private markets might initially find too risky or uncertain.

This book first builds the conceptual foundations for understanding America's innovation system and then follows its evolution. Chapters 2–4 introduce the core ideas: the translational bottleneck between scientific discovery and commercial use, the division of labour among universities, startups, and corporations, and the economic theories of Adam Smith and Joseph Schumpeter that frame specialisation and the need for coordination. Chapters 5 and 6 examine the fusion of science and technology that underpinned modern innovation. Chapters 7–12 chart the rise of the U.S. innovation ecosystem, highlighting universities, startups, incumbents, and a market for technology as the main protagonists (Chapter 7). We then trace the emergence of corporate laboratories (Chapter 8) and the federal scientific infrastructure that sustained corporate research (Chapters 9, 10). The following chapters analyse the decline of corporate research (Chapter 11) and the rise of a system defined by a division of innovative labour (Chapter 12). Chapters 13 and 14 consider policy prescriptions focusing on renewing compacts with large R&D-intensive firms, strengthening the business models of deep-tech startups, and rethinking science, technology, and industrial policy to better align translational research with broad-based economic growth.

2
The American Innovation Ecosystem

Introduction

Technological progress in the United States relies on collaboration among universities, startups, and established firms. Universities conduct basic research, startups transform discoveries into prototypes, and established companies supply capital, production expertise, and market access. When these handoffs occur seamlessly, the system operates with remarkable efficiency; examples include semiconductor foundries supporting hundreds of fabless design houses, and universities pioneering the science behind mRNA vaccines. This chapter analyses the conditions that give rise to a division of innovative labour (DOIL) and explains how it functions. We contrast Joseph Schumpeter's view of growth driven by firm rivalry and "creative destruction" with Adam Smith's earlier insight that productivity rises when tasks are divided between actors.

The division of innovative labour rests on institutions that enable specialised actors to contribute to distinct aspects of the innovation process. Four institutions are particularly important: enforceable patent rights, an effective market for technology, reliable venture finance, and public programs that support the development and adoption of new (science-based) technologies. Weakening any of these institutions undermines the functioning of the innovation ecosystem as a whole. For example, if venture finance is constrained because exit markets for startups contract, promising innovations may fail to reach scale. This chapter, together with the next, develops the economic logic of the division of innovative labour (DOIL), identifies the institutional conditions that sustain it, and explains why a specialised innovation ecosystem can fail.

Adam Smith versus Joseph Schumpeter

Robert Solow, in his seminal work, demonstrated that capital accumulation alone cannot sustain economic growth indefinitely; only technological change can do that.[1] Once equipment and education reached a certain level, further advances in productivity depended on steady technological improvement. In the 1980s and early 1990s, economists such as Paul Romer built on Solow's idea. In Romer's framework, firms conduct R&D because they expect to profit from improved products; yet the knowledge generated also spills into a shared pool, lowering the cost of future innovation for all. Each discovery thereby facilitates the next.[2]

This strand of research was later developed into Schumpeterian growth models in which innovation occurs through the displacement of older technologies and firms—a cycle known as "creative destruction."[3] The idea originated in Joseph Schumpeter's *Capitalism, Socialism and Democracy*, where he argued that the essence of competition in a market economy lies not primarily in price cutting, as classical economists had maintained, but in the deeper struggle of firms to out-innovate one another:

> The fundamental impulse that sets and keeps the capitalist engine in motion comes from the new consumers' goods, the new methods of production or transportation, the new markets, the new forms of industrial organization that capitalist enterprise creates.[4]

Whereas Schumpeter stressed competition and the role of the entrepreneur in setting the process in motion through innovation and market entry, Adam Smith saw economic growth as requiring both competition and cooperation. Smith stressed that specialisation and division of labour are sources of productivity growth. Schumpeterian growth models are based on successful inventors developing into market competitors, displacing incumbents. In this view, knowledge flows across firms are unintentional "spillovers," helping society but undermining the innovator's incentives to innovate. A Smithian view, by contrast, focuses on the flow of knowledge and ideas through market transactions.

Empirical work often relies on patent citations to measure knowledge flows; referencing another patent implies the transfer of ideas.[5] Evgenii Fadeev shows that citations cluster heavily within business relationships.[6] One of IBM's patents (on improving the packaging of semiconductor chips), for instance, is cited repeatedly, but almost exclusively by Amkor Technology, an IBM supplier, whose main business is semiconductor packaging on behalf of chip makers. IBM's invention would be valuable if Amkor could use it (and perhaps even improve upon it). Fadeev infers that IBM likely allowed Amkor to benefit from this patent and any associated know-how, perhaps licensing the patent to Amkor as part of a longer-standing business relationship. Fadeev's evidence that knowledge typically spreads through business relationships suggests that knowledge flows are not merely spillovers, open to all. Similarly, Breschi and Lissoni find that localised spillovers are not simply informal opportunities available "in the air" but instead reflect preexisting business networks.[7] This means that knowledge likely flows through market-mediated business transactions rather than circulating freely.

Knowledge can flow not only between a firm and its supplier, but also from that supplier to other firms. For example, Apple's iPhone suppliers learned to manufacture multi-touch glass and hundreds of other components and then supplied them to Chinese firms such as Huawei, Xiaomi, Vivo, and Oppo.[8] Kwanghui Lim's study of copper interconnect technology semiconductors confirms that equipment suppliers transfer knowledge from one customer to another. Equipment vendors facilitated knowledge sharing between chipmakers. TSMC worked closely with Applied Materials, while UMC partnered with Novellus, previously tied to IBM. As Lim puts it, suppliers "act as conduits through which much more information flows than is embodied in the tools they sell."[9]

This role of equipment suppliers is not new. A pioneering study in 1968 showed that specialised engineering contractors did the same for refining and chemical process technologies after World War II, first in the United States and then across the globe.[10] The study notes that American contractors offered more innovative chemical process technology, in part because American oil and chemical companies licensed process innovations to them, working closely with these contractors to design pioneering chemical plants and refineries. Moreover, in the United States, cooperation between chemical firms, contractors, and component makers was seldom based on vertical integration, which was more common in Europe and Japan.

The role of equipment suppliers goes back even further. In the late nineteenth century, textile machinery firms, such as the Platt Brothers, were responsible for diffusing textile production technology even beyond British textile firms. Gary Saxonhouse has documented their role in diffusing textile technology to Japanese textile producers:

> The famous English machinery manufacturer, Platt Brothers of Oldham, and its representatives in Japan deserve a major share of the credit for diffusing best practice among Japanese spinners. No better confirmation of the uniformity of practice among Japanese firms can be had than the findings

> that fully eighty-seven percent of all 1,800,000 spindles in Japan in 1909 had been supplied by Platt. Use of a single machinery supplier further increased the flow of technical information among firms. In advising firms as to the most appropriate design of machinery, Platt Brothers could draw on the whole range of Japanese experience. An examination of the confidential memoranda sent to particular Japanese firms finds them studded impressively often with reference to the experience of other Japanese firms. The advice given by Platt Brothers was not limited to the subject of mill design. Between 1890 and 1910 many of the larger mills kept on Platt Brothers engineers and fitters as advisors.[11]

Machine tool producers were also often responsible for diffusing knowledge from firms in one industry to other industries. As Nathan Rosenberg put it:

> All innovations—whether they include the introduction of a new product or provide a cheaper way of producing an existing product—require that the capital goods sector shall in turn produce a new product (capital good) according to certain specifications... [Firms] in this industry have typically become highly specialised, in the sense that most firms produce a relatively narrow range of output... in response to technical specifications laid down by a wide range of customers... Their success in accomplishing this improvement in turn affects the price of their machinery output and therefore is... an important determinant... of the speed with which the economy will install and apply new techniques of production once they have been discovered.[12]

Rosenberg's point is that machine-tool suppliers did more than just build equipment in the late nineteenth and early twentieth centuries: they also shared methods developed for manufacturing firearms with sectors like sewing machines, which required precise metal parts as well. Knowledge of how to produce precision machine parts did not randomly diffuse across firms. Instead, firms in one field harnessed breakthroughs from another, mediated by the machinery suppliers acting as knowledge carriers through market transactions.

The recent U.S. export controls on toolmakers such as ASML show that the ultraviolet machines used to print circuit patterns onto silicon wafers also transfer know-how. Each sale bundles hardware with complementary intangibles: control software, updated process recipes, remote diagnostics, spare parts, and on-site engineers who install the system, calibrate it, and train local staff. These ancillary services reveal proprietary optical models, process capabilities, and yield-enhancement routines. Restricting such transactions illustrates that capital-equipment markets function as channels of technology transfer and that market-mediated diffusion remains a pivotal force in the semiconductor sector.

In contrast to the Schumpeterian view of knowledge diffusion as unintended "spillovers," the Smithian view sees knowledge flows as intentional, mediated by market transactions, including licensing and acquisitions, so that knowledge creators can profit while directing their inventions to the organisations best prepared to use them. Patents, rather than restricting the use of ideas, help structure contracts that enable firms to trade and collaborate with lower expropriation risk. Specialist technology sellers can license their expertise to others, enabling them to use it at scale, thereby extending the commercial reach of each invention and boosting aggregate productivity. An effective market for technology, in turn, nurtures R&D specialists (entities that excel in invention but not manufacturing) because strong patent protection lets them profit from ideas rather than only from products.

A study based on a comprehensive survey of R&D managers in U.S. manufacturing firms in the early 1990s found that patent protection encouraged technology licensing, albeit in smaller firms lacking manufacturing assets.[13] Another study used changes in patent law to explore the effects on licensing.[14] In 2006, in the *eBay versus MercExchange* patent dispute, the U.S. Supreme Court limited the ability of a patent holder to stop an alleged infringer from using the disputed patent. In effect, this weakened patent protection. Legal scholars estimate that the ruling reduced the probability of obtaining an injunction for infringed patents by about 25 percent.[15] Using a sample of over 20,000 American firms matched to an equal number of comparable European firms from the same industry, and of the same size and profitability, the study found that the weaker patent protection reduced the propensity to licence, particularly for smaller patent holders, highlighting the importance of patents for a market for technology.

Recent studies attest to how valuable the market for technology can be. Pere Arqué-Castells and Daniel Spulber have demonstrated that U.S. public firms earn significant revenues from selling or licencing patents.[16] Aggregate revenues from licensing and selling patents can be as much as 10 per cent of annual sales. This is a sizable fraction given that these are large, publicly traded firms. In the aggregate, the annual value of such technology transactions is estimated to be about $1 trillion. Related research shows that patents can even serve as collateral, unlocking new funding channels.[17] A separate study finds that patent sales alone account for half the total value of a firm's patents.[18] For smaller and more specialised innovators, such gains may be even larger.

The Smithian framework also reframes the role of science. Over time, the interaction of scientific discovery and commercial application creates a virtuous cycle in which each advance lays the groundwork for the next.[19] The application of science in invention may itself facilitate trade in technology, both by facilitating information transmission and by clarifying property rights. Consistent with these claims, a recent study found that science-based patents are more likely to be traded.[20]

Of course, a Smithian division of innovative labour has weaknesses. Specialised knowledge chains can break down. Many firms, especially those that are not at the technological frontier, may be unable to absorb new scientific discoveries from universities. As research shifts towards universities and as established companies scale back their own research, startups, anticipating fewer partners and exit options, may not get started at all. Much of the problem hinges on whether there are enough technologically sophisticated incumbents in each sector to absorb and translate the knowledge being developed by universities and startups in their ecosystem. If not, the Schumpeterian route may dominate, wherein startups develop or acquire the assets and capabilities needed to commercialise scientific inventions themselves.[21]

Key actors in the American innovation ecosystem

The division of innovative labour draws on the specialised strengths of universities, large firms, and startups, as well as on the interactions among them. This section outlines each actor's core role. It also discusses the key role of the government.

Universities and other nonprofit research institutions: The primary role of universities and other nonprofit research institutions is to produce human capital and knowledge. Universities train the scientists and professionals who will be the innovators of tomorrow. Universities also pursue long-term fundamental research that lacks immediate applications, and this work often lays the groundwork for major technological advances. Quantum computing,genetic engineering, and artificial intelligence began as theoretical studies within universities.

Over the last few decades, a "third mission" of universities has also been increasingly emphasised. Universities are also asked to have a more direct impact on society by strengthening knowledge transfer to industry. For instance, universities license their patents and intellectual property to established firms or startups for commercialisation. Technology transfer offices (TTOs) are often established to manage these collaborations. University spinoffs or startups are another channel. Consulting for industry is another key way universities help turn science into economic production.

Large firms: Large firms are best equipped to scale and commercialise new technologies, including those invented by third parties. When startups develop new technologies, they often rely on corporate partners to bring their innovations to scale, as this requires significant investment and expertise in manufacturing, supply chain management, and marketing. For example, established pharmaceutical companies often acquire or partner with biotech startups to develop and scale up the production of new drugs or medical treatments.

Absorbing new technology requires in-house expertise. Most large firms maintain dedicated R&D labs. The preponderance of their effort is dedicated to making immediate product improvements, effecting cost reductions, addressing customer needs, and solving problems in existing product lines. A smaller fraction of R&D effort is devoted to the search for new products or processes, aimed at creating the next generation of products. Amazon began as an online bookseller and leveraged the initial foothold in internet commerce to sell other goods online. It developed more efficient ways of reaching customers and warehousing and shipping a range of goods, eventually offering these services to other merchants listed on its website. It also invested in cloud computing and machine learning (initially to manage its own data), robotics, and autonomous vehicle technology (to reduce warehousing and shipping costs). In each of these sectors, it focused on improving efficiency and reducing costs through incremental innovations. Large shipping companies such as UPS offer another example of incremental innovations. Improved mapping and routing for its drivers (including, for instance, reducing the number of left turns) to reduce the time spent in delivering packages may seem minor, but they can significantly reduce costs. Incremental innovation is critical in the automotive, telecommunications, and consumer electronics industries. A handful of firms also devote a fraction of their R&D to more fundamental, long-term projects, and their corporate labs have produced major scientific advances and technological breakthroughs.

Startups: Startups play a critical role in the innovation ecosystem by experimenting with new applications and markets. High-profile innovations across diverse sectors, including social media platforms, mobile technologies, biotechnology, and advanced materials, have originated from startups, significantly reshaping existing industries and sometimes creating entirely new ones.

Startups typically emerge either from academic research environments or from established firms. University spinoffs, in particular, commercialise ideas and technologies developed within academic institutions. These spinoffs have developed key breakthroughs in fields such as pharmaceuticals, biotechnology, and materials science.

More commonly, startups are founded by employees of established firms who leave their positions to pursue entrepreneurial opportunities identified during their professional experience. Nvidia exemplifies this process; its founders, including Jensen Huang from LSI Logic and Chris Malachowsky and Curtis Priem from Sun Microsystems, created the company to capitalise on opportunities in graphics-based processing for video game applications.

This is not a new phenomenon. Steve Klepper has documented how many industry-leading firms began as spinoffs from pioneering incumbents. For example, approximately half of the leading American automobile firms in the early twentieth century were spinoffs from Detroit's initial automakers.[22] Similarly, Silicon Valley's semiconductor industry flourished initially through "Fairchildren": new companies founded by alumni of Shockley Semiconductor and Fairchild Semiconductor, which subsequently dominated the region's semiconductor landscape. Because entrepreneurs often establish spinoffs near their former employers, successful parent firms effectively become incubators for regional innovation hubs. This pattern creates self-reinforcing clusters of expertise, suppliers, and specialised labour markets, exemplified by Detroit's automotive industry and Silicon Valley's semiconductor ecosystem.

Government: Governments can be a crucial facilitator of innovation, providing funding, procurement opportunities, and regulatory frameworks that shape the innovation ecosystem. Governments fund research and development when there may be no immediate commercial return.

Programs at the U.S. National Institutes of Health (NIH), the National Science Foundation (NSF), and European Horizon 2020 provide billions in funding to support scientific research. Governments also offer tax incentives and subsidies to encourage private-sector R&D investment. Additionally, government-sponsored grants and contracts, such as the Small Business Innovation Research (SBIR) program in the United States, offer early-stage capital to startups.

Governments can also create markets for innovative products as buyers. Government contracts for clean energy solutions, military technologies, or public health innovations provide valuable opportunities for startups and established firms. The U.S. Department of Defense (DoD) has historically been one of the largest supporters of technological advances by acting as an early (and sometimes, only) customer in lasers, microprocessors, the internet, Global Positioning System (GPS), photovoltaics, and other transformative technologies. Similarly, national health systems in many countries procure advanced medical technologies and pharmaceutical innovations, creating opportunities for innovators in the biotech and medtech sectors.

Regulation matters as well. Well-designed IP protection can encourage innovation by ensuring that creators and inventors can benefit from their discoveries while minimising practices that could stifle competition and innovation in the long run. Governments can also encourage innovation through regulations that lower commercialisation uncertainty by creating clear demand signals. Environmental rules, for example, create predictable markets for green technologies and clean energy solutions by setting carbon emission limits and resource efficiency standards. In health care, drug approval frameworks reduce uncertainty about market entry, while in telecommunications, spectrum allocation policies guide investment in new wireless technologies. Although the design of rules and their effects on innovation are important, the present volume focuses on the organisation of the innovation ecosystem and, for the most part, leaves detailed analysis of regulation to others.

Specialisation and diversity in the division of innovative labour

Universities, startups, and large corporations each specialise in a distinct slice of the innovation process, coordinating through market transactions that turn early discoveries into commercial products.

Early-stage science begins in university labs, financed largely by government grants. Startups then translate these discoveries into prototypes, test use cases, and reduce technical and commercial risk. When a technology appears to be commercially viable, large corporations provide the capital, manufacturing scale, and distribution muscle to reach global markets. Profit-seeking firms seldom fund blue-sky research. However, when scientific research becomes more closely aligned with practical goals, companies may become more willing to fund it directly. "Use-inspired" research—basic research with clear practical implications—can attract corporate investment, as companies see opportunities to directly benefit from resulting innovations.

Moderna's path to one of the first mRNA COVID-19 vaccines shows how specialisation and coordination work in a well-functioning division of innovative labour. Derrick Rossi, a faculty member at Harvard Medical School, founded the company. Rossi's work at Harvard focused on stem cells, specifically on how adult stem cells could be reprogrammed into immature cells (known as pluripotent stem cells) to be guided to become other types of cells. This process could then be used to generate healthy cells to replace damaged cells in people, with many potential medical applications.

Prior work by Shinya Yamanaka had identified four specific genes that enabled the transformation (for this discovery, Yamanaka was awarded the 2012 Nobel Prize in Physiology or Medicine). However, a limitation of Yamanaka's work was that he had used a retrovirus to insert DNA into adult cells to trigger the transformation. While viruses are very good at getting into cells, they can also produce serious side effects.

To overcome this problem, Rossi and his team experimented with mRNA to transport the four genes. Initial tests using a green fluorescent protein instead of the four genes produced mixed results. While mRNA was very effective at carrying the protein, there was also a big problem: many dead cells.

Further investigations clarified the nature of the problem. The inserted synthetic mRNA triggered an immune response, destroying many healthy cells as "collateral damage." While this problem could have derailed the whole research program, a chance conversation saved the day. Colleagues from another lab had read a paper published a few years earlier by University of Pennsylvania researchers Katalin Karikó and Drew Weissman, who had tweaked a nucleoside—a building block of RNA—which sidestepped the immune reaction of the cells while still allowing the RNA to work.

Building on the work of Karikó and Weissman, Rossi and his collaborators used modified mRNA to convert skin cells into muscle cells without provoking the immune system. Their 2010 paper pointed to wide potential in cell-based therapies and regenerative medicine. To advance those applications, Rossi licensed the invention from the University of Pennsylvania and co-founded Moderna.

Moderna's origins illustrate how startups translate academic discoveries into potentially marketable products. Shinya Yamanaka discovered how to reprogram mature cells back into a stem cell state. Derrick Rossi proposed using messenger RNA as the delivery vehicle, and Katalin Karikó with Drew Weissman solved the immune reaction that had blocked earlier messenger RNA work. Together, these advances removed key scientific roadblocks and demonstrated that modified mRNA could be safe and effective.

However, to develop COVID-19 mRNA vaccines, much research and engineering still lay ahead. One significant hurdle was safe delivery of mRNA in the bloodstream. Messenger RNA is fragile and degrades quickly. Researchers overcame this problem with lipid nanoparticles that wrap the RNA, protect it on the journey, and release it inside human cells. Once inside, the RNA instructs the cell to produce the viral protein that primes the immune system. Without the nanoparticle carrier, a messenger RNA vaccine would break down before it could trigger any protection. Some of the science behind LNPs (which themselves draw upon liposomes, an even older drug-delivery mechanism) originated at the University of British Columbia, where Pieter Cullis and his team developed lipid-based delivery systems in the 1990s. Moderna's COVID-19 vaccine uses this technology, although there are ongoing legal disputes about licensing arrangements involving Arbutus and Acuitas. Similarly, the BionTech-Pfizer COVID-19 vaccine is based on Kariko and Weissman's mRNA discoveries licensed from the University of Pennsylvania and on lipid nanoparticle technology from Arbutus and Acuitas.

Two features stand out. First, different actors in the innovation ecosystem contributed to the development of mRNA vaccines. Publicly funded university laboratories uncovered the basic mechanisms. Venture-backed startups turned that insight into viable products. Large pharmaceutical companies supplied the capital, factory capacity, and regulatory know-how required for mass deployment. Second, translation and development were just as crucial as the discovery of the basic scientific principles. Without the painstaking work that makes a concept safe, stable, and scalable, basic science would have remained on the page. This case points to a broader lesson. The American innovation system prospers because it welcomes diversity of actors and diversity of approaches. Markets test competing ideas, success is rewarded, and failure is treated as a normal cost of exploration. By advancing many technical routes at once, the system raises the chance that at least one will break through. That is, a diversity of approaches mitigates failure in the innovation ecosystem.

As with the commercialisation of mRNA technology, the success of quantum computing will heavily depend on this diversity. While classical computers operate with binary bits, representing data as either zeros or ones, quantum computers use quantum bits, or qubits, which can represent multiple states simultaneously. This phenomenon, known as superposition, along with quantum entanglement and interference, enables quantum computers to perform complex calculations simultaneously, unlocking revolutionary commercial applications.

Initially, breakthroughs in quantum computing emerged primarily from theoretical research at universities, but substantial contributions were also made by corporate labs. A notable figure is Charles Bennett at IBM, who in 1984 proposed the first quantum cryptography protocol and later introduced seminal principles such as the no-cloning theorem and reversible computation.

Peter Shor's groundbreaking algorithm developed at AT&T's Bell Labs in 1994 was equally valuable. Shor demonstrated how quantum computers could factor large numbers far faster than conventional computers, a discovery with profound implications for encryption and cybersecurity. Though Shor's algorithm remains challenging to implement in practice, it provided a critical proof-of-concept that accelerated interest and investment in quantum computing.

Founded in 1999 as a university spinoff, Canadian company D-Wave Systems was the first company to sell a working quantum computer. Its machines are purpose-built for quantum annealing, a technique that excels at optimisation tasks such as finding the most efficient delivery routes, building factory schedules, or flagging unusual spending patterns that might signal fraud. Because the hardware is tuned only for optimisation, it cannot run general-purpose quantum algorithms such as Shor's factoring method or Grover's search routine. This narrow focus, however, let D-Wave commercialise quickly: its first 128-qubit model, the D-Wave One, was purchased by Lockheed Martin in 2011, and current "Advantage" systems exceed

5,000 qubits. Today, most customers access the technology through Leap, D-Wave's cloud service, which blends classical pre- and postprocessing with quantum annealing.

Large corporations have participated actively in the race to develop more general-purpose quantum computers. Many of these firms are American (IBM, Intel, Microsoft, Google), but China is now well represented as well (Huawei, Baidu, Alibaba). In December 2024, Google introduced its Willow quantum processor, a 105-qubit chip that achieved a landmark in quantum error correction. IBM has also made notable strides in quantum computing. In December 2023, the company unveiled the Condor processor, featuring 1,121 superconducting qubits, which promised a significant leap in quantum processing power. More recently, Microsoft announced a new type of quantum processor based on topological qubits, where information is stored not in any single particle, but in the collective behaviour of an entire circuit.[23] If validated, it marks not only a significant technological advance but also a scientific one. Microsoft's qubits rely on Majorana, a new type of quasiparticle, proposing a mode of electron behaviour that is as yet unconfirmed.

Startups have joined the fray. Crunchbase data show that venture capital-backed quantum startups raised $1.9 billion in 2024, $789 million in 2023, and $1.5 billion in 2022. This represents a giant leap compared to the $100 million or so in 2015, or even compared to $200 million in 2018.[24] Some startups are trying to develop the hardware for quantum computing. A variety of designs have emerged so far. IonQ (which is now publicly traded) uses trapped ytterbium ions to perform its calculations. PsiQuantum uses photons. Others use "synthetic" qubits, such as superconducting loops of different types used by Rigetti Computing, IBM, Google, and QCI.

Other startups focus on software. Companies such as Zapata Computing, 1Qbit, Cambridge Quantum Computing, and QC Ware develop algorithms that quantum computers can use. Some focus on quantum-inspired applications, such as optimising supply chains or in finance. Finally, some startups are exploring quantum technologies that are not directly associated with computing. An active line of research, especially in China, is secure quantum communications, where firms such as QuantumCTek and Qasky are making important investments. Another area of research is the development of imaging and sensing technologies, where Qnami is active.

Although the quantum computing industry is rapidly evolving, several patterns stand out. First, it is unclear which technology path for creating and controlling qubits will prevail. Each candidate approach relies on complementary advances in error correction, ultra-low-temperature cooling, and high-vacuum systems, and so uncertainty remains high. Importantly, technological advance is not just a matter of new machines but may also involve new scientific knowledge. Second, the most promising commercial applications are unclear. The early D-Wave computer offered improvements to existing solutions, but transformative solutions to existing problems, or solutions to entirely new problems, remain out of reach. Third, national governments are providing research support and even acting as buyers. Fourth, cooperation and competition co-exist. There is Schumpeterian competition, but there is also Smithian cooperation, with firms in the ecosystem developing complementary software or searching for applications. The responsibility for frontier science is shared between businesses, particularly large ones such as Alphabet and Microsoft, and universities.

As the quantum industry matures, Smithian commercialisation will likely become more prominent. This outcome depends on a few large firms continuing to participate in scientific research. Unlike mRNA, where large firms were mainly active at the commercialisation stage, in quantum computing they are central to both advancing science and scaling up. This difference reflects the systemic nature of quantum innovation, where progress requires the integration of multiple interdependent technologies rather than advances in a single domain. Quantum computing also combines high technical risk with high market risk, unlike mRNA, which posed a primarily technical challenge once the basic science was established. For this reason, quantum depends on the involvement of large firms, which are better able to absorb dual risk, in a way that mRNA did not.

Institutions supporting division of innovative labour

The division of labour is fundamental to economic progress, but it rests on the ability to trade. When it comes to innovation, trade involves the exchange of technology in the form of licencing, acquisitions, R&D alliances, or joint ventures. Incumbent firms and university spinoffs can acquire university-based inventions by obtaining patent licences; large incumbents sometimes collaborate with or acquire startups through mergers and acquisitions. These transactions, which are part of a "market for technology," serve two primary purposes. First, they direct inventions towards those organisations that are most capable of developing or commercialising them. Second, they allow research-rich but resource-poor organisations to also contribute to the innovation ecosystem.

From the 1970s onward, institutions facilitating markets for technology began to flourish. University research became more accessible to both new and established firms, aided by stronger patent regimes that promised reliable intellectual property protections. Patents incentivise inventors to undertake risky R&D by reassuring them that the fruits of their efforts will be protected. Potential buyers become more willing to pay for technologies because they are confident that their investment will not be misappropriated. These shifts owed much to a general trend of stronger patent protection in Organization for Economic Cooperation and Development (OECD) countries following legal changes in the 1980s.[25] In the United States, the establishment of a pro-patent Court of Appeals in 1982 and the Bayh–Dole Act of 1980, which encouraged American universities to patent and license their discoveries, were among the most significant milestones. (Chapter 12 discusses the emergence of these institutions in greater depth.)

Venture capital and angel investors emerged as sources of funding, helping bridge the gap between early-stage research and commercial products. In addition to providing money, these investors contribute industry connections, mentoring, and market experience. Another important development was the proliferation of intermediaries facilitating technology exchange. Procter & Gamble, for instance, launched Connect + Develop, an online open-innovation portal designed to attract external ideas and facilitate potential partnerships. Firms such as Yet2 began scouting technologies for corporate clients, while others, like Ocean Tomo, specialised in intellectual property valuation. Intellectual Ventures, a private equity firm, entered the field by licencing and monetising patents while also developing its own science-based inventions. These intermediaries made it easier for academic innovators, small startups, and large corporations to find each other, thereby reducing friction in the market for technology.

Yet, even with robust institutional support, the efficiency of technology exchange depends heavily on the nature of the knowledge being traded. Specialisation and trade, which are interlinked in any economy, become more complex when the knowledge to be transferred is tacit and therefore difficult to articulate and contract upon. Kenneth Arrow famously remarked that when American engineers received British jet engine blueprints during World War II, they needed ten months simply to redraw them for American manufacturing standards.[26] Similar problems appeared when American companies tried to replicate cellulosic fibre production from British patents in the early 1900s. Even after buying rights to the viscose process, U.S. firms could not reproduce European successes until they partnered more closely with Britain's Courtaulds, imported key machinery, and observed the manufacturing process firsthand. DuPont also experienced major difficulties in duplicating high-quality German organic dyes. Despite spending millions of dollars and partnering with European firms, it eventually resorted to poaching German chemists to gain the know-how not disclosed in patent documents.

Science-based inventions and the market for technology

Science can reduce knowledge tacitness. It can clarify why and how something works, allowing knowledge to be written down, taught, and transferred more systematically.[27] Scientific inventions also tend to have broader potential applications: a discovery in quantum physics may spark advances in semiconductors, lasers, or telecommunications, whereas a less thoroughly understood technique might remain confined to its original niche. Photoluminescence, the phenomenon whereby materials emit light after application of an electric current, is the basis for light-emitting diodes (LEDs) as well as lasers. The principles of photoluminescence are applied not only in lighting and displays, but also in the production of semiconductor chips and vision correction surgery. This demonstrates how a deeper theoretical understanding can unlock multiple unanticipated uses.

Science accelerates the search for new applications by offering a conceptual map. Instead of stumbling through brute-force trials, researchers can rely on theories to guide them to promising paths. Studies in nanotechnology showed that molecular angles and diameters determine whether carbon nanotubes conduct electricity or exhibit semiconducting properties.[28] With these insights, researchers can focus their experiments and cut down on costly trial and error. The same approach helps in designing carbon-nanotube transistors and biosensors for medical tests and food safety checks.

Some believe that large-scale empirical observations combined with machine-learning techniques can crowd out theoretical understanding. Matteo Tranchero's dissertation instead shows that theoretical understanding complements empirical observation and machine learning, increasing the efficiency of drug discovery.[29] Genome-wide association studies (GWAS) represent a data-driven search for the genetic roots of disease. He finds that GWAS findings trigger a surge of follow-on work aimed at elucidating their causal mechanisms.

Science also lowers the cost of trading inventions by making them more modular. The more scientists understand a technology, the more they can break it down into components that can be purchased or licensed independently. Consider semiconductors. Early firms, starting with Fairchild in 1957, combined design and manufacturing because producing integrated circuits required constant coordination among designers, physicists, and engineers. As knowledge advanced, new tools and methods emerged that allowed chip design and fabrication to separate. "Fabless" firms such as Xilinx began outsourcing fabrication to specialised foundries like TSMC, while companies like ARM specialised in licensing only processor-core designs. Electronic Design Automation (EDA) tools, which were standardised in part following the publication of Mead and Conway's *Introduction to VLSI Systems* in 1978, made it possible to share design schematics without giving away proprietary knowledge.[30] Their textbook introduced modular design rules for Very Large-Scale Integration (VLSI), which allowed circuits to be described in standardised ways, and it laid the groundwork for EDA tools to become widely usable. Without such scientific and technical advances, dividing labour among multiple companies might have been unmanageable.

The same principle applies to intellectual property. Just as modular design made it easier to exchange chip designs without revealing everything, scientific understanding in other domains clarifies what exactly is being traded. Selling knowledge is challenging because the inventor must reveal the idea for the buyer to assess its value, which can reduce the inventor's ability to capture adequate returns. Patents attempt to solve this problem, but the effectiveness of a patent depends on how crisply its boundaries can be drawn. A scientific understanding helps clarify property rights. When Giulio Natta discovered the stereochemical structures of polypropylene in the 1950s, he was able to patent isotactic and syndiotactic forms separately, linking these configurations to distinctive physical properties. He shared the 1963 Nobel Prize for that breakthrough. By contrast, the earlier Phillips Petroleum patent on polypropylene emerged from trial-and-error methods that did not provide a detailed theoretical understanding. Because that patent explained only how to produce the material, rather than exactly what it was, its protection was narrower.

When scientific understanding is limited, patents tend to be imperfect, and firms keep crucial details secret to avoid giving competitors an advantage. This situation prevailed in the nineteenth-century organic-dye industry, when precise chemical structures were unknown. Patent holders such as Société La Fuchsine sometimes used overly broad patents in legal battles instead of focusing on the discovery of new dyes.[31] Some chemists fled to Switzerland, which did not recognise French patent claims, thereby catalysing the rise of the Swiss chemical sector. Only when scientific understanding matured did it become easier to define and transfer technology without crippling legal disputes.

Empirical evidence supports the view that scientific clarity makes inventions easier to trade. Patents based on scientific research are sold or licensed about 25 per cent more often than those with weaker scientific foundations.[32] This difference partly reflects higher inherent value, but it also shows that scientific inventions are more comprehensible to potential buyers. The effect is especially strong for novel inventions, which are more likely to be misunderstood, and for small firms, which are more inclined to specialise in upstream research. In such cases, a solid scientific basis helps buyers judge unfamiliar terrain, opening more space for specialisation and a finer division of innovative labour.

Safeguarding innovation diversity: how corporate labs anchor America's innovation ecosystem

As later chapters of this book show, the rise and subsequent decline of large corporate laboratories have shaped America's innovation landscape. After the 1980s, many companies pivoted away from fundamental research, leaving universities to focus on basic science and startups to pursue commercial applications. While this shift supported specialisation, it left a critical gap: corporate research had anchored the innovation ecosystem in ways that universities and startups cannot easily replicate, except perhaps in a few sectors. The dismantling of corporate labs, while perhaps privately valuable to firms, weakened America's capacity for deep-tech innovation.

Corporate labs can accelerate the translation of scientific insights into market-ready products. Michael Bikard finds that corporate-authored papers earn 23 per cent more citations from inventors than comparable university publications.[33] This is especially true for architectural innovations that require advances along a number of dimensions, often involving more than one layer of the value chain. In mobile telephony, for example, larger firms harnessed general-purpose technologies to develop far-reaching architectural changes.[34]

Coordinating such changes is much harder across organisational boundaries, as is the task of bringing together the required expertise from multiple disciplines. The transistor, for instance, resulted from interdisciplinary work at Bell Labs involving physicists, chemists, and metallurgists—drawing on wartime expertise in semiconductor purification. Although researchers at Purdue and General Electric had explored solid-state electronics earlier, only Bell Labs possessed both the theoretical insights and the practical engineering needed for success, including Henry Theurer's zone-refining technique for germanium and Gordon Teal's crystal "pulling" method.[35] Likewise, Fairchild Semiconductor's close integration of R&D and manufacturing was very valuable for the development of the planar process and integrated circuits,[36] achievements less feasible for "fabless" firms lacking in-house manufacturing.

Industrial research is also essential for an effective division of innovative labour. By building absorptive capacity, it enables firms to identify and acquire external knowledge. Knowledgeable buyers are especially important for startups, particularly early-stage ventures with promising technology but lacking the capability to commercialise it. The next chapter examines in greater detail the role of knowledgeable buyers for deep-tech startups.

Nathan Rosenberg has long stressed that diversity and experimentation are central to technological advancement and economic growth.[37] When there are different potential ways of approaching a problem, the conventional wisdom is that involving many small-scale experimenters is a more effective way than relying on a few larger experimenters conducting multiple experiments each.[38] In other words, startups are conventionally seen as the source of diversity. However, startups (and their investors) are susceptible to fashions and fads, being prone to herding into the most promising approaches. Corporate labs can offset this tendency towards herding.

A recent study illuminates why organisational variety matters. When researchers face a range of possible approaches, small firms often "herd" toward the most promising one, whereas large incumbents disperse resources across a wider portfolio.[39] The search for treatments for Alzheimer's Disease is a case in point. There are many hypotheses about the causes of Alzheimer's and how to treat it. Between 1998 and 2008, nearly 40 per cent of projects targeted beta-amyloid, and almost 60 per cent focused on just two targets: beta-amyloid and cholinergic. Moreover, this herding is largely driven by startups rather than incumbents. Of the projects initiated between 2007 and 2008, Pfizer launched six projects, of which only two focused on beta-amyloid drugs. In contrast, eight of the eighteen projects by startups targeted beta-amyloids. If the beta-amyloid hypothesis turns out to be wrong, all drug candidates relying on beta-amyloid will fail.

Markets dominated by a few big players, therefore, could exhibit greater methodological diversity and a lower probability of outright failure than the same number of trials run exclusively by startups. Even so, startups remain indispensable: while most chase the same hot leads, some startups pursue novel directions.

Is growing specialisation a natural evolution of a mature innovation ecosystem?

This new equilibrium, in which the work of innovation is spread more evenly across universities, startups, and established firms, looks like the natural next stage of a maturing innovation ecosystem. The chief catalyst is market expansion. As Adam Smith noted, larger markets make specialisation more profitable because higher output lets producers spread fixed costs, such as specialised machinery, over many units, lowering average production costs. Larger markets enable each participant to focus on its strongest activity. Given ample demand, a firm can profit by excelling at a single stage, and this deep specialisation raises overall productivity. Smith's image of the woollen coat captures the idea: shepherds, spinners, weavers, and tailors each perform a distinct step, and only their combined effort yields the final garment. Modern innovation follows a similar logic, with different organisations carrying out complementary tasks that together move new technologies from laboratory to marketplace.

Building upon Smith's insight, later economists such as Allyn Young and George Stigler extended the concept of specialisation beyond individual workers to include entire firms and industries.[40] This broader view emphasises how market growth facilitates specialisation among different firms and sectors. However, specialisation itself does not occur automatically.[41] The rapid expansion of the U.S. railroad network after the Civil War substantially lowered transportation and trade costs, but it did not produce the highly specialised economy that Smith's theory predicted. Instead, it facilitated the rise of large vertically integrated corporations. Alfred D. Chandler, in his seminal work *Scale and Scope* (1990), documented how firms used railroads and the telegraph to consolidate multiple stages of production and distribution to achieve greater operational efficiency and economies of scale.[42] By integrating supply and distribution, firms secure inputs, lower uncertainty, and curb reliance on outside suppliers. As markets grow, spreading fixed costs over larger volumes makes it cheaper to internalise several production stages than to contract with specialists, so vertical integration can outperform specialisation. But expanding demand does not always favour integration; whether firms integrate or specialise depends on the relative cost structures of each approach and on how complementary the different stages of production are.

Building on this insight, Nathan Rosenberg pointed out that market scope, not just market size, is important for specialisation. His key insight was that when the breadth of downstream demand relative to its depth increases, integration becomes less profitable. Investments in upstream inputs are concentrated in specialised upstream sectors, which then supply downstream users. In his study of the machine tool industry, Rosenberg noted that in the 1820s, machine tools were initially produced by the very firms that used them. However, as user needs evolved, internal production of machine tools became increasingly inefficient.[43] It was the diversity of demand across multiple industries that proved crucial to the development of specialised machine tool producers.

In turn, these specialised machine tools were pivotal in the industrial development of the United States in the nineteenth century. Sectors such as textiles and railroads were early adopters of machine tools, followed by arms manufacturers and sewing machine makers. Early adopters in textiles and railroads nurtured specialised machine tool firms, paving the way for later users to reap the benefits. As Rosenberg explains: "It seems clear that the extraordinary degree of specialisation achieved in the machine-producing sector of the American economy is attributable, not only to the growth of individual industries..., but also to the simultaneous growth of several industries which were technologically convergent,"[44] meaning these industries required similar types of machining operations. In essence, it was the diverse demand across different industries, not simply the size of the market, that spurred specialisation in machinery production.

Rosenberg's insight was formalised in 1998, when Tim Bresnahan and Alfonso Gambardella developed a model in which a single upstream input can serve many downstream applications.[45] Downstream firms will buy that input rather than make it themselves only if the specialised supplier's unit cost, after adding the expense of tailoring the input to each buyer, is still lower than the downstream firm's in-house cost. The key theoretical result is that, for a given total demand, specialised production is more likely when an input has many different uses (breadth) rather than being concentrated in a few large uses (depth). In other words, a specialist upstream sector is more likely to emerge when the input has a broad range of applications rather than deep demand in just a few.

The reason is that developing and producing the input entail a fixed investment. A specialist supplier would amortise this investment over all its customers. However, an individual user may have to tailor the standard input supplied for their own needs, which entails an additional cost. An individual user would produce its own input rather than buy the input if its scale of operations is large, justifying the fixed investment. The more such large users, the smaller the market for a specialist producer, and the greater the average unit cost of the producer. In turn, this would dissuade users, even those with a smaller scale of operations, from buying from the specialist producer. The result would be an industry configuration dominated by vertical integration.

Ewens, Nanda, and Rhodes-Kropf document how changes in input supply conditions—notably Amazon's introduction of cloud computing—encouraged digital startups.[46] Startups could now enter by leasing rather than buying computer equipment, reducing upfront costs. They found that startups leveraging cloud computing required 20 per cent less in initial venture capital funding. The lower entry costs allowed more risk-taking, which ultimately led to greater diversity in the web-based ecosystem. Importantly, as more startups entered, Amazon's incentives to keep improving its cloud computing business intensified, leading to even more entry and early-stage experimentation. Interestingly, Amazon had originally developed its web infrastructure for internal use, but the growth of small startups presented it with a market opportunity. As a result, Amazon became both a large user and a specialist provider of cloud services.

The same logic is illustrated in the chemical industry. Today, specialised engineering firms (SEFs) design, engineer, and construct chemical plants for companies that produce and distribute chemicals. Before World War

II, chemical companies, concerned about protecting their trade secrets, developed their own processes and designed their own plants. They only turned to external specialists for areas where they lacked specific expertise, such as electrical systems. These early specialists were the precursors to modern SEFs. As plants grew in size and complexity, larger, more diverse teams became necessary, making it increasingly expensive to keep these teams in-house. SEFs gained an advantage by spreading the costs of large teams across multiple projects, while the experience gained from working on a variety of projects improved the quality of their services. Arora, Fosfuri, and Gambardella showed that these firms facilitated the entry of new chemical producers in emerging economies, which outsourced the engineering and construction to SEFs.[47]

However, there is a chicken-and-egg problem. Companies do not outsource arbitrarily; they consider the prices set by SEFs, which in turn depend on their unit costs, and therefore, on the demand for outsourcing. This introduces a feedback loop: while Adam Smith famously observed that specialisation depends on the extent of the market, the realised extent of the market also depends on the level of specialisation. Bresnahan and Gambardella offer a resolution with the insight that upstream input providers are more likely to emerge when downstream markets are broad but shallow. Arora, Vogt, and Yoon provide empirical support from the chemical industry.[48] The key is that large companies operate in some markets, making them potentially deep. In markets dominated by large companies, which can build plants internally, SEFs face a reduced market for their services and thus have higher unit costs. A market dominated by vertically integrated large users leaves little space for specialised input providers, forcing would-be entrants to also provide for themselves. An immediate implication is that entry would be more difficult. The reverse is also true; encouraging entry will encourage specialisation. Smaller entrants grow the market by expanding its breadth rather than its depth. This enables specialised input suppliers to further lower their unit costs, pushing some not-so-small downstream firms to switch from "make" to "buy." Put differently, the process of specialisation and division of labour is self-reinforcing. Upstream specialisation in input supply fosters downstream entry, increasing the size of the market for the upstream specialists.

Bresnahan and Gambardella's economic logic also has implications for the division of innovative labour between universities and large firms. To the extent that scientific research in, say, biology or computer science is applicable to many different sectors, a specialist supplier (e.g., a university department) is more efficient. However, as depth in some industries grows, some large firms may prefer to conduct research in-house, to better tailor this research to their needs.

The recent boom in AI has indeed led many companies to invest heavily in AI research. Companies such as Google and Facebook now perform on a par with or even better than the best AI departments in universities. For instance, at the 2019 Neural Information Processing Systems conference, the premier annual conference in AI and deep learning, Google researchers contributed to 167 of the accepted papers—more than twice the amount of the second most represented institution, Stanford University.[49] There has been an ongoing brain drain of AI professors from universities that extended from 2004 to 2018.[50] The talent outflow has been most pronounced among tenured faculty, professors at top-tier universities, and among those specialising in deep learning—for example, Geoffrey Hinton to Google, Yann LeCun to Facebook AI, Ian Goodfellow to Apple after Google Brain, Zoubin Ghahramani to Uber AI, and Ruslan Salakhutdinov to Apple.

Overall, a sector that grows and matures tends to adopt a greater division of labour, as long as it is not dominated by a few large producers. Breadth, the range of distinct applications and users, matters more than sheer production scale. Incumbent firms play a mixed role in this system. Their corporate laboratories can satisfy some research needs internally, which lowers demand for specialised suppliers. Yet those incumbents also serve as the main exit route for startups through acquisition or partnership.

Chapter takeaways

The strength of the American innovation ecosystem lies in its institutional diversity and multiplicity of technological pathways for solving economic problems. Universities serve as foundational pillars, producing fundamental science and supplying the skilled workforce necessary for discovery and commercialisation. Startups and sometimes universities themselves have tried to bridge the gap between science and market applications. Established corporations, in turn, offer the scale and infrastructure required to develop complex innovations at scale and bring them to market.

Science facilitates trade in technology. A deeper understanding of how an invention works makes it more modular, clarifies patent boundaries, and lowers the cost of evaluating unfamiliar ideas. Patents rooted in scientific knowledge get traded more often and at higher values than those based on trial-and-error methods.

Lastly, we view the deepening of DOIL as a natural response to larger, and especially broader, markets. Breadth creates enough demand to support specialist suppliers, and their presence, in turn, lowers entry barriers and encourages further specialisation.

The next two chapters explore how the deepening DOIL has produced uneven progress across America's technological sectors.

3

Division of Innovative Labour and the Deep-Tech Innovation Gap

Introduction

Between 2015 and 2019, more than 75 per cent of all U.S. venture capital (VC) went to software and to consumer and business products and services. Approximately 20 per cent went to biopharmaceuticals and medical devices. Less than 5 per cent was devoted to fields such as telecommunications, batteries, fusion, and computer hardware.[1] A recent study by Namrata Narain similarly finds that VC investment is concentrated in sectors with shorter innovation lags.[2] A common policy response is to try to increase the supply of venture financing for the neglected sectors.

This chapter argues that the funding gap in neglected sectors stems from frictions in the division of innovative labour (DOIL), not from a shortage of risk capital, distorted investor incentives, or lack of scientific opportunities. These neglected domains, which we group under the umbrella term "deep-tech," include quantum computing, advanced materials, synthetic biology beyond therapeutics, energy storage, renewable fuels, and fusion power. They share two characteristics: (i) They are based on scientific discoveries but require significant translational research beyond the initial discovery; and (ii) commercial application requires complementary inventions rather than straightforward engineering.

These characteristics pose significant challenges when it comes to commercialisation. Translational work in deep-tech often requires adapting a technology to new uses. As a consequence, there is uncertainty not only about the technology itself but also about demand. Put differently, there is both technology risk and market risk.

In addition, the need for complementary inventions often requires coordinated investment. When different organisations share R&D and commercialisation responsibilities, as they do under DOIL, even highly valuable ideas can stall. Coordination is inherently more difficult across organisations to begin with. But in a market-based system, coordination also depends on expectations of how the gains will be shared between the partners. As we explain below, deep-tech startups are especially disadvantaged in their ability to capture the value they create.

The rest of the chapter examines the structural challenges facing deep-tech ventures, focusing on the challenges posed by joint technological and market uncertainty, coordinated investment, and insufficient value capture. Two case studies, light-emitting diodes and lithium-ion batteries, illustrate the arguments.

Why deep-tech is hard, especially for startups

For-profit companies invest in new technologies when they can appropriate a sufficient share of the value they create. A useful way to analyse private firms' incentives to invest is to distinguish between value creation and value capture. Value creation refers to the total value created by an invention for all stakeholders (including the inventor). Value capture refers to the share of total value that accrues to a particular stakeholder. In this discussion, we set aside the broader social value of inventions and focus only on returns that accrue to private companies. That is, we neglect issues such as customer surplus.

Value creation is complicated in deep-tech both because of technological and market uncertainty, and because these technologies often require a sequence of interdependent advances across materials, equipment, and processes to make the original "breakthrough" invention commercially viable. These tasks can be more challenging for startups. In addition, deep-tech startups face greater hurdles in appropriating a sufficient share of the value they create.

Technological and market uncertainty

To appreciate the challenges in deep-tech originating from joint technological and market uncertainty, one can contrast digital startups with deep-tech ventures. Digital startups can test product–market fit in just a few months by using cloud services and pay-as-you-go distribution; technical risks are modest and customer feedback, though noisy, arrives quickly. Instead, deep-tech ventures face two intertwined uncertainties: whether the science itself can perform at commercial scale and cost, and whether sufficient market demand will materialise at a viable price point. Market demand cannot be reliably assessed without validated technology, but technology development is itself shaped by the intended application.

Fault-tolerant qubits and ultra-durable batteries illustrate these challenges. Building qubits that remain coherent or batteries that retain 90 per cent of their capacity after ten thousand cycles pushes the limits of physics, materials science, and engineering. Yet, even if the science advances, commercial relevance depends on context. A battery's performance requirements in data centres are different from those for cars, phones, or spacecraft. Similarly, quantum computers would create value only if complementary software, algorithms, and data services were in place, assets largely outside the control of the initial innovators.

The interdependence of technological development and commercial applications generates distinctive challenges. Deep-tech entrepreneurs must iterate repeatedly between R&D and prospective uses. This function is hard under any circumstance, but especially so when decisions are distributed across multiple organisations.[3] Unlike biopharmaceuticals, where the uncertainty is primarily technical, or consumer software, where it is primarily market-related, deep-tech ventures must confront both simultaneously. A prototype may reveal the need to redesign upstream materials or upgrade downstream infrastructure, forcing the startup to renegotiate contracts or search for new partners, increasing costs, lowering value capture, and delaying commercialisation.

The biocement industry provides a good example. Founded in 2012, Biomason uses bacteria to make cement. Developing the technology was arduous because each target market demanded its own balance of cost and performance. Incumbent cement makers doubted that Biomason's process could meet industry requirements for both scale and cost. The reasons differed by segment: structural concrete demands huge volumes at commodity prices, whereas dust-control pads for temporary helipads require flexible, small-batch production more than low unit cost. Until the firm demonstrated that it could satisfy these contrasting needs at industrial scale, buyers remained unconvinced, but without validated market applications, investors were leery of funding technology development. Biomason first targeted niche applications such as dust control, earning early revenue from grants and research contracts with the Army, Air Force, and the U.S. Defense Advanced Research Projects Agency (DARPA). Eventually, Biomason succeeded in establishing a partnership with Danish concrete manufacturer IBF in 2023 for a biocement factory in Denmark to produce tiles. This partnership, together with an ongoing relationship with Martin Marietta, allowed Biomason to raise more than $100 million in VC investment.[4]

The scale-up problem

Biomason's need to demonstrate performance targets at industrial volumes also illustrates the challenges of scaling up. Scaling refers to the transition from validated experimentation "in the lab" to industrial-scale production. Scaling often involves more than just development. Additional research may be needed to adapt processes and structures so that inventions can be produced in large quantities and at acceptable cost. This research sometimes turns out to be as hard as coming up with the original discovery.

Consider Alnylam, a biotech startup that pioneered RNAi technology, which can be used to "turn off" genes in the body. The company struggled for years, not so much to develop or validate the technology, but to solve the problem of delivering the RNA molecule. After extensive experimentation with various types of nanolipid particles, Alnylam finally succeeded when it developed GalNAc conjugates that could efficiently deliver RNA to specific organs such as the liver.[5]

The problem is seen most clearly in new materials, such as carbon fibre composites. Continuous carbon fibres set in a polymer matrix yield a material that is light and strong, ideal for ultra-light bicycle frames and for aircraft wings, fuselages, and control surfaces. These composites usually emerge in university or industrial labs; yet small-batch methods keep their unit cost too high for broad commercial use. Benjamin Reinhardt explains what it takes to get new materials out of the lab and into mass production:[6]

> Leaving the lab requires bridging many orders of magnitude: from producing less than 0.001 kilograms (one gram) per day in a lab to more than 1,000 kilograms (one tonne) per day in a factory. You can think of lab-scale materials as the most artisanal products in the world, painstakingly handcrafted by people with advanced degrees. Like any artisanal product, lab-scale materials are expensive. [. . .] [W]e need to discover cheaper ways

> to produce it, since the price per quantity has a dramatic effect on how much it can be used. We call this process 'scaling', but [the term] bundles together many different problems that need to be solved to decrease cost and increase yield.

Reinhardt distinguishes between three types of scaling problems: (i) consistency, which requires ensuring that a sufficiently large fraction of the material displays a desired property; (ii) standardisation, which requires figuring out how to produce the material using conventional, low-cost equipment in an easily replicable way; and (iii) streamlining, which requires developing a continuous manufacturing process, which drastically reduces costs. This is particularly challenging for startups, which lack manufacturing experience and established relationships with equipment and material suppliers.

The large costs of scaling exacerbate the problems of joint technological and market uncertainty. Industrial-scale factories require vast capital outlays and specialised infrastructure. To justify such expense, investors demand clarity on applications and customers, but these only emerge once outputs can be produced affordably and in volume.

Take carbon fibre, a material that is now indispensable in many industries but one that involved decades of struggle to find viable applications. Early attempts included failed turbine blades and flawed aircraft propellers that helped sink Rolls-Royce into receivership in 1971. It was only much later, after production costs fell and use cases crystallised, that carbon fibre found applications in aerospace and other industries.

Uncertainty and scaling combine to create a central "chicken-and-egg" dilemma for deep-tech innovation.[7] Uncertainty makes it difficult to predict whether the technology will work and whether markets will materialise; scaling demands vast resources to demonstrate both. Iterating between prospective applications and R&D is costly as it is, and the need to commit to expensive manufacturing infrastructure amplifies the stakes. While proving demand without scaling production is difficult, raising resources to scale often requires that very proof of demand.

This interplay explains why deep-tech ventures advance more slowly than digital startups, why capital intensity is so high, and why complementary assets matter so profoundly. Overcoming these challenges often requires long-term partnerships, public support, and patient capital willing to underwrite years of technological iteration before commercial certainty emerges.

Complementary inventions and coordinated investment

In deep-tech sectors, the path from laboratory discovery to marketable product rarely consists of a single breakthrough. More often, it requires a sequence of interdependent advances across materials, equipment, and processes, each of which is necessary to render the invention commercially viable. As Nathan Rosenberg emphasised, technological progress is marked by "technological interdependence," where the utility of one innovation depends critically on parallel advances elsewhere.[8] When these complementary investments are misaligned or fragmented across multiple organisations, much of the potential value is dissipated. An example is Airbus's A380 program, where incompatible versions of computer-aided design software among consortium members contributed to multibillion-dollar overruns and delivery delays.[9]

Rosenberg also highlighted the cumulative impact of incremental innovations. While dramatic breakthroughs attract the most attention, incremental refinements such as improvements in steam engines, shipbuilding methods, or electric power generation, collectively delivered large productivity gains over time. Large firms, with the ability to amortise R&D costs over vast output, are often the principal investors in such cumulative advances. By contrast, startups must largely rely on external actors to provide these improvements.

The need for all these complementary investments, especially when spread across a vast supply chain rather than centralised within a large firm, can stall promising ideas in the lab. Startups in particular can face a formidable coordination problem, similar to the chicken-and-egg problem we discussed earlier. When early participants doubt that later ones will invest, they delay their own commitments; investors also view these early participants with scepticism. The value of prototypes may be limited if complementary inventions are not ready. The success of Tesla, for instance, hinged not only on its internal capabilities and innovations, but also on advances in battery technology by suppliers such as Panasonic and new manufacturing methods such as gigacasting, developed by the Idra Group in Italy and L.K. Technology Holdings in China.

Developing these complementary inventions typically exceeds what most startups can manage. Returning to some earlier examples, we note that qubit prototypes require cryogenic refrigerators, precision lasers, and custom chip foundries. Next-generation batteries need pilot plants with specialised reactors and quality-control systems. Those facilities cost millions of dollars and must be developed long before a single product is sold. Investors then distrust technical claims made by resource-starved startups. The chain stalls, capital dries up, and promising ideas stay in the lab.

The value-capture problem for deep-tech startups

While value creation in deep-tech is hard, especially for startups, so also is value capture. Value capture is the share of value created by an invention that a firm is able to retain. For deep-tech startups, the challenge is that even when their inventions generate considerable value, much of it is captured by incumbents, suppliers, or downstream partners. Investors in deep-tech startups, therefore, face a twofold hurdle: they must believe in the technology itself and in the willingness of downstream partners, who control essential assets such as large-scale production, distribution networks, and regulatory expertise, to adopt it. This requires estimating how much of the total value created will remain with the startup once partners take their share. Even if the overall project has a positive net present value, investment may not proceed if the startup captures only a small fraction of the surplus. When the expected return falls below the threshold investors require for the risks involved, funding dries up and development stalls.

A recent study offers a theoretical formulation of the value-capture problem for startups.[10] Startups are assumed to have an edge over established firms in developing technology, while incumbents have the advantage in commercialisation. Deep-tech startups often approach potential commercialisation partners only after committing significant resources to technology development and resolving key technical uncertainties. Without well-defined use cases and credible supporting evidence, potential partners are unlikely to engage. This challenge is compounded by the fact that many large corporations and investors find it difficult to evaluate the complex technical risks inherent in deep-tech ventures. A 2017 survey by the Boston Consulting Group found that nearly half of all deep-tech startups believed large corporations lacked the agility needed to collaborate effectively on deep-tech initiatives.[11] The sequence of investments implies that the profits startups can capture from partnering with incumbents depend on their ex-post bargaining power. Before making investments in their technology, startups are in a relatively strong position. They hold the option to walk away from unfavourable terms, and they can negotiate from a position of flexibility.

After technological investments are made, the startups' bargaining position weakens. Two factors become especially significant at this stage. The first is the size of the initial investment. When costs are relatively low, startups are more willing to proceed, even with the risk of lower value capture. The second factor is the availability of independent commercialisation pathways. Such options are plentiful in biopharma. They include contract development and manufacturing services by companies such as Lonza, ThermoFisher, Catalent, WuXi, and Fuji, and contract research by IQVIA, Labcorp (Covance), and ThermoFisher (PPD). Others offer specialised technologies. For example, Glycodisplay's proprietary process technology can standardise the production of antibodies and increase output. Startups can leverage such independent routes to market to strengthen their negotiating position.

A gap in commercialisation is more likely if independent routes to the final customer are harder to find, as is the case in biodegradable superabsorbent polymers for diapers. A handful of companies control the downstream market for diapers and sanitary pads, and competing with them would be difficult, especially for a startup. The failure of startups in this case is not necessarily due to a lack of value creation or to inadequate venture capital; rather, it is due to insufficient value capture by the startup.

Roger Masclans's doctoral dissertation provides empirical evidence that the appropriation gap is particularly severe in deep-tech sectors.[12] Masclans analyses a dataset of 5,823 venture capital–backed startups acquired by firms listed on the American stock market. The analysis covers all startups acquired between 1990 and August 2024. During this period, out of 352,390 startups that raised capital from investors, 41,484 (11.77 per cent) were acquired, while 10,303 (2.92 per cent) exited through an initial public offering (IPO). Over time, the proportion of IPOs relative to mergers and acquisitions has declined steadily (as also documented by Ederer and Pellegrino[13]). The shares of science-based startups differ sharply by sector. Roughly 95 per cent of biotechnology startups rely on science, as do 70 per cent in advanced materials and 42 per cent in medical devices. Midrange sectors include aerospace, defence, and quantum at 33 per cent, semiconductors at 24 per cent, and manufacturing, robotics, and transportation at 19 per cent. Energy and clean technology stand at 16 per cent. At the low end, only 5 per cent of computer-hardware startups and 4 per cent of artificial-intelligence startups build directly on science, and almost none in consumer electronics or digital services such as software and e-commerce do so.

Viewing value creation across the entire chain, Masclans compares the gains to startups and to their acquirers. DeepMind offers a clear example. Google bought the company in February 2014 for $650 million. By this time, DeepMind had raised $61 million in venture capital. Masclans estimates that the acquisition created $2.24 billion in gross value. DeepMind's shareholders received 29 per cent of that amount, while Google captured the remaining 71 per cent. After deducting invested capital, the net value created was $2.18 billion, of which DeepMind's shareholders kept about 27 per cent.

Contrast this with the case of Postmates, a software platform for on-demand delivery, which connects customers with local couriers. In 2020, Uber acquired Postmates for $3.9 billion. By the time of acquisition, Postmates had raised about $900 million from investors, leading to a net surplus to Postmates's equity owners of $3 billion. Uber's estimated private value gain from the acquisition was $1.4 billion, leading to a total economic value of $4.4 billion. In this case, Postmates captured nearly 70 per cent of the joint surplus. Unlike DeepMind, which developed frontier technologies, Postmates operated in a mature and competitive market where it could credibly threaten to scale independently if necessary. A large number of potential buyers further strengthened its bargaining position.

These examples illustrate the two main challenges facing deep-tech startups. They face a harder path to commercial scale because they need complementary inventions and capabilities. Their prospects are clouded by both technological and market uncertainty. At the same time, fewer incumbent firms have the research capabilities and resources to commercialise the startup's invention. As a result, deep-tech startups have fewer potential acquirers.

Masclans provides more systematic support. A comparison of firms of similar age within each sector shows that science-based startups generate 27 per cent more value. However, science-based startups capture a smaller share of the value, with the acquiring firm collecting the rest. Science-based startups capture, on average, 46 cents per dollar of surplus generated, compared to 70 cents for nonscience-based startups. In advanced materials, aerospace, computer hardware, and energy, science-based startups captured, on average, 23 per cent less value compared to their counterparts in the same industry, with the effects statistically significant. Biotechnology is an outlier, largely because virtually no startup is not science-based. Science-based startups have lower value capture in part because they face fewer potential buyers. On average, deep-tech startups have 9 per cent fewer potential buyers and up to 40 per cent fewer buyers in sectors such as energy and manufacturing.

One way startups can try to increase value capture is by commercialising themselves: being Schumpeterian entrepreneurs rather than Smithian. This requires dealing with market risk themselves. For digital startups, this is of course their *raison d'etre.* Their principal task is to validate market demand and show "product-market fit." Deep-tech startups, on the other hand, have to validate the underlying science and demonstrate that the technology is viable. Resolving market risk means going beyond their initial comparative advantage. Scaling and commercialising require capabilities that deep-tech startups do not possess, at least not initially. More to the point, these tasks are typically performed more efficiently by incumbents, who have industry connections and manufacturing expertise and who are better able to coordinate the required complementary changes. As the example of A123 Batteries discussed below shows, deep-tech startups may fail in the commercialisation phase, when the startups enter to try to capture more value.

A recent study offers an analytical framework in which startups choose whether to be acquired after resolving technology risk or try to raise additional resources to scale and resolve market risk.[14] Successfully resolving market risk increases both the number of potential buyers and the startup's negotiating position. However, it also increases the risk of execution failure. This leads to a distortion wherein startups (and their investors) tend to wait too long before getting acquired. This is particularly applicable to deep-tech startups because a decline in industrial research implies fewer potential buyers when market risk has not been resolved. The result is higher anticipated capital requirements and higher failure rates. Deep-tech startups typically exit, whether through acquisition or IPO, after a median of twelve to fifteen years, or approximately twice the duration observed in the software sector. This extended timeline suggests that internal rates of return may be modest even when headline exit valuations appear high, particularly once the higher preacquisition failure rates of deep-tech ventures are taken into account.[15]

For instance, KiOR, a VC-backed biofuel startup, switched from its initial strategy of collaborating with oil producers such as Chevron and Petrobras to competing with them, trying to become a biofuel version of Exxon.[16] It turned out that the startup's technology was not suited for bulk production of biofuel. However, it may have been suitable for producing smaller quantities of higher-value renewable fuels.[17] In essence, the investors pushed the startup to scale before the technology and market risks could be resolved. KiOR went bankrupt within a couple of years of its initial public offering.

LanzaTech, another VC-backed cleantech company using genetically modified bacteria to convert carbon emissions into industrial chemicals, such as aviation fuel, adopted a different strategy. It chose to license its technology and to partner with steel companies and chemicals producers to convert their carbon emissions into renewable fuel and chemicals. This strategy requires less investment but also reduces value capture. LanzaTech's success is critically tied to policy incentives for renewables, and so it is far from certain.

KiOR pursued what can be described as a Schumpeterian approach, seeking to disrupt existing markets by competing directly with established incumbents through new technology. In contrast, LanzaTech followed a more Smithian approach, working in cooperation with incumbents by integrating its technology into their operations and aligning its business model with their existing market structures. The contrasting strategies used reflect the harsh trade-off that deep-tech startups in particular face: partner with incumbents and give up a higher share of the potential value created, or try to resolve the technology and market uncertainty on its own and increase the risk of failure.

Why specialisation works in biopharma

This tradeoff becomes easier as the sector matures because specialist suppliers and contract manufacturers arise that can help startups reach the market without having to rely upon incumbent producers. This is the case in biopharma, where DOIL works well.

Key discoveries in molecular biology provided the scientific bedrock. The discovery of the double-helix structure of DNA in 1953 revolutionised our understanding of genetic information. This discovery was followed by the decoding of the genetic code in the 1960s, which linked DNA sequences to protein synthesis. The development of recombinant DNA (rDNA) technology in 1973 by Stanley Cohen and Herbert Boyer made it possible to create genetically engineered products, such as synthetic human insulin, which Genentech commercialised in 1982 in partnership with Eli Lilly.

Many of the applications of biotechnology were pioneered by startups. Monoclonal antibodies, discovered by César Milstein and Georges Köhler in 1975, led to targeted therapies for diseases. The initial application for transplant patients was commercialised by a startup, IDEC, in partnership with Genentech in 1985. Monoclonal antibodies became the basis for the majority of biological treatments of diseases such as cancer and autoimmune disorders.

Centocor, founded in 1979 in Philadelphia with funding from prominent VCs such as Venrock and Graylock, pioneered the use of monoclonal antibodies for diagnostic testing, licensing technology from the Wistar Institute for hepatitis and gastrointestinal cancer, and from Dana-Farber for ovarian cancer in 1981. Centocor partnered with established companies, such as Abbott, to manufacture and distribute the tests. Abbott eventually bought Centocor's tests for gastrointestinal and ovarian cancer. Centocor was acquired by Johnson & Johnson in 1994, and its diagnostics unit was sold to the Japanese firm Fujirebio in 1998.

Startups also played a critical role in advancing bioprocessing technologies, such as bioreactors and cell culture systems, bridging the gap between small-scale laboratory production and industrial-scale manufacturing. For example, Genentech's synthetic insulin project involved overcoming issues in protein production and purification. These technical challenges were resolved through innovative bacterial expression systems, ensuring the scalability and safety of insulin for diabetes care. Amgen's work on Epogen, a treatment for anaemia, required refining cell culture conditions to optimise yield and developing purification methods to maintain safety and efficacy. Similarly, startups such as Acuitas and Arbutus addressed the inherent instability of mRNA molecules through lipid nanoparticle (LNP) technology.

Three factors underpin the ability of biotech startups to capture a significant share of value. First and foremost, the principal uncertainty, particularly in biotech, is about the technology. The structured process of clinical trials provides reliable demand signals, helping startups identify optimal commercialisation partners early in the development process. Second, patents provide startups with exclusivity over their discoveries and help them to retain negotiating leverage with larger firms. For instance, in 2003, Emisphere successfully sued its joint-venture partner, Eli Lilly, for misappropriation of its drug delivery technology.[18] Finally, specialist suppliers and contract manufacturers provide startups with a route to the end user.

A recent study shows that contract development and manufacturing organisations (CDMOs) offer an alternative path to technology commercialisation.[19] Consistent with the framework developed by Bresnahan and Gambardella described in Chapter 2, biotechnology firms no longer have to invest in costly development and manufacturing assets; instead they contract these tasks out to CDMOs. Between 1995 and 2015, CDMOs grew over fivefold, helping in clinical trials and in the development and mass manufacturing of new drugs. An immediate implication is that biotechnology firms have an outside option when dealing with potential licensing partners. Indeed, the growth of CDMOs coincides with a decline in licensing deals, particularly by smaller firms. Between 2006 and 2015, the number of licensing deals by the nearly eight hundred firms in the study sample declined by 62.01 per cent, even as the R&D expenditure by the sample firms increased by more than 31.52 per cent. Further, the study reports that nearly 60 per cent of the new drugs approved by FDA were launched by smaller firms. Thus, the study concludes that CDMOs may have enabled firms to move their discoveries further downstream in the R&D funnel instead of licensing them early on.

It is important to note that although specialisation and licensing dominate biopharma today, this strategy was much harder in the industry's early years, as the cases of Genentech and Amgen show. In the late 1970s and early 1980s, the legal framework for biotechnology patents was only beginning to take shape. The *Diamond v. Chakrabarty* Supreme Court decision (1980) confirmed that genetically engineered organisms could be patented. Genentech used these tools to patent recombinant insulin and, in 1978, licensed it to Eli Lilly, receiving royalties of about 6–8 per cent on sales. Humulin, launched in 1982, became a blockbuster for Lilly, but Genentech earned only a fraction of the revenue. When Lilly used components of Genentech's insulin technology to produce human growth hormone, Genentech sued, and courts found Lilly in violation of the agreement. Genentech also licensed alpha interferon to Hoffmann–La Roche in 1980. These deals provided cash and credibility, but they also revealed the drawbacks of relying on licensing: limited royalties, risk of appropriation, and loss of control over development timelines. By 1985, Genentech brought human growth hormone (Protropin) to market with its own sales force, marking a decisive move toward vertical integration.

Amgen likewise blended both approaches before committing to integration. It formed a 1984 joint venture with Kirin Brewery for its manufacturing know-how, and in 1985 it granted Johnson & Johnson's Ortho division marketing rights for erythropoietin in Europe and some U.S. indications, while keeping the U.S. dialysis market for itself. At the same time, Amgen invested heavily in its own biomanufacturing plant so that it could control supply when Epogen was approved in 1989. With sufficient venture and IPO financing (more than $200 million raised by the late 1980s), the company built the capabilities to run clinical trials, scale production, and market its drugs directly. Both Genentech and Amgen thus experimented with licensing, but because they anticipated developing more breakthroughs in the future, they instead developed into integrated pharmaceutical firms.

Commercialising deep-tech: LEDs and lithium-ion batteries

Deep-tech sectors follow a different pattern from biopharma. This section focuses on light-emitting diodes and lithium-ion batteries, whose innovations are architectural: they must slot into larger production systems. Technical and commercial success, therefore, depends on complementary advances elsewhere, which makes it difficult for startups to bring a discovery to market. Even when such startups do successfully develop the technology and validate an application, they often fail to capture much of the value they create. After demonstrating that their technology works, deep-tech startups confront a small pool of incumbents and have few alternate paths to customers, weakening their negotiating position and shrinking their share of returns. Integrated producers, on the other hand, do not face this constraint; they can make the necessary complementary investments internally and capture a larger portion of the value their efforts generate, provided they can generate the invention themselves or acquire it. The organic LED (OLED) case shows how, once the LED display industry was established, a startup created and captured value from a breakthrough display technology through a combination of strong patent protection, collaborations with partners who offered complementary innovation capabilities, and government support. Similarly, once the lithium-ion battery had been established, a second generation of university spinoffs could find partners for collaboratively developing solid-state batteries.

Light-emitting diodes

Incandescent lightbulbs operate by burning tungsten filaments in a gas-filled bulb. The filaments heat up as electrical currents are passed through, producing light as a by-product. Ninety per cent of the energy that is put into an incandescent lightbulb is wasted as heat, while only 10 per cent is converted to light. The colour temperature of these light sources is limited to a reddish yellow hue, at around 2700 Kelvin, rendering it inappropriate for industrial applications that require "colder" colours in the blue and violet spectrum. Incandescents also suffer from a low lifespan of around 1,000 hours and a lighting efficiency of around 15 lumens (a measure of brightness) per watt. Alternative sources are more efficient. Fluorescent lights excite mercury vapour to create a colder colour temperature; Xenon-based arc lights form the basis of high intensity discharge (HID) lamps used for automotive headlights (that require brightness levels above 3500 lumens); and high-pressure sodium-vapour lamps offering lighting efficiencies of up to 150 lumens per watt have been used for street lighting since the 1930s. Ultimately, however, all of these rely on the electrical excitation of gases.

Electroluminescence from semiconductors, on the other hand, is more efficient, with a greater light-to-heat ratio and better colour profiles. Typical light-emitting diode (LED) bulbs boast around 100 lumens per watt—around 6.7 times those of incandescents; they can also be programmed to emit differing colours, such as red, green, and blue. Moreover, LEDs can be arranged in completely new form factors such as strips or panels, no longer limited by the necessity to encase gases within a glass bulb. This allowed the introduction of flat screen TVs that replaced bulky cathode ray tubes.

The theoretical foundations were established as early as 1905 when Albert Einstein clarified the mechanisms behind the photoelectric effect. The photoelectric effect can be used to create light from energy (as in lasers and LEDs) and energy from light (as in photovoltaic (PV) cells). Lab demonstrations came in quick succession: the first semiconductor-based PV cells were invented at Bell Labs in 1954 by Daryl Chapin's team; the first laser was invented in 1960 by Ted Maiman at Hughes Research Labs; and the first modern LED device is attributed to Nick Holonyak at General Electric Research Labs in 1962. Yet, the rate of diffusion differed vastly between the three: lasers saw almost immediate applications in scientific experiments and military applications such as range finding, followed by bar code scanning (1970s), industrial machining, patterning, and etching (1980s), and medical surgery and telecommunications (1990s). PV cells were initially adopted in space applications, but penetration into the mainstream market stagnated, with solar share of total U.S. energy production in 1996 at a meagre 0.09 per cent.[20] The replacement of household incandescent bulbs with LEDs came somewhere in between lasers and PVs: a viable replacement product only emerged by 2009, but diffusion has been rapid since then, with around 47 per cent of U.S. households reporting use of LED bulbs for a majority of their indoor lighting needs by 2024.

Part of the reason for the delayed diffusion of LEDs was that early LEDs could not produce blue light. The first movers in LEDs focused on refining their beachhead markets, such as pocket calculators, where the blue light problem was not important.[21] RCA was an exception: as a TV manufacturer, it had a vested interest in finding green and blue LEDs to allow complete rendering of the visible colour spectrum, to replace the bulky cathode ray tubes (CRT) in TVs. Paul Maruska and Jacques Pankove at RCA's Materials Research Division researched ways to make gallium nitride (GaN) LEDs work. They achieved green and blue light emission, but the devices were unsuitable for commercial use: the RCA architecture consisted of a metal insulator semiconductor (MIS) structure that only contained an n-type GaN semiconductor. The lack of a p-type layer (which most modern LED devices also use) implied that more electricity was required to emit light, making the RCA technology impractically inefficient. When RCA ran into financial troubles relating to its abortive Videodisc project and experienced a leadership transition, it exited LED research. By the 1990s, large American firms had also washed their hands of large-scale research projects in optoelectronics: RCA closed its LED research program while HP (Agilent) and Monsanto (Litronix) spun their programs off as independent companies. The search for blue LEDs stagnated until the late 1980s when Japanese firms entered the foray.

The Japanese catch-up in optoelectronics was kicked off by the Ministry of International Trade and Industry's (MITI's) research consortium from 1975 to 1978, following a proposal submitted by Izuo Hayashi, a celebrated former Bell research scientist.[22] The project, while unsuccessful, inspired Nagoya University's Isamu Akasaki to collaborate with Toyoda Gosei (a parts manufacturer for Toyota) to continue the research. Akasaki and a close collaborator, Hiroshi Amano, invented the p-type GaN layer, allowing for the introduction of a p-n junction blue LED. Shuji Nakamura at Nichia Chemicals subsequently introduced a process innovation (thermal annealing) that made it possible to produce high brightness blue LEDs on a large scale. Akasaki, Amano, and Nakamura would share the Nobel Prize in 2014 for their discoveries.

Nichia and Toyoda Gosei first targeted the automotive market, applying their white lights to headlamps and internal displays. American startups, such as Color Kinetics and TIR, used the technology for outdoor signage, capitalising on the programmability and form factor of the LEDs. However, neither the Japanese first movers nor the American startups were successful at penetrating the far larger indoor lighting market. The LED market share in this sector was a mere 1 per cent in 2010. Part of this low adoption rate had to do with the high unit price of an LED lamp at $80–100 (in 2008), longevity, colour-rendering issues, and flickers.[23] Fixing these issues required dedicated effort to improve the design of the LED chip as well as improvements in phosphor design (which affected colour), heat sink, and driver configurations (which affected longevity and flicker). Hence, the "last mile" delivery of LED technology to households occurred through Philips, which introduced a 60 Watt A-Lamp replacement as part of its submission to the U.S. Department of Energy's (DOE) L-Prize competition in 2009. Combined with generous consumer subsidies for energy-efficient lighting products, large incumbents such as GE and Osram Sylvania quickly followed suit by licensing LED technology from firms such as Nichia to compete with Philips. By 2016, the price of LED lightbulbs had dropped by 90 per cent (to less than $3), and GE had completely exited the U.S. compact fluorescent light market. Around half of all general lighting demand in the United States is now met by LEDs.

The causes of the delayed diffusion of LEDs can be better understood by a comparison to lasers, which rely on the same physical principles.[24]

Technological uncertainty. LEDs suffered from greater technological uncertainty than lasers. Some LED researchers tried alternatives to GaN, with ZnO being popular with academics. However, most of the proposed alternative LED materials had claimed theoretical advantages that never came close to matching GaN LED performance.[25]

The messy nature of LED fabrication also frustrated attempts at replication: while there were multiple paths to build and improve lasers (as crystals, gas, and liquids), there was a narrower path to build LEDs, as these are semiconductor diodes. Various forms of epitaxy needed to be tried, from liquid phase epitaxy (LPE) to chemical vapour deposition (CVD), while new "tricks" to dope substrates needed to be developed (such as the RCA MIS and Nakamura's thermal annealing process). These techniques suffered from erratic results because they involved chemical reactions at high temperature and exacting atomic-level precision.

Technological effort in one domain often depended on progress in another. Blue LEDs increased in value after red and yellow LEDs appeared;

GaN emerged as a prominent research topic because researchers determined that silicon-carbide-based blue LEDs were inefficient; solving the passivation problem (and finding a p-doped GaN layer) would not have emerged as a high- value research topic had RCA not introduced the MIS architecture and, further, showed the deficiencies of an n-type only GaN LED. Nakamura may never have worked on thermal annealing had he not seen the inefficiencies of the low-energy electron beam irradiation (LEEBI) technique that Akasaki's team used to solve the passivation problem. In short, the process was sequential, nonlinear, and messy.[26]

Market uncertainty. LEDs suffered from greater demand uncertainty than lasers. At first glance, the total addressable market for LEDs may have seemed larger since there were established markets for lighting, and TV sets. However, the presence of incumbent technology often complicates projecting demand for a potentially "disruptive" innovation.[27] For one, the legacy technology may improve: compact fluorescent bulbs improved in their efficiency as well as in colour characteristics. Additionally, consumers had become accustomed to the notion that lighting products needed to be encased in a "bulb" form attached to a socket, which ironically was technically more demanding for LEDs. Lasers also suffered from demand uncertainty, but given their novelty, they were spared the direct competition with an established industry. Moreover, the prospect of generous defence contracts for laser products for artillery ranging, communications, and guidance systems encouraged research. A similar public sector role for LED research did not appear until the DOE L-Prize, potentially because the defence applications were limited.

Despite the $10 million reward and promises for priority in federal procurement of future LED bulbs, the winning submission for the DOE L-Prize for a 60-Watt A-Lamp replacement came from Philips, an integrated consumer electronics firm. Philips played no part in the early development of the technology, but instead made strategic acquisitions related to LED fabrication and luminaire design. Philips bought Lumileds (a spinoff from HP's LED business) for LED fabrication in 2005. For luminaire design, the firm acquired TIR systems (along with its Lexel lighting platform), Colour Kinetics, and Partners in Lighting in 2007. These acquisitions gave the firm a comfortable position in designing sconces, chandeliers, pendants, track lights, and floor and desk lamps, all of which required a customised approach to thermal management. With 100W incandescent lamps selling for as little as 50 cents, an LED bulb's consumer value proposition depended on reducing its unit price, while also improving on erratic flickers, high heat, and limited lifespan. After resolving the major technical problems by the late 2000s, Philips turned its attention to scaling and process improvements.

To sum up, creating value in deep-tech is challenging because it requires the concurrent resolution of technological and market uncertainties, which is easier to manage for integrated firms than for startups. Partnerships with established firms may help, but information exchange is harder across firm boundaries, and decision-making is also slower when multiple partners have to agree. In LEDs, no startup before the 1990s contributed to the development of LED technology; most (except Cree) struggled to find a viable market. Startups like Color Kinetics focused mainly on smaller downstream niches such as outdoor signage at landmarks (replacing the neon signs at Times Square with LED signage, for instance) or upstream components such as remote phosphor technology at Intematix (and to a lesser extent, Cree).

Organic light-emitting diodes: An American success story

Organic light-emitting diodes (OLEDs) do much the same thing as LEDs. However, in OLEDs, a startup succeeded by leveraging partnerships with specialist suppliers and building on early support from DARPA and other government agencies.

In 1987, Ching W. Tang and Steven Van Slyke at Eastman Kodak Company published a seminal paper, "Organic Electroluminescent Diodes," in *Applied Physics Letters*, announcing the first practical, low-voltage, multilayer OLED device, using fluorescent organic materials.[28] Kodak focused primarily on licensing their foundational OLED technology to companies such as Pioneer, LG, Sanyo, TDK, eMagin, and Univision Technology. The technology, at this time, was best suited for simpler applications such as displays for car audio systems, introduced by Pioneer in 1997.

The next generation of OLED was based on phosphorescence rather than fluorescence. Universal Display Corporation (UDC) was founded in 1994 by Sherwin Seligsohn to commercialise research on self-emissive organic materials by Princeton researchers Stephen Forrest and Mark Thompson. UDC's commercial success was based on a breakthrough development of phosphorescent OLED (PHOLED), the result of collaborative research with

Princeton University, the University of Southern California (where Mark Thompson had moved), and the University of Michigan (where Stephen Forrest had moved). PHOLED technology has significantly higher energy efficiency, allowing it to be used in various applications, including smartphones, televisions, wearables, and automotive displays. A recent consulting report estimated the global market for OLED in 2023 at about $46 billion, with the display market accounting for nearly three-quarters of the market.[29]

A publicly listed company since 1996, UDC has only four hundred employees and is highly profitable, with profits of $220 million on revenues of about $650 million and a market cap of about $7.5 billion. It holds over six thousand patents. UDC's business model is based on the supply of its OLED materials, especially PHOLED, licensing revenues, and contract research. The company has also strategically acquired OLED intellectual property portfolios from companies like Fujifilm (2012), BASF (2016), and Merck KGaA (2023). It has also acquired Adesis, a contract research organisation that had previously performed contract R&D for UDC. It has a long-term partnership with PPG to manufacture its PHOLED materials, which are used by UDC licensees—Asian manufacturers such as Samsung, LG, AU Optronics, and BOE Technology Group—who use PHOLED in their display panels.

UDC benefited from government initiatives aimed at improving lighting efficiency, enabling the company to diversify beyond the display market. The DOE instituted a program on solid-state lighting as part of its energy efficiency objectives.[30] UDC, along with its university partners, Princeton, the University of Michigan, and the University of Southern California, benefited from DOE grants and contracts, starting in 2002, which funded research in implementation of UDC technology in downstream applications, such as a 2014 project with IDD Aerospace, which involved developing an energy-saving OLED lamp for use in aircraft cabin interiors. In addition to grants supporting technology development, UDC also had some procurement support. Between 2008 and 2016, UDC received forty-five SBIR grants and contracts, and an additional seven contracts from the DoD, in all worth nearly $23 million. Importantly, the Department of Energy also tried to bring together industry incumbents to develop technology roadmaps for lighting, enabling UDC to develop its technology for applications other than display panels.[31] According to Mike Hack, UDC's Vice President of Business Development,

> DOE R&D funding has been invaluable to UDC. In the early years, it provided validation of our technology and reduced the financial risk of pursuing new technical approaches and focusing on lighting in addition to the more immediately profitable display market. Later on, it was instrumental in allowing us to form key partnerships with other U.S. lighting companies.[32]

The company continues to improve its technology, developing new materials, as well as new processes such as organic vapour jet printing for OLED fabrication. It is also engaged in scientific research, and its research staff publishes extensively in scientific journals and conference proceedings. A notable example is a recent paper in *Nature* in 2020, in collaboration with university researchers, which has already been cited 181 times.[33] It also sponsors research at universities, resulting in over fourteen papers published in the *Journal of the American Chemical Society* alone.[34]

UDC is an example of where the division of innovative labour has worked in deep-tech. The company developed a university discovery for display applications. It partnered with a specialised materials manufacturer, PPG, itself an established company, to produce the patented materials, which were supplied to UDC licensees to produce display panels embodying the technology. Leveraging government R&D grants and contracts, it invested in collaborative research with universities and in-house efforts to improve the technology and develop complementary process technologies. A key difference with LED is that the target market, display panels, was already established, unlike LEDs themselves. This made it arguably easier for the company to focus on technology development and just license the results to downstream producers.

Lithium-ion batteries

The development of lithium-ion batteries illustrates the defining characteristics of deep-tech sectors. Transforming early scientific breakthroughs into commercially viable technologies required extensive translational research. Early prototypes faced significant hurdles, particularly around energy density and safety, which had to be systematically addressed. Some of this translational work was ultimately recognised with the Nobel Prize in Chemistry in 2019.

The problem of storing chemical energy and converting it into electrical energy occupies an important place in the history of physics. Its origins are often traced to 1799, when Alessandro Volta, a professor of chemistry at the University of Pavia, constructed the first battery by stacking alternating zinc and copper discs separated by cloth or cardboard soaked in brine. The invention led to a wave of empirical and theoretical research that quickly established electromagnetism as a major scientific field. A second major discovery occurred in 1859 when Gaston Planté, a lecturer in physics at the Conservatory of Arts and Crafts in Paris, invented the lead-acid battery, the first that could be recharged by passing a reverse current through it.

Transportation was quickly perceived as an important application for the new technology. In 1900, electric vehicles accounted for 38 per cent of total vehicles in the United States, with steam and petrol making up 40 and 22 per cent, respectively.[35] Thomas Edison understood that increasing energy density—how much energy a battery can store in relation to its weight or volume—was vital for success in the automotive market, along with making batteries safer and last longer. In 1909, after spending more than a million dollars of his own money on the venture, he developed the A-12 nickel storage battery. Unfortunately, the internal combustion engine had improved much faster in the meanwhile, making this technology uncompetitive in the automotive market. Applications of Edison's battery came later, in smaller electrical devices rather than in electrical vehicles.[36]

Further progress in battery technology was made in the 1970s and 1980s with the development of the lithium-ion battery. Surprisingly, it was Exxon, an American multinational oil and gas corporation, which spearheaded the effort. The oil shocks of the 1970s, along with concerns about pollution, had led to a search for alternatives to oil. As part of these efforts, in 1972 Exxon hired M. Stanley Whittingham, a post-doc from Stanford University who had been doing research on intercalation in batteries.

The basic unit of the battery, the cell, is made of a small number of components. At opposite ends there are two electrodes, one negatively charged (the anode), the other positively charged (the cathode). To produce electricity, electrons must travel through a substance, the electrolyte, that transports ions between the anode and the cathode, allowing the battery to charge and discharge. Improvements in battery performance are largely driven by advances in how these components are designed and manufactured.

Intercalation refers to the process in which ions are inserted into the lattice of host materials without causing significant structural disruption.

The host materials, often crystalline solids, have layered or open-framework structures that provide ion pathways and storage sites, acting as figurative "bookshelves" for ions. In this analogy, the best bookshelves are light, sturdy, and durable, can pack many ions, and allow for rapid circulation. The challenge is to identify materials that would result in safe and reliable structures.[37]

Based on his research on intercalation at Stanford, Whittingham at Exxon developed a battery that worked by pairing a titanium-disulfide cathode with a lithium metal anode. Titanium disulfide has a layered crystal structure, which allows lithium ions to easily intercalate during charging and discharging without causing major structural breakdown. This was a big breakthrough. Whittingham's battery was rechargeable, lightweight, and very high in energy output. Up to that time, the best rechargeable battery was based on nickel-cadmium, providing a maximum of 1.3 volts. Whittingham's battery increased that to 2.4 volts.[38] However, the battery also had significant safety challenges: lithium metal is highly reactive and prone to forming dendrites, which can lead to short circuits and thermal runaway. Recognising the limitations of titanium disulfide and the dangers posed by lithium metal, John Goodenough searched for a safer material for the cathode. In 1980, Goodenough and his team at Oxford University discovered that lithium cobalt oxide ($LiCoO_2$) could serve as an excellent cathode material, effectively doubling the energy density of lithium-based batteries. Akira Yoshino, a researcher at Asahi Kasei Corporation, built on the foundational research of Whittingham and Goodenough to create a safer and more practical battery in 1985. Instead of using a highly reactive lithium metal as the anode, he replaced it with carbon-based materials such as petroleum coke, which could intercalate lithium ions. This innovation drastically improved battery safety by reducing the risk of dendrite formation. In recognition of their contributions, Whittingham, Goodenough, and Yoshino were jointly awarded the 2019 Nobel Prize in Chemistry.

The lithium-ion battery was commercialised in portable electronics in 1991 by Sony and in 1992 by a joint venture between Asahi Kasei and Toshiba. Like most new technologies, the lithium-ion battery was initially very expensive, and its performance specifications were not always satisfactory. Its high-energy density made it valuable for applications like portable electronics; however, its high cost per unit of energy (among other specifications) made it impractical for other applications such as electric vehicles.

Given the size of the potential electric vehicle (EV) market, it is not surprising that innovation in battery technology has often been driven by the requirements of the EV industry.[39] The NMC system, typically combining nickel, manganese, and cobalt, was developed in the early 2000s by researchers at Argonne National Laboratories and is now the most widely used cathode material in EV batteries. It balances energy density, thermal stability, and cost-effectiveness. Its lower reliance on cobalt, an expensive and ethically problematic material, reduces costs and increases sustainability. Manganese substitution further lowers costs while enhancing stability.

Lithium nickel cobalt aluminum oxide cathodes, introduced in 2001, offer slightly higher energy density than nickel-rich NMC but have a lower discharge voltage. They became popular after Panasonic used them in Tesla's first Model S in 2011, but they have since lost ground to other battery chemistries due to their higher cost, shorter lifespan, and need for robust thermal management, which can reduce safety.

Arguably, the critical challenge for batteries in transportation nowadays, even more than energy density, is cost. Lithium iron phosphate (LFP) batteries have emerged as a lower-cost alternative. Invented in the United States in 1997 and further developed in Canada, their production became concentrated in China during the 2010s. By 2023, two-thirds of EVs sold in China featured LFP batteries, compared to less than 10 per cent in Europe and the United States, where nickel-based chemistries remain dominant.[40] Globally, LFP batteries accounted for more than 40 per cent of the EV market by capacity in 2023, more than doubling their 2020 share.

Batteries have evolved in a number of dimensions in addition to innovations in cathode design. Early lithium-ion batteries used soft carbon anodes, but switching to hard carbon and eventually to graphite significantly improved energy density, enabling better performance. Graphite, combined with a newly discovered electrolyte additive, ethylene carbonate, became the standard anode material. This additive forms a solid electrolyte interphase (SEI) layer, preventing undesirable reactions while allowing ion flow. More recently, manufacturers have incorporated small amounts of silicon into graphite to further boost performance.

Electrolyte solutions have also evolved. They typically comprise a solvent like ethylene carbonate and a lithium salt, but proprietary additives significantly enhance battery performance. These additives, often seen as a manufacturer's "secret sauce," can make substantial differences in efficiency and longevity.

Material efficiency has been a key focus area. Battery layers—current collectors, anodes, separators, and cathodes—have steadily become thinner. For example, copper current collectors have reduced from 20 to 6 microns in thickness over two decades. Simultaneously, the proportion of active, electricity-generating materials in a battery's total weight has increased, improving overall efficiency. The adoption of "cell-to-pack" designs has also eliminated intermediary modules, streamlining production and reducing material usage. This innovation alone has cut EV battery pack costs by approximately 15 per cent in recent years.

Manufacturers are also scaling up individual cell sizes to leverage surface-area-to-volume effects. Larger cells require less material for enclosures, though historical concerns about thermal runaway risks limited their use. Advances in more stable chemistries, such as LFP, have made larger designs possible. Tesla's 4680 cylindrical cells and BYD's "blade" LFP batteries are examples of this trend. Tesla's 4680 battery demonstrates the impact of incremental improvements. Between its first and second generations, changes like thinner casings, updated chemistries (from cathode NMC811 to NMC955), and reduced anode and cathode thickness resulted in an 11 per cent increase in energy density while lowering costs.

Manufacturing has also seen dramatic efficiency gains. Electrode coating machines, for instance, have improved tenfold in speed, reducing capital requirements per unit output by 90 per cent. Double-sided coating machines and faster stacking processes for separators are further enhancing productivity. Machinery has also scaled up, producing wider material sheets to boost throughput. Tesla's "dry" electrode manufacturing process is an innovation aiming to eliminate solvent use, potentially cutting electrode production costs by 50 per cent. Battery factories have grown significantly, with production volumes rising from fractions of a gigawatt-hour to tens of gigawatt-hours annually. These improvements and economies of scale have further reduced unit costs.

Challenges of commercialising lithium-ion batteries

The development of lithium-ion batteries illustrates the extensive translational work required to turn early scientific breakthroughs into commercially viable technologies. Beyond the technical challenges, however, there was also significant uncertainty surrounding market demand. Lithium-ion batteries held promise across diverse sectors—transportation, consumer electronics, power grids, and medical devices—each with its own distinct requirements. Furthermore, success depended not only on improving core battery performance but also on complementary innovations in materials, manufacturing, and supply chains.

Scaling and complementary innovations. A123 Systems, founded in 2001 and headquartered in Massachusetts, was arguably the brightest hope in the U.S. battery startup ecosystem. The company's technology was based on a lithium-iron-phosphate chemistry developed at MIT.[41] The company attracted significant attention and investment, including a $249 million grant from the U.S. Department of Energy. It went public in 2009, raising $380 million. However, by 2012 the company's fortunes had shifted drastically. Some of A123's problems stemmed from its excessive reliance on a single customer, an EV startup named Fisker Automotive. Scaling up the technology was also very costly and fraught with risks. Between 2008 and 2012, A123 had invested more than $300 million in equipment and infrastructure. Like other battery manufacturers, it struggled with a market where prices were too low to cover production costs. In October 2012, A123 filed for bankruptcy.

The company was caught in a classic chicken-and-egg dilemma, as described in previous sections. Scaling up was essential to drive down production costs, but that required large orders from automakers. Yet automakers hesitated to commit without stronger consumer demand, which in turn depended on cheaper batteries and complementary innovations. A123's problems—encouraging complementary investments and achieving scale—are common to all deep-tech innovators. However, some problems were specific to A123's position as a startup. In choosing A123's batteries, automakers and suppliers had to be able to count on the company being around for many years to fulfil warranty obligations and respond to design changes. However, A123's financial troubles raised doubts about its survival, scaring off some potential partners. In principle, the government could have helped by providing loans to battery suppliers or purchase incentives for electric vehicles. To some extent, this is what happened. Many battery producers, including A123, received government support, typically in the form of subsidised loans and grants. Whether this support was enough, however, is a different (and difficult) question.

Value-capture problems. In ecosystems where innovative labour is divided among many participants, firms will only invest if they can secure a sufficiently large share of the value created. Yet collaboration within such ecosystems carries significant risks. As the case of Asahi below shows, alliances with incumbents can expose technology suppliers to knowledge leakage and loss of control over commercialisation. One partner may reap most of the profits, while the other may obtain very little.

Recall that it was Akira Yoshino of Japan's Asahi Kasei who created a safer and more practical lithium battery in the 1980s by pairing John Goodenough's cathode with a carbon-based anode. Despite this breakthrough, Asahi struggled to commercialise its prototype because it lacked experience in battery manufacturing. Seeking support, it approached Sony, but the collaboration soon turned problematic.

When Isao Kuribayashi of Asahi demonstrated the prototype to Sony's camcorder division in 1987, the timing was ideal: Sony was developing what would become the Handycam, which required a lightweight, compact battery. Sony initially sought a partnership with Asahi. However, after negotiations broke down, Sony pursued the development of the battery independently. Here, accounts diverge. Sony claims that the battery it eventually created was developed in-house. However, as Charles Murray notes, "Sony's battery used the same essential chemistry as Asahi Chemical's. The cathode was lithium cobalt oxide, the anode was petroleum coke, and the liquid electrolyte contained lithium ions."[42] What is more likely is that Sony researchers, at the very least, learned a great deal from Asahi's prototype.

The example highlights both the benefits and the limitations of a division of innovative labour. Knowledge was distributed, with different companies and actors possessing different pieces of the puzzle. Asahi's expertise in organic chemistry and carbonaceous materials was crucial to develop the initial prototype; however its lack of battery manufacturing expertise hindered its ability to commercialise the technology. It sought a partnership with Sony, which left it exposed to the risk of unwanted knowledge leakage to the partner. Unlike Asahi, Sony was both a consumer electronics manufacturer and a battery producer, giving it unique insights into the needs of both markets. Sony's engineers addressed key production challenges, such as improving the durability of cathode powders, developing effective separators, and enhancing electrolyte stability. In 1991, Sony introduced the first commercial lithium-ion battery, revolutionising the electronics industry. (Asahi followed shortly after, in collaboration with Toshiba.)

The example underscores the fact that important scientific and technological discoveries do not automatically translate into profits. Very often, it is the companies that possess the manufacturing and distribution capabilities that benefit from innovation. Sony's manufacturing prowess and knowledge of the consumer electronics market were key to its ability to capture the bulk of the value from the discoveries by Whittingham, Goodenough, and Yoshino. Battery manufacturing today is dominated by large firms such as BYD, CATL, LG Energy Solution, and Panasonic.

Next-generation battery startups

It is noteworthy that A123's strategy differed from that of UDC, the OLED technology leader. A123 chose to produce batteries itself for a range of automobile producers, whereas UDC focused on supplying technology and materials to display panel producers. Further, UDC collaborated with PPG to produce the key materials, whereas A123 set up manufacturing facilities in the United States, China, and the Czech Republic. In this sense, A123's experience reflects the risks Schumpeterian entrepreneurs take on.

Some recent battery startups appear to be taking a leaf out of UDC's playbook. Consider QuantumScape, a Stanford University spinoff founded in 2010.[43] Its core invention is a ceramic electrolyte separator, instead of a porous polymer separator and liquid electrolyte between a carbon-based anode and a cathode, as in a typical lithium-ion battery. Crucially, by 2012, QuantumScape had formed a partnership with Volkswagen, mitigating the hold-up problem discussed earlier. Volkswagen's initial collaboration and validation provided a route to market for the nascent technology. VW invested $100 million in 2018 and an additional $200 million in 2020, making Volkswagen QuantumScape's largest shareholder.

QuantumScape also partnered with Murata, a Japanese materials firm, to produce its key ceramic electrolyte separator, reminiscent of the UDC–PPG partnership. Its current business model is to develop the technology where the batteries can be efficiently produced at scale and to license to partners such as VW, which will invest in plant and equipment. Other solid-state battery startups, such as Solid Power and SAE, follow the same business model: licensing their technology, and providing know-how and key materials, while the partner invests in large-scale manufacturing capacity. Solid Power, a spinout from the University of Colorado in 2011, was initially supported by ARPA-E and Air Force grant and contract funding until it managed to form partnerships with BMW in 2017. BMW later made a significant investment in the startup, along with Ford. In 2021, Solid Power entered into a collaboration with SK Innovation to manufacture automotive-scale batteries based on Solid Power's technology.[44]

Whether these firms will succeed remains to be seen. What is noteworthy is that these deep-tech startups are dealing with the combination of technology and market risk by seeking early partnerships with incumbents, collaborating with specialist materials suppliers, and licensing their technology and know-how, rather than manufacturing themselves. Collaboration helps with value creation, but it also implies lower value capture.

Chapter takeaways

The benefits of DOIL are distributed unevenly across technical fields. The barrier is neither a lack of ideas nor a shortage of capital. Instead, deep-tech startups are challenged in creating and capturing value. They need to collaborate with industry partners, and they must rely on others to provide complementary inventions. Without validated use cases and without proven technology, potential partners are hard to attract. And even if they succeed, negotiations with asset-controlling incumbents tilt the surplus away from the startup.

Light-emitting diodes and lithium-ion batteries illustrate this pattern. The underlying science emerged in American laboratories, yet Dutch, Japanese, Korean, and later Chinese conglomerates captured most of the value. The withdrawal of large integrated corporate labs in the United States left startups with few partners and little leverage. OLEDs added an instructive wrinkle. Universal Display Corporation combined strong patents with a clear target market and close partnerships, enabling the startup to preserve its leadership share even in a globally fragmented supply chain.

Biopharma remains the one science-intensive sector where the division of innovative labour functions well: patents are enforceable, a structured regulatory pathway in the form of clinical trials for resolving technology risk also minimises market risk, research-intensive incumbent firms readily understand the underlying scientific base, and a dense network of contract development and manufacturing organisations provides credible outside options that soften hold-up risk.

4

America's Evolving Innovation Ecosystem

What We've Lost and Why It Matters

Introduction

For most of the twentieth century, corporate laboratories played an important integrative role. Their scientists pursued fundamental discoveries, and others translated them into marketable products and processes, to be commercialised by business units. The retreat of these labs over the past four decades has shifted virtually all exploratory research to universities, except in a select few areas, and has pushed early commercialisation onto startups. (The decline of industrial research is discussed in Chapter 11.)

The consequences for innovation have been uneven. Digital sectors, such as cloud software, selected areas of biomedicine, and artificial intelligence, have raced ahead but deep-tech sectors have fallen behind. This chapter documents those divergent outcomes and links them to the withdrawal of industrial research.[1] It then shows that venture-backed startups have failed to fill the void created by this exit. The chapter highlights what has been lost with the demise of the large corporate lab and shows that U.S. technological leadership remains strong in fields where large corporations continue to invest in scientific research. Meanwhile, rivals—especially China—are advancing rapidly in areas where American corporate research has receded.

The uneven translation of research and its organisational origins

We began Chapter 1 by showing that the translation of disruptive science has declined. Figure 1.3 from that chapter showed that the probability of a high-quality disruptive paper being cited by a patent had dropped from around 19 per cent in the first half of the 1990s to 6 per cent in the 2010s. Simply put, disruptive science was more likely to be used in patents when industrial research was more prominent.

Investments in industrial research are positively correlated to the translation of science. We measure the translation of science by the share of highly cited papers that are cited in a U.S. patent document. Industrial research is measured by the share of highly cited papers that are authored by corporate scientists. We find that in fields where corporations reduce their investments in scientific research, patents also exhibit lower use of science (as measured by citations). Figure 4.1 shows that halving the share of corporate papers year on year is associated with a 4 per cent drop in patent citations to science. Thus, there is evidence that the slower translation of science documented in Figure 1.3 may be related to the withdrawal of large corporations from scientific research. Industrial research is much more likely to be used in invention than university research. As a result, a decline in industrial research is likely to reduce the share of high-quality research that is also relevant for inventors.

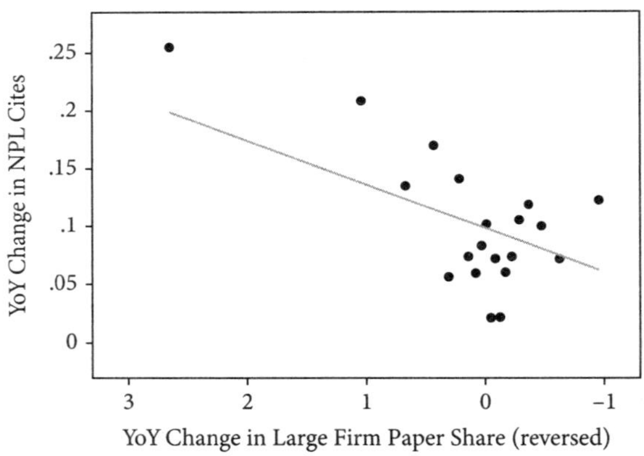

Figure 4.1 Commercial Application of High-Quality Papers and Large Firm Share by Scientific Field (1980–2015)

Notes: This binned scatterplot relates changes in the commercialisation of science against large firm participation in science at the scientific subfield-year level. The y-axis measures the year-on-year changes in the share of scientific papers cited by patents within 5 years of paper publication. The x-axis measures the change in the share of public firm publications taken from the DISCERN database.[2] The sample is limited to papers that are in the top 10 per cent of forward paper citations for the field and year. Scientific publication data is sourced from the SciSciNet database[3]

Next, we also examine the contribution of universities and VC-backed startups to the translation of science. While only a very small minority of all new firms are funded through venture capital (VC)—about one-sixth of 1 per cent on average per year in the United States and less in most other countries—VC-backed startups feature disproportionately among the fastest growing and best performing companies. From 1999 to 2009, over 60 per cent of initial public offerings (IPOs) in the United States originating from industrial startups received VC funding.[4]

VC-backed startups punch above their weight in innovation. In a study published in 2000, Kortum and Lerner estimated that, on average, a dollar of venture capital was three to four times more potent in stimulating innovation (at least as measured by patents) than a dollar of traditional corporate R&D. Thus, although the VC industry financed on average less than 3 per cent of corporate R&D in the United States from 1983 to 1992, it might have been responsible for a much greater share—perhaps 8 per cent—of U.S. patents in that decade.[5]

Figure 4.2 plots the share of scientific papers cited by patents against the share of startups, large firms, and universities that cite papers in their patents. Science is more likely to be used in inventions when there are more VC-backed startups and universities using science. Overall, the results suggest two complementary views. Industrial research is more likely to feed into inventions than university research, but areas of science with a deeper division of innovative labour also show greater translation of science.

However, VC-backed startups have reduced their translational efforts in some fields. Figure 4.3 shows how translation, measured as use of science in patents, has evolved over time. The square-dotted line tracks translational efforts by all inventors, not just VC-backed startups. It shows that, although translation of science increased up to the mid-1990s, it dropped thereafter. The diamond-dashed line focuses on the translational efforts by VC-backed startups. The pattern is similar: VC-backed startups increasingly translated scientific research into technology until the 2000s, but since then, these efforts have plateaued. This suggests that as the VC sector has grown since the early 1990s, VC funds have been increasingly unwilling to bet on science-based startups involved in translation.

Analysing data from the consulting firm Sand Hill Econometrics, Josh Lerner observes that VC funds have increasingly been focusing on technologies in which the innovation cycle is shorter, such as social media and software, rather than on technologies in which innovation cycles are longer,

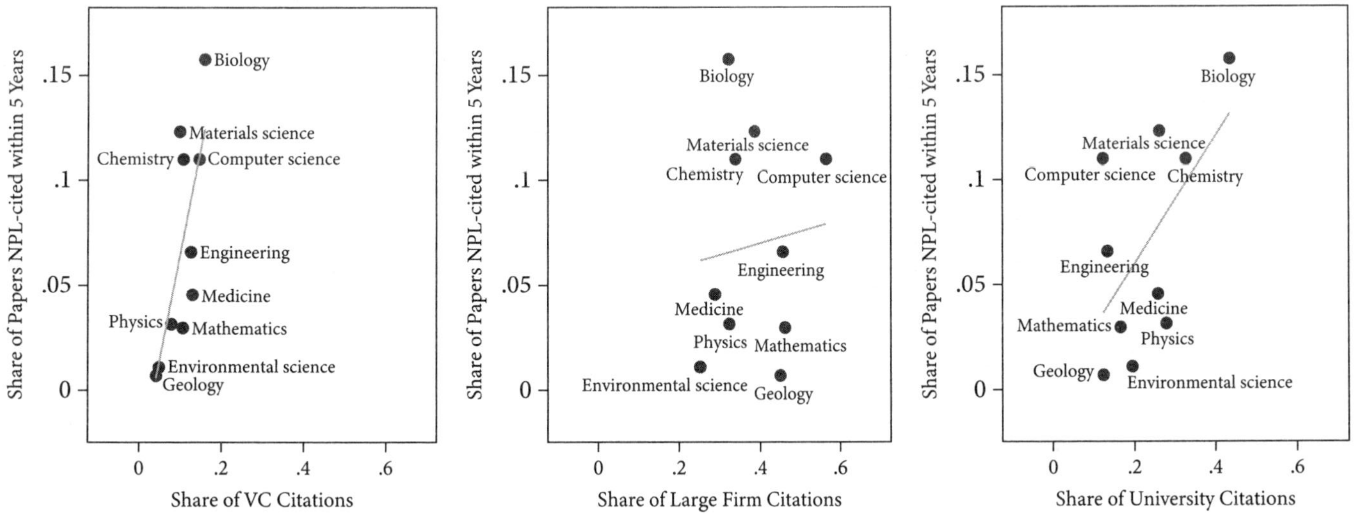

Figure 4.2 Commercialisation of Scientific Fields by Types of Users (1980–2010)

Notes: Scatterplots at the scientific field level graph the share of papers cited by patents against the types of users citing science. “Share of VC citations” in the x-axis of the left panel divides the number of papers cited by at least one VC-backed startup patent by papers cited by any patent (pairwise correlation with forward patent citations is 0.74). “Share of Large Firm Citations” in the middle plot changes the numerator to papers cited by patents of U.S.-headquartered publicly listed firms from the DISCERN project ($r = 0.10$). “Share of University Citations” in the right plot changes the numerator to papers cited by patents of universities and national laboratories ($r = 0.59$). VC-backed firms, public entities, and national laboratories are identified through data from Ewens & Marx (2024).[6] Sample is limited to papers that are in the top 10% of forward paper citations for the field and year. We count patent citations of papers that occur up to five years after the focal paper’s publication. Scientific publication data is sourced from the SciSciNet database.[7]

such as advanced materials and cleantech.[8] The reason is simple: venture funds have discovered that they perform much better financially in the former areas, which arguably rely less on science, than in the latter areas, where costs are higher and successful exit takes longer. This finding is consistent with an MIT study showing that VC-funded cleantech startups had lower rates of return than software and medical technology startups.[9] Lerner notes, for instance, that funds whose initial mandate was in unpopular areas—such as Ampersand Ventures in advanced materials and CMEA Capital in specialty chemicals and advanced materials—were forced to reinvent themselves or perish.

Recent work by Honggi Lee, Matt Marx, and Lia Sheer provides further systematic evidence that VC groups have been retreating from deep-tech to focus more on less science-intensive or "shallower" technological areas.[10] They tracked VC-backed startups in the United States from 1995 to 2013 and found that the share of science-based startups in venture capital had declined. Specifically, they document that over time VC-backed startups have become (i) less likely to cite scientific articles as prior art in their patents (our measure of translation), (ii) less likely to publish scientific articles themselves, and (iii) less likely to have a PhD founder. These changes occurred as VC funds invested more in IT (and, in particular, in IT firms that were less science-intensive), while their retreat from science was less evident in the life sciences.

The retreat of VC groups from science is concerning, especially given the concurrent decline of the large corporate lab. Nevertheless, different organisational forms may specialise in different areas of innovation. Perhaps VC-backed startups are focusing on scientific fields that large firms have exited, whereas large firms are leaving areas where startups are active. We examine this "specialisation" hypothesis in Figure 4.4.

Scientific fields where large firms withdrew from science can be seen in the second (top left) and third (bottom left) quadrants in Figure 4.4, split by changes between decades. Fields where startups translated less research over time are shown in the third (bottom left) and fourth (bottom right) quadrants.

The withdrawal of large firms from science has been sustained over time and is most marked in the physical sciences (physics, materials, engineering), including chemistry, from the 2000s. Consistent with the evidence in Figure 4.3 (the diamond-dashed line), VC-backed startups translated increasingly larger amounts of scientific research into technology across

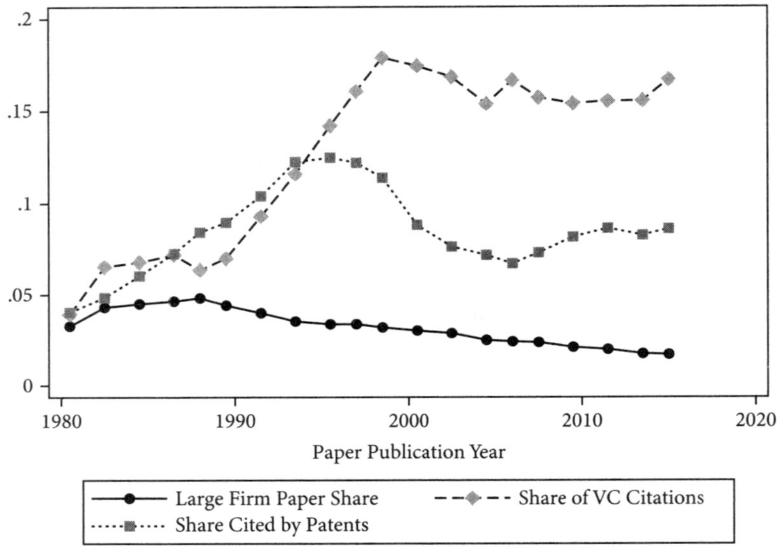

Figure 4.3 Translation of Science and Corporate Participation by Firm Type (1980–2015)

Notes: The binned scatterplots summarise scientific field-year level data. "Large Firm Paper Share" divides the number of papers authored by publicly listed U.S. firms by all scientific publications.[11] "Share of VC citations" divides the number of papers cited by at least one VC-backed startup patent by the number of papers cited by any patent in the field-year.[12] "Share Cited by Patents" divides the number of papers cited by patents by all scientific publications in the field-year. The paper sample is limited to those within 10 per cent of forward paper citations in their field-year. We count patent citations of papers that occur up to five years after the focal paper's publication. Scientific publication data is sourced from the SciSciNet database.[13]

all scientific fields, up to the 2000s; however, since then, these efforts have plateaued. The stability in Figure 4.3, however, hides considerable heterogeneity across scientific fields. Translational efforts by VC-backed startups declined in the physical sciences (physics, chemistry, materials, engineering) and increased in the life sciences (biology and medicine) and computer science. The MIT study on cleantech ventures found that after 2010, VCs reduced series A funding for cleantech ventures and transitioned any remaining cleantech investments to focus on software and deployment rather than physical sciences. A subsequent analysis in 2023 by the consulting firm Cambridge Associates found that this shift improved the financial performance reported by cleantech ventures.[14]

Thus, the evidence from Figure 4.4 is inconsistent with the "specialisation" hypothesis. Both large firms and VC-backed startups are withdrawing from

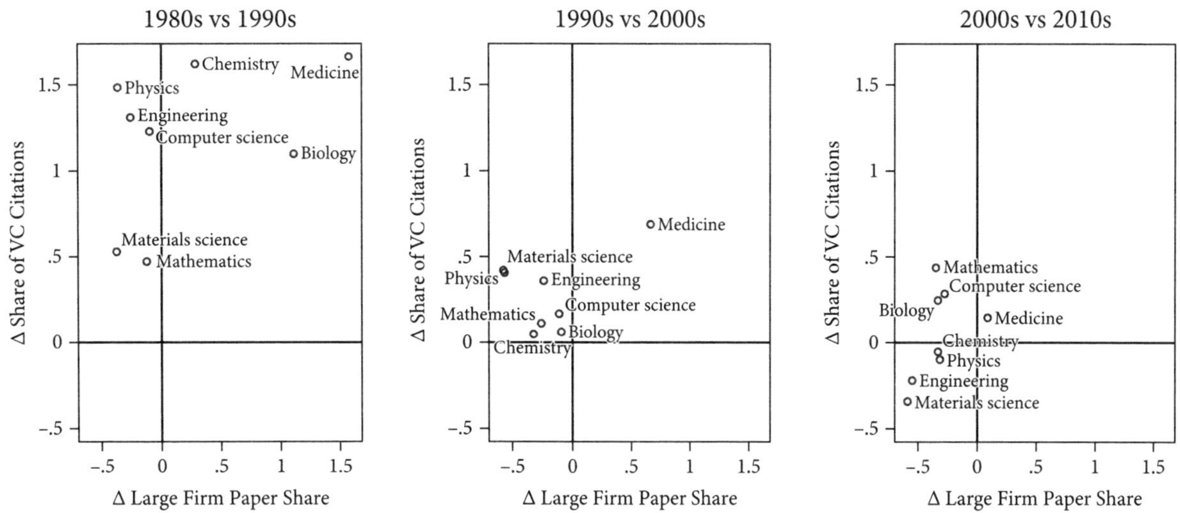

Figure 4.4 Large vs VC-backed Firm Participation in Science (1980–2019)

Notes: The scatterplots are at the scientific field level. "Share of VC citations" divides the number of papers cited by at least one VC-backed startup patent by the number of papers cited by any patent in the field.[15] "Large Firm Paper Share" divides the number of papers authored by publicly listed U.S. firms by all scientific publications.[16] The left panel plots the change in average VC citation share between the 1990s and 1980s against the change in average large firm paper share in the 1990s against the 1980s. The middle and right panels plot these changes for the subsequent decades. The scientific publication sample is limited to those within the top 10% of forward paper citations in their field-year. Patent citations to papers are limited to those that occur up to five years after paper publication. Geology and environmental science are omitted. Scientific publication data is sourced from SciSciNet.[17]

science, especially the physical sciences. Life sciences and computer science do not show a similar withdrawal. One interpretation is that both large firms and VC groups have learned that investing in science is unrewarding. This is the standard interpretation wherein the social value of innovation exceeds its private value. The standard prescription is to subsidise R&D by universities and private firms. A different possibility, though not mutually exclusive, is that industrial research complements startups' own translational efforts. That is, deep-tech startups depend upon scientifically sophisticated corporate partners (and potential acquirers) to innovate successfully. The same prescription (to support upstream university research) in this case would be insufficient to revive translation in deep-tech.

There are three sources of complementarities between startup and incumbent research. First, startups often arise as spinoffs from incumbent firms to explore commercial applications of inventions made in corporate labs, which the parent company is unable or unwilling to pursue itself. Second, startup prototypes (especially in deep-tech) require a sophisticated incumbent to absorb and scale the innovation. Unlike a new molecule produced by a biotech firm, innovations introduced by deep-tech startups are not discrete, modular inputs. Deep-tech innovations often require embedding in a larger architecture fielded by incumbent firms. Carbon nanotubes have to be incorporated into sensors, organic light-emitting diodes (OLEDs) into displays, innovative cathodes into batteries, and batteries in devices and vehicles, absorbent polymers into water purification systems, and so on. Third, successful exit may depend on the acquisition of a science-based startup by a research-intensive incumbent. Taken together, these three complementarities suggest that the research activities of startups and large firms are closely intertwined. Policies that support the former while allowing the latter to weaken may therefore prove ineffectual.

These considerations apply to non-deep-tech startups as well. However, innovations in software have an easier path to the market because the interfaces with other components of the overall system are better defined, thanks to a variety of agreed-upon standards. With a few exceptions, incumbents have offered Application Programming Interfaces (APIs) that allow components made by other firms to interoperate within their products, and often with the products offered by other incumbents. For instance, Dropbox offers a widely used cloud storage and sharing service, available on a variety of devices and operating systems. As a startup, Dropbox was able to offer this service because it used Python, a widely available cross-platform language.

Dropbox's core logic, written in Python, could run on Windows, macOS, and Linux with minimal modifications. Many deep-tech startups do not enjoy the same advantage. Standardised interfaces and interoperability are not as easily achieved in the world of atoms as they are in the world of bits.

What we lost with the demise of corporate labs

Why is it so difficult to replace the functions of the industrial research lab? The next three subsections consider the unique role played by industrial research in bridging the gap between academic discovery and commercial application.

Identifying and overcoming roadblocks to commercialisation

There is considerable evidence that industrial research is more potent than university science in spurring technological advances. For instance, Michaël Bikard, examining simultaneous papers written on the same discovery (e.g., Newton and Leibniz's invention of calculus), found that inventors pay less attention to discoveries "made in academia" than discoveries "made in industry."[18]

The commercial imperatives that guide corporate labs help focus their research on materials and phenomena relevant to the corporation. Andrew Odlyzko, who spent over two decades at AT&T Bell Labs, emphasised the importance of this connection to the market:

> It was very important that Bell Labs had a connection to the market, and thereby to real problems. The fact that it wasn't a tight coupling is what enabled people to work on many long-term problems. But the coupling was there, and so the wild goose chases that are at the heart of really innovative research tended to be less wild, more carefully targeted and less subject to the inertia that is characteristic of university research.[19]

This unique positioning enables corporate laboratories to combine the best of both worlds: research grounded in real-world problems, ensuring significant industrial applications, while maintaining the flexibility to pursue scientific exploration beyond immediate commercial needs.

This use-inspired focus in research does not diminish its scientific impact. Louis Pasteur's work, which addressed the practical issue of wine spoilage, led not only to the invention of pasteurisation but also to the development of the germ theory of fermentation. Pasteur's work, driven by a specific commercial need, also laid the groundwork for modern bacteriology, immunology, and vaccination science. Research focused on solving practical problems can lead to significant advancements in fundamental scientific knowledge. The close engagement with applications creates a problem-rich environment, opening up potentially fruitful areas of deep scientific inquiry.

The development of Bell Labs' Holmdel Horn Antenna provides another example of how industrial research, even when initially driven by practical goals, can result in groundbreaking scientific discoveries. The Horn Antenna was originally designed to improve microwave communications by detecting weak radio signals. However, when Arno Penzias and Robert Wilson began using the antenna in 1964, they encountered persistent background noise that they could not explain. After ruling out all possible sources of interference, they realised that they had stumbled upon evidence of cosmic microwave background radiation: residual heat from the Big Bang that permeates the universe. This discovery provided concrete evidence supporting the Big Bang theory, a cornerstone of modern cosmology, and earned Penzias and Wilson the Nobel Prize in Physics in 1978.

The evolution of research at DuPont is an example of the complexities involved in balancing fundamental research with a focus on practical applications. Wallace Carothers, a pivotal figure in DuPont's history of innovation, joined the company with the understanding that he would have the freedom to engage in fundamental research without the immediate pressure to deliver tangible results. This assurance was crucial in attracting Carothers, who was driven primarily by the pursuit of scientific knowledge. Under this arrangement, Carothers and his team were able to do fundamental research, demonstrating that polymers were large molecules, not simply colloidal aggregates of many small ones. In doing so, they also synthesised nylon, a synthetic polymer that revolutionised the textile industry. Thereafter, the further development of nylon, including finding ways of producing key intermediate inputs, was shouldered by other parts of the company.

Nylon and other synthetic polymers, such as neoprene, polyester, and polyacrylonitrile (Orlon), were sources of immense profits for DuPont in the decades that followed. This story highlights a critical nuance: had DuPont initially emphasised a strictly practical orientation, it might have deterred

Carothers from joining the company. His contributions were fundamental to these discoveries, suggesting that the initial freedom to explore basic science was a key ingredient in DuPont's later successes. There is a delicate balance that corporate labs must navigate between translational research, targeting specific practical goals, and curiosity-driven research, which is more exploratory and open-ended. Striking this balance is challenging but essential for fostering an environment that supports both immediate innovation and long-term scientific discovery.[20]

Scale and multidisciplinary approach

One may argue that startups staffed with capable founders can emulate corporate labs. Yet, this is insufficient. Solving practical problems requires expertise that spans multiple fields of knowledge. Bell Labs, for instance, was renowned for its ability to marshal resources from diverse scientific disciplines to tackle some of the most challenging problems in technology and science. As E. B. Craft of Bell Labs described it:

> Perhaps the outstanding characteristic of this organisation, the one that sets it apart a little from others, is its conduct of research and development by a group method of attack.... So in all of these technical departments, we have specialist chemists, metallurgists, physicists, engineers, statisticians, mathematicians, men that are trained and skilled in their particular branches of science and engineering.... When a problem is put up to the Labs for solution, it is divided into the elements, and each element is assigned to that group of specialists who know the most about that particular field, but they all cooperate and make their contribution to the solution of the problem as a whole.[21]

The creation of the transistor is a testament to the essential role of interdisciplinary collaboration, where theoretical and practical expertise across physics, metallurgy, and chemistry converged at Bell Labs. Before Bell Labs' success, other entities like Purdue's Karl Lark-Horovitz and General Electric had made efforts to advance solid-state electronics, but they lacked the interdisciplinary coordination needed to overcome the material and theoretical challenges of developing a practical transistor. Bell Labs, however, assembled a team that included physicists like John Bardeen and

Walter Brattain, who brought expertise in quantum mechanics and solid-state physics, and metallurgists like Gordon Teal, who specialised in the purification and doping of semiconductors. Bell Labs' capability to achieve such breakthroughs was further enhanced by the wartime collaboration between MIT's Radiation Lab and AT&T's Western Electric, which equipped Bell Labs' metallurgists with advanced skills in semiconductor purification and doping—key techniques for semiconductor production. The synergy between these diverse disciplines allowed Bell Labs to solve complex technical problems that had stymied other research efforts, ultimately leading to the creation of the transistor.

The development of Google Translate by the Google Brain team is another case in point. Quoc Le, a leading scientist, developed advanced algorithms that software engineers then translated into Google's TensorFlow programming language. Concurrently, hardware engineers meticulously refined Google's Tensor Processing Units (TPUs), custom-designed circuits for executing neural network inference tasks with remarkable efficiency. The first TPUs, deployed in Google's data centres in 2015, outperformed existing Graphical Processing Units (GPUs) by up to twenty-six times in speed. Google's ability to continually advance TPU technology—rolling out four iterations in just two years—showcases a development cycle that is far more accelerated than what is typically seen in academic settings.

A second, and related, feature of industrial research is its scale. The Google Translate paper has thirty-one coauthors, many of whom are leading researchers in their respective fields. The difference between corporate and university research is clearly visible in artificial intelligence (AI). Since 2010, large corporations such as Google, IBM, and Facebook have invested heavily in AI research. A 2019 study already showed that the share of corporate publications in top AI journals, including the International Conference on Machine Learning (ICML), had tripled between 2004 and 2016. These firms have pioneered research in specialised fields such as deep neural networks, producing landmark publications like the "Cat Paper" and the "Google Translate Paper," validating the effectiveness of new algorithms, such as Long-Short Term Memory (LSTM), for image recognition and language translation, respectively.[22]

Between 2011 and 2018, research publications by large firms featured, on average, one more coauthor (4.3) than those from other institutions (3.4). The top AI publishers, including Microsoft, Google, IBM, Yahoo, Toyota, Baidu, NEC Corporation, Facebook, Adobe, and LinkedIn, make up 10 per cent of the papers published with fewer than eleven authors (2,168 out of 20,989) but 28 per cent of the papers published with more than eleven authors (twenty-two out of seventy-nine). High-quality papers show the same difference in team size: among the Machine Learning Conference papers in the top decile by citations received, corporate publications have 4.4 authors, while non-firm publications have 3.6. This pattern also holds for the top 1 per cent of cited publications. Corporate publications involve more authors, with 4.4 authors per publication compared to 3.6 for noncorporate publications. In NeurIPS, a top Machine Learning conference, the average number of authors per paper steadily increased from around three in 2014 to nearly five in 2023.[23]

In addition to large teams, AI research is also very demanding in terms of computational resources and large datasets. For example, Google's proprietary dataset, JFT-300M (introduced publicly in 2017), contained more than 375 million labels for 300 million images. In comparison, Stanford's Imagenet dataset, one of the largest datasets made publicly available by a university, contained around 14 million images in the same period. Nur Ahmed and coauthors at MIT have analysed AI papers to show that in 2021, the average number of parameters used in industry publications was twenty-nine times larger than that of their university counterparts.[24] Large language models (LLMs) require vast amounts of text and code data. Big firms curate massive datasets from a wide variety of sources, covering virtually all public websites, including Wikipedia, news outlets, forums, e-commerce sites, social media sites, video transcripts, as well as digitised books, and academic and scientific papers.

Training and operating LLMs require specialised AI accelerators and data centres to handle the massive datasets required to train the models. The resource cost of training state-of-the-art LLMs is staggering. For instance, Meta's Llama 3 training costs are estimated at over $500 million. These figures represent just the compute costs, not the extensive R&D, data acquisition, and personnel expenses.

The AI case also shows that the common assertion that private capital will not finance long-term and risky projects is not universally true. Some of the firms engaged in the development of LLM models are startups (extremely well-funded ones at that). OpenAI reported losses of $5 billion on revenues of $3.7 billion in 2024 and was reportedly valued at $300 billion. When the potential commercial payoff is high enough, as it appears to be for chatbots and related applications of LLMs, private financing appears to be in abundant supply.

Industrial research creating external benefits

The third reason why the new ecosystem struggles to substitute for the loss of industrial research is that it delivers substantial spillovers. Given how widespread and unexpected the fruits of scientific progress are, the sponsoring firm often fails to capture a significant fraction of the returns to its investment. For instance, current LLMs such as ChatGPT, Gemini, and Claude are based on a breakthrough announced in a 2017 paper, "Attention Is All You Need" by Google researchers. This seminal work introduced the "transformer" model, which revolutionised natural language processing by allowing for the simultaneous processing and interpretation of whole sentences rather than the traditional word-by-word translation method. The transformer model has since become foundational to a wide range of advanced AI applications, from generating images to sequencing DNA, due to its ability to recognise patterns effectively.[25] All eight co-authors of the seminal Google paper left Google shortly after its publication to co-found or work in AI companies. For example, Lukasz Kaiser, another key contributor of the attention paper, joined OpenAI, a direct competitor of Google.

This type of spinoff activity has been recognised as an important conduit through which the external benefits generated by corporate laboratories accrue to society. Steve Klepper's research, for instance, found that spinoffs in high-tech industries such as the early automobile, semiconductor, and laser industries performed better than other startups in the industry.[26] The comparison between Fairchild Semiconductor and Texas Instruments illustrates this point well. While Texas Instruments was better managed than Fairchild, it spawned far fewer spinoffs. Many of Fairchild's employees left to start their own companies, including Intel, founded by Robert Noyce and Gordon Moore, and AMD, founded by Jerry Sanders. In contrast, the Dallas-Fort Worth cluster near Texas Instruments, although significant, became less economically influential.

As Bob Metcalfe, of the eponymous Metcalfe's Law, put it:

> Bell Labs' greatest contribution may have been driving Shockley out. Shockley Semiconductor, his start-up, was a fiasco, but the man was good at recruiting talent, especially Gordon Moore from Caltech and Robert Noyce from MIT. Those two men would later found Fairchild Semiconductor, which over the years spun off Intel, National Semiconductor and Advanced Micro Devices. Those companies, in turn, spun off more

start-ups, which grew to become Silicon Valley, the world's pre-eminent innovation machine, clustered around Stanford and the University of California at Berkeley.[27]

Spinoffs may not discourage private investment in research as long as the sponsoring firm captures adequate returns. Large firms, with their diversified activities and strong market positions, are better equipped than smaller firms and startups to capture sufficient private returns from their scientific research, even when significant external benefits also accrue to others. Google itself continues to reap significant benefits from the attention mechanisms introduced in the "Attention" paper, as these have become foundational to many of its AI-driven products and services, such as Google Translate and Bidirectional Encoder Representations from Transformers (BERT).

The external benefits of industrial research are not a new phenomenon. Xerox Palo Alto Research Center (PARC), founded in 1970 to spearhead advanced research and innovation, has significantly contributed to the American economy through groundbreaking inventions such as the mouse-controlled graphical user interface, Ethernet for local area networks, and the laser printer. A widely recognised lesson from Xerox PARC's legacy is the wedge between the societal value of its groundbreaking innovations and Xerox's ability to capture this value privately. While the laser printer was a notable success for Xerox, the company captured only a fraction of the benefits from many other PARC inventions, particularly those in industries beyond its core business. Companies such as Apple and Microsoft capitalised on PARC's research. Apple's Macintosh computer drew heavily from PARC's graphical user interface, and Microsoft incorporated elements of PARC's research into its Windows operating system.

IBM and the commercialisation of Giant Magnetoresistance

Giant Magnetoresistance, or GMR for short, is a notable example of the value of industrial research. GMR was a significant innovation in computer disk drives, making it possible to shrink drives while greatly increasing capacity. The GMR effect was independently discovered in 1988 by Albert Fert at Université Paris-Sud (supported by Thomson-CSF, a French electronics firm) and by Peter Grünberg at Forschungszentrum Jülich, a German research institute. Although a major scientific advance, the discovery initially appeared to have limited commercial potential. The experiments demonstrating GMR relied on molecular beam epitaxy (MBE), which required large magnetic fields operating at very low temperatures. Commercial applications, on the other hand, would require smaller magnetic fields and room temperature.[28]

Fortunately, Stuart Parkin, an IBM researcher who was present at the conference where the discoveries were announced, was intrigued by the potential for advancing storage technology. This required fundamental research in physics, not just engineering research. Contrary to Fert's hypothesis that the GMR effect arose from the internal structure of chromium and iron and was specific to these materials, Parkin theorised that the effect was due to the interlayer coupling of materials, and therefore might be found with other materials as well. Parkin successfully reproduced the GMR effect with silver, copper, gold, cobalt, ruthenium, and nickel oxide. He also demonstrated that the effect could be produced with just two magnetic layers separated by a spacer layer in small magnetic fields. These were significant scientific advances in their own right—Parkin was nominated for the Nobel Prize, which, however, went only to Fert and Grünberg.

The commercial impact of Parkin's research is indisputable, however. GMR substantially improved upon the existing technology used for hard disk drives (HDDs), anisotropic magnetoresistance (AMR). IBM was the first company to commercialise heads based on GMR, and it took just ten years to move from the discovery to an HDD product on the market, half the time required to commercialise the earlier technology. Just three years after the discovery of GMR, Parkin had developed very small, multilayered sandwiches of materials called "spin valves." In December 1997, IBM announced a 16.8 GB 3.5-inch HDD product using GMR heads for the desktop market. IBM began production of a 6.48 GB 2.5-inch HDD for the mobile computer market in early 1998.

The remarkable part of the story is the rapidity with which a scientific discovery was applied, at scale. What made this possible was that IBM had both the upstream research capability and the necessary downstream engineering and commercial capabilities. Stuart Parkin possessed both the scientific expertise and the knowledge required to translate the discovery of GMR into a commercially viable technology. The Disk Storage Research Unit of IBM Research took on the task of developing a physical sensor that could be incorporated into a hard drive. IBM's Storage Division integrated the head into a new drive for large-scale production. IBM had pioneered thin films as well as AMR-based disk drives earlier. AMR heads had required changes in several aspects of the drive, including the electronics, data format, and head/disk interface. GMR heads were compatible with other components of the drives using AMR heads; even the processes and tooling were the same. Hence, IBM and other manufacturers could readily integrate the GMR heads with other drive components.

The diffusion of this technology was as swift as its translation. IBM published many of Parkin's key findings. As Mark Kryder, head of research at Seagate (and professor at Carnegie Mellon University), put it, "Once the IBM research was out, everybody began working on GMR product development at the same time."[29] Jülich, which had filed the basic patent on GMR, licensed liberally. Importantly, so did IBM, which had done much of the follow-on work. IBM licensed this technology shortly after it commercialised GMR to Seagate and Western Digital. The similarity of AMR and GMR production technology helped the entire HDD industry to switch to GMR within two years after IBM.

This example illustrates all three aspects of industrial research. IBM Research employed Parkin, without whom GMR might have remained a mere scientific discovery. Parkin did more than recognise the potential of the discovery. He also undertook the research necessary to understand its implications, such as that GMR was not specific to chromium and iron, and not dependent on their internal structure, but rather was a property of layered materials. Parkin's understanding of the manufacturing technology for disk drives helped him translate and develop GMR for commercial applications. Second, the scale and scope of IBM Research were invaluable. Researchers in the Disk Storage unit could build on Parkin's advances and integrate them into the other components. Finally, the entire industry benefited from IBM's investments. IBM published many of its research findings and licensed its patents and technology to other manufacturing companies, many of which were started or run by former IBM engineers.[30]

Leadership at a crossroads

As discussed earlier in the section The Uneven Translation of Research and Its Organisational Origins, the withdrawal of large American firms from science was partially compensated by the corresponding entry of universities and VC-backed startups, notably in the software and biotech sectors. However, deep-tech areas did not experience this influx. The resulting vacuum, in turn, has begun to be filled by foreign rivals. Over the past decades, East Asian countries have poured public and private funds into catching up to the technological frontier and subsequently pushing the frontier itself in solid-state electronics (liquid crystal display [LCD], light-emitting diode [LED], semiconductor processing) and material sciences (batteries and photovoltaics).

China, in particular, has emerged as a powerful challenger in many high-technology sectors. China enjoys many of the structural advantages that propelled the United States past European countries in the nineteenth century: notably, a vast internal market and deep pools of scientific, technological, and entrepreneurial talent. Two recent studies highlight the rapid progress China has recently made across a wide range of high-technology fields.

The first study, the 2025 Harvard University Critical and Emerging Technologies Index, assesses the capabilities of twenty-five countries across five key technology sectors: artificial intelligence (AI), biotechnology, semiconductors, space, and quantum.[31] The study finds that while the United States continues to lead across all five sectors, China is closing the gap, particularly in biotechnology and quantum technologies.

Even in AI, where the United States has a considerable advantage, China has made significant strides, thanks to its vast pools of human capital and data. In this sector, China appears to prioritise the rapid development and commercialisation of AI-enabled products over the pursuit of frontier scientific breakthroughs.[32] The 2025 releases of DeepSeek's R1 model and Alibaba's Qwen3 family of models suggest that the U.S. lead in this field may be more vulnerable than previously thought.

In advanced semiconductors, no single country controls the entire supply chain. The United States excels in chip design, tools, and equipment. Taiwan, Japan, and South Korea dominate in manufacturing and fabrication, specialised materials, and wafers. China has considerable strengths in assembly and testing, as well as in the mining and refining of inputs.

The study finds that China appears to have the most immediate opportunity to overtake the United States in biotechnology. While the U.S. leads in biosecurity, genetic engineering, vaccine research, and agricultural technologies, China's advantages lie in its human capital and scale of pharmaceutical production.

The second study is by the Australian Strategic Policy Institute (ASPI), an independent think tank established by the Australian government in 2001. This study analyses the top 10 per cent most highly cited research publications across sixty-four critical technologies over a twenty-one-year period (2003–2023). ASPI's results highlight a remarkable shift in research leadership over the past two decades. Between 2003 and 2007, the United States led in sixty of sixty-four technologies, but by 2019–2023, it led in only seven. Conversely, China, which led in just three technologies in the early 2000s, now leads in fifty-seven. In terms of institutions, U.S. technology firms, including Google, IBM, Microsoft, and Meta, hold leading or strong positions in artificial intelligence, quantum, and computing technologies. U.S. government agencies and national laboratories also perform well, notably NASA in space and satellite systems. However, the Chinese Academy of Sciences (CAS) is now the world's single most influential institution, holding a global lead in thirty-one of the sixty-four technologies analysed.

These results reflect the rapid maturation of China's innovation ecosystem. Chinese universities now produce far more STEM PhDs than their U.S. counterparts.[33] Since 2013, annual R&D investment in China has increased by over $480 billion in purchasing-power-parity terms—a greater rise than in the United States.[34]

Foreign firms are challenging American leadership in several research-intensive technology segments

Display technologies. An early example of Asian firms closing the gap with American science and technology can be found in display technologies. From black and white to colour cathode ray tubes used in television sets to liquid crystal displays to (organic and inorganic) LEDs and, most recently, quantum dot flat panels, displays have become thinner, crisper, and more flexible thanks to the diligent application of scientific advances. The cathode ray tube itself was an instrument of science used by a British physicist, J. J. Thomson, to discover the electron in 1897. However, it was an American firm, RCA, that provided the funds for Vladimir Zworykin's research to introduce the first television set for mass consumption in the 1939 New York World's Fair. RCA pioneered research into colour televisions and licensed its patents globally. Following David Sarnoff's vision for a TV that could "hang on the wall," RCA researchers made fundamental scientific advances, with

George Heilmeier inventing the first Liquid Crystal Displays in 1968 and Herbert Maruska creating a blue LED in 1972.[35]

However, as these advances were being made, basic research at RCA labs was experiencing several setbacks. Public sponsorship for industrial research in defence and aerospace, an important source of support for RCA labs, declined after the Sputnik shock had subsided. The arrival of a new CEO in Robert Sarnoff (the founder's son) in 1967 also directed lab personnel towards more downstream developmental efforts, such as the Videodisc project.[36] Research at RCA suffered, with scientific publications at RCA dropping from a high of over eighty in 1966 down to around ten per year in the 1970s.[37] This cutback implied that more exploratory, basic research projects in LCD and LED technology went unfunded. Henry Kressel, a former lab manager at RCA labs, recounts the story as follows:

> It was clear that investments in the hundreds of millions of dollars over years would be needed to reach major product objectives given that all aspects of the technology were new. . . . The corporate decision was made to license the liquid crystal display technology rather than pursue internal product development. So it was licensed to the Sharp Corporation in Japan, which invested many millions of dollars to bring displays to the market—initially for calculators and computer terminals.[38]

Building on licensed technology from RCA, Sharp introduced the first wall-mountable LCD TV in 1992. Other Japanese firms such as NEC, Hitachi, and DTI would join LCD panel production during the 1980s and 1990s, followed by Taiwanese and Korean firms. The story for LED displays, recounted in Chapter 3, has been similar: technological opportunities seeded by American corporate labs were not followed through in the United States. The bulk of the labour (and reward) for commercialising display technologies belonged to corporate labs overseas.

Electrical technologies. Entrepreneur and venture capitalist Peter Thiel quipped in 2011, "We wanted flying cars, instead we got 140 characters." Today, thanks to advances in battery technology, lightweight composite materials, and autonomous flight systems, flying cars are finally moving from concept to commercialisation. Yet the companies leading this emerging sector are predominantly Chinese.[39]

China's prominence in this space is part of a broader pattern. Across virtually all electrical and clean technologies, including batteries, electric vehicles, solar and wind power, drones, and robotics and automation, Chinese firms have established dominant positions.

Take battery technology, which we discussed in Chapter 3. China now leads global battery manufacturing by a wide margin. In 2023, it accounted for nearly 90 per cent of global installed cathode active material capacity and more than 97 per cent of anode active material capacity. Outside China, only Korea (9 per cent) and Japan (3 per cent) hold significant shares of cathode material production. At the level of specific chemistries, China hosts almost all global production of lithium iron phosphate (LFP) batteries and more than three-quarters of lithium nickel manganese cobalt oxide (NMC) and other nickel-based chemistries, compared to 20 per cent in Korea.[40]

More broadly, China now holds commanding positions across most clean technology industries. According to the International Energy Agency's 2024 Energy Technology Perspectives, in 2023 China accounted for roughly 80 per cent of global production of solar photovoltaic (PV) modules and battery cells, more than 60 per cent of wind nacelles, over 50 per cent of electrolysers, and nearly 40 per cent of heat pumps.[41]

Kyle Chan argues that China has created a network of interconnected "tech-industrial ecosystems," in which progress in one area accelerates advances in others. This interdependence allows China to compound its industrial advantages through shared supply chains, technologies, and human capital.[42]

A good example is the electric vehicle (EV) industry. China's early expertise in lithium battery production for smartphones gave firms such as CATL and BYD a head start in scaling up EV batteries. Its large smartphone and electronics sectors supplied EV makers with advanced components such as touchscreens, sensors, and control systems. The rapid diffusion of innovative manufacturing processes provides another advantage. Gigacasting allows automakers to produce large vehicle structures as a single piece, replacing the traditional method of welding multiple components. Originally developed by Idra, an Italian company acquired in 2008 by China's LK Group, gigacasting significantly reduces factory space requirements, production times, labour costs, and material waste. Tesla first employed the process for its Chinese-made Model Y in 2021, but the LK Group is now supplying several other Chinese automakers.[43]

A dominant position in manufacturing does not, of course, mean that Chinese companies also lead in research and development. Nevertheless, manufacturing and R&D are closely intertwined. Consider the early history of BYD, the battery and EV manufacturer.[44] When the company pivoted to lithium-ion batteries, it did not merely imitate Japanese technology and production methods. Instead, it completely reengineered the manufacturing process to suit China's economic environment. While Japanese firms relied on expensive, capital-intensive automation, BYD took advantage of lower labour costs by developing a labour-intensive, yet highly efficient, production system.

Efficiency was further enhanced by more finely subdividing manufacturing tasks, reducing the variability inherent in manual labour. Most importantly, BYD engineers invested heavily in designing simple tools, or "jigs," that improved both worker productivity and consistency. About two-thirds of BYD's R&D expenditures were devoted to process improvements. This strategic focus on incrementally refining and reengineering the manufacturing process enabled BYD to compete with more established players at a fraction of their capital costs.

The electric vehicle industry illustrates the growing innovative capacity of Chinese firms.[45] Until recently, the Chinese firms' main competitive advantage over Tesla or other EV automakers was in having significantly lower prices. However, in February 2025, BYD unveiled "God's Eye," an advanced driver-assistance system seen as a precursor to fully autonomous driving. A month later, BYD announced a battery-charging system capable of adding about 470 km of driving range in five minutes—a fraction of the time required by Tesla's current technology.

Chinese manufacturers are now not just replicating Tesla's innovations but are advancing beyond them. The original gigacasting process used by Tesla relied on a specially formed aluminium alloy developed by SpaceX engineers. When Xpeng released its G6 SUV in 2023, however, it had already adopted a gigacasting system that was both lighter and more rigid than the one used by Tesla. Xpeng and other Chinese brands have also improved on Tesla's lightweight aluminium cabling used in charging and cooling systems. Engineering services company Caresoft estimates that BYD has introduced around 100 cost-saving improvements across various components and materials that, if adopted by Tesla, would reduce costs by $350–$885 per vehicle.

Semiconductors. The American "footprint" in semiconductor research is also shrinking. For three decades, the United States enjoyed a near-monopoly on major technological breakthroughs in the field. The transistor was invented at AT&T Bell Labs; the integrated circuit (Texas Instruments and Fairchild Semiconductor) and the planar process enabling its mass

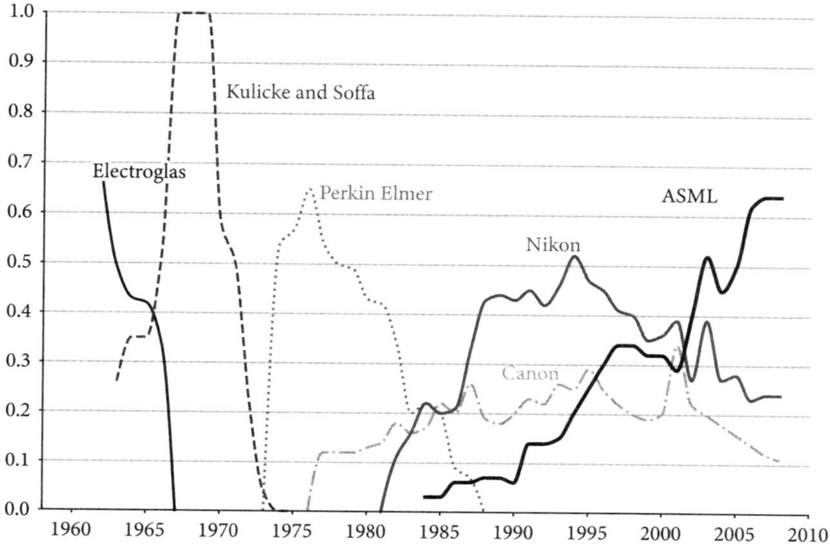

Figure 4.5 Market Shares of Leading Lithography Tool Suppliers (Reproduced from Pillai 2023)

Notes: Reproduction of Figure 7 from Pillai (2023).[46] Global market shares of photolithography exposure tool suppliers is displayed. Data for 1962–1982 is from Henderson (1993) and data for 1982–2008 is from Gartner Inc.

production (Fairchild Semiconductor) emerged from industrial research. The CMOS transistor architecture (RCA), along with key advances in photolithography tools (GCA and PerkinElmer) during the 1960s and 1970s, were likewise American contributions. Until the 1980s, U.S. firms such as Electroglas, Kulicke & Soffa, and PerkinElmer dominated the semiconductor equipment market, as Figure 4.5 shows.

Beginning in the 1980s, however, competition from Japanese rivals such as Nikon and Canon intensified, and American firms lagged behind in the transition from contact/proximity aligners to step-and-repeat projection aligners (steppers).[47] Japanese dominance continued into the 1990s as the industry moved into deep UV lithography (in the 193 and 248 nm range) using excimer lasers. Even as the industry transitioned to extreme UV lithography (in the 13.5 nanometer range), American tools suppliers failed to make a comeback. As with displays, large American firms seeded the initial research: as early as 1992, Intel invested $200 million in its Extreme Ultra Violet (EUV) development efforts, and under SEMATECH sponsorship, formed joint ventures with public and private labs to form EUV LLC in

1997.[48] Billions more would be sunk, while IBM and Bell Labs explored parallel approaches to generating EUV resolutions, such as X-ray lithography and electron beam lithography. However, even as the industry converged around laser-produced plasma (LPP) as the dominant solution, no American firm was ready to finish the advanced engineering that was required to produce a complete EUV lithography system: large firms (integrated device manufacturers and foundries) had washed their hands of producing tools, while the only surviving American photolithography firm, Silicon Valley Group (SVG), was absorbed by the Netherlands' ASML.[49]

As the science behind semiconductor production matured, it became possible to modularise production and divide the labour into ever-narrower niches. After the introduction of Carver Mead and Lynn Conway's Very Large-Scale Integration (VLSI) design methodology, it became possible for computer scientists without a materials background to design chip layouts *in silico*. An Electronic Design Automation (EDA) tools industry consisting of Cadence (1983) and Synopsys (1986) was founded to service these designers, while specialist foundries such as TSMC complemented fabless firms such as ARM, Qualcomm, Broadcom, and NVIDIA, which purely focused on chip designs. The founding firms of Silicon Valley did not resist this fragmentation. On the contrary, they welcomed the gains from specialisation. Recounting the founding of Electroglas, which built furnaces for chip manufacturers, Gordon Moore rationalised this business model:

> Interviewer: So you started buying from Electroglas eventually and stopped making your own? Gordon Moore: [Yes]. . . . But that's been repeated over and over again, that a company dedicated to supplying the equipment that has a broad market ends up doing a better job than an in-house equipment supply capability can. *So, when we set up Intel, we decided we'd do nothing on equipment internally, we'd work with the vendors, and even if this resulted in technology we developed getting transferred to the rest of the industry, it would be the most effective way for us to continue to grow.*[50]

Beyond photolithography systems, the photo-resist materials that are applied to silicon wafers in the etching process are dominated by Japanese firms such as JSR, TOK, Shin Etsu, and Fuji, which serve over 70 per cent of the market. Even the market for ultra-pure water used to wash the wafers is dominated by Veolia (France) and Kurita (Japan) outside North America.

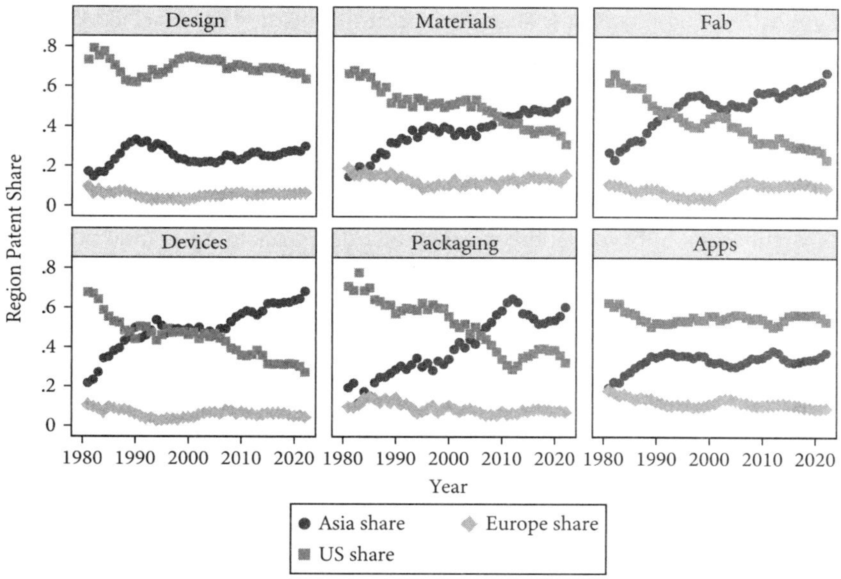

Figure 4.6 Regional Shares in Semiconductor Patenting (1980–2022)

Notes: These graphs plot the regional share of U.S., Asian, and European assignees in granted USPTO patents within six areas of the semiconductor supply chain. "Asia" refers to assignees from Japan, Korea, Taiwan, China, and Singapore. "Europe" refers to assignees from Germany, France, Sweden, Switzerland, the United Kingdom, the Netherlands, and Finland. The six categories are constructed by aggregating Cooperative Patent Classification (CPC) subclasses. "Design" includes patents in G06F30 (computer-aided design of circuits) and related G06F subclasses for processor and system architecture. "Materials" covers C30B (single-crystal growth), C23C (thin-film deposition), and C23F (etching). "Fab" comprises H01L21 (manufacture of semiconductor devices) and G03F (photolithography and patterning). "Devices" includes H01L (general semiconductor devices), H01W (optoelectronics such as LEDs, lasers, and solar cells), and G11C (memory). "Packaging" draws on H05K (printed circuits, IC packaging, substrates, and 3D integration). "Applications" captures patents in H04L (wired digital communications), H04W (wireless networks), and H04N (imaging and video technologies). CPC data is sourced from Google Patents; Assignee data is sourced from the Dimensions dataset.

American firms still hold their own in design and application. Figure 4.6 plots the regional assignee share of United States Patent and Trademark Office (USPTO) patents, beginning from upstream (chip design) to downstream (communications and memory applications), with process technology related to chip fabrication (materials, equipment, fabrication, device manufacture and packaging) in between. The United States still dominates electronic design automation (through firms such as Synopsys, Cadence, and Mentor) and chip design (Intel and Nvidia), as seen in the "Design" subgraph—the U.S. share briefly dips in the 1990s but never below 60 per cent, and it has stayed above this threshold throughout the past four decades.

Downstream applications, such as in communications (Cisco, Broadcom, Qualcomm), are another area where the U.S. share has remained steady, though with Japanese strength in imaging and optical sensing applications, the absolute share is lower than in design, at around 60 per cent. The United States has ceded control in all areas relating to process technology. Crystal growth and deposition (the "Materials" subgraph), photolithography (the "Fab" subgraph), the manufacture and packaging of final products ("Devices" and "Packaging") are all areas where U.S. dominance has been ceded to Asian firms.

American leadership remains strong where American firms invest in scientific research

Even as American firms ceded positions to Asian rivals in displays, electrical technologies, and parts of the semiconductor value chain, they continued to invest heavily in emerging fields such as artificial intelligence and quantum computing. This has allowed the United States to maintain its technological leadership, for now.

Artificial intelligence. American firms have produced major breakthroughs in AI. Google, Microsoft, and IBM are among the leading publishers of scientific papers in the five top AI conferences (AAAI, ICML, IJCAI, KDD, and NIPS), as shown in Table 4.1. Nonetheless, Chinese firms and universities are making rapid advances. Between 1990 and 2025, the top 15 U.S. institutions collectively published 22,627 conference papers, compared with 10,812 from China. Yet the gap has narrowed sharply in recent years (Figure 4.7). By volume, the Chinese Academy of Sciences now produces as many top AI conference papers as the entire University of California system. Chinese firms such as Alibaba (25th), Tencent (35th), and Huawei (44th) also appear among the top fifty institutional publishers.

Foreign catch-up has been far less pronounced in AI patenting, as shown in Figure 4.8. U.S. firms account for roughly 70% of all AI patents granted in the United States since 2010, a share that has remained stable across most AI subfields. Although Japanese firms experienced a brief surge in AI patenting in the early 1990s, U.S. firms have dominated all major categories of AI patents in the subsequent decades, at least within the U.S. patent system.

Table 4.1 Top AI Conference Author Affiliations (1990–2024)

Rank	Affiliation	Paper Count	Region	Affiliation Type
1	Chinese Academy of Sciences (CAS)	5,882	China	Government
2	University of California (UC System)	5,880	U.S.	University
3	**Alphabet**	**5,630**	**U.S.**	**Corporate**
4	**Microsoft Corporation**	**2,845**	**U.S.**	**Corporate**
5	University of Illinois System	2,478	U.S.	University
6	ETH Domain (Switzerland)	2,329	Europe	University
7	Tsinghua University	2,185	China	University
8	University of Texas (UT System)	2,167	U.S.	University
9	Carnegie Mellon University	1,915	U.S.	University
10	Massachusetts Institute of Technology (MIT)	1,712	U.S.	University
11	**IBM (International Business Machines)**	**1,651**	**U.S.**	**Corporate**
12	Peking University	1,591	China	University
13	Stanford University	1,474	U.S.	University
14	University of Washington	1,252	U.S.	University
15	Zhejiang University	1,154	China	University

Notes: The table lists the number of total conference proceedings authored by the top 15 publishing organisations in the Advancement of Artificial Intelligence Conference (AAAI), the International Conference on Machine Learning (ICML), the International Joint Conference on Artificial Intelligence (IJCAI), the Special Interest Group on Knowledge Discovery and Data (KDD), and the Conference on Neural Information Processing Systems (NIPS) since 1990 to 2024. Proceedings data is sourced from Clarivate Web of Science.

Quantum computing. Another scientific and technological field in which American corporations have made major contributions is quantum computing. As discussed in Chapter 2, American firms have pushed the frontiers in this field in tandem with academia. Table 4.2 shows that, since the 1990s, IBM and Alphabet combined have produced more high-quality publications than MIT, the leading academic institution. Similar to AI, the U.S. share in quantum patenting has held up better than its share in quantum publications (Figure 4.9). Since 2000, American assignees have received 54 per cent of all quantum computing patents (in CPC Class G06N 10/00); this share increases to 61 per cent when we restrict attention to patents granted after 2010. By contrast, the U.S. share of quantum publications has declined from roughly 30 per cent in the 1990s to about 20 per cent after 2010. Still, the United States maintains a strong position in high-impact work: its share of top publications—those in the top quintile of

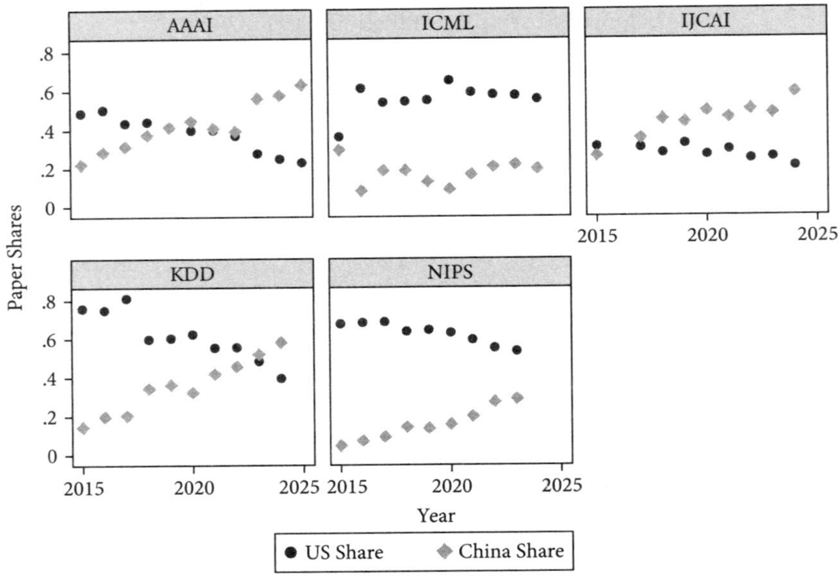

Figure 4.7 Artificial Intelligence Publications (2015–2024)

Notes: The graphs plot the share of papers by authors with a U.S. affiliation ("US Share") versus Chinese affiliation ("China Share") in prominent artificial intelligence (AI) journals listed in AAAI, ICML, IJCAI, KDD, and NIPS.[51] Publication and affiliation data are sourced from the Clarivate Web of Science.

forward citations—remains above its overall share of publications, exceeding one-third even in the 2020s.

Unlike AI, where leadership is concentrated in the United States and, secondarily, in China, quantum computing features a far more distributed landscape. The United States, Europe, and China, as well as Canada and Japan, all possess significant research strengths and have made substantial investments in quantum technologies. Table 4.2 lists the top 15 institutions publishing in quantum computing. Notably, four European universities account for 24 per cent of high-quality quantum papers. Oxford University, for instance, is home to David Deutsch, who, together with Richard Jozsa (now at Cambridge), developed one of the earliest quantum algorithms to outperform its classical counterparts.

Two Chinese institutions—the University of Science and Technology of China and Tsinghua University—also rank among the top 15. Government-backed industrial hubs, most notably Hefei's "Quantum Avenue," play a central role in advancing China's quantum sector by linking academic

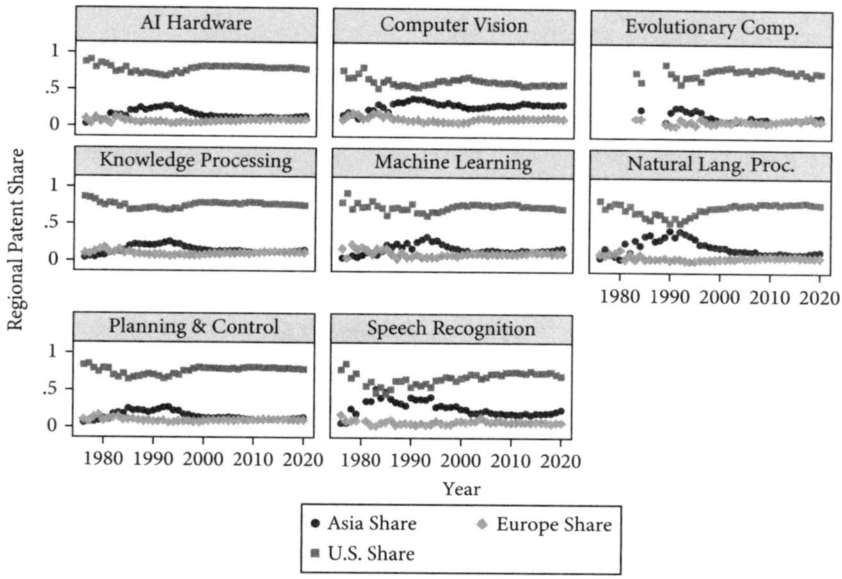

Figure 4.8 Artificial Intelligence Patents (1980–2022)

Notes: The graphs plot the share of patents by assignees with a U.S., European, and Asian affiliation, by domain within artificial intelligence. Assignee disambiguation and location data is sourced from Patentsview. AI patent data is sourced from the AI Patents Database from the USPTO Office of the Chief Economist.[52] The domains follow the USPTO's taxonomy of AI component technologies: *Machine learning* refers to computational methods that learn from data; *Computer vision* extracts information from images and video; *Speech recognition* processes audio to recover sequences of words; *Evolutionary computation* applies biologically inspired algorithms such as genetic search; *Knowledge processing* covers approaches to represent information and derive new facts from existing knowledge bases; *Natural language processing* develops methods to analyse and generate human language; *AI hardware* refers to specialised hardware designed to accelerate AI computation; and *Planning and control* covers methods that generate and execute plans to achieve specified goals.

research to industry. China holds advantages in applied quantum domains such as quantum communications and sensing. In quantum communications, China has achieved global leadership, highlighted by its successful in-orbit testing of quantum communication technologies. In quantum sensing, Chinese firms excel in market-ready applications, whereas the United States maintains an edge in earlier-stage, less mature segments. However, China remains significantly behind in quantum computing, particularly in hardware and the practical implementation of quantum systems.[53]

To sum up, both AI and quantum computing are fields in which American corporations have made pivotal contributions. The importance of their role

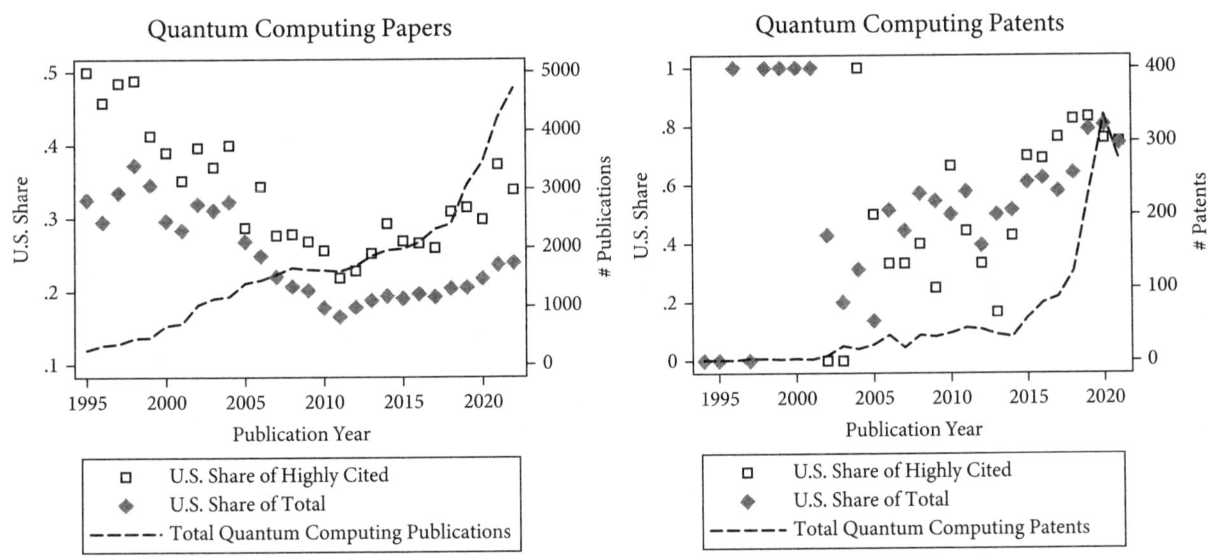

Figure 4.9 Quantum Computing Papers and Patents (1994–2021)

Notes: The graphs plot the share of USPTO patents and publications by assignees and authors with a U.S., European, and Asian affiliation. Patent assignee disambiguation and location data is sourced from Patentsview. Paper author affiliation data is sourced from OpenAlex. The dashed lines plot the number of publications (in the left plot) and patents (in the right). Publications are limited to those whose Open Alex topics include the following terms: *Quantum Computation, Quantum Computing, Quantum Entanglement, Quantum Measurement, Quantum Memory, Adiabatic Quantum Computation, Quantum information processing, Quantum Machine Learning, One-way quantum computer.* Patents are limited to those with the G06N 10/00 CPC. The grey diamond markers plot the U.S. share of all publishing (left plot) and patenting (right plot). The hollow black square markers plot the U.S. share of the top cited papers (left plot) and patents (right plot). "Top" papers and patents are those in the top quintile of 2-year forward citations for years with 50 or more papers and patents respectively.

Table 4.2 Quantum Computing Paper Author Affiliations (1994–2024)

Rank	Affiliation	Paper Count	High-Quality Paper	Region	Affiliation Type
1	Massachusetts Institute of Technology	755	215	U.S.	University
2	California Institute of Technology	566	198	U.S.	University
3	University of Oxford	631	183	Europe	University
4	University of Science and Technology of China	1017	177	China	University
5	University of Waterloo	643	165	Canada	University
6	**IBM**	**516**	**161**	**U.S.**	**Corporate**
7	Harvard University	381	155	U.S.	University
8	Los Alamos National Laboratory	474	145	U.S.	Government
9	Tsinghua University	675	139	China	University
10	Universität Innsbruck	381	136	Europe	University
11	University of California, Berkeley	374	116	U.S.	University
12	University of Geneva	269	104	Europe	University
13	**Alphabet**	**229**	**103**	**U.S.**	**Corporate**
14	National Institute of Standards and Technology	326	102	U.S.	Government
15	Imperial College London	377	97	Europe	University

Notes: The table lists the top author affiliations in quantum computing for quantum papers sourced from the OpenAlex database (full details on the topics listed are in Figure 4.9). "High- Quality Paper" refers to the number of quantum computing papers in the top quintile of two-year forward citations each year. "Paper Count" refers to all papers in quantum computing. U.S. corporate authors are bolded.

stems in part from the deeply interdisciplinary nature of these technologies, which require tight coordination between hardware engineers, software developers, and domain specialists. Large firms are uniquely equipped to operate at this intersection: the instruments, data resources, fabrication facilities, and compute infrastructure necessary to achieve meaningful advances in AI and quantum research often demand investments far beyond the reach of most startups, frequently running into the tens of millions of dollars.[54] Thus, in fields where American companies continue to invest in scientific research, the United States is better positioned to sustain and extend its leadership in science and technology. Industrial research remains an essential pillar of the national innovation ecosystem.

Chapter takeaways

The translation of scientific breakthroughs into innovations in deep-tech sectors is uneven. We argued that this unevenness can be explained by the reorganisation of the American innovation ecosystem in the past four decades. The new coalition of universities, startups, and their VC-backers reaps the benefits of specialisation in select sectors such as the life sciences. However, this new system still runs into trouble in fields that require the resolution of both commercial and technical uncertainty. The coordination between technology development and potential use cases is more easily accomplished within a single organisation that is experienced in research, translation, and commercial application.

Historically, American industrial laboratories managed this task. They assembled and maintained multidisciplinary teams of scientists that were connected to manufacturing and to market-facing divisions. The dominant market positions of many of these firms also allowed them to stomach spillovers to potential rivals, often in the form of spinoffs or employees moving to competitors. As these laboratories fade from prominence, the gaps between academic discoveries and commercial applications will be more pronounced.

The consequences of this erosion are not confined to individual firms. The withdrawal of corporate research diminishes the complementarities that once linked incumbents and startups. Deep-tech ventures depend on sophisticated partners to absorb prototypes, modify architectures, and scale new technologies. Without such partners, many face protracted valleys of death, especially in sectors like semiconductors, advanced materials, and clean energy. The decline of corporate laboratories also weakens the spillovers that once diffused widely through licensing, publications, and spinoffs. These external benefits were central to the growth of regional clusters and to the dynamism of the broader innovation system.

The uneven pattern of American leadership illustrates these dynamics. In areas where firms have continued to invest in science, such as artificial intelligence and quantum computing, the United States remains at the frontier. In contrast, in domains where corporate research has retreated, from display technologies to semiconductor manufacturing tools, leadership has shifted abroad. East Asian and European competitors have capitalised on the absence of U.S. incumbents by sustaining research programs and building the institutional capacity needed to integrate discovery and commercialisation.

5
The Rise of Science-Based Innovation

Introduction

On a September morning in 1962, John F. Kennedy asked his audience at Rice University to imagine the whole of human history compressed into fifty years. In that accelerated timeline, writing and wheeled carts would have appeared only five years ago, the steam engine scarcely two months ago—and humankind would be "reaching for the stars before midnight tonight." Kennedy's thought experiment crystallises the main question of this chapter: how did the once-glacial pace of progress quicken into the burst that defines modern economic growth?[1]

This chapter argues that the decisive turn came from a belated but transformative fusion of two knowledge realms that had long evolved on separate tracks: science, the systematic study of nature, and technology, the application of knowledge to practical ends. For millennia, these realms advanced largely in parallel. Roman concrete, medieval shipbuilding, and Gutenberg's press all flourished through ingenuity and empirical tinkering, while Scholastic thinkers pursued natural philosophy largely through abstract reasoning, with little connection to workshops or markets. Even the early Industrial Revolution fit this pattern: Newcomen's and Watt's steam engines predated a formal theory of thermodynamics by decades.

Beginning in the seventeenth century and decisively by the nineteenth, an empiricist scientific method dismantled this compartmentalisation. Observations from telescopes, barometers, and factory floors fed emerging theories; theoretical breakthroughs in turn looped back to improve practice. By the time Irving Langmuir solved the "bulb-blackening" problem at General Electric, corporate laboratories staffed with chemists and physicists had replaced the lone trial-and-error inventor, creating a self-reinforcing feedback loop between propositional (scientific) and prescriptive (technical) knowledge.[2]

The convergence of workshop practice and formal science was long in coming. It began with craft-based trial and error before giving rise to systematic inquiry. Removing the informational and organisational barriers that once separated "knowing why" from "knowing how" enlarged the stock of economically useful knowledge and raised the rate at which science could be applied to the problem of economic production.

Modern economic growth: Integrating science and technology

The application of scientific knowledge to technological problems has been the hallmark of modern economic growth. Science, for this book, refers to generalised knowledge about the mechanisms of nature. Laws of motion (Newton), thermodynamics (Carnot, Kelvin, Nernst), fluid dynamics (Bernoulli), and electromagnetism (Maxwell) demonstrate how science strives to simplify the complex and "to make the wonderful comprehensible," in Herbert Simon's words.[3] Technology, in contrast, concerns itself with the workings of artifacts (i.e., human-made objects).[4] Our discussion below is based on the prior scholarship of Nathan Rosenberg, Walter Vincenti, and Paul David, as well as Joel Mokyr, who argues that the Scientific Revolution and the diffusion of abstract knowledge about nature expanded the "epistemic" base of inventions, which in turn produced more empirical facts to enrich scientific understanding itself.[5]

Most, if not all, areas of technology have relied on an understanding of nature; the cultivation of corn and the breeding of domesticated animals were based on folk wisdom later formalised in Mendelian genetics. Building canals and cathedrals required basic knowledge of hydrology and geometry, passed through skilled artisans. Maritime navigation relied on known positions of celestial bodies and was later aided by the invention of the compass. However, the fusion of the scientific and technological realms only happened implicitly, as doctrines of Scholastic philosophy kept the two separate. The rise of Baconian empiricism helped demolish some of these barriers, and a century later, the application of science to inventions emerged in the Industrial Age. By the eve of the second Industrial Revolution in the mid-to-late nineteenth century, inventions in the chemical (synthetic dyes) and electrical (telegraph and dynamos) industries became impossible to produce without a deeper understanding of the natural laws underpinning them. The Haber–Bosch process for producing fertiliser, which enabled the capture of nitrogen from the air and in doing so broke the age-old

Malthusian curse of chronic food scarcity, was a wholly synthetic innovation that could never have emerged from trial-and-error empiricism alone. It required knowing that nitrogen is a distinct element, that it is abundant in the atmosphere, and that while crops need nitrogen to grow, they cannot absorb it directly from the air and must obtain it from nitrogen-rich fertiliser.

We distinguish between pre-industrial, trial-and-error innovations and science-based innovations. Brewing beer is an example of the pre-industrial, which relied on "brute empiricism" during its invention and refinement; pasteurisation is an invention in the same domain that relies on an abstract understanding of the underlying mechanisms of brewing (i.e., germ theory).

Given how influential science-based inventions are, it is puzzling why science and technology were not combined before the Industrial Revolution. The next section finds the reasons in a doctrinal "firewall" set up by the Scholastic approach to science during the Middle Ages, which was in turn deeply influenced by the Aristotelian separation between the abstract (celestial) and natural (sublunar) worlds. The subsequent section studies how these barriers were brought down by the empiricist project pioneered by Francis Bacon, among others, during the Scientific Revolution. The empiricist project culminated in the creation of state-sponsored organisations such as the Royal Society. These institutions championed the use of empirical observation to guide the pursuit of knowledge. The fusion of the study of nature with the study of artifacts became the foundation on which the Second Industrial Revolution built upon the first.

What is science-based invention?

The distinction between science-based invention and trial-and-error invention can be illustrated by historical examples. In 1763, James Watt was working as an instrument maker at the University of Glasgow when he was asked to repair Newcomen engines. Through his investigations, he was intrigued by how inefficient early steam engines were. Through conversations with Joseph Black, who had introduced the concept of "latent heat," Watt reenvisioned steam condensation, eventually inventing a steam engine with a separate condenser that significantly improved efficiency. Yet when Watt first developed his engine, no comprehensive theory of thermodynamics existed.

The detailed scientific explanations of how steam engines function at varying temperatures and pressures emerged later thanks to theorists such as Sadi Carnot, transforming Watt's partly theory-inspired invention into a fully science-based innovation.[6]

The contrast between Watt's initial design and the refined physics that subsequently supported it highlights two categories of inventions: those based on largely empirical observations alone (what we will term black-box inventions) and those rooted in a generalised understanding of the mechanisms of nature (science). Black-box inventions rely on trial-and-error methods, guesswork, and pattern recognition, without a deeper understanding explaining their success.

But why does this deeper understanding matter? Humans progressed from stone tools to bronze, iron, and steel through trial and error. Some of the most important inventions for economic growth, such as the Gutenberg press, rely on hardly any science at all. In this chapter, we contrast the cases of vulcanised rubber and the incandescent lightbulb to illustrate the benefits of relying more deeply on scientific understanding—that is, identifying the underlying mechanisms that explain *why* an invention works, rather than simply demonstrating that it works.

Mechanism-agnostic invention: The story of vulcanisation

The invention of vulcanised rubber by Charles Goodyear in 1839 serves as an example of an innovation achieved without a theoretical understanding of the mechanisms behind it. Goodyear's breakthrough transformed an unruly natural substance into one of the most essential industrial materials of the modern era, demonstrating how inventions can arise purely from observation and experimentation, without a deeper explanation of why they work.

In the early nineteenth century, natural rubber attracted interest for its elasticity and water resistance, but it proved to be unstable. It melted in heat, cracked in cold, and offered limited utility beyond narrow applications. Lacking formal scientific training, Goodyear addressed rubber's shortcomings through trial and error. He mixed different substances into rubber, particularly sulphur, and varied the heat conditions, observing the results closely. His aim was to correct rubber's defects, not to uncover its molecular properties.

Goodyear's breakthrough occurred by accident. One day, a piece of rubber mingled with sulphur fell onto a hot stove and, instead of melting, took on a tougher, yet still elastic, form. Fascinated, Goodyear painstakingly experimented with sulphur and heat ratios until he perfected a repeatable process he called vulcanisation. He could not explain why sulphur and heat stabilised rubber. He only knew that it worked. Goodyear had no theoretical understanding of vulcanisation, so his process was inconsistent. He knew that heating rubber with sulphur produced a tougher material, but he could not explain the reaction or control it reliably. This absence of mechanistic understanding limited early attempts to optimise the process. It was not until scientists later unravelled the chemical foundations of polymer bonding that manufacturers could refine quality control and scale up production.

Goodyear's experience captures both the promise and the hazards of mechanism-agnostic invention. By relentless observation and experimentation, he solved an important practical problem. Still, the enduring impact and widespread optimisation of his breakthrough would ultimately hinge on the theoretical insights that followed.

Mechanism-informed invention: Solving the "bulb-blackening" problem

The early twentieth century saw a shift in industrial innovation, as companies like General Electric (GE) recognised that increasingly complex technologies required more than trial-and-error solutions. Nowhere was this clearer than in the problem of "bulb blackening," a persistent issue in incandescent lamps. Thomas Edison's earlier success with carbon filaments had relied on brute-force experimentation. Finding a material that glowed for a long time required little scientific theory. But as lighting technology advanced, so did the challenges. The blackening of lightbulbs, caused by tungsten evaporating from filaments and depositing inside the bulb, could not be solved by tinkering. Instead, it required both an explanation of why the technology was reaching its limits and a systematic way to control the processes at play.

Irving Langmuir, a research chemist at GE Research Labs, took on this problem, guided by newly emerging scientific theories. One key concept was Owen Richardson's theory of thermionic emissions, which allowed Langmuir to hypothesise that heated filaments emit charged particles that are adsorbed on the inner surfaces of bulbs. Langmuir's theory then led to his solution of introducing an inert gas such as argon or nitrogen into the bulb to scatter the evaporating tungsten particles. This solution went against the prevailing, "intuitive" solution at the time, which surmised that blackening was caused by impurities within the bulb. This approach had pointed to the opposite (unsuccessful) prescription to create a more perfect vacuum within the lightbulb. Langmuir's approach, on the other hand, built on the emerging fields of surface chemistry and high-temperature physics. In his experiments, Langmuir adjusted the pressure of the gas within the bulb and was able to reduce blackening dramatically. The filament's operating temperature could also be increased, boosting luminosity and offering a more efficient lamp.

As we detail in Chapter 8, Langmuir's solution yielded commercial benefits for GE and marked a broader shift in how American corporations approached technological problems. The days of "Eureka" moments from lone inventors were giving way to laboratories staffed with scientists who combined theoretical knowledge with carefully designed experiments. Whereas Edison's methods had been sufficient to discover a workable filament, Langmuir's deeper understanding of molecular interactions from thermionic processes enabled him to optimise filament behaviour, overcome blackening, and even pave the way for additional innovations in lighting. The significance of Langmuir's work was underscored by his 1932 Nobel Prize in Chemistry, which recognised his contributions to surface chemistry and atomic-scale processes. More than a single-product improvement, his triumph set a model for corporate research: deploy scientific theory to explain the mechanisms behind technological challenges, then harness those explanations to improve and extend performance.

Three links between science and invention

The examples above set the stage for understanding how science-based invention created opportunities for economic growth that neither science alone nor trial-and-error invention could achieve on their own. Below, we theorise on three mechanisms.

First, science by its very nature is generalisable. A general understanding of the process of polymerisation in the 1930s enabled not only the invention of synthetic rubber but also the proliferation of entirely synthetic substitutes of natural substances such as silk (nylon). Scientific knowledge reduces the costs of applying an insight from one application to other areas of application. CRISPR Cas-9, for instance, was discovered by Danone to extend strain life for yogurt production. It has since been used in gene therapy to cure congenital diseases in humans. Thanks to their generality, scientific inventions can more easily apply to contexts beyond their own, while those based on trial and error cannot. At the same time, it is important to underscore that science would not advance far without the accumulation of empirical observations. Thermionic emissions, theorised by J. J. Thomson and Owen Richardson, was itself based on a serendipitous discovery by Thomas Edison who had observed electric current flowing through the vacuum of his lightbulb. (Edison even termed the effect after himself and took out a patent for an "Electrical Indicator" based on it in 1883 (US 307031).) The development of chemistry owed as much to the theoretical work of Boyle, Dalton, and Lavoisier as to the empirical patterns uncovered through the combinatorial experiments of earlier alchemists.

Second, scientific claims are precise. This matters because "the stronger the underlying scientific theory, the less the degree of empiricism" (trial and error) is required.[7] The failed trials in the trial- and-error method may be avoided when science codifies the underlying reason behind the failure. Once we learn through the stoichiometric works of Gay-Lussac (1808) and Avogadro (1811) that the molecular ratio of hydrogen atoms to oxygen-forming water molecules is 2:1, we remove a critical part of guesswork when designing a rocket engine that combusts liquid hydrogen and oxygen together.[8] Einstein's special (1905) and general (1915) theories of relativity similarly help with time dilation corrections in Global Positioning System (GPS) satellites. Einstein's key prediction was that time does not pass at the same rate for everyone: it moves more slowly for objects travelling at high velocities (special relativity) and for objects in stronger gravitational fields (general relativity). GPS satellites orbit Earth at speeds of approximately 14,000 km/h (about 3.9 km/s) and at altitudes of around 20,200 km (mid-Earth orbit).[9] Due to their velocity and their distance from Earth's gravitational field, the onboard atomic clocks on these satellites experience time differently than clocks on the ground. Special relativity predicts they tick more slowly due to their speed, while general relativity predicts they tick faster because they are farther from Earth's gravitational pull. The net effect is a time discrepancy of roughly 38 microseconds per day. Left uncorrected, the cumulative error would result in a GPS inaccuracy of up to 10 kilometres per day. The point is that these errors are not adjusted after the fact through trial and error (which would risk mid-air collisions, shipping disasters, and other navigation failures). They are corrected in advance through equations such as the Schwarzschild metric formulated over a century ago. These relativistic corrections to GPS systems are a testament to how the precise nature of science can eliminate waste.[10]

Third, scientific claims are falsifiable, thereby opening science to constant improvement and refinement. A hallmark of prescientific belief systems is their infallibility against empirical observations. Delphi's oracles were notoriously (and perhaps strategically) equivocal in this manner. The practice of rain-making rituals found across ancient cultures is a similar case: the implicit hypothesis offered by the shamans is merely that it will rain at some point after the ritual, rendering the claim empirically irrefutable.

Scientific claims, by contrast, expose themselves to the possibility of being proven wrong. One of Antoine Lavoisier's greatest achievements was to refute the phlogiston theory of combustion, which hypothesised that materials burn by releasing fire-like substances called phlogistons. A prediction from the theory was that materials should then become lighter after combustion. Lavoisier's careful measurements after burning sulfur and phosphorus showed this to be untrue. Instead, he found that a substance in the air (which would later be identified as oxygen) was consistently involved in combustion. Science advances precisely because its claims can be falsified.

The path to "industrial enlightenment"

Despite its payoffs, the fusion of science and technology occurred relatively late. This subsection traces the intellectual history of natural philosophy and inventions preceding the Scientific Revolution.

The separation of science and technology

According to Joel Mokyr, propositional knowledge is factual understanding of how nature works (for example, that water boils at 100°C), while prescriptive knowledge is the set of rules, recipes, and techniques for making or doing things (for example, instructions for distilling clean water). Throughout most of human history, these two forms of knowledge met only sporadically. Insights about nature rarely translated directly into practical routines, and when they did, the linkage was usually accidental rather than systematic. Both grew nonetheless, but largely independently.

The great industries of premodern times, such as agriculture, shipbuilding, metallurgy, and textiles, advanced more through the experience of skilled labourers than through systematic scientific exploration. Pre-industrial agriculture, for example, progressed through incremental changes in crop rotation and the use of animal-drawn ploughs, developments that were largely empirical in origin. The mostly atheoretical approach to inventions characterised many Roman technical achievements, including their development of concrete. This versatile material underpinned structures like the Pantheon and aqueducts; yet it owed its success to experimental builders and engineers, not learned philosophers and scientists. Likewise, in seafaring, improvements in hull design, sails, and navigation routines emerged from iterative knowledge rather than formal research centres. The invention of the compass and gunpowder, while momentous for the history of navigation and human conflict, was not inspired by systematic investigations into magnetism or combustion.

Exceptions to this rule, while remarkable, were rare. Scientific projects of this era could not keep their flame alive through history, unlike the critical mass of seventeenth-century thinkers who ignited and sustained the Scientific Revolution. One such polymath was Archimedes of Syracuse (ca. 287–212 BC), widely regarded as one of antiquity's greatest mathematicians and scientists, who also devised practical devices like the Archimedean screw. The Antikythera mechanism, an advanced Greek analogue computer for astronomical predictions, showcased the theoretical sophistication some classical thinkers possessed. Yet it remained an isolated marvel, unscaled to broader technological domains. Despite its intricate system of gears modelling celestial movements, neither its knowledge nor its methods saw widespread application. Where science and technology did gain traction, it was often for military use. Archimedes created formidable war machines (including the "Claw of Archimedes") that stymied Roman forces during the siege of Syracuse. Other engineers, such as Ctesibius in Alexandria, fashioned advanced pumps and artillery devices. Such feats underscore the potential synergy between science and real-world applications. However, this synergy was typically contained within military contexts.

Occasionally, rulers supported centres of learning where scientists and engineers could collaborate, even in the absence of immediate military aims. The Museum of Alexandria, closely tied to its famed library, was arguably the leading research institute for science and technology in the Greco-Roman world. Founded in the early third century BC by Ptolemy I Soter (and expanded by Ptolemy II Philadelphus), it produced celebrated scholars like Euclid, Archimedes, Ctesibius, and Hero. They forged a unique mix of basic science (geometry, astronomy) and engineering (pumps, water clocks, early steam-powered devices). Even so, no ruler ever systematically leveraged these inventors to boost agriculture or general industry. Technology in the ancient and classical periods advanced through incremental improvements shaped by the trial and error of craftsmen. Public sector investments went mainly into infrastructure, impressive in scale but rarely guided by formal scientific thought.

The private sector, meanwhile, tended to rely on craft traditions rather than scientific knowledge. Craft knowledge is more likely to be tacit, requiring years of painstaking apprenticeship to diffuse. Norms within private producers' associations such as guilds were also secretive in stark contrast to academia. Galasso, Comino, and Graziano studied the adoption of patenting by inventors after the Venetian Republic's introduction of a patent statute in 1474 and found that guilds that barred outsiders and capped prices rarely filed patents.[11] Patenting was instead concentrated in guilds located far from Venice or operating in cities with weak elite connections, where inventors could not rely on informal privilege and thus substituted formal patent protection. Restrictive guilds hoarded craft secrets and slowed the outward flow of technical information, limiting opportunities for theory to inform practice. More open or politically peripheral guilds used patents to codify and publicise invention, lowering the boundary between workshop know-how and abstract knowledge. Even under the world's first comprehensive patent law, it was the micro rules of local organisations that determined whether the new institution could accelerate the integration of science and technology.

The separation of science and technology (and of scientists and inventors) in the West was a by-product of the Aristotelian view of natural philosophy inherited by the Scholastic tradition of the medieval period. Aristotle's definition of the physical sciences (or "natural philosophy" as it was known) dealt with the activity of "natural bodies" such as the fall of an apple toward the centre of the Earth (which was considered the centre of the universe). Inventions such as the pulley or lever fell under the study of the artificial, which pursued goals contrary to nature's teleological purpose (i.e., lifting an object went against its natural purpose to fall). This is not to deny that Aristotle was an empirical thinker. He was celebrated for his studies of zoology, basing his political philosophy on the observation that the human species' telos (purpose) was social (*zoon politikon*). However, his scientific taxonomies were informed more by his metaphysics than by experiences gathered from the physical world.[12]

For example, the Aristotelian framework imposed compartmentalisation between disciplines, arguing for distinct laws governing each realm: the study of earthly phenomena (what he called the "sublunar world") was to be defined by the mixture of the four primary elements: Earth, water, air, and fire, while the study of celestial bodies beyond Earth involved a fifth element—the "quintessence." The celestial physics that Kepler inherited from the Greeks argued that celestial bodies should move differently from the rectilinear paths natural bodies on Earth would take: while a falling apple would fall straight, the planets would have to move in perfect circles. This pattern is more broadly attributable to the Greek way of thought, which posited that inquiries into nature (physics), knowledge itself (epistemology), and fundamental existence (metaphysics) formed a continuous intellectual endeavour. This imposition of metaphysical assumptions on physical phenomena continued largely unchecked into the Middle Ages.

Though a pagan thinker, Aristotle had a profound hold on the medieval scientific paradigm. Daniel Garber quotes the Jesuit *Ratio studiorum* (Plan of Studies) of 1586, which instructs that at least in the classroom "in logic, natural philosophy, morals and metaphysics, the doctrine of Aristotle is to be followed."[13] The Latin term *scientia* referred to any rigorous body of knowledge syllogistically derived from self-evident premises. Theology, in this sense, could be elevated to the "queen of sciences" by Thomas Aquinas as its premises were considered the most certain of all. Other studies on physical motion, cosmology, meteorology, and natural history would be included in this category. On the other hand, medicine, alchemy, architecture, navigation, and engineering fell outside *scientia*, as it was believed that they could not be derived from universal principles. In this sense, the Scholastic view of science was closer to mathematics than to modern physics.

The fusion of science and technology

This strict compartmentalisation of science and technology began to crack as successive waves of "anti-Aristotelian" attacks by scientists marshalled empirical contradictions against the orthodoxy. Johannes Kepler led the way by revising his theories of orbital paths based on empirical observations of planetary paths. In his *Mysterium Cosmographicum* (1596), Kepler had posed that planetary distances could be derived from nesting the five Platonic regular solids within one another.[14] However, closer examination of the data showed that orbits were in fact elliptical.

Aristotle's "plenist" position that denied the existence of a vacuum was refuted in a similar fashion by Evangelista Torricelli (a student of Galileo), who in 1643 devised a glass tube filled with mercury to show the existence of unfilled space. The emergence of the mechanical and corpuscular philosophy of Robert Boyle and René Descartes around the same time reopened the elemental debates that pervaded Greek thought. Contrary to Democritus's atomic view of matter, Aristotle himself believed that all matter could be reduced to four elements: earth, water, air, and fire, which combined to manifest hot, cold, wet, and dry qualities. By contrast, the mechanical view, first formalised by Descartes's *Principia Philosophiae*, stated that a single matter and a single set of laws governed the material world. Gottfried Wilhelm Leibniz shared this outlook, positing the monad as the single building block of reality, and Isaac Newton echoed it by distilling classical mechanics into three laws of motion. Crucially, the doctrinal barriers between the study of celestial bodies and earthly natural bodies would soon be demolished under the mechanical program, as better modes of observation (such as advanced telescopes) added confidence to the belief that the same laws governed both the celestial and terrestrial realms.

The key quality of the Scientific Revolution that sets it apart from other forms of resistance against the Scholastic view of the universe (such as the sixteenth-century Reformation and the Confessional conflicts that followed it) was the mode in which they carried out their resistance. One pillar of this resistance was René Descartes's embrace of methodological doubt, which holds that all suppositions are false until proven otherwise by experimentation and observation.

The other pillar was empiricism, which Francis Bacon promulgated in his 1620 *Novum Organum*,[15] which presented a manifesto advocating for a radically new approach to science. Bacon criticised Scholastic thinkers for their excessive reliance on deductive reasoning, a method effective in mathematics but sterile when applied to the study of nature. Drawing inspiration from the works of Kepler, Copernicus, and Galileo, Bacon argued that the ancient Greek assumption of a perfect cosmos deducible from axioms was fundamentally flawed. Instead, Bacon insisted that nature must be observed and understood without preconceptions. The frontispiece of Francis Bacon's *Novum Organum* (1620) captures the spirit of the Renaissance: a ship sailing boldly beyond the classical Pillars of Hercules symbolises humanity's newfound courage to explore intellectual realms beyond the authority of ancient traditions. During the fifteenth and sixteenth centuries, European curiosity about nature underwent a profound revival. Established classical authorities increasingly faced scrutiny as explorers, artists, and engineers uncovered new perspectives and previously unknown continents.

Bacon's vision redefined science as an inductive enterprise informed by empirical observations. He urged scientists to collect extensive data through experiments and careful observation, subsequently generalising cautiously. This "bottom-up" method contrasted sharply with adherence to axioms—fundamental assumptions or self-evident truths posited by Aristotle. Bacon analogised scientists to bees: diligently gathering nectar (empirical facts) and transforming it into honey (general truths). Like the method of Cartesian doubt, Bacon's approach applied the same disciplined skepticism to the "idols of the mind," the biases and misconceptions that distort judgment, and it relied on rigorous experimentation. Remarkably, Bacon even anticipated modern hypothesis testing by recommending targeted experiments to decisively adjudicate between competing theories, which he labelled the "Instance of the Fingerpost."

The empirical turn reshaped invention itself. Bacon argued that, before long, knowledge would begin to move in the opposite direction as well: inventors would draw on abstract scientific principles to create new artifacts, turning theoretical insights into practical designs. Bacon contrasted these from "timeless" inventions that did not owe their provenance to deductive applications of knowledge, such as gunpowder, silk, the magnet, sugar, and paper.[16] He further wrote that nature still contained "many secrets of excellent use, having no affinity or parallelisms with anything that is now known, but lying entirely out of the beat of the imagination, which have not been found out."[17] To aid with this endeavour, in his *New Atlantis* Bacon proposed establishing a "House of Solomon" which would act as a state-sponsored research laboratory, systematically producing new knowledge and technology.[18] Rather than relying on accidental brilliance, his method of invention would be deliberate and cumulative.

By the seventeenth century, Europe had a new type of institution that would fit this description: the scientific academy. Italy's Accademia dei Lincei (1603), the Royal Society of London (1660), and the Académie des Sciences in Paris (1666) were created to advance open inquiry into nature and to connect theoretical insight with practical application. Unlike guilds or universities, these academies emphasised experiment, empirical evidence, and useful knowledge. The Royal Society gathered practitioners, scholars, clergy, and courtiers who embraced experimental philosophy and built an international network for practical and philosophical investigation of the physical world. This broad membership let artisans, instrument makers, physicians, and gentlemen scholars exchange ideas in a common forum.

The academies' working norms strongly promoted the fusion of propositional and prescriptive knowledge. Members met weekly to demonstrate experiments and debate results. The Royal Society adopted the Latin motto *Nullius in verba* ("take no one's word for it"), signalling a commitment to first-hand evidence over received authority. At Gresham College, its fellows investigated mechanics, magnetism, air pressure, gunnery, anatomy, and astronomy, directly linking scientific theory such as Newtonian mechanics or Boyle's law to improvements in pumps, artillery tables, and surgical methods. The academies also formalised publication and correspondence; journals like the *Philosophical Transactions* launched in 1665 ensured systematic recording and wide dissemination of new discoveries. This culture of transparency and circulation of knowledge stood in sharp contrast to the secrecy typical of many guilds.

Importantly, the academies enjoyed state patronage without direct state control. The French Académie received crown funding, and the Royal Society held royal charters. Yet both bodies governed their own affairs, setting agendas guided by curiosity and practical value rather than by theology. This semi-autonomy gave scientists a shared identity and an incentive to pursue knowledge useful to the public and to national prestige. Early members such as Robert Boyle, Christiaan Huygens, and Gottfried Leibniz exchanged ideas across borders, combining mathematical theory with engineering practice. The result was a faster feedback loop between understanding why and knowing how. Academy projects converted scientific insight into improvements in navigation, astronomy, clockmaking and agriculture.

Thus the scientific academies of the seventeenth and eighteenth centuries stand out as clear institutional catalysts of knowledge fusion. They fostered a culture that prized both explanation of natural phenomena and practical application of that understanding. Although they were elitist and were largely confined to Western Europe, they paved the way for the modern research university by demonstrating the power of organised, collaborative science.

Of course, the First Industrial Revolution did not unfold in strict accordance with Bacon's predictions. Much like early breakthroughs in fire, metalworking, and agriculture, which owed their success to serendipity, Thomas Newcomen's steam engines preceded the formal development of thermodynamics. Peter Mathias notes that even the great inventions of the English Industrial Revolution were, by and large, "not the result of the formal application of applied science [. . . but] the products of inspired amateurs, or brilliant artisans trained as clock-makers, wheelwrights, blacksmiths or in the Birmingham trades. William Murdock, Boulton's greatest mechanic, was more representative than James Watt."[19] These amateurs, artisans, and tradespeople "were mainly local men, empirically trained, with local horizons, often very interested in things scientific, aware men, responding directly to a particular problem. [...] Richard Arkwright had been a barber."[20] Indeed, Joel Mokyr highlights the role of trained mechanics and engineers in the technological advancements of the Industrial Revolution. William Hanlon argues that the success of this period relied heavily on the ingenuity of a few individuals but also significantly depended on a broader base of skilled artisans and mechanics who could implement, adapt, and refine new technologies.[21] These mechanics possessed a combination of practical skills and technical knowledge, enabling them to understand, operate, and improve upon new machinery. For example, the development and refinement of the steam engine by James Watt required the skills of mechanics who could construct, adjust, and maintain the engine's complex components.

According to Joel Mokyr, the collaboration between inventors, often from scientific or engineering backgrounds, and skilled mechanics was essential for the successful development and diffusion of new technologies.[22] These mechanics played a crucial role in the iterative process of innovation, where initial designs were continually improved through practical experience and problem-solving on the shop floor. For instance, Richard Arkwright's spinning frame, which revolutionised textile manufacturing, was refined and perfected through the contributions of skilled mechanics who worked alongside Arkwright to address operational challenges and enhance the machine's efficiency. Mokyr also notes that the rise of a class of trained mechanics was facilitated by the institutional and educational developments of the time.[23] Apprenticeship systems provided young workers with the opportunity to learn from experienced craftsmen, gaining valuable hands-on experience. Technical schools began to emerge, offering formal training in various trades and technical subjects. The establishment of professional societies, such as the Institution of Mechanical Engineers in the United Kingdom, helped disseminate technical knowledge and skills, fostering a more capable and adaptable workforce.

This is not to claim that inventions were entirely a-scientific: though the era's scientific knowledge was incomplete, it was not irrelevant. Steam power owed a conceptual debt to Evangelista Torricelli and Otto Von Guericke's studies of atmospheric pressure, and craftsmen like James Watt or Richard Trevithick owe an intellectual debt to past investigations into vacuum. As Mokyr notes, an indirect culture of rational, systematic experimentation contributed to the Industrial Revolution's success. Entrepreneurs like Josiah Wedgwood, renowned for revolutionising the pottery industry, embodied this bridging role. Even if they lacked fully formed scientific theories, they embraced "experiment books" and meticulous observation, drawing sporadically on chemical understandings and exchanging ideas with known scientists such as Joseph Priestley.

Moreover, thanks to the establishment of empiricism in scientific inquiry, the data produced from these experiments was not lost on scientists who waited with a "prepared mind." In Bacon's terms, the Industrial Revolution enabled experimental conditions that would normally not be attainable, allowing scientists to "twist the lion's tail"—that is, force nature to yield secrets that were not perceivable under usual circumstances. The best example probably comes from Sadi Carnot, who is often credited with founding thermodynamics. Carnot's greatest scientific contributions occurred while efforts were being made to improve the efficiency of steam engines. In the early nineteenth century, steam engines were vital to industrial progress, but their efficiency was limited. Motivated by the practical goal of maximising engine efficiency, Carnot formulated his eponymous cycle. This theoretical construct defines the maximum possible efficiency for a heat engine operating between two temperature reservoirs, and it laid the groundwork for the field of thermodynamics. Carnot's insights also contributed to development of the second law of thermodynamics, which states that entropy in an isolated system always increases. His work provided a fundamental understanding of energy conversion processes, establishing that no heat engine can be 100 per cent efficient. By addressing a practical engineering problem, Carnot's research advanced scientific knowledge and also had a lasting impact on theoretical and applied physics.

In similar fashion, the development of spectroscopy was indebted to Joseph von Fraunhofer, who started his career as an industrialist in the glassmaking business and applied his expertise to replacing Newton's prism with a diffraction grating to create wavelength dispersion (1814).[24] Pasteur's foundational works in microbiology took place under a commission from the French wine industry, which faced a mounting problem of spoilage that occurred with mass production and long-distance transportation for an increasingly urbanising French consumer base. Mass production also created by-products that could be studied by chemists. The coal tar industry's new waste materials provided chemists, such as William Perkin, with ample raw materials to try to synthesise new substances, including quinine. Of course, a happy accident allowed him to create mauveine dye (1856), which would in turn spawn the synthetic dye industry.

Indeed, Peter Mathias remarks that by the mid-nineteenth century, "increasingly the stimulus behind innovation [became ...] largely a matter of applied science in one industry after another."[25] Burgeoning scientific disciplines began to intersect more directly with technological development. The establishment of formal research institutions and the professionalisation of science created new avenues for the application of scientific principles to practical ends (the subject of the next chapter). The result was a second Scientific Revolution, when new instruments (the telescope, the microscope, the vacuum pump, the barometer, the thermometer, and others) opened up hitherto neglected fields, like meteorology, and eventually created entirely new ones like thermodynamics and organic chemistry.

Chapter takeaways

This chapter examined the evolving relationship between science and technology. For much of history, the two domains advanced separately. Inventors and artisans relied on hands-on experimentation and feedback from markets, while natural philosophers sought knowledge of the world with little interest in application. When connections between them did occur, they were incidental rather than systematic, and as a result the pace of transformative breakthroughs was limited.

The Scientific Revolution and the rise of empiricism broke down these barriers. Observation and experiment became central to inquiry, enabling theories to be anchored in evidence. This shift not only displaced outdated Aristotelian doctrines but also created the scientific method itself, a structured process that allowed craft knowledge and theoretical reasoning to inform each other.

The First Industrial Revolution remained largely the product of artisanal ingenuity, but it generated streams of data and new puzzles that invited scientific explanation. Steam engines, coal mines, steel furnaces, and large-scale wineries provided the raw observations that scientists began to incorporate into emerging theories. In the nineteenth century the relationship deepened. Scientific discoveries informed industrial practice, while industrial challenges created new fields of scientific inquiry.

This feedback loop marked a decisive turning point. Science and technology ceased to be parallel traditions and instead became mutually reinforcing. Scientific advances expanded the scope of technological possibilities, and technological problems opened new domains of scientific research. The United States, which industrialised rapidly during this period, absorbed this model and began to institutionalise it. The convergence of science and technology became the foundation for the country's later leadership in innovation.

The central takeaway is that modern economic growth rests on this integration. Once science and technology became linked, innovation was no longer episodic but cumulative and self-sustaining. The next chapters examine how the organisation of innovation in Europe and the United States evolved to direct and harness this fusion, and how institutions were built to coordinate discovery and application at scale.

6

Smithian and Schumpeterian Models of Translation

Commercialising Inventions in the First and Second Industrial Revolutions

Introduction

The First Industrial Revolution, which lasted roughly from around the 1760s to the 1830s, brought about the mechanisation of the textile industry, the adoption of steam power for locomotion and manufacturing, and cheaper iron production. As momentous a change as this was, its impact on economic productivity was uneven, mostly concentrated in the cotton and textile industries.[1] Gregory Clark summarises prior work on British data and shows that the productivity growth from the First Industrial Revolution was modest: from 0.2 per cent per year between 1600 and 1760 to 0.33 per cent per year during the period from 1760 to 1869.[2] The "modern" annual growth rates of 2–3 percent in Western Europe became possible only after the Second Industrial Revolution, which started in the middle of the nineteenth century.

The defining difference between the First and Second Industrial Revolutions is that the latter was powered by the deliberate, systematic application of scientific knowledge to industry. By contrast, the advances of the First Industrial Revolution sprang from inspired tinkering and trial-and-error, not from formal science. Although James Watt did make some use of James Black's theory of latent heat, the inventions of the First Industrial Revolution were mostly a testament to design ingenuity rather than applications of scientific discovery.[3] The Spinning Jenny and the Cotton Gin both delivered efficiency gains, but they did not rely on generalisable scientific principles as inventions in the electrical or chemical industries during the Second Industrial Revolution did.

How were innovation ecosystems in Europe and the United States organised to commercialise inventions in each epoch? We use the framework established in Chapter 2 that contrasts Smithian paths of innovation to Schumpeterian ones. In the former, the locus of invention is different from the locus of commercialisation, and new ideas are traded through Markets for Technology (MFT). In the latter, the inventor carries the idea through the full process.

We argue that the innovations of the First Industrial Revolution used both Smithian and Schumpeterian routes. The choice depended on the maturity of the downstream market for which innovations were being traded at the time. This is consistent with our discussion in Chapter 2 that DOIL is a natural outgrowth of a mature innovation ecosystem. Although the era yielded seemingly radical breakthroughs, most innovations still sprang from familiar markets. Watt's steam engine, for instance, began as an improved Newcomen pump for draining mines; only later did Watt add the rotary mechanism that displaced waterwheels and horsepower in factories, breweries, and blast furnaces. Likewise, the steam engine, cotton gin, sewing machine, and equipment for signalling and maintaining railways and steamboats all flourished in markets thick with both suppliers (inventors) and buyers (licencees) of new designs. Smithian specialisation coexisted with extensive markets for technology.

With the Second Industrial Revolution, inventions became more science-based. The application of new science gave rise to inventions that required complementary inventions and market validation. Innovators were forced to adopt the Schumpeterian path. The earliest inventions of the Second Industrial Revolution came from self-taught, independent inventors such as Henry Bessemer (steelmaking), Ernest Solvay (alkali chemicals), Alfred Nobel (explosives), the Siemens brothers (steelmaking and electricity), Ezra Cornell (telegraph), Thomas Edison (lightbulbs and dynamos), Alexander Graham Bell (telephone), and Charles Martin Hall (aluminium). Some tried the Smithian route, knocking on the doors of incumbent firms that would license their ideas. Met with a lack of willing buyers, they gathered venture financing to build the factories and sales organisations required to manufacture and sell their own products: the companies of these inventor entrepreneurs eventually engaged in cross-geographic licencing to diffuse their technology, but the introduction of the first product occurred unmistakably through their own firms.

The age of the inventor–entrepreneur gradually gave way to established firms that integrated research by erecting the first corporate labs. These firms, concentrated in the synthetic chemicals and electrical industries, had similarly attempted a Smithian route by trying to source inventions from outside, but they realised that the supply of science-based inventions was paltry and dwindling. It would take another century for academia to take commercial application of scientific discoveries seriously, while scientific innovations were growing in complexity and sophistication that overwhelmed even the sharpest of savants. The first industrial labs in Germany aimed to fill this gap and were able to extend their lead against competitors as a result. American firms in the twentieth century took note of this success and quickly followed suit, a subject we explore in full detail in Chapter 8.

Both in Europe and America, the independent inventor was the primary source of invention in the nineteenth century. American inventors were more likely to patent and license their inventions, particularly mechanical inventions related to textile and agricultural machinery, transport equipment, and inorganic chemical processes. Even as the incumbent producers, such as railroads, mines, and textile firms, grew in size, they largely remained dependent on external sources of invention. In this sense, there was a market for technology and perhaps even a Smithian DOIL. As the complexity of inventions grew, inventors with breakthrough innovations transitioned into Schumpeterian entrepreneurs, such as George Westinghouse (air brakes) or Charles Martin Hall (aluminium), who chose not to license their ideas to incumbents but formed their own companies to manufacture and sell directly to the downstream market. Once established, firms initially looked to external inventors to supply them with improvements and refinements, as AT&T did till the end of the nineteenth century. (Chapter 7 discusses this case in further detail.) However, over time, some of them began to invest in internal research as well. The model of large industrial labs as the source of invention was new but sufficiently impressive that Schumpeter concluded, in 1942, that giant corporations would routinise invention itself (the subject of Chapter 8). And indeed, for a time, they did. Alfred Chandler, writing in the 1980s, concluded that large integrated firms would dominate both invention and commercialisation. In effect, Schumpeterian entrepreneurs transitioned to Chandlerian firms, which both originated and commercialised innovations. Ironically enough, the 1980s also marked the beginning of a new division of innovative labour: the era of startups, research specialists, and the large-scale production of government-funded university science.

Both Schumpeterian entrepreneurship and the Smithian routes remained open, even as the corporate labs in Chandlerian firms declined.

The remainder of this chapter examines the pathways through which science-based inventions were commercialised in the nineteenth century and the roles played by universities, independent inventors, startups, and incumbent producers. The next chapter turns to the American experience in greater detail.

Organising "translational" labour: Smith versus Schumpeter revisited

The central thesis of this book is that the key to unlocking the innovative potential of scientific advances is in accelerating their translation into inventions and the diffusion of those inventions into products and services. Among other things, one must deal with two types of challenges: that related to the technical feasibility of the invention and that related to its market potential. The former requires a deeper understanding of the scientific principles underlying a new artifact; the latter involves identifying latent consumer demand. One type is not more trivial than the other. The vastness of the scientific and technological search spaces for new inventions is difficult to overstate: had the invention of the Shockley junction transistor not arrived after Bardeen and Brattain's point-contact prototype, Jack Kilby would have struggled to introduce compact integrated circuits, and without integrated circuits, the follow-on process innovations in the planar process by Intel's co-founders would seldom have materialised. On the other hand, resolving market uncertainty may be just as difficult: in Henry Ford's words, customers often express an interest in a faster horse, even though they actually want an automobile.

In this chapter, we describe how deep-tech inventions of the nineteenth century in the chemical and electrical industries often struggled to find their "early adopters" who would unlock the adoption "S-curves" and simultaneously develop the inventions themselves.[4] A key issue, which we introduced in Chapter 2, is whether the tasks of developing the innovation and finding early adopters should be divided (as in a Smithian DOIL) or integrated (as in a Schumpeterian go-to-market strategy). The answer depends on two opposing forces: the gains from specialisation and the losses from a lack of coordination.

The commercialisation of nylon highlights the importance of close coordination for the commercialisation of a new science-based product.[5] DuPont organised its nylon project as a duarchy of Elmer Bolton from the Chemical Department (who dealt with developing the technology for the new polymer) and Leonard Yerkes, manager of the Rayon Department (who oversaw the production scale up and go to market strategy for the new product). By 1934, the Chemical Department's synthetic fibre group led by Wallace Carothers had formulated five compounds that could be candidates for commercialisation. Of these compounds, the "6–6" polymer was chosen over the "5–10" polymer because the feedstock, benzene, was cheaper. The ammonia division at DuPont was responsible for producing one of the key inputs, hexamethylene diamine, because it required high-pressure equipment. The Chemical Department was tasked with developing methods to produce the 6–6 compound at scale; a major roadblock was to find a way to mix the two main ingredients, adipic acid and hexamethylene diamine, in exact proportions (1:1). The Department solved this engineering problem by combining the two in a salt form first and then converting it into a fibre. The Department also developed a new way to draw fibres from the solid polymer, "melt spinning," which required that molten nylon compounds be pushed through small pinholes. To solve frequent clogging in these spinning assemblies, the lab constructed a glass version to diagnose the problem, extending continuous spinning times.

The Rayon Department had extensive experience in producing and marketing fabrics. As the development work at the Chemical Department progressed, the Rayon Department took prototype nylon yarn to the Union Manufacturing Company in Maryland to be knitted into hosiery. Further tests were carried out at another apparel manufacturer, Van Raalte of New Jersey. The Rayon Department relayed feedback on dyeing, wrinkling, and other issues to the Chemical Department for further improvements. After in-house wear tests among employees and their families, a pilot sale was staged at a Wilmington department store. The Rayon Department also co-ran a pilot plant that identified further roadblocks to large-scale production. For instance, nylon yarn, unlike silk filaments, did not contain a natural coating (sericin) to protect it during textile processing. The Rayon Department enlisted the help of a German consultant and other departments in the company to develop a custom coating for nylon. The company also tested its production capacities by supplying the Plastics Department with the compound, which marketed nylon as toothbrush bristles under the trademark

"Exton" in 1938. It was only after the resolution of both technical and market uncertainties that DuPont orchestrated a national release on 15 May 1940 (named "N-Day"), selling four million pairs within four days.[6] Nylon stockings became an instant sensation, being repurposed into parachutes during World War II and opening a new business division for the company. The case illustrates the advantages of specialisation, albeit within the bounds of a company. At the same time, close coordination between technology and market specialists was critical: even the product name, nylon, was chosen after a leading candidate "no-run" was abandoned after it was found that the new hosiery still suffered from runs.

Indeed, as the LED and battery case studies in Chapter 3 make clear, coordinating the disparate tasks of technical and market uncertainty resolution in the open market is fraught with unexpected costs. A critical assumption in Smith's pin factory model is task modularity: that tasks flow in one direction, that they are strictly independent, and that deliverables can be specified. The "linear" model of science-based innovation conceives of these tasks as sequential: it begins with basic research through which scientists explore curiosity-driven questions without practical applications in mind.[7] Applied research shifts focus to using scientific principles to solve narrower problems, while technological development works on specific modes of market deployment. In such a model, the flow from theoretical understanding to practical application is unidirectional.

However, at the frontier of science, knowledge flows both ways, with empirical discoveries in the lab or in the field updating the prior findings of basic research. The "chain-linked model" of innovation by Stephen Kline and Nathan Rosenberg features such feedback loops. While science generates new ideas, guides research, and helps avoid dead ends, technology also provides new tools and methods that, in turn, stimulate scientific inquiry. In Rosenberg's words:

> In fact, a major, neglected theme in the 20th century science is that prior progress in the technological realm has come to play a critical role in formulating the subsequent research agenda for science. The natural trajectory of certain technological improvements has served to identify and to define the limits to further improvement which, in turn, has served as a focusing device for subsequent scientific research [. . .] That is, technological progress serves to identify, in reasonably unambiguous ways, the direction in which scientific research needs to be conducted, and at the same time, it

holds out the prospect of a large financial return should the research prove to be successful.[8]

As discussed in Chapter 3, organising the activities of science, technology, and commercialisation through a network of contracts may be inefficient compared to an internalised solution such as an inventor entrepreneur or a corporate lab in an established firm. Within such organisations, there is greater capacity to match roadblocks in commercialisation with relevant technological and scientific solutions. The transition from the First to the Second Industrial Revolution decisively shifted the balance from Smithian to Schumpeterian paths of innovation.

Commercialising inventions in the First Industrial Revolution

During the First Industrial Revolution, some inventors monetised their ideas through a market for technology licencing patents or selling rights to established manufacturers that could integrate the innovations into existing or new production lines. Others followed the Schumpeterian path of entrepreneurship, founding new firms or radically reorganising old ones to deploy those inventions themselves and disrupt incumbent industries. This interplay of licensing and venture creation propelled rapid diffusion and commercial success. In what follows, we outline several hallmark cases that show how these twin mechanisms operated in practice.

Sewing Machine. The experience of Elias Howe illustrates one of the earliest examples of a Smithian inventor: someone who profits from ideas through a market for technology rather than by building a firm.[9] Howe patented the lock-stitch sewing machine in 1846, but with little capital, fragile health, and no factory of his own, he focused on licencing instead of manufacturing himself. Crucially, the 1836 U.S. Patent Act gave him enforceable property rights, while an eager corps of machine builders such as Isaac M. Singer, Wheeler and Wilson, and Grover and Baker already possessed the plants, skilled labour, and sales networks needed to reach the booming ready-made clothing market. Instead of waging ruinous, case-by-case patent wars, Howe turned those complementary assets to his advantage. He first demanded a steep royalty of about $25 (nearly half the price of an early sewing machine) from anyone using his lock-stitch mechanism; then, in 1856, he joined with Singer and two other rivals to form the Sewing Machine Combination, the nation's first patent pool. The Albany Agreement merged their critical, overlapping patents (Howe's lock-stitch, Wheeler & Wilson's four-motion feed, Singer's horizontal bed, and others) and set a standardised per-machine royalty—about \$5 on domestic and \$1 on exported units—that any manufacturer could pay for a blanket licence. By farming out production risk while collecting royalties, Howe is estimated to have collected over \$2 million (nearly \$50 million today) between 1856 and 1867 when his patent expired.

Steam engine. The story of James Watt and his steam engine is well known. Perhaps also well known is the importance of his partnership with Matthew Boulton, an established industrialist from Birmingham, who acquired the patent rights to Watt's patent and formalised his collaboration with Watt. However, what is less well known is that Boulton and Watt did not sell steam engines. Instead, they licensed the technology, which included detailed drawings and know-how. The firm arranged for the installation and construction of its engineers, monitored their operation, and oversaw any needed repairs. Licencees typically paid royalties based on the estimated savings in fuel costs relative to the older Newcomen engine.[10]

Though Boulton and Watt were principally Smithian entrepreneurs monetising their inventions through licensing, they borrowed some parts of the Schumpeterian playbook: the duo assiduously persuaded potential users of the benefits of their technology. By the 1760s, use of the older Newcomen steam engine was already well established in mines and mills. Therefore, Boulton and Watts mostly had to establish the technical superiority of their engine, rather than persuade users to replace horse or water power. To appeal to breweries and other industries that used horses for power, they developed the term "horsepower" to make it easy for potential adopters to quantify the efficiency gains. Boulton and Watt remained focused on the technology, leaving the main task of manufacturing steam engines to licencees. Smithian entrepreneurship typically entails identifying the ultimate customer who derives value from the invention and, when necessary, undertaking complementary downstream investments to enable its adoption.[11]

As discussed in Chapter 2 and in the sewing machine example, a strong intellectual property (IP) regime is critical for the functioning of markets for technology. In 1775, Boulton pushed through an Act of Parliament that extended Watt's patent to 1800, securing a twenty-five-year monopoly, which they enforced relentlessly. The pair successfully sued Jonathan Hornblower in the 1780s for infringement, forcing his compound engines off the market.[12] Boulton and Watt continued to make improvements in the technology over the life of the patent. Watt, for instance, adapted the initial design for pumping water out of mines to one for use in blast furnaces, and he later developed a more efficient two-stroke engine. Another key innovation by Watt was the development of a rotary design for driving machinery, replacing horses and waterwheels. Watt, along with John Southey, also developed a mechanism for measuring the operating efficiency of their engines in 1796. By concentrating on low-pressure condensing engines covered by their patents, withholding detailed specifications, and combining legal action with strategic secrecy, Boulton and Watt preserved technological leadership long after competitors emerged.

Railroads. George Stephenson, a self-taught mechanic, tested his initial design for a locomotive at a colliery where he was employed. In 1823, following the introduction of his engines, Killingworth Colliery was able to remove all horses from the haulage process. In 1823, he (along with his son, Robert) started the world's first locomotive factory, with financing from Edward Pease, a banker and wool merchant from Darlington. Pease also helped Stephenson get a job in 1821 at a company that built and operated a railway line between the towns of Stockton and Darlington. The commercial success of this venture increased demand for steam locomotives. Stephenson also contributed greatly to other aspects of railways, such as standardising tracks.[13]

Stephenson was a quintessential Schumpeterian entrepreneur whose partner provided financial investment and business connections to customers. Initially, Stephenson had to compete against horsepower and later against other types of steam locomotives. This competition had both technical and marketing facets. Stephenson made a number of improvements to his original design. For example, he introduced a steam blast that improved combustion efficiency, a more efficient drive train, a more efficient multi-tubed boiler, and a better method for fastening rails.

Once the railroad industry was established, incumbent firms began relying on external inventors to supply innovations for their components. In America, innovations initially focused on expanding coverage and subsequently on increasing throughput by introducing more powerful locomotives, larger cars, and stronger and heavier rails. These advances arose from practical experience, improved materials (especially steel), and inventions by employees and independent inventors. Between 1852 and 1865, the number of patents pertaining directly to railroads increased from about 50 to over 500 per year, comprising a significant share of total patenting activity at the time.[14] Some independent inventors amassed fortunes through Smithian innovation routes. For example, Elijah McCoy, a mechanical engineer forced to work as an oiler for the Michigan Central Railroad because of racial prejudices, invented an automatic oiling system in 1872. The system was adopted so widely on railroads that engineers were sceptical of any locomotives that did not use "the real McCoy." In 1873, Eli H. Janney, a clerk at a dry goods store and an amateur inventor, designed a knuckle-style coupler for railway cars with an automatic locking system, which remains the standard coupler even today. Understandably, railroad executives were very attentive to the development and acquisition of new technology. However, they strongly preferred to manufacture the licenced inventions themselves, adapting the invention as needed and scaling its production to their needs. The invention would thereby also contribute to the accumulated technical expertise of the acquiring company.

Exceptions to this pattern arose when breakthroughs needed to be introduced. George Westinghouse's braking system is one such example. After Westinghouse demonstrated his compressed-air braking system in 1868, one of the largest railroad companies at the time, the Pennsylvania Railroad, approached him for a licence. However, instead of licensing it, he founded the Westinghouse Air Brake Company to produce and sell the system in 1869. The decision was partially born out of Westinghouse's experience with his first anti-derailment mechanism ("the frog"), where the patent had been put into a railroad patent pool that minimised his ability to extract rents.[15] He continued to improve on the original invention, designing a "triple valve" system in 1872 that would allow automatic braking.[16] Westinghouse also pushed for the standardisation and interoperability of railroad design to increase demand for his uniform airbrake system. Westinghouse further introduced an integrated signalling and switching system for railroads that used compressed air to move switch points and signal arms, controlled from electrical switch boxes. The increased speed and density of railroad traffic made collisions at junctions even more dangerous, greatly increasing the value of Westinghouse's signalling devices and interlocking switches. Instead of licencing his electropneumatic signalling system to incumbents, Westinghouse founded Union Switch & Signal in 1881 to manufacture and sell the entire signalling system. Alfred Nobel's dynamite and Henry Bessemer's steelmaking process, inventions requiring commensurate levels of precision and complexity, followed similar patterns of commercialisation.

In sum, commercialising inventions in the First Industrial Revolution proceeded primarily via Smithian methods. The inventions, though not based in scientific discovery, represented advances in mechanical engineering that still bore substantial technical uncertainty. Yet, many of these inventions enjoyed clarity in the types of markets and applications they could be sold to, explaining their heavy reliance on Smithian paths of innovation through markets for technology. The experience of Westinghouse's Air Brake Company shows that upstream inventors could also take the Schumpeterian route and forward integrate into the market, particularly for more complex and systemic innovations.

The Second Industrial Revolution: science-based inventions complicate DOIL

The Second Industrial Revolution can be framed as a century-long exercise in commercialising the deep-tech inventions of the times. Unlike mechanical inventions of the First Industrial Revolution, the inventions of the Second carried significantly greater technical uncertainty (as the underlying science was still being developed); they also faced greater market uncertainty as large incumbents were often uninterested in acquiring new inventions. For these reasons, paths to commercialisation were more diverse, with more entrepreneurs following Schumpeterian strategies, at least early in the industry life cycle.

The rise of Schumpeterian inventor-entrepreneurs

During the Second Industrial Revolution, Smithian innovation was soon dominated by eponymous entrepreneurs who would go to market themselves, rather than wait for a licencee to appear. Justus von Liebig's beef extract process is a rare example of a Smithian path to commercialisation. Liebig, together with Jöns Jacob Berzelius, is widely regarded as one of the early pioneers of organic chemistry. As a faculty member at the University of Giessen, Liebig invented a method to reduce beef into meat extracts in 1847. Liebig publicised the process for industrialists to commercialise, and George Giebert, a Belgian engineer working in Uruguay, established the Liebig Extract of Meat Company (LEMCO, later Oxo) in 1865 to process cow carcasses that were otherwise being wasted in South America (at the time, cattle were slaughtered for their hide, not for their flesh). Importantly, this was a new product, and a considerable marketing effort was invested in establishing it as a food product. Giebert hired Liebig to perform quality checks on the meat extract and lend his name and scientific credentials to the company.[17] The LEMCO case represents a prototypical example of university-industry collaboration: the original invention originated with an agricultural chemist, whereas a firm provided the necessary capital, secured raw materials, and managed commercialisation. Implementing Liebig's idea required relatively little technical sophistication. The beef cubes themselves also integrated easily into Western European diets, finding a large and ready market. Other science-based innovations were not so lucky. Instead, the earliest science-based innovations during the Second Industrial Revolution required Schumpeterian paths of commercialisation, first by inventor entrepreneurs and later by industrial research laboratories.

The earliest inventor-entrepreneurs focused on providing improved means of producing existing products. As such, the market risk was lower. However, the novelty of their inventions required that substantial technical uncertainty be resolved through internal research. Consider the introduction of the Bessemer process in 1856 to enable the mass production of steel. Steel had traditionally been produced through small-scale, artisanal processes. Henry Bessemer, an autodidact, was inspired by an accidental discovery that blowing air on molten iron could produce steel.[18] He patented the process in 1856. At first, he took the Smithian route, licensing his discoveries to local iron manufacturers. However, the resulting quality of steel was erratic, leading Bessemer to enter production in partnership with W&J Galloway & Sons, a steam engine manufacturer in Sheffield. One of the problems identified was that the process was too rapid, removing too much of the carbon and manganese, thereby creating wrought iron that was too soft. The solution, found by Robert Mushet, was to reintroduce trace amounts of carbon by adding spiegeleisen (an alloy of iron and manganese) to the furnace. Having found the solution, Bessemer acquired the rights to the patent and began licensing his technology widely. Andrew Carnegie, for instance, took note of this innovation and constructed his Edgar Thomson works in 1875 specifically to exploit the process. Twenty years later, Carl Wilhelm Siemens and Pierre Martin developed an improved process with finer quality control and the ability to use scrap metals—the open hearth furnace.[19]

The Pennsylvania Steel Company would start operating the Siemens-Martin process a mere three years after its introduction.

Two decades after its initial introduction, the Bessemer process had spread widely, allowing Smithian routes of innovation to reopen. Percy Gilchrist and Sidney Thomas, for instance, enhanced the applicability of the Bessemer process by dealing with impurities such as phosphorus and sulphur found in some types of iron ores. By this time, the underlying scientific basis of steelmaking was better understood. Their presentation to the Iron and Steel Institute in 1879, titled "The Elimination of Phosphorus in the Bessemer Converter," articulated their findings and the chemical principles at play. After demonstrating that their process was commercially viable, with the help of Bolckow, Vaughan and Company, a large iron-making concern in Middlesbrough, they widely patented and licensed their process to existing iron and steel producers.

The often rudimentary nature of science-based inventions meant that commercial implementation required significant translational work. Potential licencees put a low value on technologies that had not yet been commercially validated. This often meant that inventors needed to start their own firms to commercialise their discoveries. The inventor-entrepreneurs of this category include Alfred Nobel and Ernest Solvay.

Ascanio Sobrero, while studying under Jules Pelouze, successfully synthesised nitroglycerin in 1846. While Sobrero stopped work after safety concerns were raised on the highly reactive compound, Nobel, an alumnus of the Pelouze training lab, continued work on stabilising the explosive and invented dynamite in 1867. Rather than relying on licencing to diffuse his inventions, Nobel opted to found subsidiaries with local partners to enter what was often a heavily regulated sector of the economy (explosives).[20] Within seven years of his Dynamite patent (1863), he was running five factories in Europe; the number grew to fifteen by 1873. One of the reasons to opt for internalisation may have been that key steps of this process still relied on tacit knowledge. The steps to produce dynamite involved carefully settling nitroglycerin in a bed of sorbents and stabilisers. Mistakes could lead to accidents that could tarnish his (and his product's) reputation. Nobel's industry experience probably made him especially sensitive to this possibility. For example, a Nobel factory in New Jersey, which was manufacturing nitroglycerin (then known as "blasting oil") before the invention of dynamite, exploded in 1869.

Solvay also chose to commercialise his eponymous process by integrating downstream rather than license it to existing soda ash producers. Sodium carbonate (Na2CO3) was a critical input into glassmaking and the manufacture of detergents. As its name suggests, the traditional method to obtain soda ash was by burning wood. Because of the widespread deforestation in Europe, this became unsustainable. The first industrial process to produce soda ash was developed by Nicolas LeBlanc, who responded to a 1783 competition by the French Academy of Sciences for producing alkali from sea salt. LeBlanc's process involved heating a mixture of sea salt with sulphuric acid, limestone, and charcoal. LeBlanc himself would not emerge as an inventor-entrepreneur, as he met an early demise during the French Revolution. The British alkali industry, however, adopted the method to dominate global markets until the introduction of the Solvay method. In the 1860s, Ernest Solvay, another autodidact who gained familiarity with industrial chemistry through his family's chemical business, developed a process that extracted soda ash using ammonia, thereby eliminating the pollutants associated with the LeBlanc method. Solvay's process was also 20 per cent cheaper than LeBlanc's.[21] Rather than license, Solvay invested in plants in Belgium, France, Germany, and Russia. He did license the British rights to Brunner Mond & Co. in 1873, and accepted a minority equity stake for the American rights from the Solvay Process Company in 1884.[22]

A general theme that emerges is that initial discoveries had to be commercially validated. That is, there was considerable uncertainty and many technical challenges in scaling up production and ensuring consistent quality of output. Few potential licencees were able and willing to take on these challenges. As a result, inventors typically had to launch companies to do it themselves. Once launched, there was little incentive for the innovating company to license to competitors in markets it could supply itself.

The embryonic years of industrial research

As the nineteenth century drew to a close, the success of the Schumpeterian inventor-entrepreneurs was studied and emulated by incumbent firms that had heretofore stayed away from the business of scientific research. This section traces the emergence of industrial research in general; Chapter 8 studies how this embryonic model became firmly entrenched in the United States in the twentieth century.

Industrial labs in synthetic chemicals

For most of history, chemical innovation relied on trial and error. Researchers prior to the introduction of analytical chemistry lacked a clear understanding of molecular structures or the interactions of atoms within compounds. Breakthroughs were as much a result of serendipity as they were of methodical experimentation. Advances across several branches of chemistry in the nineteenth century transformed the field into a more systematic and predictive science. In organic chemistry, Aleksandr Butlerov and August Kekulé developed the theory of chemical structures to explain how atoms were arranged within molecules. Kekulé, for instance, clarified in 1865 how benzene consisted of a six-carbon ring. This structural insight helped explain why the molecule was surprisingly stable, despite being unsaturated (i.e., being composed of fewer hydrogen atoms per carbon atom than other stable hydrocarbons). Around the same time, Dmitri Mendeleev introduced the periodic system to reveal underlying regularities among the elements by their atomic weights. The 1860s also saw advances in analytical chemistry through spectral analysis which were pioneered by Robert Bunsen and Gustav Kirchhoff. Later in the century, Wilhelm Ostwald, Jacobus Henricus van't Hoff, and Svante Arrhenius applied principles of thermodynamics to chemical reactions and established the field of physical chemistry.[23]

The emerging systemisation of chemical knowledge had two implications for innovators. First, as it became easier to synthesise novel products, new markets opened up. Second, since discovery relied less on blind luck and more on systematic investigations, the returns to large-scale research and team-based innovative efforts increased. Both margins tilted the balance in favour of industrial research.

An illustration of this transformation can be seen in the history of the synthetic dye industry, which began in 1856 with the discovery of mauveine. William Henry Perkin, a student at London's Royal College of Chemistry, was attempting to synthesise quinine for malaria treatment when he inadvertently created a vibrant purple dye from aniline, a coal-tar derivative. Recognising its potential, Perkin patented and commercialised the dye, pioneering synthetic dyes that were brighter, more durable, and cheaper than their natural counterparts. Similar to Solvay, Perkin set up his own firm to commercialise this process. Departing from prior inventor-entrepreneurs, he also established a private laboratory at Greenford Green, near his dye factory.[24] However, labs were still an ad-hoc part of the organisation, as seen from the decision to leave the Greenford laboratory out during the sale of Perkin's company to Brooke, Simpson & Spiller at the end of 1873.

Perkin's breakthrough highlighted the possibility of replacing natural dyes with synthetic ones. However, the supply of talented chemists with the ability and wherewithal to discover new synthetic dyes was limited. Companies had to discover their own dyes or depend on competitors to obtain licences. Germany was well supplied with trained and talented chemists, some of whom were working in countries with larger industrial sectors, such as Great Britain. The combination of growing scientific opportunities and a ready supply of human capital prompted German chemical companies to establish corporate labs. The application of science to the problem of economic production was becoming institutionalised.

The first firm to introduce this concept was BASF (Badische Anilin und Soda-Fabrik), which recruited Heinrich Caro in 1868 to "execute operations in the laboratory that are necessary from both a theoretical and a practical point of view."[25] Caro was trained in chemistry and textile colouring and had worked for nearly a decade for a British dyestuff manufacturer, where he developed an improved version of Perkin's process. He was recruited for the job after returning to work under Robert Bunsen's lab in Germany. By 1874, Caro was directing the company's indigo dye inventions, discovering successful products such as methylene blue. More laboratories would be added to BASF's corporate structure, with eighteen established by 1887, organised by type of dye and subfield of chemistry.

Hoechst, another major German chemical firm, also established a separate *Analytisches Laboratorium* headed by Hermann Strecker by 1870. While the lab in its early years did not produce novel products, it was more than a quality control shop attached to a factory, organised at the "corporate level."[26] Later, Hoechst started its *Zentrallaboratorium* to support its decision to enter drugmaking. To run the lab, the firm recruited two academics from Giessen—August Laubenheimer and Eduard von Gerichten. Links to academia were nurtured carefully, with future Nobel Prize laureate Paul Ehrlich being employed as a contractor in 1894 to supply diphtheria antitoxins. The collaboration was mutually beneficial: Ehrlich had discovered that methylene blue could be used to selectively stain bacteria cells in vivo, a critical step in studying diseases such as tuberculosis and syphilis. This work culminated in Ehrlich's discovery of Salvarasan, which became a blockbuster Hoechst drug for the treatment of syphilis. By the 1880s, a corporate laboratory had become part of managerial considerations, with Oehler (1882),

Kalle (1882), Agfa (1882), Cassella (1885), and Bayer (1886) establishing laboratories within a four-year period.

Why synthetic dyes? Why were synthetic dye firms especially likely to internalise research? Commercialising coal tar-based dyes was fraught with scientific and technological challenges. For instance, early synthetic dyes, while visually striking, often lacked durability. They were prone to fading, particularly under light or after washing, which limited their commercial viability. Translational research tackled this problem by applying advanced chemical insights to improve the stability of dyes. Scientists improved dye molecules to withstand light, heat, and repeated washing, and they perfected mordanting methods that chemically bind colour to fibres. Perkin's first scientific task after discovering that mauveine worked only on silk was to find a mordant capable of anchoring the dye to cotton, a much larger market. Acting as a molecular adhesive between dye and cellulose, the mordant solved the adhesion problem. These advances made synthetic dyes durable, versatile, and compliant with the textile industry's demanding performance standards, boosting their commercial appeal.

The transition from laboratory-scale experiments to industrial production posed another challenge. Early methods of chemical synthesis were inefficient, yielding inconsistent results and low quantities of usable dye. Translational research focused on optimising industrial processes, including distillation, crystallisation, and filtration. These refinements increased yields, reduced impurities, and ensured consistent quality, enabling the large-scale production of dyes needed to meet the growing market demand. Even after overcoming technical hurdles, synthetic dyes initially faced resistance from manufacturers and consumers who were accustomed to natural dyes. Early synthetic products were sometimes criticised for lacking the brightness or longevity of their natural counterparts. Through ongoing experimentation in industrial labs, synthetic dyes became brighter, longer-lasting, and more versatile, ultimately surpassing the performance of natural dyes.

This early investment enabled the German chemical industry to go from strength to strength, maintaining its global dominance until the conclusion of World War II. The general-purpose nature of chemical knowledge meant that the research that the firms invested in yielded opportunities to diversify beyond dyestuffs by the late nineteenth century. For instance, Bayer and Hoechst expanded into pharmaceuticals and synthetic materials.

The most famous Bayer success story is Aspirin, which was synthesised by Felix Hoffmann in 1897. BASF had also expanded into fertilisers, introducing the Haber–Bosch process to enable large-scale ammonia synthesis. This breakthrough, developed by Fritz Haber and scaled by Carl Bosch, revolutionised agriculture by producing synthetic fertilisers that significantly boosted global crop yields. The process also catalysed advances in other sectors, including the production of polymers, resins, and explosives.

Why Germany? Why were German firms the first to implement this experiment in industrial research? German university education probably played an important role. Compared to the British and French systems, the German education system may have done a better job of supplying academically trained chemists able to invent at the technological frontier.[27] The research university paradigm pioneered by Humboldt University had spread throughout German-speaking regions, with chemists at Heidelberg (Robert Bunsen and Gustav Kirchhoff), Gottingen (Friedrich Wohler), and Berlin (Jons Berzelius) rising to global renown. Alumni such as Carl Duisberg (Bayer) and Carl Bosch (BASF) later revolutionised industrial chemistry. Supporting the organic chemists was a cadre of engineers produced by the technical schools at the time. By 1870, Germany already boasted eight Technische Hochschulen (predecessors to the modern Technical University system) in Berlin, Karlsruhe, Munich, Dresden, Stuttgart, Hanover, Braunschweig, and Darmstadt. Three more schools, at Aachen, Danzig, and Breslau, were added by 1910. After 1899, the schools were granted the authority to award doctoral degrees. Between 1900 and 1914, these schools graduated over ten thousand students who had completed five to seven years of tertiary instruction and could supply the managerial echelons of optical, chemical, and electrical industry firms.

By contrast, the French system failed to establish a robust pipeline of technically trained personnel to industry. The grandes écoles system instituted after the French Revolution (École des Mines, École des Ponts et Chaussées, École d'Artillerie, École de Genie Militaire) was primarily intended to produce civil servants and military officers, rather than innovators. The École Polytechnique integrated modern scientific subjects such as mechanics and electricity only by the twentieth century. The "lower" grandes écoles, such as the Écoles des Arts et Métiers, were set up to train engineers, but they did not engage in research to discover new knowledge. The "new" grandes écoles (the École Supérieure for physics, chemistry, electricity, and aeronautics) that were closest to the German Technische Hochschulen were established only by the 1880s. Britain was similarly lacking in standardised technical education at scale: prior to the establishment of University College London in 1836, Cambridge and Oxford were the only universities offering instruction in the sciences. From around the 1820s, industrial towns began establishing mechanics institutes, but their functions were limited to training labourers in basic arithmetic and some proficiency in mechanics.[28] Compared to the French Écoles des Arts et Métiers, which required a rigorous two-year coursework, records suggest that curricula at mechanics institutes were haphazardly put together, and dropout rates were high.

The rapid progress of the chemical sciences in the latter half of the nineteenth century brought promises of novel products such as synthetic dyes. Commercialising new products inevitably involves both technology and market risk. Often innovators founded companies to commercialise their innovation, but with the rising cost of doing frontier chemical science, the inventor-entrepreneur began to recede as the primary source of inventions. Firms, seeing the sources of external science dwindle, were compelled to cultivate their own. They established laboratories with teams of researchers and supplied them with materials and equipment to aid their research. This trend began with German firms in the 1860s, which tasked their labs with combining discovery, development, and market deployment. Supported by growing academic research in chemistry and trained chemists, these labs sought to routinise the process of invention that had hitherto relied more on serendipity and personal flair. The investments paid off handsomely, allowing them not only to develop new dye colours but also to enter new industries such as pharmaceuticals and fertilisers.

Industrial labs in the electrical industries

Unlike chemicals, where synthetic products replaced existing products, such as dynamite for gunpowder, or steel for iron, the electrical industries that sprang up in the nineteenth century were creating entirely new markets.[29] Physicists were learning more about electromagnetism as the technology was improving. So were the users, who were introduced to a general-purpose technology that could light lamps, power factories, play music on phonographs, and allow instant communication over seas and continents. Though slower, the search to find commercial applications for electromagnetism proceeded similarly: first, with inventions being traded in a market for technology, and later with an embryonic form of internalised research.

The foundations of modern electrical and electronic industries are rooted in the study of two distinct, yet interrelated, forces: electricity and magnetism. The relationship between the two remained elusive until the early nineteenth century. In 1820, Hans Christian Ørsted made a groundbreaking discovery: a compass needle placed near a current-carrying wire deflected, revealing that electricity generates a magnetic field. This observation provided the first empirical evidence linking the two forces. Ørsted's discovery set the stage for a new era of exploration into electromagnetic phenomena. Building on Ørsted's findings, André-Marie Ampère formulated Ampère's law in 1823, which quantified the magnetic force between electric currents. Ampère demonstrated that parallel currents attract, while antiparallel currents repel, providing a mathematical foundation for understanding electromagnetic interactions. He also introduced the concept of "electrodynamic molecules," an early precursor to electron theory, which posited the existence of particles within matter responsible for magnetic effects.

Inspired by Ørsted's work, Michael Faraday conducted a series of experiments that culminated in the discovery of electromagnetic induction in 1831. Faraday demonstrated that a changing magnetic field could induce an electric current in a conductor, providing the theoretical basis for generating electricity. His concept of "lines of force" illustrated how electric and magnetic fields exist in space, offering a visual model for field interactions. Faraday's work was transformative. It not only deepened the understanding of electromagnetic phenomena but also laid the groundwork for practical applications. The principle of electromagnetic induction became the cornerstone of electric power generation. Within decades, Faraday's discoveries were applied to build electric generators capable of producing power on an industrial scale, addressing a critical barrier to the commercialisation of electricity. The culmination of these advancements came in the 1860s, when James Clerk Maxwell formulated his equations, mathematically unifying electricity and magnetism into the theory of electromagnetism. It was now understood that electric currents create magnetic fields and that the motion of a conductor through a magnetic field generates electric currents.

As indispensable as Maxwell's equations were, the commercial application of electromagnetism required effective dynamos and transformers to generate, control, and amplify electric currents. Moreover, electricity was a solution looking for a problem. New applications in lighting, household appliances, factory machines, and streetcars would need to be found. In other words, electrification faced two-sided uncertainties. Schumpeterian inventor-entrepreneurs, therefore, had to establish firms and, in effect, create new industries. As electrical inventions, such as dynamos, wireless communication, and vacuum tubes, became more complex and scientifically sophisticated, firms began hiring researchers to understand the scientific basis for how their own products worked.

The widespread adoption of electrical technologies hinged on cost-effective electricity generation and distribution. The invention of the dynamo, a device that converts mechanical energy into electrical energy, was a pivotal step in this process. The earliest practical dynamo designs emerged in the mid-nineteenth century. Werner von Siemens, in 1867, introduced the principle of self-excitation, which improved the efficiency of dynamos by enabling continuous electricity generation. In 1871, Zénobe Gramme built on Siemens's work, developing a machine capable of generating direct current (DC) at an industrial scale. These inventions made large-scale electricity generation technically feasible, but they still faced significant barriers to commercial application. In 1877, Charles F. Brush refined the dynamo to power arc lamps for street lighting and industrial applications. His design improved reliability and reduced costs, making DC electricity more accessible.[30]

The early inventor-entrepreneurs, while full of initiative, carried little formal scientific training or required teamwork. For instance, Ezra Cornell, who had designed a plow to lay underground telegraph cable in the 1840s, realised that telegraph signals would attenuate underground due to inadequate insulation. Instead, he proposed stringing wires on glass-insulated poles. This simple idea was sufficient for him to attract investors, eventually leading to establishment of the Western Union Telegraph Company. When Alexander Graham Bell asked for $100,000 for the rights to his telephone invention in 1876, Western Union dismissed the idea as a toy.[31] Bell proceeded to establish his own telephone company with the backing of Gardiner Hubbard and Thomas Sanders (both connected through Bell's interest in activism for the deaf). Particularly in America, this type of Schumpeterian entrepreneurship coexisted with a Smithian division of innovative labour between independent inventors and manufacturers, which we describe in Chapter 7.

As the electrical industry matured, further improvements required a deeper understanding of the science, and those investigations became increasingly costly to develop and coordinate (as in the synthetic chemical example above). While early dynamos exploited the fact that movement of a coil generates magnetic flux (and hence, electrical currents), their efficiency was very low (Brush's prototype was strapped to farm animals to create rotary motion). To reduce energy loss, increase durability, and produce stable electricity flow, follow-on innovations in coil design, insulation, and commutation were needed. Follow-on innovators such as Elihu Thomson and Edwin J. Houston built an extensive patent portfolio to protect their ideas around these problems. By the 1890s, Thomson–Houston had vertically integrated into the first large-scale electricity market, arc lighting, and acquired Brush's company.

Despite its brightness and efficiency, arc lighting faced significant hurdles in reaching widespread use. Its reliance on carbon rods that evaporated during use necessitated constant adjustments, and its short lifespan made it impractical for many applications. The incandescent bulb, invented by Edison in 1879, used a heated filament encased in a vacuum-sealed glass bulb, offering several advantages over arc lighting. It was more durable, required less maintenance, and was suited to domestic use. Edison's focus was not just on creating a functional bulb but also on building an entire electrical system, including power generation and distribution, to rival gas lighting. His Pearl Street power station, built in 1882, demonstrated the practicality of centralised electricity distribution, laying the foundation for modern electrical infrastructure. After a spate of competitive bouts, Edison Electric Light and Thomson–Houston merged to form General Electric (GE) in 1892, combining innovations in lighting with power distribution.

As leading firms reached the frontiers of existing technology, they began to see the promise of internal research, as their German predecessors in chemicals had a few decades earlier.[32] An example that demonstrates the importance of internalised research is the "current war." George Westinghouse entered the electrical industry with his advocacy for alternating current (AC) systems. AC, based on patents acquired from Nikola Tesla, allowed electricity to be transmitted over longer distances with less power loss compared to Edison's direct current (DC) systems. By the 1880s, Westinghouse knew that his competitor, Thomas Edison, had been operating a research lab in Menlo Park from around 1876. He therefore commissioned a similar research facility a year after founding his company in 1886. Benjamin Lamme headed research into optimising AC performance, while Tesla was retained as an independent consultant to demonstrate AC's superiority against DC. The turning point came at the 1893 World's Columbian Exposition in Chicago, where Westinghouse's AC system lit the event, publicly demonstrating its superiority. Subsequent projects, such as the Niagara Falls power plant, cemented AC's dominance. After some initial resistance, GE adopted AC technology, and the two companies eventually created a patent pool to share innovations. Ironically, the key conceptual advance that improved AC motors came from Charles Proteus Steinmetz at GE, who introduced the use of complex numbers to understand magnetic hysteresis in AC motors. In recognition of his stature in the scientific community, Steinmetz would serve as the president of the American Institute of Electrical Engineers from 1901 to 1902.

While the translation of chemical knowledge was a mostly European (and increasingly German) affair, the commercialisation of key electrical inventions happened in the United States.[33] However, the arc of experimentation in both innovation ecosystems seemed remarkably similar: the first applications of the new science often involved trial-and-error experiments by talented individuals, who typically commercialised their inventions by starting new companies. With time, these companies, seeking growth by expanding scale or introducing new and improved products, could not rely on external inventors. Inventions themselves became technically more demanding. Firms, therefore, began to internalise research. These were primitive versions of the large research labs that would rise to conduct fundamental research (described in Chapter 8). Importantly, however, most managers in these "deep tech" industries had been introduced to the idea of industrial laboratories by the turn of the century.

Chapter takeaways

The Second Industrial Revolution had an arguably greater impact on economic development than the First, thanks to the systematic application of science to innovation. Starting with dyestuffs and telegraphs, the chemical and electrical industries gave birth to industrially produced fertilisers, pharmaceuticals, electrified factories, incandescent lightbulbs, and the radio. This chapter illustrates how scientists, inventors, and innovators coordinated the "translational" labour required to bring the insights of Kekule and Maxwell to market as finished products.

Unlike the First Industrial Revolution, which chiefly produced mechanical inventions with clear downstream uses, few potential licencees could take on the task of translating scientific breakthroughs in chemistry or electromagnetism. Therefore, translational tasks typically fell to the inventors themselves, who became Schumpeterian entrepreneurs to demonstrate the technical and commercial viability of their discoveries. This pattern is evident in a whole range of discoveries, be it Bessemer's process for producing steel in large volumes or Charles Brush's improved arc lighting system. Even when inventors were inclined to license to existing producers and take the Smithian route, the latter often lacked the ability and imagination to see the potential of what was being offered, as Alexander Bell's unsuccessful attempt to license his invention to Western Union shows. However, improvements to existing discoveries could be licensed more readily. Once validated at scale, the Thomas–Gilchrist basic process for enabling the Bessemer process to use phosphorus-rich iron ores was readily licensed the world over. Similarly, as Chapter 7 describes, AT&T maintained an entire department in the 1880s and 1890s to evaluate and acquire external inventions.

Beginning with the German chemical pioneers, such as BASF and Hoechst, the leading companies of the Second Industrial Revolution invested in strengthening the scientific basis of their technologies, to absorb external developments and make incremental improvements in products and processes, ultimately generating their own inventions. By integrating basic research, applied science, and production, they accelerated technological development and ensured that breakthroughs could be scaled rapidly to meet market demand. The institutionalisation of industrial research and development in the late nineteenth and early twentieth centuries heralded the transformation of the Schumpeterian entrepreneurs of the Second Industrial Revolution into the corporate giants that Alfred Chandler would admiringly describe in his book on the Visible Hand of managerial capitalism.[34]

7
The Origins of the American Scientific–Industrial Complex

Introduction

Building on the previous chapter's discussion of the Second Industrial Revolution and the emergence of modern science-based industries, the next four chapters trace how the American innovation ecosystem has evolved. This historical journey highlights the junctures that shaped its current structure and the challenges it now faces, setting the stage for examining the policies and institutional changes needed to strengthen it for the future.

We begin with the half-century that followed the Civil War, from 1865 to the 1920s. During this period, the United States advanced from an industrial follower to a global leader. This transformation rested on distinguishing features of the American economy: its vast and rapidly growing domestic market, its abundant natural resources, and its decentralised political and economic institutions.

Early American growth drew on imported technologies. Creative tinkerers and entrepreneurs absorbed advances in textiles, transport, and chemicals, tailoring them to domestic needs. They soon pioneered manufacturing methods featuring standardisation and scale. In parallel, several elements of the innovation ecosystem coevolved, yielding a distinctively American synthesis. The first element was the university. Throughout much of the nineteenth century, American higher education was primarily geared toward "practice and vocation."[1] By the 1890s, though many universities put a stronger emphasis on research, their main contribution during this period was to train the workforce to meet industry demands.

While universities served the nation as a talent foundry, industry was perfecting mass production and multidivisional management. The nineteenth century saw the rise of giant corporations such as Carnegie's steel works, Standard Oil, and the Western Union Telegraph Company. These giant corporations grew in the face of an enduring suspicion of monopoly power that marked American antitrust policy. A variety of antimonopoly statutes were enacted at both the federal and state levels. Along with the rapidly growing domestic market and the increasing potential of the application of science to the problems of economic production, stricter antitrust enforcement led many of the leading companies to invest in internal research (instead of growing through acquisitions).

The other noteworthy aspect of the institutional structure was the inventor-friendly American patent system. Compared with European regimes, it was cheap, quick, and transparent. Independent tinkerers could secure exclusive rights for a modest fee, pledge those rights as collateral, or license them. In the early 1900s, more than one-third of all new U.S. patents changed hands. This fluid market for technology shepherded inventions into factory lines and consumer products. It also tempered corporate power. Even a monopolist had to court outside inventors or risk being leapfrogged by a rival buyer of their patents.

American universities at a crossroads

A patchwork of local institutions

Through much of the nineteenth century, American universities lagged behind their European counterparts. Their main objective was to prepare students for specific professions such as the ministry, teaching, law, or business. Many of them were established by religious denominations to train clergy and educators. As a result, American universities offered little in the way of advanced instruction and allocated minimal resources to research.

By the time the United States gained independence in 1776, there were only nine colleges in the country to serve a population of about 2.5 million.[2] However, by the beginning of the Civil War, approximately nine hundred colleges had entered the market, although many of these quickly exited due to high competition and limited resources. The college mortality rate was extraordinarily high at 80 per cent. In stark contrast, the U.K. had just eleven universities, and France and Germany had twenty-two each during the same period. The contrast is starker when we note that the three countries were roughly similar in population size: 40 million for the United States, 38 million for France, and 31 million for Britain. Historian Richard Hofstadter famously remarked that college creation in America during this time got "completely out of hand."[3]

Miguel Urquiola attributes the early backwardness of American universities to specific structural features of the U.S. education system.[4] Unlike Europe, where universities were often centralised and state-supported, American higher education was decentralised and market-driven. Before the Civil War, U.S. universities operated with limited federal government support for research and minimal oversight. Colleges catered to the needs of their local communities, offering denominational sorting (so that Presbyterians could study with other Presbyterians, for instance) and physical proximity to students' homes. The focus was on the humanities and classical education rather than science or engineering. Science education was based on ancient texts, with minimal experimentation or hands-on learning. The limited curriculum did not necessitate the hiring of specialised professors, resulting in a system where faculty were often poorly compensated and hiring decisions were influenced more by school connections, religious affiliation, or independent wealth than by academic expertise.

For example, Henry D. Rogers, the first professor of geology at the University of Pennsylvania, was appointed because, as a man of independent wealth, he offered to serve without compensation. Even into the 1860s, professors' salaries at Harvard and Yale were below the cost of living, with tutors earning barely more than artisans. Willard Gibbs, arguably the greatest American scientist of his time, who was awarded the first doctoral degree in engineering in the United States in 1863, worked as an unsalaried professor at Yale University from 1871 to 1880. Yale agreed to pay him $2,000 per year only after he received a competing offer from Johns Hopkins in 1880. Reflecting the values of the time, Harvard's president, Charles Eliot, in his inaugural address in 1869, commented that "The poverty of scholars is of inestimable worth in this money-getting nation. [. . .] Luxury and learning are ill bed-fellows."[5] As late as 1926, resource constraints at Harvard pushed Wallace Carothers to work at DuPont, which doubled his salary and provided him a newly constructed lab staffed with newly minted PhDs from Colorado, Johns Hopkins, Illinois, MIT, and Michigan.[6]

Because American universities had not yet developed strong research capabilities, many of America's leading scientific minds at the time had to seek advanced training abroad. Before 1914, between 5 and 10 per cent of all foreign students in Germany came from America, more than from any other country.[7] In 1880, 39 per cent of all scientists listed in the *American Men of Science* had a foreign PhD, while that share is 22 per cent in 1900 and only 3 per cent in 1924 (For further details, see Chapter 8, Figure 8.9.).[8] The experience of Ira Remsen illustrates the limited support for scientific research during this period. After studying under renowned German chemist Friedrich Wöhler at the University of Göttingen and obtaining his PhD in chemistry, Remsen returned to the United States with ambitions to advance American chemical research. Upon joining Williams College in 1872, he requested a space to establish a small laboratory, planning to fund it himself. However, the college administration declined his request, reportedly stating that Williams was "a college, not a technical school."[9] Remsen left Williams College for Johns Hopkins University in 1876, where he went on to establish the *American Chemical Journal* and laid the foundation for modern chemical education in the United States.

In Germany, by contrast, the Humboldtian model of higher education, attributed to the German philosopher and education official Wilhelm von Humboldt, promoted the integration of research and teaching.[10] The model encouraged the advanced, specialised study of different fields, enabling German universities to become not just transmitters of knowledge, but also creators of it. The University of Berlin (now Humboldt University of Berlin), which Humboldt helped establish, was one of the first institutions to embody this philosophy. Specialised research centres became a hallmark of German universities, notably influencing fields such as chemistry, physics, and medicine.

Building a skilled workforce for an industrialising nation

In the second half of the nineteenth century, American universities gradually adapted to evolving local needs, shifting from basic vocational training to more advanced scientific and technical education. Although they were not yet global leaders in scientific research during this period, universities played a crucial role in America's industrialisation by training skilled professionals to meet the demands of a rapidly growing economy.

The decades after the Civil War were marked by unprecedented economic growth. One of the most significant developments was the expansion of the railroad network and the industries it supported, such as steel and coal. Railroads became the arteries of the American economy, facilitating commerce on a national scale and integrating previously isolated regions into a single market. Electrification began transforming American cities. This period also saw the rise of large firms in new, fast-growing industries, including Standard Oil, AT&T, and General Electric (as we detail later in Section 7.3).

The rapid growth of industries created an urgent need for technically trained people who could design, operate, and improve complex systems. American universities responded by expanding graduate programs and forging close links with industry. For example, the steel industry needed metallurgists to refine production processes and improve product quality. Institutions like the Colorado School of Mines specialised in metallurgy and materials science, providing students with practical skills for immediate use in industry.

From the 1890s onward, university–industry collaborations focused on ensuring that universities provided graduates with the appropriate skills and qualifications. Corporations helped shape curricula and training programs to align them with industry needs. Cooperative education programs such as those at Northeastern and Drexel universities rotated students between classroom instruction and industrial placements, ensuring they were not only well versed in theory but also gained hands-on experience. Universities tailored their curricula to the needs of their local economies. Mining districts emphasised metallurgy and geological engineering, textile centres stressed mechanical design and dyes, and rail hubs emphasised civil and electrical engineering.

Founded in 1861, the Massachusetts Institute of Technology (MIT) emerged from William Barton Rogers's effort to create an independent university that served the needs of a rapidly industrialising United States. MIT launched the first U.S. electrical engineering curriculum in 1882.[11] Early courses blended mathematics (algebra, calculus, and differential equations) with theoretical electricity, mechanical design, and extensive laboratory work. Charles Cross built laboratories for electrical and heat measurements, encouraging precision and hands-on experimentation. These programmes focused on applying scientific principles in practice. The University of Oklahoma added petroleum-focused engineering courses in 1916.[12] Its first petroleum-focused degree, then called engineering geology, was awarded in 1919. The School of Petroleum Engineering was established in 1924.

Early petroleum courses combined mechanical, electrical and chemical engineering with soil chemistry and geology to meet industry needs.

The mining of precious metals helped transform Colorado into an urbanised, industrial state, spurring the development of railroads, smelters and heavy industry. The Colorado School of Mines traces its origins to 1873, when it was opened under the Episcopal Church; it became a territorial institution in 1874 and joined the state system after Colorado attained statehood in 1876.[13] Early curricula included chemistry, metallurgy, mineralogy, mining engineering, geology, botany, mathematics, and drawing. The school integrated theory and practice by scheduling lectures in the morning and laboratory work in assaying and chemical analysis in the afternoon. The Stratton Assay Laboratory, completed in 1900, gave each student a furnace and assay station, enabling undergraduates to roast ores and analyse metals. By 1906, Mines offered two four-year degrees (Engineer of Mines and Metallurgical Engineer), and seniors undertook a six-week "Senior Trip" visiting mines, mills, and smelters.

Founded in 1899 at the heart of North Carolina's mill belt, North Carolina State's School of Textiles was one of the first U.S. institutions purpose-built for industry. By the 1930s, its curriculum paired organic chemistry and fibre physics with dye labs and pilot looms, enabling students to tackle real problems such as colour fading, yarn breakage, and shrink resistance. The program's hallmark was experiential learning: undergraduates logged hours in campus dye houses and finishing rooms before confronting full-scale operations during summer placements.

The expansion of higher education in science and engineering was buttressed by reforms such as the Morrill Acts of 1862 and 1890. During the Civil War, Congress passed the Morrill Act of 1862, granting federal aid to several states for founding colleges of agriculture and mechanic arts. The Act of 1890 expanded this model to the former Confederate states. State legislatures and existing colleges embraced the moment by adding departments of agriculture and engineering to their programs.

The Morrill Acts transformed engineering education in the United States. Within fifty years of the passage of the Morrill Act, the United States had managed to rapidly increase its stock of skilled human capital to levels comparable with Western European countries. From four engineering schools in 1860, the number increased to seventeen by 1870 and to eighty-five by 1880. By 1917, there were 126 engineering schools of college grade in the United States.[14] The annual number of graduates in engineering tripled from around 300 in 1870 to 866 by 1880. By 1911, the United States was graduating around ten times as many engineers annually.[15] In total, 55,000 American degree holders in engineering were produced between 1870 and 1915. For comparison, Germany granted 1,800 engineering degrees per year in 1911 and produced 14,215 degree holders by 1915.

Charged with spreading "useful" knowledge, land-grant colleges applied scientific knowledge to address practical problems faced by rural communities.[16] At the University of Minnesota, plant pathology research in the early 1900s yielded rust-resistant wheat varieties that stabilised grain production across the Great Plains. In Alabama, Tuskegee's George Washington Carver promoted crop rotation and soil-conservation practices that restored exhausted cotton land. Another important example is Stephen Moulton Babcock's butterfat test, developed in 1890 at the Wisconsin Agricultural Experiment Station. Babcock devised a simple, low-cost assay—sulfuric acid plus a hand-cranked centrifuge—that accurately measured milk-fat content. Within five years, it had become a national standard, catalysing rapid improvements in butter and cheese production. Importantly, this also facilitated industrial-scale production because milk from multiple dairy farms could be combined and processed together.

After the Civil War, American universities pivoted from purely classical instruction to hands-on training calibrated to industrial demand. By training a generation of engineers and technicians, universities became a fundamental engine of economic transformation. These institutions had not as yet climbed to the frontiers of science: MIT, the Colorado School of Mines, and NC State did not yet aspire to publish in the "pure" sciences; they aimed to supply electrical engineers for General Electric, mining specialists for Anaconda, and textile chemists for Burlington Industries.

The turn toward research

Although nineteenth-century American universities were not at the forefront of scientific research, the seeds of their future research capabilities were planted during this period. In the late nineteenth and early twentieth centuries, a select few American universities underwent significant transformations to become research-oriented institutions. Johns Hopkins University, under the leadership of Daniel Coit Gilman, pioneered this shift by establishing faculty-led research and graduate education as central to its mission, setting a new standard that influenced other institutions. Cornell University, led by its first president, Andrew Dickson White, expanded beyond its land-grant roots by investing in research facilities and attracting top scholars, reinforcing its mission to advance knowledge. Harvard University, under Charles W. Eliot, restructured to include graduate education and a strong emphasis on research. MIT, Yale, and Chicago followed by expanding graduate programs and research initiatives.[17]

Several forces propelled these changes. First, as American universities expanded their graduate programs, demand for competent teachers who were experts in their fields grew as well. Many leading American universities also started emulating the German model of higher education, which combined teaching with research. Reinforcing this cultural shift was the migration of leading scientists from Europe. The influx brought advanced knowledge, research methods, and a commitment to scientific inquiry. German-born physiologist Jacques Loeb moved to the United States in 1891. His pioneering research on tropisms and artificial parthenogenesis at the University of Chicago and the Rockefeller Institute helped establish the United States as a centre for experimental biology. Others, such as Hermann von Helmholtz, influenced American science from afar by providing training for study abroad students such as Henry Rowland, who would later be appointed professor of physics at Johns Hopkins.[18]

Funding for a broader, multifaceted curriculum that could accommodate advanced instruction, including some research, came from students and donors. At the turn of the twentieth century, federal support for scientific research in the United States was minimal, accounting for only 4–7 per cent of university revenue between 1909 and 1939, according to data from the Biennial Survey of Education by the Department of Education.[19] This limited federal support made universities reliant on state funding, which provided around 20–30 per cent of their revenue, student fees, and contributions from industry and philanthropic foundations.

Universities that reformed their teaching, offering more advanced and specialised instruction, drew larger numbers of students and secured greater resources. At Harvard, President Charles Eliot introduced an elective system that allowed undergraduates to choose their courses. The university's graduate and professional schools expanded. Between 1889 and 1891, the Lawrence Scientific School was partly absorbed into a newly established graduate school, and the business school followed in 1908. These institutional changes were matched by a shift in pedagogy. By 1880, rote recitations had largely given way to lectures and discussions.

These reforms were well received by the market. Urquiola reports that Harvard's enrolments increased by 66 per cent in the 1880s and 89 per cent in the 1890s. These were the highest growth rates among all U.S. colleges, with the exception of Cornell and Princeton. This growth enabled selectivity in admissions, which Harvard and Columbia were the first to implement, soon followed by others. A virtuous circle had started, with the best teachers and peers attracting large numbers of high-quality students, who subsequently donated to their alma mater. As Urquiola puts it: the "reforms procured minds and money, which allowed them [the research universities] to procure more of each."[20] During Eliot's four-decade presidency, Harvard's faculty grew from about sixty to six hundred, and "major scholars began to be more than an occasional fluke."[21]

The turn toward research by a select number of universities was facilitated by philanthropy. In 1865, Ezra Cornell, who had made a fortune with the commercial application of the telegraph, donated half a million dollars to Cornell University, which was among the first universities to implement teaching reforms. In 1874, the recently deceased Johns Hopkins, a wealthy investor in railroad companies, donated seven million dollars, the largest philanthropic gift up to that time, to the establishment of Johns Hopkins University. Influenced by the German ideal, Johns Hopkins became the first research university in the United States—a "Göttingen in Baltimore." Philanthropists like Andrew Carnegie and the Rockefeller Foundation provided significant support, especially in areas of basic research and medical sciences.[22]

In 1902, Andrew Carnegie endowed $10 million to establish the Carnegie Institution of Washington (now Carnegie Institution for Science). Carnegie envisioned an institution dedicated to fundamental, long-term research, allowing scientists the freedom to pursue innovative ideas without immediate practical applications. This commitment led to groundbreaking discoveries, including Edwin Hubble's work at the Mount Wilson Observatory, which revolutionised the understanding of the universe and laid the foundation for modern cosmology, as well as Thomas Hunt Morgan's pioneering research in genetics done at Columbia University.[23]

The Rockefeller family played an important role in advancing scientific research. In addition to its support for founding the University of Chicago as a research-oriented university, it was especially influential for biomedical research. Established in 1901, the Rockefeller Institute for Medical Research (now Rockefeller University) was the first American institution dedicated solely to biomedical research, and it quickly became a leader in the field. Among its notable contributions were the identification of the yellow fever virus by Hideyo Noguchi in 1918 and Peyton Rous's discovery in 1911 that viruses can cause cancer (a finding that later earned him a Nobel Prize). In the 1940s, Rockefeller researchers, led by Oswald Avery, also identified DNA as the molecule responsible for heredity, a discovery that reshaped the fields of genetics and molecular biology.[24]

By the early twentieth century, the combined impact of structural reforms in leading universities had driven a significant increase in both the quantity and quality of American research. Between 1870 and 1915, publications in mathematics, physics, and chemistry rose sharply, with American contributions to prestigious foreign journals doubling or more.[25] The number of doctorates awarded in these disciplines also grew, while fewer American students needed to study abroad, signalling that American science was beginning to catch up with Europe. Up until 1897, Americans had earned a mere 56 PhDs in mathematics, 73 in physics, and 101 in chemistry. By 1915, these numbers had increased 2.6-fold (to 149), 3.4-fold (to 252), and 4.1-fold (to 419), respectively.[26]

The rise of corporate giants

The rapid growth of the American economy following the Civil War and the integration of its vast markets thanks to the telegraph and the railroads profoundly transformed the industrial structure of the nation. Between 1870 and 1913, its GDP grew 5.3 times and 2.1 times on a per capita basis. On the eve of World War I, Americans were slightly richer than the richest Western Europe country (Great Britain), which had a per capita GDP of $4,921 compared to the United States' $5,301.[27] Raw steel output per capita rose seventy-five times between 1870 and 1900. Value added in manufacturing grew 6.6 times during this period.[28] Local workshops and family-run enterprises gave way to giant corporations with integrated operations. In sectors such as steel, transportation, mining, and finance, nineteenth-century America developed novel mechanisms for coordinating operations and managing risk.[29]

No industry captured the late nineteenth century ethos of "bigger, faster, cheaper" better than steel. And no one personified this more than Andrew

Carnegie, whose mills were producing more steel than all of Britain by 1900.[30] Steel was the critical material for railroads, bridges, machinery, and later skyscrapers, but in the 1860s, it was expensive and scarce. Carnegie changed that by fostering technical and organisational innovation. His company pursued the newest processes, such as the Bessemer converter, and later, the open-hearth furnace, to mass-produce steel at a fraction of the old cost. Just as importantly, Carnegie pioneered continuous productivity improvements on an unprecedented scale. In 1875, when Carnegie opened his first plant (the Edgar Thomson Steel Works, named for a major railroad client), steel rails cost about $100 per ton. By the 1890s, the price had plummeted to about $18 per ton. Carnegie instituted rigorous cost accounting and production targets, insisting that each plant's performance be quantitatively measured so that the best methods could be identified and replicated.

Like many other American firms at that time, Carnegie Steel grew by importing advanced technologies from Europe and by refining them through experimentation. Carnegie's initial breakthrough came with the adoption of the Bessemer process, a method for producing steel by oxidising impurities from molten iron (see Chapter 6). Originally developed and patented in Britain in 1856, the process was brought to the United States by Alexander Lyman Holley. Carnegie saw its potential and commissioned Holley to build the Edgar Thomson Steel Works in 1875, which later became part of Carnegie Steel. In 1886, Carnegie also adopted the open-hearth furnace process at Homestead Steel Works, then the largest steel mill in the world. Developed in Europe by German-British engineer Carl Wilhelm Siemens and French engineer Pierre-Émile Martin, the Siemens–Martin process allowed for more controlled and flexible steelmaking. Homestead also moved increasingly toward continuous production by installing advanced material-handling systems such as overhead cranes, hoists, charging machines, and rail-mounted buggies.

Foreign technology was not, however, the only source of competitive advantage for Carnegie. Other steel mills in the United States had adopted the Bessemer process and the open-hearth furnace. However, larger scale meant that the benefits of new production technology and efficiency improvements were greater. Companies tend to have stronger incentives to develop innovations, especially process innovations, when they are larger, because their R&D costs can be spread over a greater level of output.[31] Thus, while experimentation with furnace design and metallurgical processes may have been a good idea for Carnegie, it may not have been economical for a smaller steel company.

Another sector in which foreign science and technology were of paramount importance was the pharmaceutical industry. Before 1920, American companies were responsible for only a few of the new drugs introduced to the market. The foundational discoveries in bacteriology, immunology, and pharmacology came largely from Germany and France. American firms, lacking an indigenous scientific infrastructure, relied heavily on European journals, visiting scientists, and imported methods.

Parke-Davis, founded in 1866 in Detroit, initially focused on traditional formulations: extracts, pills, and elixirs.[32] However, under the leadership of George S. Davis, the firm aggressively sought to modernise. Davis spearheaded expeditions to remote regions to discover medicinal plants and hired trained scientists, often from the University of Michigan. Its initial successes were largely driven by innovations in manufacturing and quality control. At a time when medicinal extracts varied wildly in strength and reliability, Davis recognised the urgent need for consistency and safety in drug formulations. In 1879, Parke-Davis introduced the first chemically standardised medicinal drug. By 1883, the company had developed and marketed a list of twenty "normal liquids," each standardised through chemical assays. In 1897, it pioneered physiological standardisation by testing the effects of drugs on animals. These methods helped ensure that patients received predictable and safe dosages, promoting confidence in mass-produced medicines. Another important innovation was the practice, initiated in 1886, of using lot numbers on the labels of each product. This practice allowed Parke-Davis to trace the entire production history of each product and ingredient, including the source and testing. This type of quality control, decades ahead of regulatory requirements, positioned Parke-Davis as a leader in pharmaceutical quality assurance.

A key milestone in the company's history was the decision in 1895 to produce diphtheria antitoxin, just a year after it had been developed in Europe. Recognising the potential of the antitoxin, Parke-Davis recruited two scientists from the University of Michigan to replicate and enhance the German process, thereby establishing the first commercial biological laboratory in the United States. Parke-Davis went on to build close ties with the University of Michigan, supporting numerous graduates working on projects of common interest, and then hiring them when they completed their studies.[33] A second example of imported technology was the collaboration with Japanese chemist Jokichi Takamine, who brought a novel enzyme called Taka-Diastase to Parke-Davis in the 1890s. Davis, recognising its potential as a digestive aid, successfully marketed it in 1895. This was one of the first examples of trans-Pacific pharmaceutical collaboration. Takamine would later go on to isolate adrenaline, another breakthrough that Parke-Davis refined and commercialised. By the turn of the twentieth century, Parke-Davis had established itself as one of the most advanced and respected pharmaceutical companies in the world.

Parallel to the stories of steel and medicine was the story of capital. By the turn of the twentieth century, finance had emerged as the great enabler and organiser of industry, embodied in figures like John Pierpont Morgan.[34] During the frenetic growth of the 1870s and 1880s, many industries (railroads especially) had overbuilt and suffered crashes like the Panic of 1873 and 1893. Morgan made his mark by swooping in to reorganise bankrupt railroads — a process so common it gained a nickname, "Morganization." He would broker peace among warring railroad tycoons, rationalise their routes to reduce competition, and in return often secure banking control or board seats.[35] By the 1890s, Morgan had used this approach to control a significant share of railroad mileage. Morgan's crowning act of industrial finance, however, was in manufacturing. In 1901, as noted, he assembled United States Steel Corporation by merging Carnegie Steel with a host of other steel companies. The deal created a corporation with a capitalisation of $1.4 billion (more than twice the U.S. federal budget that year, which amounted to $588 million[36]) and a workforce of 168,000.[37] The new U.S. Steel combined an array of subsidiaries from mines to mills to distribution, effectively controlling the processes by which steel was made, and the finished steel products all under one corporate roof. The formation of U.S. Steel marked the apogee of the trust-building era, where many industries saw similar consolidations: Standard Oil, American Tobacco, General Electric, and International Harvester.

Breaking up the giants: The birth of U.S. antitrust policy

Men like John D. Rockefeller, Andrew Carnegie, and James B. Duke became the faces of unprecedented industrial consolidation. Rockefeller's Standard Oil, for example, started the 1870s controlling only a modest share of U.S. oil refining, but through acquisitions and relentless expansion by 1879 it commanded over 90 per cent of the nation's refining capacity.[38] In tobacco, James B. Duke similarly swept up competitors: after gaining control of a new cigarette-making machine, Duke's American Tobacco Company gobbled up almost all major tobacco firms, controlling four-fifths of the U.S. tobacco market by 1906. These behemoths, known colloquially as "trusts," achieved dominance not through innovation but through acquisitions, economies of scale, and anticompetitive tactics.

The rise of trusts provoked a fierce public reaction. The clamour for government to rein in the trusts culminated in the U.S. Congress passing the Sherman Antitrust Act in 1890, which outlawed "every contract, combination . . . or conspiracy in restraint of trade" and any monopolisation or attempted monopolisation of interstate commerce.[39] Notably, nothing in the law spoke of innovation or technological progress; its target was market dominance.

While in the 1890s enforcement was weak, the tide turned with Theodore Roosevelt's election to the presidency in 1901. In rhetoric, he distinguished between "good" trusts and "bad" trusts, arguing that he was not against bigness per se, only against corporations that abused their dominance at the expense of the public. In 1902, his administration launched a successful antitrust suit against Northern Securities Company, a railroad holding company recently put together by J. P. Morgan and James J. Hill. Roosevelt's administration brought around forty antitrust cases over seven years, targeting beef, oil, tobacco, and other monopolies, but he also struck deals with firms he deemed well behaved.

Roosevelt's successor, William Howard Taft, proved even more zealous in enforcing antitrust statutes, bringing ninety-nine antitrust suits.[40] Taft's tenure at the office also saw the conclusion of two high-profile suits brought by his predecessor against Standard Oil and American Tobacco. In May 1911, the Supreme Court ruled unanimously against John Rockefeller, notwithstanding Standard Oil's argument that it had introduced important innovations in refining, such as the Frasch-Burton process, which improved the production of kerosene from high-sulphur crude oil.[41] In 1912, the courts also ruled that DuPont had to split its gunpowder business into three companies. In 1911, GE entered into a consent decree regulating its incandescent bulb pricing. Importantly, however, the decree allowed patent holders to control pricing and distribution by their licencees. In a later ruling in 1926, the Supreme Court reiterated its conclusion that fixing the prices at which direct licencees (e.g., Westinghouse) sold their products was a condition "normally and reasonably adapted to secure pecuniary reward for the patentee's monopoly."[42]

Crucially, these early antitrust efforts were overwhelmingly focused on size, market structure, and the competitive process, rather than the implications for corporate innovation: the trusts were not accused of stifling technological progress. On the contrary, Standard Oil argued that it had innovated vigorously. Frederic Scherer cites a brief in which Standard Oil's lawyers claimed that "[Standard Oil] have been unremitting in their efforts to improve the processes of refining, to diversify the useful by-products to be obtained from the refining of petroleum and to introduce them into general use, [. . . .] They have made great efforts to solve the problem of refining refractory oils and through the success of these efforts they have been able to utilise to their great advantage oils that otherwise were useless except for fuel purposes."[43]

Antitrust was, in this sense, a form of economic checks and balances, a way to prevent private power from becoming so concentrated that it could dictate terms to society. Supreme Court Justice Louis Brandeis distilled the sentiment with his famous distrust of "the curse of bigness."[44] In Brandeis's view, giant corporations not only squeezed out smaller rivals but also amassed undue political influence and bred inequality, ultimately threatening democracy. Brandesian views still resonate in the American antitrust culture: mere market dominance and the potential to "drive honest men from business" remains a red flag.

With growth through acquisitions impeded by antitrust pressure, some behemoths began to view innovation as a means of entering new markets. Innovation and patents could also provide some defence against antitrust enforcement. In the cellophane case against DuPont, the district court noted in its 1953 judgment that

> [D]u Pont's position is the result of research, business skill and competitive activity. [. . .] The record reflects not the dead hand of monopoly but rapidly declining prices, expanding production, intense competition stimulated by creative research, the development of new products and uses and other benefits of a free economy.[45]

Independent inventors and the market for technology

While late-nineteenth-century America witnessed the rise of powerful corporate giants, it also remained a fertile ground for independent inventors.

These Smithian entrepreneurs, working in workshops or modest labs, fuelled a dynamic market for technology. Helped by an accessible U.S. patent system and supported by capable intermediaries, inventors thrived even in the shadow of larger enterprises, contributing to the nation's ascent as an innovator.

Many opted to license or sell patents to established firms. By the late 1800s, patent transfers had become a defining feature of the American innovation landscape. According to Naomi Lamoreaux and Kenneth Sokoloff, the share of patents by inventors unaffiliated with firms peaked at 45 per cent in 1890, dropping thereafter to 22 per cent in 1910.[46] Over one-third of newly issued patents, and more than 60 per cent in some industries, were transferred to third parties. This created a mutually beneficial system: inventors focused on developing ideas and designs, while corporations provided manufacturing expertise, supply chains, and access to markets. At the centre of this exchange stood a patent system that was open, and affordable. U.S. law granted inventors exclusive rights quickly and at low cost, allowing individuals of modest means to transform inventions into tradable assets. This stood in stark contrast to Europe, where steep fees and complex patent application processes often stifled innovation at the outset.

From the early years of the Republic, the American patent regime was designed to democratise innovation. Guided by the constitutional mandate to "promote the Progress of Science and useful Arts," the United States adopted a system that lowered entry barriers and made intellectual property accessible to nonelites.[47] This accessibility fostered a culture of grassroots innovation. Thousands of mechanics, farmers, and tinkerers patented improvements to everyday machinery, from ploughs to cotton gins, embedding innovation in the routines of daily production. A market for technology grew, complete with patent agents, brokers, and attorneys who connected inventors with manufacturers or investors, facilitating deals that brought inventions to scale.[48]

Markets for technology fostered specialisation in inventive activity across two dimensions.[49] First, among individuals, a class of highly productive inventors emerged. From the first third of the nineteenth century to the last third, the fraction of patents produced by inventors with ten or more patents over their careers rose from less than 5 per cent to between 25 and 36 per cent. These highly productive inventors were also the ones most active in technology markets, either selling or licensing their patents to other firms or individuals.

Second, specialisation increased across organisations. Individual inventors coexisted and often collaborated with the industrial giants that arose after the Civil War. While corporations like Standard Oil or U.S. Steel thrived on scale, small inventors carved out specialised niches. If someone invented a better valve or loom attachment, the American patent system allowed them to secure protection affordably, then sell or license the invention to larger firms or regional manufacturers.[50]

Highly productive inventors exhibited what Zorina Khan and Kenneth Sokoloff term "contractual mobility": the propensity not to be attached to any specific firm or industry but instead to sell different patents to different buyers. A typical example was that of Richard Gatling, who received many patents for inventions ranging from agricultural machinery (like a rice-sowing machine, a wheat drill, a hemp-breaking machine, and a motor-driven plough) to his famous Gatling gun, over a career spanning sixty years. Gatling was highly entrepreneurial. He was never attached to any single firm for very long, and he relied largely on the sale or licensing of his patents to a wide array of different manufacturers to extract the returns to his efforts.[51]

Licensing and patent transfers allowed new technologies to reach markets through firms with the means to mass-produce them. In this way, independent inventors often acted as de facto R&D arms for larger companies, earning royalties or lump-sum payments for innovations, because few incumbents had in-house invention capability. Instead, in this DOIL, they relied upon independent inventors, including those from the ranks of their own employees.

Indeed, a major focus for companies was to evaluate and acquire external inventions. In 1908, commenting on the responsibilities of T. D. Lockwood, the longtime head of AT&T's patent department, the firm's CEO Theodore Vail noted that

> Mr. Lockwood's duties were, first to examine every patent that was issued [. . .] connected with the telephone or electricity to see whether it had any bearing on our business, and if so we tried to get some rights under it and possession of it. Next he was to examine all the devices in the carrying on of the business. [. . .] Of course new devices in the new business were all the time occurring to the people. Those were submitted to us from our licensees, and Mr. Lockwood would examine them as to the patentability and as to the value, and whether they had been gone over before, and all that sort of thing.[52]

Clearly, the most important responsibility of AT&T's patent department was not to generate inventions, patentable or otherwise. It was to gather information on technology developments, evaluate them for relevance to telephony, and if necessary, acquire those technologies. Acquiring patents had become a strategic priority for corporations. Firms that missed key inventions risked falling behind, especially in fast-moving sectors such as communications. Intellectual property, in other words, became as central to industrial strategy as access to raw materials.

In the late nineteenth century, this two-sided marketplace, with independent inventors on one side and enterprises on the other, had reached a significant scale. Between a fifth and a third of patents changed hands annually, sustaining a characteristically American system of invention. To facilitate this marketplace, patent attorneys, brokers, and agents linked inventors to corporate buyers. Private syndicates and early "angel" backers funded those without manufacturing capabilities. These early financial mechanisms foreshadowed modern venture capital by giving proven inventors a financial runway and by normalising the notion that technological risk could be priced and shared.

The system was not without flaws. Patent disputes were common, and "patent wars" occasionally erupted, especially in industries like sewing machines and farm equipment. The system also tended to favour quick patents on incremental tweaks. Yet overall, the system gave small players a genuine opportunity to profit from their ingenuity and contribute to a broader wave of industrial expansion.

Of course, not all inventors during this period took the Smithian route and sold their inventions to others. As we saw in Chapter 6, many took the Schumpeterian route and leveraged their patents to attract risk capital and establish their own companies. For instance, in the 1840s, Ezra Cornell and Samuel Morse helped commercialise telegraph technology. Their partnership culminated in 1851 with the formation of Western Union, through the consolidation of competing telegraph firms. Thomas Edison used his patents on electric lighting and power systems to secure investor backing, founding the Edison General Electric Company in 1889, which merged in 1892 to become General Electric. Alexander Graham Bell's telephone invention gave rise to the Bell Telephone Company in 1877, which eventually evolved into AT&T. In 1888, Charles Martin Hall's innovation in aluminium production, the Hall–Héroult process, enabled him to attract risk capital and establish the Pittsburgh Reduction Company, later renamed Alcoa in 1907.

Although individual inventors flourished during the second half of the nineteenth century, their decline had begun by the turn of the century. As documented by Lamoreaux and Sokoloff, the share of inventors unaffiliated with firms dropped by half from 45 per cent in 1890 to 22 per cent in 1910. In the Northeast, inventors often became employees of large firms, while in the Midwest, they more frequently established their own firms.[53]

Contributing to the decline of independent inventors was the shift towards more complex, capital-intensive innovations in sectors such as chemicals and electricity. Nevertheless, independent inventors still accounted for over half of U.S. patents by 1930, significantly outpacing corporations.[54] Corporations maintained links with independents by purchasing patents to complement in-house R&D.

To summarise, the interplay between an accessible patent system, independent inventors, and large manufacturers gave the United States a powerful advantage during the late nineteenth and early twentieth centuries. While corporate trusts consolidated power, small-scale innovators continued to develop and license technologies. This synergy powered sectors such as sewing machines, reaping equipment, and telegraphy, where the accumulation of incremental improvements led to rapid technological advancement.

That blend of grassroots inventiveness and industrial scale adoption still runs through American innovation. Today's fights over "patent trolls" and pharmaceutical patents echo an older tension: how to protect the lone inventor's access to markets while safeguarding R&D.

Chapter takeaways

The early shortcomings of American universities in research did not significantly hinder the development of American industries during the nineteenth and early twentieth centuries. This was largely because America grew rich before it became a scientific and technological leader. American industries leveraged European technologies and innovations, combined with the country's vast domestic market, to become the dominant global industrial power by the early twentieth century. What the United States lacked in scientific depth, it compensated for with an unusually open patent system. Low filing fees and reliable courts let independent tinkerers monetise their ideas through licensing or sale, acting as crucial suppliers of incremental improvements for capital-rich corporations. American firms focused primarily on improving efficiency, scaling production, and capitalising on their large consumer base, which allowed them to grow rapidly without needing cutting-edge scientific research.

For example, industries like steel, textiles, and railroads borrowed heavily from European innovations, particularly from the United Kingdom and Germany. This allowed the United States to industrialise quickly without needing to pioneer new technologies. It was not until the early twentieth century, as America reached the technological frontier, that companies recognised the need for advanced scientific knowledge to drive further innovation.

Around the turn of the century, however, American universities absorbed the Humboldtian ideal of merging teaching with inquiry and, boosted by waves of émigré scholars, gradually built research capacity at institutions such as Johns Hopkins, Harvard, Illinois, Berkeley, Wisconsin, and the University of Chicago. Also, mounting international competition and the growing technical complexity of electricity, chemicals, and telecommunications convinced firms that organisational scale alone could no longer secure leadership. Companies like AT&T and General Electric responded by founding in-house laboratories, consciously emulating the German dye firms that had fused chemistry with industrial production decades earlier.

By World War I, these trends—a large and integrated domestic market, vocational yet increasingly research-oriented universities, a liquid market for intellectual property, and nascent corporate labs—had created the institutional scaffold for what would become the American scientific-industrial complex. The United States was now equipped not merely to import technologies, but also to generate, absorb, and continuously renew science-based innovation on its own soil.

8
The Rise of Industrial Research in America

Introduction

The opening decades of the twentieth century marked the beginning of a fundamental transformation in how the American economy organised innovation. In the century prior, the United States divided the innovation supply chain between Smithian inventors who originated new ideas and incumbent firms that licensed inventions from markets for technology to commercialise them. Many of the great inventors of this era such as Edison, Tesla, and DeForest would raise the seed funding for their ventures through patent sales.

As discussed in Chapter 7, American businesses in the nineteenth century grew primarily by importing technology from Europe or refining it via trial and error. Andrew Carnegie (covered in Chapter 7), who built his fortune by licensing the Bessemer process for steel production from Britain, is a poster-child of this early model. This success, however, was largely driven by practical improvements and mass production efficiencies rather than scientific advances per se. Over four decades after the turn of the century, this decentralised, market-mediated division of innovative labour was gradually replaced by one where scientific research, technology development and commercialisation were consolidated within corporate laboratories.

The industrial research lab was an "institutional innovation in which the scientific research agenda is largely shaped by technologies."[1] Industrial scientists were tasked with improving existing technologies and inventing new ones. This shift shaped science to respond better to the needs and goals of the economy. In turn, science helped industrial societies achieve consistent productivity growth during this period. As we show in Chapter 10, around 80 per cent of patenting firms in America had established a research laboratory by 1960, completing the paradigm shift. Initially, corporate labs focused on quality control and solving operational problems rather than conducting fundamental research. Early corporate researchers, such as Charles Dudley at the Pennsylvania Railroad Company, primarily tested materials like iron and steel for rails. Over time, these labs began to attract renowned scientists, including future Nobel Laureates Irving Langmuir of GE (Chemistry, 1932) and Clinton Davisson of AT&T (Physics, 1937), and gradually shifted towards more foundational scientific research.

This chapter explains the three economic forces that precipitated this transformation: First, inventions increasingly relied on science. Second, some American firms had reached the technological frontier, having exhausted the opportunities for innovation through trial and error and the importation of technologies from Europe. Third, industrially relevant science from universities was inadequate. The confluence of these forces encouraged American firms that were at the technological frontier to produce for themselves the scientific knowledge they could not obtain from public sources.[2]

Scientific foundations of early-twentieth-century innovation

As we recounted in the latter parts of Chapter 6, the beginning of the twentieth century was marked by a burst of scientific advances in chemistry and physics and a greater reliance by industry on these new discoveries. The electrification of industrial economies was well underway, with arc lighting (Yablochkov candles) illuminating Parisian streets as early as 1878 and the Edison incandescent lightbulb being invented the following year. Edison's observation of thermionic emissions in lightbulbs inspired a theoretical explanation by Owen Richardson in 1901, paving the way for vacuum tube electronics. In the same year, Guglielmo Marconi demonstrated the first transatlantic wireless communication between Newfoundland, Canada, and Cornwall, England. Dynamos and alternators to power the new appliances and factories using electricity, built on laws of electromagnetism developed decades earlier by James Clerk Maxwell and Heinrich Hertz, also appeared. Advances in chemistry were equally rapid. After William Perkin's discovery of synthetic dyes in 1856, organic chemists had synthesised cures for fevers and headaches (Aspirin, 1897) and nitrogen fertilisers (Haber-Bosch process, 1910) to replace the dwindling supply of Chilean guano. Newly developed processing techniques for cellulosic fibres led to rayon (1884), celluloid (1869), and cellophane (1908). Steady improvements in hydrocracking since the 1910s led to the efficient refinement of petrochemicals, fuelling the rapidly improving internal combustion engines of the day and providing feedstock for the impending plastics revolution (neoprene, nylon, polyester) in the 1930s. These were nothing if not the systematic application of science to the problems of economic production.

Patent data show the growing dependence of inventions on science. Figure 8.1 shows that patents in the two decades preceding World War I rarely cited the scientific literature. The following period, between 1920 and 1940, on the other hand, showed a marked increase in citations to science, especially by breakthrough patents.[3] Breakthrough chemical patents, for instance, were up to three times more likely to cite a scientific article than nonbreakthrough ones, while breakthrough communication patents (telephone, radio, and vacuum tube) were more than seven times more likely to do so than nonbreakthrough ones.

American firms were often at the forefront of these innovations, but they faced fierce, science-based competition across the Atlantic. GE's control over electric lighting in the 1890s was based on the carbon-filament high-vacuum incandescent variety (first invented by Thomas Edison). But German chemists such as Carl Welsbach and Walther Nernst (the 1920 Nobel Laureate in Chemistry) invented, respectively, incandescent mantels for gas lamps (a substitute product) and a glower which required no vacuum to operate and was 50 per cent more efficient. Patent rights to the Nernst glower in turn were first sold to the German firm AEG for $1 million and later to GE's rival, Westinghouse, in 1894.[4] In the case of the chemical industries, firms lagged European leaders and chose to import technology. In petrochemicals, methods for refining hydrocarbons were often licensed from European inventors. Eugene Houdry's semicontinuous catalytic cracking process, developed in 1927, was licensed by the Socony-Vacuum Oil Company and was widely diffused around the industry. In response, firms such as Standard Oil of New Jersey would develop their own technology (fluid catalytic cracking). In chemicals, DuPont, Hercules, Dow, Monsanto, and Allied would largely rely on processes from German firms for manufacturing dyes, fertilisers, fibres, and explosives from coal tar derivatives. Given that America was an industrial powerhouse and its per capita GDP was greater than that of France and Britain by World War I,[5] it may not have been obvious to the average American firm that they needed to change the way they organised innovation. Yet, those at the cutting edge felt their need for science unfulfilled as global competition intensified.

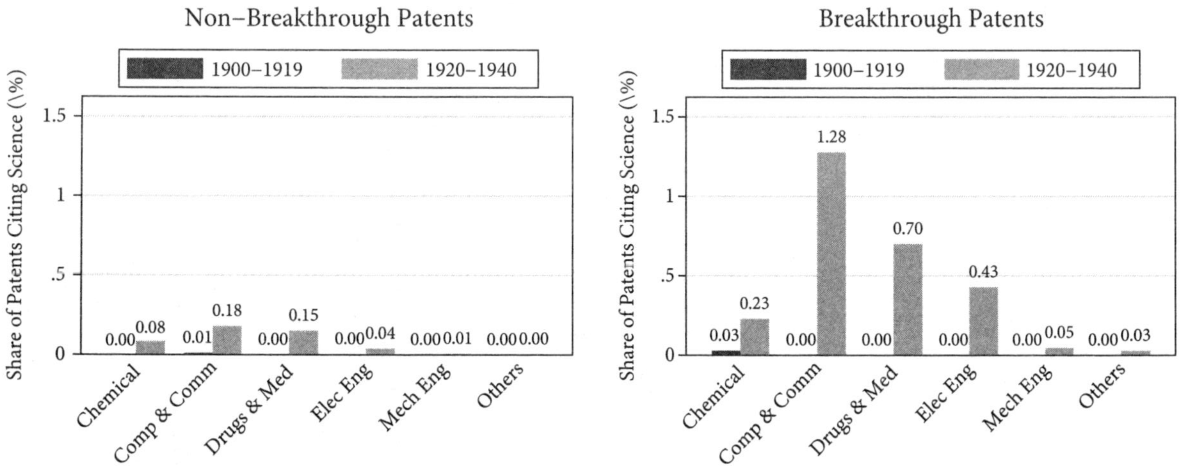

Figure 8.1 Patent Citations to Science, by Breakthrough Patent Status and Technology Category (1900–1940)

Notes: This is a reproduction of Figure 1 of Arora, Belenzon, Kosenko, Yafeh, and Suh (2024, hereafter ABKSY).[6] The right panel plots the percentage share of "breakthrough" patents that cite scientific articles for patents issued between 1900 and 1919 and 1920 and 1940, by National Bureau of Economic Research (NBER) patent categories. The left panel plots the same for all other ("non-breakthrough") patents. Breakthrough patents are defined as those that are in the top 10 per cent of the importance measures from Kelly, Papanikolaou, Seru, and Taddy (2021)[7], where importance is calculated by dividing similarity with future patents (ten years after focal patent issuance) by similarity with past patents (five years before focal patent issuance), comparing patents granted in the same year. Scientific citation data for patents is sourced from Marx & Fuegi (2020).[8] NBER categories for patents are sourced from Hall, Jaffe, and Trajtenberg (2001).[9]

Universities did not produce relevant science

As innovation became more science-based, companies initially looked to external suppliers and specialised contract research organisations, such as the Mellon Institute. The institute, established in 1913, grew steadily in contract revenues (from $300,000 to $800,000) and in the number of sponsoring firms between 1919 and 1929. Over the same period, the number of industrial fellows sponsored by firms grew from 83 to 145. Union Carbide's contract with the institute yielded ethylene glycol, an antifreeze, which became a key product for the firm.[10] But contract research worked best for generic, well-specified problems, where contracting problems were less severe. It also required that the sponsoring firm itself possess significant scientific capabilities.[11] Contract research could complement internal research, not substitute it.

Universities were another source but were slow to provide the types of frontier knowledge in organic chemistry and electronics that firms in the electrical and chemical industries demanded. As discussed in Chapter 7, American land grant colleges such as the University of Oklahoma, the Colorado School of Mines, and NC State had traditionally developed specialities specific to industrial activity around their location. Faculty in top chemical engineering departments also often established research firms that served corporate clients, but their job was to troubleshoot engineering problems rather than to make fundamental discoveries on the natural phenomena that firms were facing. Arthur D. Little at MIT, for example, formed a successful consulting practice that catered to the petroleum industry of the time. MIT's Research Laboratory of Applied Chemistry (RLAC), under the leadership of William Walker, aggressively pursued industrial contracts throughout the 1920s. Recognising the potential for mutually beneficial relationships with industry, MIT launched an endowment fund drive in 1919, resulting in the 'Technology Plan'. The plan was designed to secure corporate financing by offering tailor-made conferences, targeted research, and access to alumni files for recruitment purposes. By 1920–1921, sponsored industrial research at MIT exceeded $100,000, and by 1930, it had risen to over $270,000.[12] These funds supported research projects that were directly relevant to industrial needs, such as chemical process optimisation, materials development, and improvement of manufacturing techniques.

As companies turned to universities for research, industry–university partnerships grew. Yet, these efforts alone were insufficient to keep pace with the rapid advancements required by industry. Though universities provided valuable research services in established domains such as hydrocracking (for petroleum refinement) and metallurgy (for steel production), they lagged in chemistry (organic and polymer) and physics (electrical engineering and electronics). This vulnerability surfaced more than once as American chemical firms relied heavily on technology imports from Europe. However, this reliance on foreign know-how was exposed as a vulnerability during World War I. After hostilities commenced, DuPont was cut off from its dyestuffs supply from Germany. The company could only resume production after it entered into a collaboration with a British company (Levinstein Ltd of Manchester) that had acquired a confiscated Hoechst plant in Britain, and engaged a consultant, Maurice Poucher, who was familiar with the dyes BASF sold in America. DuPont also had to lure away several chemists working in German companies.[13]

A similar pattern emerged in the electrical industries.[14] Much of the scientific foundation in electronics until the 1920s was provided by European institutions such as the Cavendish laboratory in Britain (Faraday, Maxwell, Thomson, Richardson, and Bragg) and German research universities (Hertz, Siemens, Hittorf, Roentgen, Wehnelt, and Braun). The British lead in electromagnetism was established early with Maxwell's equations, but it was also aided by the Royal Society and government-sponsored projects such as the construction of a global telegraph line during the nineteenth century.[15] Germany's traditional strength in chemistry also allowed for the discovery of new rare-earth substances that were applied as new vacuum tube filaments. Until World War I, American universities were well behind: They published only nine papers per year in the *Transactions of the American Institute of Electrical Engineers*, between 1920 and 1925, accounting for fewer than 10 per cent of total publications.[16] Electrical engineering departments were routinely staffed by instructors with only bachelor's degrees. Although enrolment in electrical engineering programs increased after the end of World War I, research in the field remained dominated by firms until the late 1920s. No doctorates in electrical engineering were awarded at MIT until 1910. No leading American university produced more than two electrical engineering doctorates a year until the 1930s. Two decades later, MIT alone produced thirteen per year between 1950 and 1954.

American universities, therefore, did not provide for the scientific needs of leading firms prior to World War II. Figure 8.2, which compares the focus

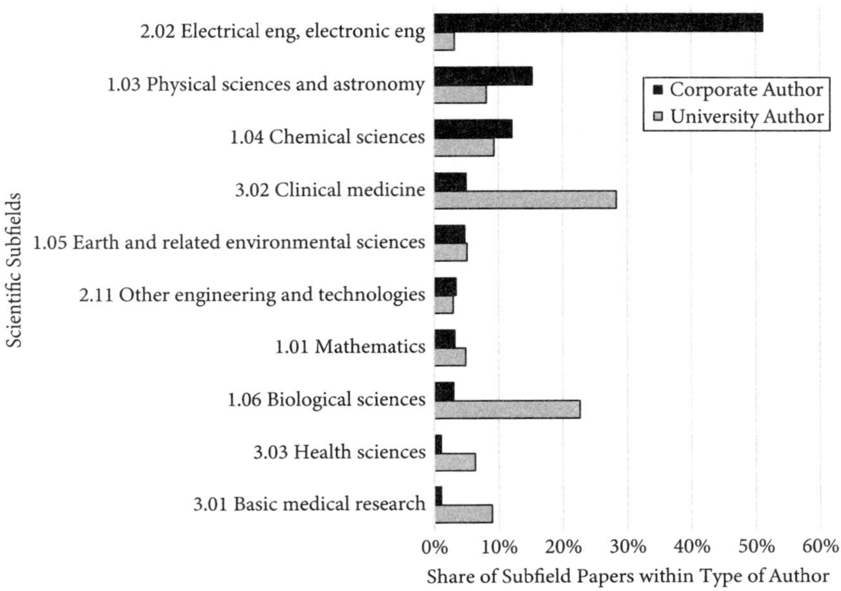

Figure 8.2 Scientific Publications by Subfield and Type of Author (1900–1940)

Notes: This is a reproduction of Figure 3 of ABKSY (2024). The black bars divide the number of corporate papers in a scientific subfield by all corporate papers. The grey bars divide the number of U.S. university papers in a scientific subfield by all U.S. university papers. Scientific subfields with at least 1,000 papers during the sample period are included in the analysis. See https://www.oecd.org/science/inno/38235147.pdf for a list of the fields of science, based on the 2002 revision (6th edition) of the Frascati Manual.

of corporate and university publications, shows that electrical engineering, physics, and chemistry account for the top three corporate scientific subjects, with electrical engineering accounting for over half of all corporate publications between 1926 and 1940. In contrast, the top three university fields are clinical medicine (28 per cent), biology (23 per cent), and chemistry (9 per cent). Comparing university and corporate papers published in the same year and the same scientific journal, we found that university papers were 76 per cent less likely to be cited by a patent than a comparable corporate paper.[17]

This suggests that university science received less attention from inventors than corporate science. This trend aligns with modern findings that academic papers are less likely than corporate papers to be cited by inventors, even for simultaneous discoveries in the life sciences.[18] While university scientists were instrumental in establishing the American Physical Society (1889 at Columbia University) and the American Chemical Society (1876 at

New York University), scientific associations for commercially relevant fields were founded by corporate scientists: the American Institute of Electrical Engineers, established in 1884, was headed by Norvin Green from Western Union. The first president of the Institute of Radio Engineers, established in 1912, was Robert Marriott from the Wireless Company of America. Similarly, the Optical Society was founded in 1916 by Peter Nutting of Kodak, while the Acoustical Society of America was founded in 1928 by Harvey Fletcher and V. O. Knudsen from Bell Telephone Laboratories.

After World War II, public support and coordination at the federal level would often direct university research towards national priorities, such as solid-state electronics and computer science, following the Sputnik shock in the 1950s. (The construction of the federal scientific establishment is explained in Chapter 9.) However, the federal infrastructure for such coordination was underdeveloped prior to 1940. The only federally supported national research organisations in the United States by 1914 were the National Bureau of Standards, the Census Bureau, and the National Advisory Committee on Aeronautics (NACA) under the Smithsonian institution. At the outbreak of World War I, the U.S. Navy created a consulting board chaired by Thomas Edison with the purpose of crowd-sourcing patents and screening them for defence purposes. The Naval Consulting Board considered innovations ranging from ordnance to torpedoes, wireless communications, and medicine. However, without congressional authority or appropriation, the organisation could not accomplish much: only 110 patents were examined, and a single patent went into production.[19]

To do better, a group of physicists, including George Ellery Hale at Caltech and Robert Millikan at the University of Chicago, lobbied the Wilson administration on behalf of the National Academies to create the National Research Council (NRC) in 1916. The NRC failed to receive federal funding and was instead supported by the Carnegie Corporation ($150,000) and the Rockefeller Foundation ($50,000). Even with a relatively late entry into the war in 1917, American scientists managed to develop submarine detection devices, such as C, T, and MT tubes, as well as chemical weapons, including lewisite. However, these achievements owed little to any coordination or planning from the federal government. In stark contrast, the Office of Scientific Research and Development (OSRD) during World War II spearheaded several national efforts to solve "big science" problems such as mass producing penicillin, developing radar, and developing the atom bomb.

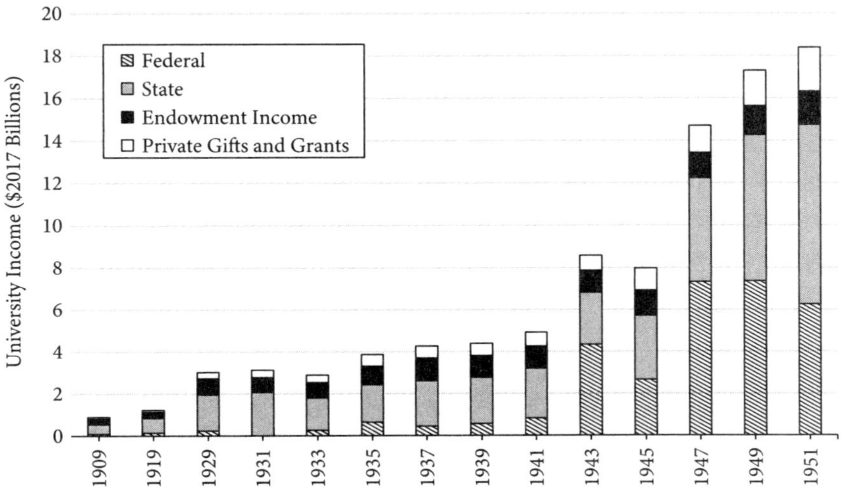

Figure 8.3 Sources of University Revenue in the United States (1909–1953)

Notes: This graph plots the sources of revenue for the institutions of higher education in the United States. Data is sourced from Snyder (1993), Table 33, and is based on the U.S. Department of Education's Annual Report of the Commissioner; Biennial Survey of Education in the United States.[20] The figure for federal funding sources in 1919–20 is included under state government funding for those years. Dollar values from 1929 onwards are deflated to 2017 using the GDP deflator from the Federal Reserve Bank of St. Louis (https://fred.stlouisfed.org); for years prior to 1929, data from David & Solar (1979) is used (https://www.measuringworth.com/datasets/usgdp/constructiongdp.php).

Unsurprisingly, federal support of academic research was paltry. As shown in Figure 8.3, universities up until World War II relied heavily on state and industry funding instead of federal funding.[21] According to the Biennial Survey of Education compiled by the Department of Education, the share of federal funding as a source of university revenue had hovered around 4–7 per cent between 1909 and 1939. The share of state funding, on the other hand, was somewhere between 20 and 30 per cent in the same period.[22] In absolute terms, university research budgets during this time paled in comparison to their corporate counterparts. For its 1938 report, the National Resources Planning Board under the National Research Council (NRC) surveyed 1,450 American colleges and universities and found that the top 150 institutions spent an average of $333 thousand per university on research.[23] The University of Chicago ($2.6 million in 1929–1930), and the University of California ($2.4 million in 1928–1929) were the top research spenders. By comparison, DuPont alone spent as much as the two universities put together: DuPont's budgets for 1925, 1930, and 1935 were $1.99 million, $5.5 million, and $6.6 million, respectively.[24] AT&T's R&D expenditures were even larger: the 1925, 1930, and 1935 budgets were $11.7 million, $23.2 million, and $15.4 million, respectively.[25] The state of public science during that period encouraged leading firms to fill the void.

Corporations responded to poor public science by developing internal scientific capabilities

Faced with a gap in knowledge between the innovative and scientific frontiers, research managers like Willis Whitney at GE Research Labs, Frank Jewett at AT&T Bell Labs, C.E.K. Mees at Kodak, and Charles Stine at DuPont lobbied top management to establish a centralised laboratory. This period marked a significant expansion of corporate research activities across the American industrial landscape. We measure corporate participation in three ways. First, we match the authors of peer-reviewed scientific publications from Microsoft Academic Graph (MAG) to American industrial firms. Second, we obtain data on R&D labs operated by firms from a national survey conducted by the NRC since 1920.[26,27] Third, we use the employment of prominent scientists by a firm as an additional indicator of corporate investment in science. For this purpose, we collected information on the employment affiliation of American scientists from the 1921 and 1938 editions of the Cattell Directory of *American Men of Science* (AMS).[28]

Average corporate laboratory staff approximately quintupled from 13.7 in 1927 to 65.9 in 1940, while the share of firms operating a lab rose from around 18 per cent to 35 per cent, as shown in Figure 8.4. The share of firms employing prominent scientists increased threefold, from 6.5 per cent in 1915 to around 20 per cent in 1938. The increase in publishing is starker: in 1915, less than 1 per cent of firms published in the sciences, whereas by 1940, just over one out of ten firms published (11.1 per cent). The top publishing firms during this period are chiefly concentrated in the electrical and chemical industries, as shown in Table 8.1. Note that there is substantial skew in this distribution, with the top 5 firms accounting for 82 per cent of all corporate publications. This skewness is an enduring feature of American corporate science throughout the twentieth century, as we revisit in Chapter 10.

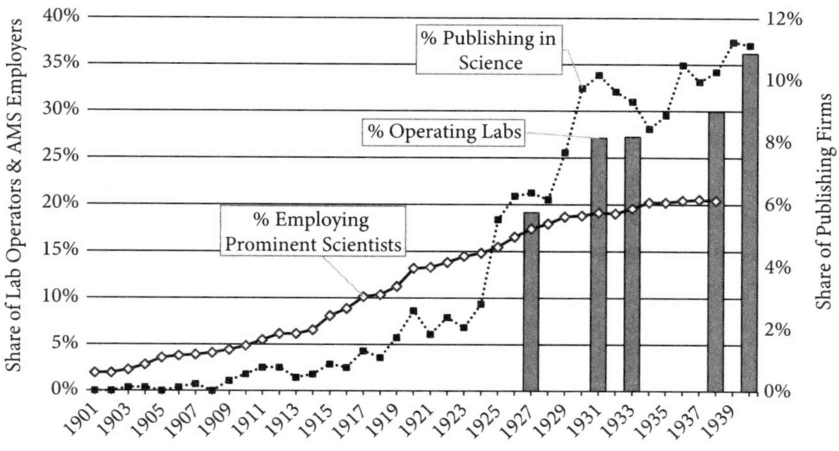

Figure 8.4 Rise of Corporate Science, 1900–1940

Notes: The graph plots the rise of corporate science for patenting firms in the ABKSY sample, which consists of American industrial firms and their subsidiaries identified from Berle & Means (1932) combined with listed firms from the Center for Research in Security Prices (CRSP). The share of firms operating labs (grey bar) and the share of firms employing prominent scientists in the AMS directory (solid line) are plotted on the left axis. The share of firms producing scientific publications (dashed line) is plotted on the right axis. Corporate publications in peer-reviewed scientific publications are matched from Microsoft Academic Graph; industrial labs data are matched from the Industrial Research Labs (IRL) directory; prominent corporate scientists are identified from the *American Men of Science* (AMS) directory.

The rise of corporate science is more pronounced in areas where innovation began to rely more heavily on basic science and where American universities were lagging. Figure 8.5 shows that, by 1920, the chemical industry employed 133 scientists listed in the *American Men of Science* directory, compared to only 18 in 1900. Overall lab employment in this sector also increased by almost five times between 1927 and 1940, which accords with prior work.[29] Figure 8.5 also shows the growth in corporate publishing to be concentrated in chemicals and electrical engineering, with elevenfold and twenty-ninefold increases, respectively. The quality of corporate research was also on the rise, as evidenced by the recognition of corporate scientists with prestigious awards. Irving Langmuir, whose work we recounted in Chapter 5, was awarded the Nobel Prize in Chemistry in 1932 for his work on surface chemistry. Similarly, Clinton Davisson at Bell Labs won the Nobel Prize in Physics in 1937 for his discovery of electron diffraction, which confirmed the wave nature of electrons and was a foundational achievement in quantum mechanics.

Table 8.1 Top U.S. Corporate Scientific Publishers (1900–1940)

Firm Name	Paper Count	Cumulative Share	Industry
General Electric	1,154	35%	Electric transmission & distribution equipment & electrical industrial apparatus
AT&T	664	56%	Communications, except radio & television broadcasting
Westinghouse	475	70%	Electric transmission & distribution equipment & electrical industrial apparatus
RCA	207	77%	Communications, except radio & television broadcasting
Eastman Kodak	182	82%	Amusements
Western Electric	105	85%	Communications, except radio & television broadcasting
Commonwealth Edison	50	87%	Communications, except radio & television broadcasting
Swift & Company	45	88%	Glass & glass products
Humble Oil and Refining	41	90%	Petroleum refining & related industries
Procter & Gamble	41	91%	Chemicals & selected chemical products
Sharp & Dohme	40	92%	Drugs, cleaning & toilet preparations
Parke Davis	37	93%	Drugs, cleaning & toilet preparations
Southern California Edison	34	94%	Communications, except radio & television broadcasting
Corning Glass Works	30	95%	Primary nonferrous metals manufacturing
Detroit Edison	29	96%	Communications, except radio & television broadcasting
Western Union	29	97%	Communications, except radio & television broadcasting
Westinghouse	29	98%	Other fabricated metal products
DuPont	24	98%	Chemicals & selected chemical products
General Motors	24	99%	Motor vehicles & equipment
U.S. Steel	23	100%	Primary iron & steel manufacturing

Notes: The table presents the number of total scientific publications in Microsoft Academic Graph (MAG) from 1900 to 1940 matched to ABKSY sample firms. The top 20 publishing firms are included.

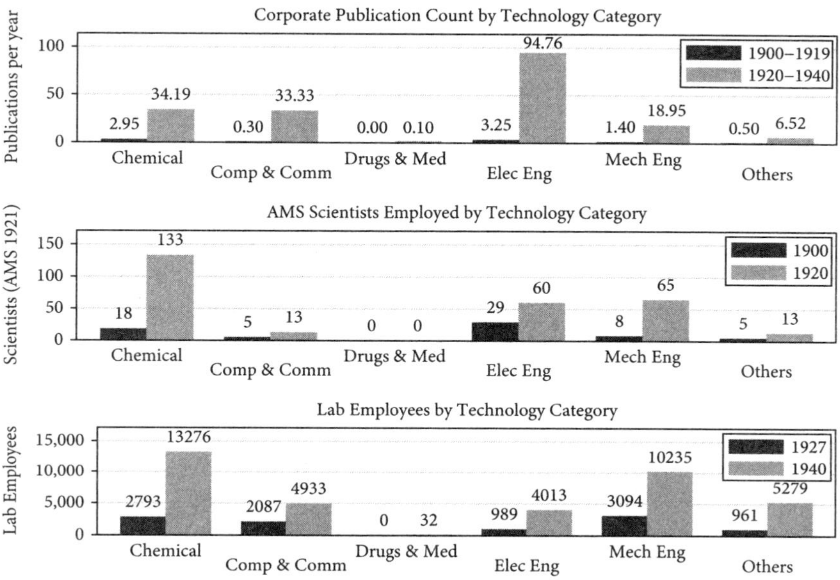

Figure 8.5 Corporate Investments in Science, by Technology Category (1900–1940)

Notes: This is a reproduction of Figure 2 from ABKSY (2024). The top panel plots total corporate publications in each NBER patent category per year produced between 1900 and 1919 and between 1920 and 1940 respectively. The middle panel plots the number of scientists from the AMS directory affiliated with firms in each category in 1900 and 1920. The bottom panel plots total employees at industrial laboratories in each category per year for 1927 and 1940. A technology category for a firm is defined as the NBER patent category in which it is granted the most patents during our main sample period, between 1926 and 1940.[30]

Overcoming scepticism: DuPont, General Electric, and AT&T

Initially, many in industry and academia were sceptical about the viability of embedding research within large, profit-driven corporations. T. D. Lockwood (head of AT&T's patent department mentioned in Chapter 7) stated that he was "fully convinced that it has never, is not now, and never will pay commercially, to keep an establishment of professional inventors, or of men whose chief business it is to invent."[31] Even after the establishment of Bell Labs in 1925, its founder, J. J. Carty, who also served as AT&T's chief engineer, had asserted that the lab was not intended to pursue scientific research for its own sake, but rather to focus on improving and extending AT&T's services.[32] This reflected a broader hesitation within industry to invest in research that did not offer immediate commercial applications. While there was an emerging consensus that innovation was increasingly based in science, it was not obvious that corporations could succeed where external contract organisations or universities failed. Pilot research programs at firms were one way to test this question.

DuPont

DuPont's early research efforts encountered resistance as well. When DuPont established its first laboratory for testing explosives in 1888, the primary focus was on quality control rather than on innovation. The idea of investing in scientific inquiry was met with scepticism by the company's executive committee. DuPont, founded in 1802 as a gunpowder manufacturer, had grown into one of the largest industrial firms in the United States by the early twentieth century. However, as traditional growth strategies became less effective, the firm began integrating scientific research into its business strategy. In 1902, DuPont established its first research laboratory at the Carney's Point plant in New Jersey, initially focused on improving and testing the quality of explosives, the main function of industrial labs at the time.

However, as DuPont was preparing to ramp up production of explosives such as smokeless powder and trinitrotoluene (TNT) around 1914, it found itself hamstrung by German embargoes on critical inputs, including diphenylamine and toluene, which are stabilisers for smokeless powders and TNT, respectively. Upon learning that DuPont's reserves of the materials were dwindling, the firm's chemical director, Charles Reese, tasked chemists at DuPont's Eastern Lab and Experimental Station to reverse engineer the process. After scouring the scientific literature, researchers deduced that aniline and aniline hydrochloride were heated to 230 degrees centigrade in a pressured reactor, at which point ammonium chloride split off as a by-product and diphenylamine was produced. The firm started producing fifty thousand pounds of diphenylamine per month by December 1914 and ramped up output to one hundred and fifty thousand pounds by late 1916, thanks to a critical refinement that owed to a footnote in a German journal (*Journal für Praktische Chemie*). Estimates at the beginning of the war showed that DuPont's existing stocks of diphenylamine would be exhausted by March 1915; investment in scientific research had therefore been vindicated. Similarly, Reese also tasked the Eastern Lab with producing toluene. It not only produced a replacement product (trinitroxylenes) but also helped the firm produce tetryl (trinitrophenylmethylnitramine), a key fuse ingredient hitherto only produced in Germany.[33]

DuPont's postwar successes with products such as automotive lacquers (Duco finishes developed with General Motors) meant that new research would once again face neglect. Arguing that "applied research is facing a shortage of its principal raw materials," Charles Stine (Reese's successor) thereby proposed to the executive committee to establish a central research organisation in 1926.[34] In the following year, a research organisation similar in purpose to those of its German rivals, such as Bayer and Agfa, would be established, focusing on colloidal chemistry, catalysis, and organic synthesis. Thanks to this commitment to basic science, DuPont was able to recruit chemists such as Wallace Carothers from Harvard. Carothers's work on polymer chemistry in turn enabled DuPont to synthesise and commercially produce large, chained molecules that could be formed into synthetic rubber (neoprene) and fibre (nylon), starting the plastics revolution.

General Electric

GE Research Laboratory (GERL) was established in Schenectady, New York, in 1900. The initiative, championed by Charles P. Steinmetz, one of General Electric's leading electrical engineers (and president of the American Institute of Electrical Engineers), was rooted in the understanding that to maintain and enhance General Electric's market position, the company needed to focus on fundamental scientific research. Unlike Edison's Menlo Park facility that preceded it, GERL was envisioned as a hub for advancing the scientific understanding necessary to outpace competitors, domestic (Westinghouse) and foreign (AEG, Siemens). The founder of GERL, Willis Whitney, would state to future Nobel Prize winner Irving Langmuir that while "the laboratory will have to pay for itself,... in addition, *it should make a contribution to the advancement of science and knowledge*."[35] A commitment to scientific research paid dividends early: development of the tungsten filament by William Coolidge in 1906, for instance, addressed the efficiency challenges posed by the Nernst glower. The tungsten filament allowed GE's bulbs to operate at higher temperatures, produce more light, and reduce energy waste, effectively countering the technological threats from Europe. GERL researchers also sought to solve the problem of bulb blackening. Competing hypotheses on the cause of bulb blackening required a deeper scientific understanding to resolve. Irving Langmuir, an American chemist hired by GE after completing his PhD at the University of Göttingen in Germany, was tasked with investigating this issue. Langmuir applied Owen Richardson's theory of thermionic emissions and proposed filling the bulb with inert gases to scatter the evaporated particles from the tungsten filament, a solution that emerged from his research on surface chemistry.[36]

AT&T

AT&T's early approach to innovation was relatively modest. Rather than pioneering new technologies, the company primarily relied on purchasing patents and inventions from outside sources and adapting them for its own use. In 1892, Hammond Hayes, the head of AT&T's Mechanical Department, decided to focus the company's resources on practical, rather than theoretical, advancements. Hayes believed that theoretical expertise could be outsourced through collaborations with institutions like MIT or Harvard, while the department concentrated on perfecting engineering methods. As late as 1906, AT&T had no internal capacity for inventing new technologies, instead focusing on refining and adapting existing solutions. This conservative stance began to change in 1907 when AT&T found itself facing significant financial challenges. Following the expiration of key patents, thousands of independent phone companies emerged, intensifying competition. Between 1902 and 1907, AT&T's debt tripled, and its stock price dropped sharply, limiting the company's ability to secure additional financing. In response, AT&T turned to a group of bankers led by J. P. Morgan, who installed Theodore Vail as president. This leadership change marked a fundamental shift in AT&T's approach to research and development. Vail had previously served as AT&T's general manager in 1878, when he had initiated projects like developing underground telephone cables. However, in 1887, disagreements with the company's owners, who prioritised short-term profits over long-term investments in technology, led Vail to leave the company. Upon his return in 1907, he had broader authority to shape AT&T's direction, enabling him to make innovation and technological advancement a core part of the company's strategy.[37]

Vail's vision was to unify the entire telephone industry under AT&T's control. He believed that the telephone system was a "natural monopoly" and that the public would be best served by a single, government-regulated entity providing universal service. Achieving this goal required not only integrating all telephones into a single network but also pushing the technological boundaries necessary to overcome the physical limitations of long-distance communication. Under Vail's leadership, AT&T moved away from relying on external patents and began developing its own innovations. By 1910, the company had established extensive research laboratories and experimental departments, marking a major departure from its previous focus on adapting existing technologies.

A key challenge that emerged during Vail's tenure was the problem of long-distance signal transmission. At the time, telephone signals could only travel about 1,800 miles, which meant that connecting cities like New York and Denver was possible, but reaching the West Coast was not. The signals would weaken over long distances, making transcontinental communication impossible without some form of amplification. In 1909, AT&T's new head of research, John Carty, along with physicist Frank Jewett, took on the challenge of developing a solution. They explored several methods of signal amplification, including mechanical and magnetic techniques, but these proved ineffective. Jewett, who had a background in physics, suggested looking into emerging research on electrons, leading to the hiring of physicist Harold Arnold in 1911 to explore electronic amplification. Arnold initially experimented with mercury vapour tubes but found them unsuitable. In 1912, however, he recognised the potential of the Audion, a device invented by Lee de Forest that could amplify electrical signals. Although de Forest himself did not fully understand the science behind his invention, Arnold saw its potential. Over the next few years, Arnold and his team refined the Audion into a functional telephone amplifier, allowing the company to overcome the limitations of long-distance communication.[38] By 1915, AT&T had established a research division with forty-five employees, including several PhDs, and had successfully completed the first transcontinental telephone line between New York and San Francisco, powered by vacuum-tube-based amplifiers. This breakthrough brought Vail closer to his vision of a national, unified telephone network. An improved understanding of wireless technology by Arnold's group also made possible the opening of a wireless relay on this line in the same year.

Successfully leveraging physics research into vacuum tubes for long-distance telephony justified establishing a consolidated research lab engaged in scientific research: by 1925, AT&T merged its various research and engineering functions into Bell Telephone Laboratories. In the same year that Bell Labs was established, Clinton Davisson began work that would later earn Bell Labs its first Nobel Prize in Physics. In 1927, Davisson and Lester Germer conducted an experiment on electron diffraction that would provide the first direct evidence of the wave nature of electrons, a key prediction in quantum mechanics. In all three cases, early experiments with industrial research allayed managerial fears that investing in science was too unpredictable to be a profitable enterprise.

To recapitulate, the technologically advanced industries of the early twentieth century increasingly relied on science. Leading firms concluded that the cost of accessing science through contract organisations or partnerships with universities was becoming prohibitive. With foreign sources imperilled by geopolitics, firms began investing in science.

Corporate science was a minority concern

Investments in science were highly concentrated. While up to 66 per cent of all patenting firms during this period operated a lab, only around 25 per cent employed more than fifty staff members, as shown in Figure 8.6. Similarly, around 43 per cent of firms published in the sciences, but only five firms published more than five papers per year.[39] This concentration requires an explanation. The gap between the technological frontier and the state-of-the-art public science exposed so far was a constraint faced by all firms in the industry: why did some firms invest while others did not?

Comparing firm characteristics by their investments in science in Figure 8.7, we find that they are more technologically advanced and tend to be larger. On the x-axis, we categorise firms by how intensively they invest in science: "3 Indicators" implies that firms (i) publish, (ii) operate a lab, and (iii) employ prominent scientists, while "2" and "1 Indicators," respectively, imply that the firm engages in at least two or one of these activities. On the left panel of this plot, we find that just over a fifth of the firms that engage in all three activities cite scientific articles in their patents—significantly more than the other groups. The results are qualitatively similar for other patent-based measures of proximity to the technological frontier that measure the textual novelty of patent documents[40] (middle-left) and that indicate whether a firm patents for the first time in a new patent class (bottom-left).

The right panel of Figure 8.7 shows that investments in science are strongly correlated with size: firms that are positive in all three indicators are around 4.4 times larger than firms that do not invest at all in science; they also tend to command around twice as much market share compared to noninvesting

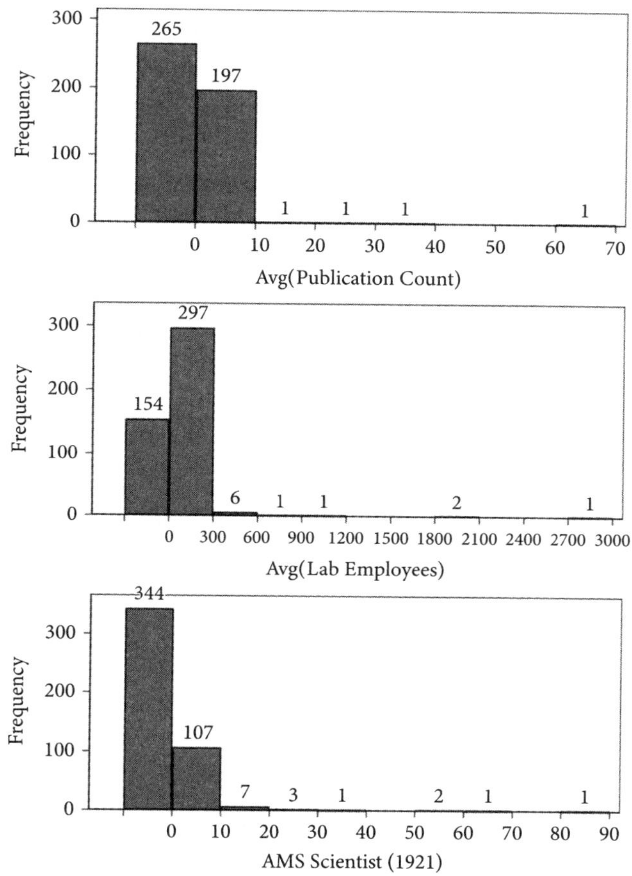

Figure 8.6 Heterogeneity of Corporate Science (1926–1940)

Notes: This is a reproduction of Appendix Figure B2 in ABKSY (2024). The upper histogram bins the number of publications per year authored by sample firms. 265 firms (the leftmost bar) do not author any scientific publications from 1926 to 1940. The middle histogram bins the number of personnel per year employed at corporate laboratories. 154 firms (the leftmost bar) report no employed lab personnel. The lower histogram bins the number of corporate scientists found in the 1921 edition. 344 firms (the leftmost bar) do not employ any AMS scientists.

firms. One may conjecture various reasons for this pattern. A classic explanation attributed to Joseph Schumpeter states that only large firms have the wherewithal and incentive to conduct research.[41] The fixed costs of setting up a lab are considerable, and only firms with large market shares may have been able to justify these costs by appropriating rents through their market power. Another explanation attributed to Richard Nelson is that because the fruits of science are unpredictable ex ante and technology markets are

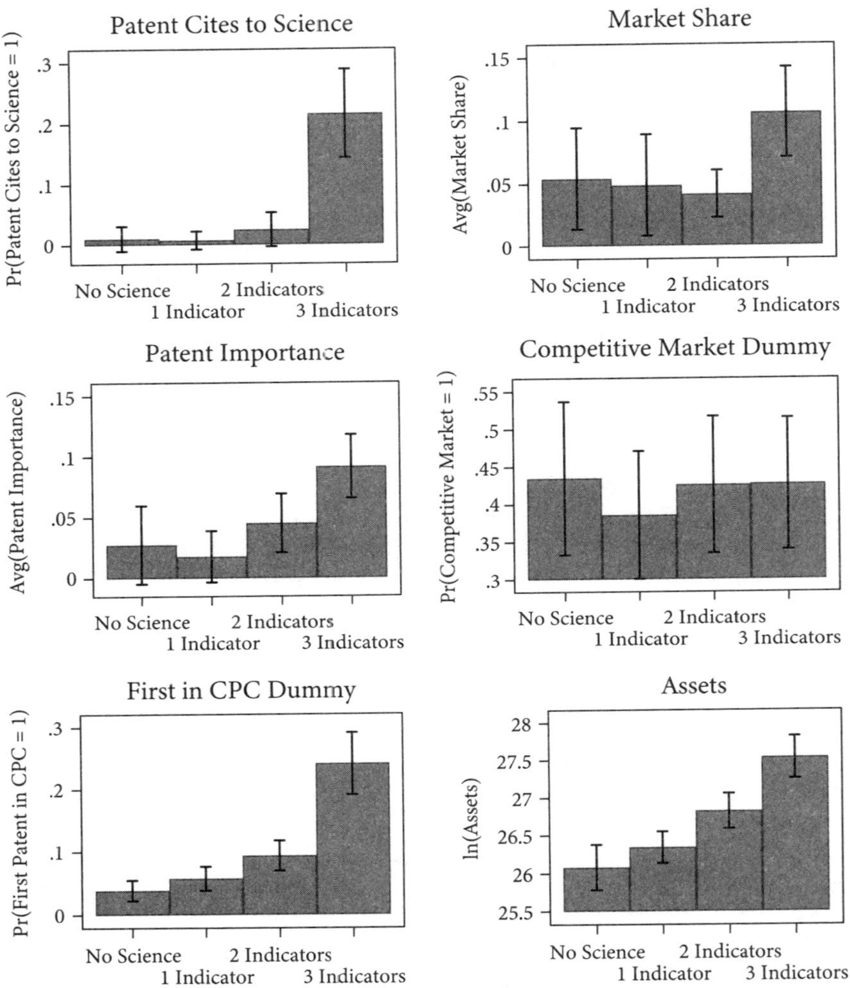

Figure 8.7 Indicators of Corporate Science and Distance to Technological Frontier and Firm Characteristics (1926–1940)

Notes: This is a reproduction of Figure 4 of ABKSY (2024). The left panel plots measures of technological leadership by investment in science, while the right panel plots market share, size (assets) and concentration (competition dummy) analogously. The three indicators of investment in science on the x-axis measure whether the firm i) produces a scientific publication; ii) operates an industrial laboratory; iii) employs a scientist from the AMS directory. The "No Science" group consists of firms that engage in none of these three activities. The "3 Indicators" firms engage in all three activities. The "2 Indicators" firms engage in two of the three activities. "1 Indicator" firms engage in one of the three activities. "Market Share" and "Assets" are averaged between 1926 and 1930.

often inefficient, larger and more diversified firms would be more likely to have the manufacturing and distribution channels that could effectively commercialise scientific discoveries than smaller ones.[42] We may speculate yet another reason: given that public knowledge supply was constrained, leading firms may have seen scientific investments as a strategy to build up moats against potential competitors. In any case, large firms with significant market shares and at the technological frontier were the ones driving scientific research. This trend continued through the Golden Age of corporate innovation post-World War II (Chapter 10), and it remains true today.

The 1930s intensified concerns about the concentration of market power and potential abuses thereof. The concentration of research activity we documented led the Temporary National Economic Committee to observe in 1940 that "there is probably no other basic function of general economic activity so dominated by a few enormous concerns."[43] Because only the largest firms had the resources to maintain industrial labs, the fruits of science were unevenly distributed in the economy. This led to concerns that the concentration of research further reinforced the market power of dominant American corporations.

Yet, the federal government exercised considerable forbearance in the regulation of large, innovative corporations. For example, recognising that AT&T's aspirations to maintain a monopoly on long-distance phone service sat uncomfortably with federal regulators, the firm's vice president, Nathan Kingsbury, committed to ceasing buy-ups of local phone companies in 1913. It also started allowing local phone companies access to its long-distance system. The U.S. Congress responded by formally exempting the telephone business from federal antitrust laws in the Willis-Graham Act of 1921.[44] Radio was a related industry in which the government had a direct hand in consolidation when creating the Radio Corporation of America (RCA) in 1919. Shortly after World War I, concerns grew within the U.S. Navy that wireless communications, a strategically important sector, was controlled by a British concern (Marconi Wireless Company). Moreover, the three leading companies in the sector (GE, Westinghouse, and AT&T) were embroiled in litigation that retarded technical progress and standardisation. Franklin Delano Roosevelt, in his role as Assistant Secretary of the Navy, took on the suggestion from GE's Vice President Owen Young to broker a deal between the three companies, creating a spinoff in the form of RCA that would hold a patent pool. This solution simultaneously mitigated foreign competition and patent coordination problems that were plaguing the industry at the time.

The production of corporate science has always been concentrated within a few dominant players, a pattern that has persisted throughout the past century. Recognising this enduring relationship between economic concentration and corporate science is essential for understanding the role of large firms in driving technological innovation. The vignettes from AT&T and RCA also give pause for policymakers to consider balancing the benefits of corporate research with the challenges brought by greater market power.

Corporate science and firm performance

If firms invested in research to solve pressing technological problems, such firms ought also to have produced better and more valuable inventions. This was indeed the case. Firms that invested in industrial research produced more influential patents (those cited more by future inventors). The three left subfigures of Figure 8.8 show the number of patents in the top 5 per cent of forward citations against publication stock, lab size, and scientists (normalised by assets). We find that highly cited patents are positively correlated with all three measures (The correlations are $r = 0.366$ for publications, $r = 0.213$ for lab size, and $r = 0.128$ for AMS scientists.) A similar positive correlation also holds when (in separate tests) we replace high-impact patents with those that are in the top 5 per cent of stock market value. A standard deviation increase in publication stock is associated with around 2.7 times more high-impact patents, relative to the sample mean.

The payoffs from corporate science were noticed not only by inventors but also by the stock market. The right panel of Figure 8.8 shows that firms investing in research enjoyed a stock market premium in terms of their stock price relative to the book value of assets: a standard deviation greater publication stock was associated with around 3.6 times greater market-to-book ratios relative to the sample mean. The results show that corporate science was considered valuable by investors during this period.

Structural advantages accelerating the privatisation of research

How were firms able to staff and equip these newly built facilities? After all, the emerging intellectual climate at American universities generally discouraged academics from engaging with industry: Henry Rowland's

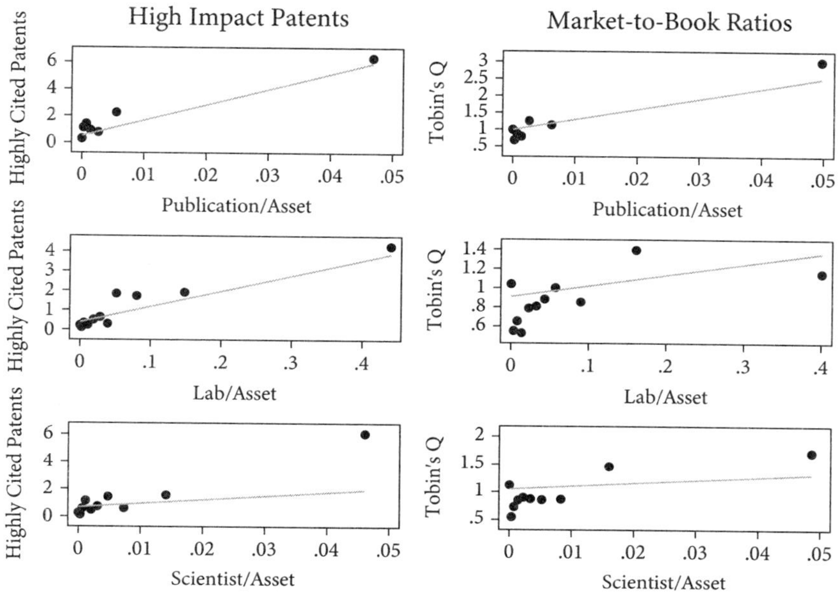

Figure 8.8 Corporate Science and Firm Performance (1926–1940)

Notes: The left panel consists of binned scatterplots (at the firm-year level) that plot the relationship between high-impact patents and the three measures of corporate research. The right panel plots the relationship between market-to-book ratios (Tobin's Q) and measures of corporate research. "Publication/Asset" refers to publication stock divided by assets; "Lab/Asset" refers to the number of lab personnel recorded in the IRL directory divided by assets; "Scientist/Asset" refers to the number of prominent scientists found in the 1938 edition of the AMS directory divided by assets.

1883 address to the American Association for the Advancement of Science (AAAS), titled "A Plea for Pure Science," famously implored that he was "tired of seeing our professors degrading their chairs by the pursuit of applied science instead of pure science."[45] Some academics also actively pushed back against industrial influence on university research. Chemist G. N. Lewis left MIT for Berkeley, claiming that "industrial intrusions into university research" were becoming too onerous. The establishment of the California Institute of Technology (Caltech) represented a countermovement against the proliferation of industrial consulting work on campuses and MIT's Technology Plan of the 1920s. On advice from George Hale, Caltech would refrain from direct research contracts with firms and focus on "fluid" fundraising from foundations for general, basic research.[46] In spite of this climate, firms were helped by three structural advantages: limited support for research in universities, a growing supply of trained researchers, and the growing importance of science-based inventions.

Private-public gap in research support

Working for poor pay and heavy teaching loads, academics began to find corporate labs attractive alternatives, offering higher salaries than academia and greater research freedom. In some cases, firms would offer flexible arrangements to lure top talent, allowing researchers to retain academic positions while working part-time in industry. Scientific results, conditioned on patent protection, were generally liberally published such that researchers could maintain their prestige in the scientific community. Leonard Reich notes that Irving Langmuir, for instance, was disenchanted with the lack of research support at Stevens Institute of Technology, where he joined as a faculty member in 1906:

> To his chagrin, he found few students with an interest in science. His attempts to upgrade laboratory facilities and the quality of student work met with hostility from students and indifference from his colleagues. To make matters worse, he had little time for research. When he left in 1909 to join the GE Research Laboratory, Langmuir found a position that met his needs far better. [47]

Access to advanced equipment was another draw. Research equipment was becoming more expensive. For instance, the generation of high vacuum—a prerequisite to studying thermionic emissions—required Langmuir to adopt and modify Wolfgang Gaede's molecular pump imported from Germany. Ultra-centrifuges, Svedberg's Nobel prize-winning scientific instrument used to separate chemical substances by their molecular weights, were vital to polymer research. In the 1920s, apart from DuPont, only the University of Wisconsin (where Svedberg had visited in 1923) had an ultra-centrifuge.[48]

High-energy physics research at Berkeley and Stanford during the 1930s was a key area where universities were compelled to cooperate with firms to build large capital equipment for scientific use.[49] While Ernest Lawrence at Berkeley's Radiation Lab conceived of the concept for the cyclotron, building it required extensive support from private sources. The 84-ton magnet used for the cyclotron, for example, was supplied by the Federal Telegraph Company of Palo Alto, which had previously used it to amplify intercontinental radio signals. Stanford's physics department, in an effort to compete with rival developments at Berkeley, sought corporate support to conduct research using the rhumbatron (an electron accelerator) and the klystron (a vacuum tube for modulating microwaves). Both devices were built by the Sperry Gyroscope Company, with extensive engineering support provided by its lab personnel. The ability of firms to manufacture sophisticated research instruments allowed for those entering atomic physics research to recruit top talent. Westinghouse, for instance, had established a laboratory in 1916 and counted a Nobel Prize winner in Arthur Compton (Physics, 1927) as a staff alum. By 1935, Westinghouse began to conduct research in nuclear medicine and industrial mass spectroscopy with the recruitment of Princeton physicist Edward Condon.[50] Under his guidance, the world's first industrial electrostatic nuclear accelerator (known as the Westinghouse Atom Smasher) was built in Forest Hills in 1937. The firm's experience later allowed it to build the world's first commercial nuclear power plant in Shippingport, Pennsylvania.

Rise of human capital supplied by American universities

Universities produce two inputs for corporate research: knowledge and human capital. As we have shown above, university *knowledge* before World War II was inadequate for innovative companies. However, the skilled labour produced by doctoral programs around the country helped staff

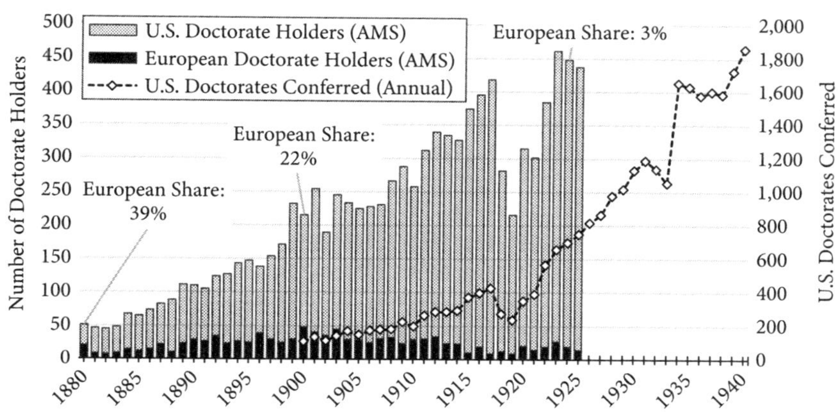

Figure 8.9 U.S. PhD Production and Alma Mater of *American Men of Science* (1900–1940)

Notes: The stacked bar chart plots the number of scientists listed in the 1906, 1910, 1921, and 1927 editions of *American Men of Science* who received their PhD each year from 1880 to 1925. The black bar represents those receiving their degrees from European institutions, while the dotted bar represents those with U.S. degrees. The dashed line (plotted in the right axis) represents the number of doctoral dissertations completed in science and engineering disciplines in U.S. universities. The data is from the Proquest Dissertation and Theses database.

the industrial labs. Whereas in the past century, the best training in the natural sciences was conducted in Europe, American universities gradually established themselves as centres for learning as expatriate academics began staffing chemistry and physics departments in research universities throughout the country.[51] The dashed line in Figure 8.9 shows how production of U.S. doctorates in the natural sciences remained at just over one hundred in 1900 and climbed rapidly after 1920 to reach close to two thousand on the eve of World War II. The stacked bar graphs show the doctoral alma mater of prominent scientists listed in the 1906, 1910, 1921, and 1927 editions of the *American Men of Science* directory. Of the fifty-one AMS scientists receiving their doctoral degrees in 1880, twenty (39 per cent) hailed from European institutions. This number drops to around 22 per cent for the cohort receiving doctorates in 1900 and to 3 per cent in 1925. The increased human capital produced by universities should have aided in staffing the new corporate labs of the time. Indeed, Jeff Furman and Megan MacGarvie argue that early pharmaceutical laboratories benefited from their proximity to universities. George Davis, for instance, recruited two scientists from the University of Michigan for the laboratory of his firm Parke-Davis (located nearby in Detroit) in an effort to mass-produce an antitoxin for diphtheria that was discovered by German and French scientists in 1894.[52]

The Great Depression and the decline of the individual inventor

The economic collapse following the Great Depression led to severe financial strain for universities, small firms, and individual inventors. For smaller firms, the Depression's financial strain crippled R&D activities. Recent research by Ramanan Nanda and Tom Nicholas highlights a strong negative correlation between bank failures, which disrupted financing and patenting activity, especially among smaller firms dependent on loans, and external funding for R&D.[53] Tania Babina, Asaf Bernstein, and Filippo Mezzanotti show a similar result by comparing individuals against corporations: the decline in patents by inventors unaffiliated with corporations after 1929 was around 13 per cent greater for counties with failed banks.[54] Independent inventors who were the dominant constituents of the American innovation ecosystem in the nineteenth century had already begun to be subsumed by firms around the turn of the century. According to Naomi Lamoreaux and Kenneth Sokoloff, the share of inventors unaffiliated with firms dropped by half from 45 per cent in 1890 to 22 per cent in 1910.[55] The age of the "heroic inventor"—an Edison (GE), a Bell (AT&T), a Cornell (Western Union), or a Hall (Alcoa)—who could attract risk capital based on a blockbuster patent was fading as the task of creating and capturing value from increasingly complex technologies had come to demand teamwork between large groups of scientists and engineers. The rise of the salaried R&D personnel may have been accelerated by the financial distress of the Depression era.

In contrast to smaller entities, large incumbent firms were more persistent in research. DuPont's invention of nylon (1935), Kodak's introduction of Kodachrome (1935), GE's invention of the fluorescent lamp (1934), the development and diffusion of television and commercial air travel all occurred during this period thanks to extensive investments in research. Unlike small firms and independent inventors, larger firms could reach into internal capital markets to sustain their R&D programs. The economic historian Alex Field termed the 1930s the "most technologically progressive decade of the century": much of this progress was thanks to the industrial labs that persisted on science-based innovation strategies.[56]

Top universities adapted to financial distress by forging deeper partnerships with industry which provided financial backing for their research. Under President James Bryant Conant, Harvard emphasised research in fields such as chemistry and biology, helping the university remain relevant in applied sciences. MIT, led by Karl T. Compton, concentrated on defence-related research, positioning itself to later house the Radiation Laboratory during World War II. Stanford, guided by Ray Lyman Wilbur, leveraged its location in California to partner with emerging aerospace and technology industries, which laid the groundwork for its future role in Silicon Valley.[57]

Chapter takeaways

In sum, the corporate laboratory replaced the heroic inventor as the chief translator of science into invention in the decades leading up to World War II. This was driven by the increasing reliance of frontier inventions in the chemical and electrical industries on new science and by the undersupply of university science responding to these needs. To fill the shortfall between the technological frontier and the state of American scientific knowledge, leading firms set up industrial labs that went beyond the old workshop model limited to quality control and product development: staffed by the nation's growing scientific talent, the labs opened new vistas of science in electrical engineering, vacuum tube (and later solid state) electronics, surface, photo, organic and polymer chemistry, as well as early atomic physics. The early movers in these research enterprises enjoyed dominant market positions with radically novel products such as nylon, colour photography, and long-distance radio.

Inspired by these successes, other industries began to follow the lead of electrical and chemical companies by establishing their own research laboratories. In 1908, Charles Goodyear and Paul Litchfield established the first rubber industry research lab, Goodyear Research, which played a pivotal role in advancing rubber technology and production methods. General Motors' research department was set up in 1911. In the 1920s, the petroleum industry emerged as a major player in industrial research, with companies like Standard Oil, Shell, Gulf, and the Universal Oil Products Corporation leading the way. The pharmaceutical industry followed suit: Abbott Laboratories, Eli Lilly, Parke, Davis and Company, and E. R. Squibb established research facilities to explore new drugs, improve manufacturing processes, and ensure product safety and efficacy. By the end of this period, more than a third of all patenting firms had established a lab.

As we show in Chapter 10, by the start of the Cold War, industrial research had become a widespread phenomenon in the U.S. economy. However, though pervasive, corporate investments in frontier science (firms which we term "Leaders") remained highly skewed, concentrated in large firms with market power, and occupying technological leadership.

9

Science Becomes a National Priority

Introduction

In the interwar years, most of the leading American firms carried out only tentative experiments with in-house research, but the end of World War II precipitated a wholesale reconfiguration of the American innovation system. From 1946 to 1960, the share of patenting public companies that operated a research laboratory leapt from one-third to more than three-quarters.[1]

Our point of departure is the federal government's decision, forged in wartime urgency and refined in the early years of the Cold War, to treat science as a strategic national resource. World War II offered a dramatic proof that radar, proximity fuses, mass-produced penicillin, and nuclear fission could determine the outcome of a Great-Power conflict. This conviction as to the importance of science expressed itself through three channels. First, the government poured money into college education. The G.I. Bill (1944), the National Defense Education Act (1958), and an expanding palette of graduate fellowships trebled university enrolments and turned the doctorate into the basic credential of professional research. Second, the state financed a vast expansion of research, propelling American universities to the front rank of global science. Third, the federal government acted as a lead customer for the downstream fruits of science, using mission-oriented procurement in defence, aerospace, and nuclear power to underwrite expensive pilot runs and soak up early production.

Those three policies shaped the scientific-industrial complex. Universities, national laboratories, and defence contractors were the first beneficiaries of the policies, but the social benefits were broader. Industry giants, such as DuPont, IBM, General Electric, and AT&T, and others such as General Motors, RCA, Raytheon, Westinghouse, Pfizer, and Merck, responded to the new flow of graduate talent, government grants, and assured public markets by expanding their own laboratories and by ratcheting research ambitions from short-term technical service to long-horizon exploratory science. The result was a "Golden Age" of corporate research, a period roughly from 1945 to the end of the 1970s, when industrial labs produced Nobel Prize-worthy discoveries and pioneered new science-based industries, such as semiconductors, lasers, plastics, and antibiotics.

This chapter reconstructs the federal side of that story, first examining how wartime lessons about mobilisation, coordination, and scale shaped postwar agencies and their funding mechanisms. Next the chapter traces the explosive growth of university science and national laboratories, documenting how federal dollars shifted campuses from regionally oriented teaching institutions into world centres of basic research. This research not only produced new knowledge but also newly trained STEM PhDs who embodied this knowledge. Finally, the chapter details the rise of mission-oriented procurement, first in defence, then in space and energy. This combination of push and pull policies shortened the time from proof-of-concept to full-scale production, and it also encouraged firms to develop in-house scientific and technological capabilities.

World War II

World War II showed that mastery of scientific knowledge was indispensable for success in modern warfare. Hitler's advance into Poland and through the Low Countries would have been harder without the emergence of mechanised warfare combined with close air support. The Battle of Britain would have similarly been more protracted had the Dowding system, which exploited the latest cavity magnetron designs, not been deployed by the Royal Air Force. The cryptanalysis of the German Enigma machine by Marian Rejewski and Alan Turing gave the Allies a decisive advantage in the Battle of the Atlantic. The flow of new science-based instruments of war continued unabated until the end of the war: the invention of jet propulsion by Hans Von Ohain (applied in the Heinkel 178 in 1939), the production of Nylon parachutes by DuPont in 1938, the mass production of penicillin in 1944, the successful launch of the V2 rocket in 1942, and the detonation of two atomic bombs in 1945 conclusively demonstrated that science was a resource no less strategic than petroleum or steel.

Furthermore, the scientists and engineers engaged in wartime projects such as the Rad Lab and the Manhattan Project earned a seat at the policymaking table. Soon, federal agencies such as the National Science

Foundation, the National Institutes of Health, the National Aeronautics and Space Administration, the Atomic Energy Commission, the Advanced Research Projects Agency, and the scientific offices of each branch of the military (such as the Office of Naval Research, the Air Force Office of Scientific Research, and the Army Signal Corps) came into existence.

We examine three wartime science projects: the radar, proximity fuse, and penicillin. These projects became touchstones for postwar policymakers, who drew two key lessons from their success. First, the United States was still a net importer of scientific knowledge in many technologies; second, the commercialisation of science-based inventions required overt coordination between research (university academics), development (firms), and deployment (the government). The first lesson influenced the sheer scale of federal support for the sciences after 1945; the second lesson influenced the manner in which it was administered.

Taking radio to the limits: radar and proximity fuse

By the 1930s, radios offered a reliable means of two-way communication and broadcasting, with over six hundred stations serving news and entertainment to American households. However, the full potential of radio wave technology had yet to be explored. One of those functions was radio detection and ranging, which allowed objects to be located by bouncing electromagnetic waves off of them. Early radar systems, though innovative, were limited by their use of low-frequency waves, restricting range, resolution, and the ability to detect smaller, fast-moving targets. The state of the art in radio detection and ranging shifted in 1940 with the invention of the cavity magnetron by British scientists John Randall and Harry Boot. By allowing radar to operate at higher microwave frequencies, the magnetron significantly enhanced detection capabilities. The technology's full potential, however, was realised only through a partnership between academia, industry, and government.

Upon receiving British know-how from the Tizard mission of 1939,[2] the U.S. government established the MIT Radiation Laboratory (Rad Lab) the following year. The lab assembled over three thousand scientists and engineers, including Luis Alvarez and Isidor Rabi. Supported by a $1.5 billion investment (equivalent to over $20 billion today), the lab developed over one hundred radar systems tailored to diverse military needs.[3]

New radar

Key breakthroughs included pulse radar, which allowed precise distance measurements, and airborne radar, enabling aircraft to track targets at night or in poor visibility.

The collaboration between the Rad Lab and American industry was instrumental in scaling radar from lab prototypes to battlefield-ready systems. Companies like Raytheon, General Electric (GE), and Westinghouse tackled the engineering challenges required for mass production and operational reliability. Raytheon's Percy Spencer (head of the power tube division) refined the cavity magnetron for mass production, delivering tens of thousands of units by 1943. Magnetrons required a hollowed-out cavity within solid metal. Conventional methods required either casting or carving the cavity out of solid metal blocks, which was time-consuming. Spencer's innovation was to stamp thin cross-sections of copper and to solder the pieces together in a conveyor-belt system. This increased production from around one hundred per day to twenty-six hundred. Spencer later capitalised on his wartime experience to invent the first commercial microwave oven.[4] GE and Westinghouse contributed by miniaturising radar units for deployment on fighter aircraft and naval vessels.

Radar's impact on World War II was profound. By 1943, radar-equipped aircraft patrolling the Atlantic had significantly reduced the U-boat threat, securing vital Allied supply lines. Anti-submarine radar installed on ships further bolstered naval capabilities, turning the tide in the Battle of the Atlantic. By 1944, radar-guided bombing missions enabled Allied forces to target enemy positions accurately in low-visibility conditions. The technology was crucial in campaigns such as the Normandy landings, where radar guided landing craft to designated beaches and coordinated air support.

Radar's wartime success spurred its adaptation for peacetime applications, particularly in aviation and meteorology. Private industry benefited immensely for years thereafter, though radar sales to the military of about $3 billion alone exceeded the size of the commercial radio industry.[5] By the late 1940s, the Federal Aviation Administration (then the Civil Aeronautics Administration) began integrating radar systems into air traffic control, enhancing flight safety and managing increasingly crowded airways. Similarly, meteorologists quickly recognised radar's potential for tracking precipitation and severe weather. By the 1950s, weather radar had become an essential tool for storm monitoring, paving the way for modern meteorological techniques.

Raytheon's work on radar systems led to the development of the microwave oven, culminating in the launch of the Radarange in 1947. Westinghouse and GE applied their radar engineering skills to telecommunications and consumer electronics, contributing to the postwar boom in broadcasting and home appliances. A recent study by Daniel Gross and Maria Roche identifies three ways in which the radar program had a persistent effect on post-World War II innovation, namely, the production of new knowledge, the training of engineers and managers, and the creation of an industrial ecosystem.[6]

The estimated thirty-six hundred person-years of research and development laid the scientific and technical basis for microwave communications (useful later for mobile telephony), information processing, and solid-state electronics, where Bell Labs' postwar work on transistors built directly upon its wartime work on germanium-based diodes. Gross and Roche estimate that approximately fifteen hundred patents, accounting for between half and two-thirds of the patents essential to radar production, were developed as part of the war effort, primarily by firms involved in the radar project. The radar effort also resulted in a twenty-seven-volume introduction to radar and microwave engineering, which became a standard reference in scores of American physics laboratories, being cited by more than twenty thousand academic articles and over twenty-five hundred U.S. patents.

In addition, the program also trained people. Gross and Roche show that researchers involved in the radar project were far more likely to continue patenting in radar after the war ended. In addition to patenting, many became entrepreneurs and industrial R&D directors themselves. By 1960, Rad Lab and Harvard's Radio Research Lab (RRL, a spinoff organisation for developing radar countermeasures established in 1942) alumni were a third more likely than comparable researchers to be in managerial roles. This difference was due entirely to the higher propensity for Rad Lab and RRL alumni to become R&D managers.

Growing the industrial base was an explicit project goal. Gross and Roche show that out of a sample of eighteen companies with contracts for Rad Lab-designed systems, fourteen were new to the radar technology. Of these, ten remained in the industry after the war. These companies would then support a network of subcontractors that would supply components. According to a *Fortune* magazine article, there were around eight thousand subcontractors by the conclusion of the war.[7] Simply put, the radar project created an entire industry, one that was larger in size than the radio industry.

Proximity fuse

The proximity fuse, designed to detonate explosives automatically when near a target, marked a revolutionary advance in military technology. Before its invention, shells would explode on impact ("percussion fuses"), blunting the explosive potential of a shell as half of the force would be absorbed by the ground where it fell. Innovations such as the "time fuse" were introduced, which would detonate after a predetermined time of flight, but accuracy would vary, especially in the heat of battle. The proximity fuse would automatically detect how far away the shell was from its target and detonate it a few feet from the target. This was especially critical in anti-aircraft artillery that needed to intercept enemy bombers and fighters. As simple as the idea seems on paper, the development of the proximity fuse required two technical feats: miniaturising radar components to fit within the confines of an artillery shell and ensuring they could withstand the extreme forces of launch and flight.[8]

RCA and GE played pivotal roles in solving these challenges. RCA, drawing on its background in radio technology, pioneered the production of compact vacuum tubes and other essential electronic components that would fit into artillery shells. Its engineers redesigned the radar circuits and hardened them to withstand the intense acceleration forces—up to twenty thousand *gs*—experienced during the launch of a projectile. Innovations in vibration-resistant circuit designs and high-speed testing allowed RCA to ensure the reliability of these miniaturised systems under extreme conditions. Power management posed another hurdle. Traditional radar systems required substantial energy, but proximity fuses had to function with minimal power. RCA addressed this problem with breakthroughs in battery technology and low-power circuit design, ensuring the fuse could operate efficiently from the moment it was fired to its detonation near a target. Raytheon adapted ruggedised versions of miniature tubes it had designed for possible portable applications such as hearing aids.[9] These advances not only facilitated the fuse's success but also found later applications in consumer electronics, including portable radios.

GE's contributions were equally vital. The company developed shock-absorption technologies and durable casings to protect the sensitive electronics within the fuse. Its materials engineers worked to ensure these components could endure the punishing environments of artillery use, ranging from intense heat and vibration to high-speed rotation during flight. This was important because the battery powering the internal radio of the shell would be activated by breaking a glass casing containing electrolytes, "arming" the device to explode upon finding a nearby target. The glass casings, therefore, needed to be strong enough to stay inert until firing and sensitive enough to break upon firing. GE repurposed its lamp division's Christmas light plants to engineer and manufacture these lamps. Its innovations proved essential in maintaining the fuse's functionality and accuracy in diverse combat conditions. The sheer scale of production required for proximity fuses added another difficulty. Manufacturing millions of highly precise devices demanded stringent quality control and advanced assembly-line techniques.[10] In the end, five different companies—Crosley, RCA, Sylvania, Eastman Kodak, and McQuay Norris—were contracted for the final assembly of the fuses, whose contract value jumped more than sevenfold between 1942 and 1945, from $60 million to $450 million.[11]

These feats did not occur in a vacuum: the coordinating role of the government was key. The National Defense Research Committee (NDRC, the predecessor of the OSRD) had commissioned research on the proximity fuse as early as June 1940. The Navy, concerned about the aerial threat to surface warships, had pushed the NDRC to accelerate the development of advanced directional fuses that could be used in Anti Aircraft Artillery (AAA). The government organised the fundamental research in "Section T" that would work in the Carnegie Institution in Washington, D.C. It then contracted Johns Hopkins University to establish an Applied Physics Laboratory with seven hundred personnel to improve on a British prototype that could not yet withstand the G-forces of a spinning AAA shell. On the demand side, government procurement programs guaranteed demand for proximity fuses, de-risking the R&D investment, and they also created a clear feedback loop between military needs and corporate production capabilities. This enabled the companies to focus on solving critical technical challenges without market uncertainty, accelerating the timeline from prototype to deployment.

The proximity fuse succeeded because university scientists, corporate engineers, and field operators worked in tight coordination. Feedback from live tests let RCA and GE refine the design, correct unexpected flaws, and ensure reliable performance in combat. Their collaboration blended electronics, materials science, and mechanical engineering, speeding problem-solving and setting a model for later innovation ecosystems. Interestingly, the proximity fuse was an application for innovations in solid-state electronics that would follow in the wake of World War II: the first market for the

AT&T's transistor, invented in 1947, for instance, was to replace vacuum tubes in fuses used in the Korean War; two decades later, RCA's miniaturised diode lasers would see action as fuses for the sidewinder heat-seeking missile.

The radar and proximity fuse illustrate the consequential, yet laborious, application of science to innovation. None of the participants—the government, the firms, and the universities—would by themselves have been able to adapt the British prototypes for deployment and mass-produce them within two to three years. Faced with compressed schedules, the government needed to align the capabilities of each sector through the NDRC/OSRD, while aligning incentives by signalling that R&D investments would yield financial returns.

Penicillin and the antibiotic revolution

The mass production of penicillin during World War II marks a turning point in medical history. While Alexander Fleming discovered penicillin's antibacterial properties in 1928, it languished as a scientific curiosity for over a decade, constrained by challenges in production and stabilisation. It was only in 1940, when British scientists Howard Florey and Ernst Boris Chain at the University of Oxford demonstrated penicillin's therapeutic potential, that the groundwork for its widespread use began to take shape.

Turning penicillin into a scalable medical treatment required overcoming formidable technical hurdles in fermentation and chemical engineering. This task fell to the unique ecosystem of government-funded translational research, academic expertise, and corporate innovation. The U.S. government, recognising the strategic importance of the drug, partnered with companies such as Pfizer, Merck, and Eli Lilly to develop deep-tank fermentation, a mass production method that revolutionised penicillin production. Before this breakthrough, penicillin was grown in surface cultures, a labour-intensive and inefficient process. With funding and technical support from the OSRD's Committee on Medical Research (CMR) and the U.S. War Production Board (WPB), scientists at the United States Department of Agriculture's Northern laboratory in Illinois adapted a submerged fermentation process used by Pfizer for gluconic acid, discovered a more effective strain of Penicillium, and introduced corn steep liquor as a more effective nutrient medium. This method dramatically increased yields and reduced production time. By early 1944, Pfizer's Brooklyn plant had become the world's largest supplier of penicillin, producing enough doses to support the Normandy landings. Merck and Eli Lilly also played crucial roles. Merck developed methods to extract active penicillin from impurities, while Eli Lilly introduced crystallisation techniques to concentrate and standardise doses. These innovations ensured that penicillin could be reliably transported to battlefield hospitals, where it reduced infection–related mortality rates by up to 75 per cent.

The success of penicillin during World War II positioned firms like Pfizer, Merck, and Eli Lilly as leaders in the burgeoning pharmaceutical industry. The deep-tank fermentation process became a standard for producing biologics, vaccines, and other antibiotics. By the 1950s, these companies were expanding their portfolios, developing treatments for tuberculosis, pneumonia, and other diseases that had previously been major causes of mortality.

Though large-scale production of penicillin was primarily a chemical engineering accomplishment, medical research efforts initiated during World War II continued to bear fruit for decades after. Some of it was inspired by war needs but not directly funded by the federal government. The discovery of the antibiotic, streptomycin, by Selman Waksman's group at Rutgers University, supported by Merck, is a case in point. Streptomycin would prove to be effective in combating tuberculosis and other diseases caused by gram-negative bacteria. In other cases, such as Oswald Avery's fundamental discovery that DNA was the carrier of genetic information, the work was part of an effort to combat bacterial pneumonia at the Rockefeller Institute.

Gross and Sampat argue that federal research and procurement projects, coordinated by the Committee for Medical Research and the War Production Board, had profound long-term effects.[12] It did so by creating new fundamental knowledge, including extensive data on diseases and chemicals. The authors provide evidence that focal areas for the CMR and WPB, such as physiology and blood, saw sharp increases in scientific publication activity in the two decades after the war had ended. For example, CMR had launched a massive program on blood products because wounded soldiers frequently needed blood transfusions. A first step was to separate the different components of blood. Gross and Sampat argue that this created a research platform that facilitated the discovery of a range of drugs and therapies in the decades after World War II:

> For example, CMR's massive drug screening efforts—including in the hunt for antimalarials, treatments for other tropical diseases, and insect repellents, which collectively screened nearly 20,000 compounds—later became a model for cancer chemotherapy research and other efforts at the NIH. . . . Techniques developed by the blood substitute research program "provided a technical framework for [a] productive research field" after the war on blood-related disorders and blood-derived therapeutics. . . . the separation of blood "[made] possible the [further] discovery of the function and the uses in therapy" of different components in blood fractions.[13]

More broadly, companies involved in the war effort changed how they discovered drugs; they began to rely on scientific discoveries to inform and guide their search. This change can be seen in two pieces of evidence that Gross and Sampat provide. First, they show that the late 1940s and 1950s were a revolutionary period for drug discovery, especially for firms that received contracts from the CMR and WPB. For these firms, the average annual new drug introductions more than tripled to over ten per firm every five years. Other firms increased their average five-year drug introductions from 0.7 to 1.5 per firm. Prior to the late 1940s, total annual drug patenting by both groups of firms was more or less constant, and few of their patents were based in science (as measured by citations to the scientific literature). Both patterns changed after World War II: starting in the late 1940s, drug patenting grew, and they were more heavily reliant upon science. The growth in patenting and the growing reliance on science are far more significant for pharmaceutical firms involved in the war effort.[14] Pfizer's postwar transformation is a case in point. It entered the war as a producer of chemical products using biological processes. It emerged as a successful producer of penicillin. Thereafter, it searched for new antibiotics, developing terramycin in 1949, the fruit of systematically screening soil samples from around the world. In its efforts to develop therapies for chronic diseases, Pfizer increasingly grew scientifically oriented, with a growing staff of biologists and organic chemists, and engaging leading academic scientists as consultants.[15]

The examples of radar, proximity fuse, and penicillin illustrate several common themes. First and foremost, these innovations required a deep scientific understanding of the phenomena involved, along with complementary advances in engineering and design. Second, a combination of push and pull policies, where the federal government funded fundamental work but also stood ready to purchase successful solutions, seemed to work better than either policy alone. Third, getting working devices into the field required coordinated complementary initiatives.

Federal support of science

As discussed in Chapter 7, federal funding of research was minimal prior to World War II. The largest research appropriations were directed at agriculture rather than industry. Universities were largely funded by states and businesses, necessitating a focus on applied research relevant to local industries and regional public interests.

The Cold War featured heavy involvement of the federal government in sponsoring research. The shift reflected the main lesson drawn from the wartime "deep-tech" projects run by the OSRD. When hostilities began, the United States lacked a commanding lead in key scientific fields. Though the United States was home to some of the most advanced electrical companies, the cavity magnetron needed to be transferred through the Tizard mission. Penicillin itself was prototyped (albeit in petri-dish form) at a British institution. Most of the leading physicists of the Manhattan Project received training from European institutions, while the first fission reaction was a German achievement (by Otto Hahn and Fritz Strassmann). As the Berlin blockade (1948–1949) and the Korean War (1950–1953) heralded a new geopolitical competition with the Soviet Union, American policymakers were keen to gain a scientific edge. This sometimes meant literally capturing former Nazi scientists and engineers to redeploy them in national projects. Operation Paperclip, run by the Joint Intelligence Objectives Agency, relocated an estimated sixteen hundred scientists to the United States.[16] On the home front, the federal government entered the business of science, both in the production of knowledge and human capital and the procurement of products embodying science.

Building the federal research infrastructure

The zeitgeist was captured by Vannevar Bush, the director of the OSRD which performed major wartime R&D programs. In "Science, the Endless Frontier," Bush articulated an expansive vision for government sponsorship of upstream research. Science, he argued, was the "pacemaker of technological progress," and he emphasised that "[t]he most important ways in which the Government can promote industrial research are to increase the flow of new scientific knowledge through support of basic research and to aid in the development of scientific talent."[17]

Bush's vision called for a single "National Research Foundation" to be run solely by scientists with no political interference. While there was bipartisan support for such an organisation, there was also pushback against Bush's request for the agency's political independence.[18] By the time the NSF was established, five years had elapsed, allowing for legacy partnerships during the war (such as the Atomic Energy Commission [AEC], the Office of Naval Research [ONR], and the Public Health Service) to receive congressional approval to be established as standing agencies.

The AEC was responsible for both military and civilian nuclear advancements, inheriting the Manhattan Project sites of Oak Ridge, Argonne, and Los Alamos, while breaking ground on new particle accelerators that would continue to advance high-energy physics. The AEC also spearheaded the peaceful applications of nuclear energy in power generation. As well, the commission funded ecological studies that were foundational to understanding the environmental impacts of nuclear radiation.[19] A by-product of this research was the introduction of radiation therapy in the biomedical field.[20]

The ONR, established in 1946, was crucial for funding research with applications that spanned both military and civilian sectors. At its founding, the ONR's mission was articulated as "planning, fostering, and encouraging scientific research in recognition of its paramount importance as related to the maintenance of future naval power and the preservation of national security."[21]

The ONR initially concentrated on naval and marine technologies, including deep-sea exploration, which proved essential for submarine warfare, underwater navigation, and the radar and acoustic detection of enemy vessels. These innovations also contributed to broader scientific knowledge in oceanography.[22] The ONR was also one of the early funders of computer science research. Taking inspiration from the Army's support for Electronic Numerical Integrator and Computer (ENIAC) at the University of Pennsylvania, the ONR contracted MIT's Servomechanisms Laboratory for Project Whirlwind, one of the first digital computers with real-time output. Whirlwind I and II would become prototypes for the more advanced Semi-Automatic Ground Environment (SAGE) air defence systems used by the Air Force.

NASA traces its roots back to 1915 in the National Advisory Committee on Aeronautics (NACA). By 1946, NACA had already been engaged in research involving rocket-engine powered aircraft such as the Bell X-1, which became famous for the plane Chuck Yeager rode to break the sound barrier. These early experiments set the stage for NASA's future achievements in aerospace and space exploration. In response to the launch of Sputnik in 1957, Dwight Eisenhower signed the National Aeronautics and Space Act of 1958: NASA inherited NACA's eight thousand employees, an annual budget of approximately $100 million, and three major research laboratories: the Ames Aeronautical Laboratory in California, the Langley Aeronautical Laboratory in Virginia, and the Lewis Flight Propulsion Laboratory in Ohio (later the Glenn Research Center).[23] This infrastructure was augmented with the absorption of facilities such as Caltech's Jet Propulsion Lab. This allowed the agency to conduct R&D to support human spaceflight and planetary exploration, beginning with the successful launch of the Explorer 1 satellite in 1958, which provided crucial data on the Van Allen radiation belts and demonstrated the United States' capabilities in space.[24]

The Advanced Research Projects Agency (ARPA, later DARPA, the Defense Advanced Research Projects Agency) was another response to Sputnik, created with a unique mandate to focus on breakthrough technologies that could significantly enhance national security. DARPA's accomplishments include the development of stealth technology, pioneering time-sharing computing and seeding artificial intelligence research in the 1960s. Stealth was the latest iteration of the U.S. Air Force's attempt to increase the survivability of reconnaissance aircraft. The potential strategic fallout of a shoot-down of spy planes had become evident in 1960, when a U-2 plane was downed by Soviet-made surface-to-air missiles (SAMs). The DoD's first response was speed—to develop the SR-71 in 1964 and outrun missiles with a top speed above Mach 3. A second solution was stealth, proposed by Robert Moore, deputy director of DARPA's Tactical Technology Office.[25]

By the 1970s, it had become possible to design flight surfaces with minimal radar cross sections using the physical theory of diffraction developed by Pyotr Ufimtsev in the 1960s.[26] DARPA initiated the Experimental Survivable Testbed (XST) program, which contracted Lockheed Martin and Northrop Grumman to research and produce stealth aircraft. DARPA was also an early sponsor of artificial intelligence in the 1960s, an idea far ahead of its time. DARPA sponsored blue-sky research projects such as "Shakey the robot" at the Stanford Research Institute as well as the Speech Understanding Research program at Carnegie Mellon University in the 1970s.

Advances in time-sharing computing were also made under the leadership of J. C. R. Licklider at the Information Processing Techniques Office (IPTO), who led Project Machine Aided Cognition (MAC) and proposed the idea for Advanced Research Projects Agency Network (ARPANET) (the early version of the internet).

Initially founded as the Hygienic Laboratory within the Marine Hospital Service in 1887, the NIH was conceived as a response to the growing need for scientific investigation into public health challenges.[27]

In 1930, the Ransdell Act renamed the Hygienic Lab to the National Institute of Health. In 1937, the National Cancer Institute was established, and the 1944 Public Health Service Act integrated it under a unified NIH. A pivotal provision extended the National Cancer Institute's grants program to all of NIH by 1946. This extramural funding mechanism grew rapidly, from $4 million in 1947 to over $100 million by 1957, then surpassing $1 billion by 1974. The full NIH budget similarly expanded from $8 million in 1947 to over $1 billion by 1966. The period from 1955 to 1968, under the leadership of Director James A. Shannon, came to be known as NIH's "golden years."[28]

Federal agencies not only became more prominent actors in the innovation ecosystem, but federal funding for university research and development also rose rapidly during this period. Figure 9.3 illustrates how federal support for research at higher education (the pattern-filled bar) jumped from $2.6 billion (2017 dollars) in 1945 to $25.3 billion in 1970.

The federal laboratories established for World War II were redirected toward peacetime research and housed within universities as federally funded research and development centers (FFRDCs). These included the Jet Propulsion Laboratory (JPL) at Caltech, Lincoln Laboratory at MIT, and the atomic research facilities at Brookhaven, Argonne, and Lawrence Livermore.[29] These centres made significant contributions across a range of technologies. MIT's Radiation Laboratory, pivotal for wartime radar, evolved into the Lincoln Laboratory, where early work on the Semi-Automatic Ground Environment (SAGE) helped to establish the foundations of modern computer networking.[30] At Caltech's JPL, rocket research broadened into pioneering space exploration programs—including the Viking and Voyager missions[31]—while Brookhaven National Laboratory, founded in 1947, introduced the Brookhaven Graphite Research Reactor to advance peaceful nuclear technology, making substantial strides in nuclear medicine, diagnostic imaging, high-performance computing, and fusion energy; Lawrence Livermore's Shiva and Nova laser programs helped to pioneer inertial confinement fusion.[32]

Expansion of human capital

Heeding Vannevar Bush's call to develop scientific talent, the United States embarked on a dramatic expansion of its scientific and engineering workforce. A key driver was the expansion of higher education. In the United States, the GI Bill of 1944 and the NDEA of 1958 enabled millions of young people to attend college, transforming the American workforce and democratising higher education.

Prior to World War II, higher education in the United States was predominantly accessible to the upper classes. The GI Bill significantly broadened access, leading to a surge in college enrolments. By 1947, veterans comprised nearly half of U.S. college admissions. The bill, officially known as the Servicemen's Readjustment Act of 1944, provided tuition assistance and living stipends to veterans pursuing college, vocational training, or on-the-job programs. Between 1944 and 1956, over 7.8 million veterans utilised the education and training benefits offered by the GI Bill.[33] The influx of educated veterans laid the foundations for eventually expanding graduate education in the United States. The Sputnik shock deepened these investments in the sciences through the NDEA of 1958 which allocated over a billion dollars to improve science and foreign language curricula and provide loans to thousands of "promising, yet needy" students in STEM disciplines through the National Defense Student Loans (NDSL).[34] The NDEA was followed by the Higher Education Act (HEA) of 1965. Title IV of the HEA established an array of student financial aid programs, including the Federal Pell Grant program, which offers need-based grants to millions of low-income undergraduate students to this day.

Individual agencies also played a role by starting their own grant programs to nurture doctoral talent. The NSF's Graduate Research Fellowship Program (GRFP), for instance, provided support to graduate students pursuing research careers since 1952. The NIH's Clinical Associates Program during the Vietnam war (nicknamed the "Yellow Beret" program) allowed young life science researchers to continue their work at the institutes instead of serving in the front lines.[35] The program counts four Nobel Laureates (Michael Brown, Joseph Goldstein, Harold Varmus, and Robert Lefkowitz) among its alumni.

The expansion of human capital post-World War II was unprecedented for its depth and breadth. Data from Biennial Surveys of Education in the United States show that between 1949 and 1969, the number of degree-granting higher education institutions grew 36 per cent, from 1,851 to 2,525, while total student enrolment grew more than threefold from 2.4 million to 8 million; the number of doctorates produced grew 4.6 times, from 6,420 to 29,912.

Firms absorbed these personnel to staff their research labs. As science and engineering doctorates grew from around forty thousand to just under one hundred twenty thousand between 1954 and 1970, the share of those working at private corporations stayed steady between 19 and 28 per cent (Figure 9.1). Workplace affiliations are taken from the National Register of Scientific and Technical Personnel (NRSTP) survey. The survey data reveals a significant growth in industry-based research scientists over this period, from 12,239 in 1958 to 19,849 by 1970. Within this group, those specifically designated as research scientists grew from 9,293 to 15,036 over the same time. Figure 9.2 shows that the chemical (20 per cent), pharmaceutical (13 per cent) and petroleum industries (12 per cent) employed close to half of all NRSTP Scientists from 1964

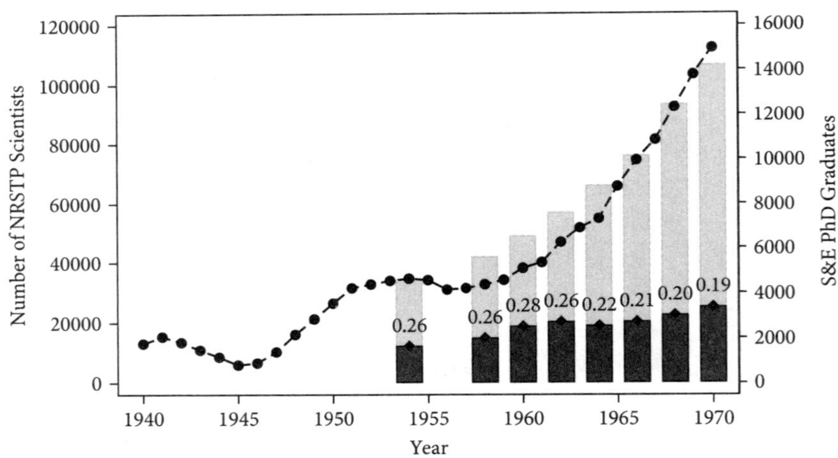

Figure 9.1 Production and Employment of Science and Engineering Doctorates (1925–1970)

Notes: This figure tracks the production and employment of Science & Engineering (S&E) PhDs from 1925 to 1970 in the United States. The bars represent the total number of scientists in the National Register of Scientific and Technical Personnel (NRSTP) survey, split between those working in industry (dark grey) and non-corporate sectors (light grey). The black diamonds show the proportion of NRSTP survey scientists working in industry. The dashed line with circle markers shows the number of S&E PhD graduates from American universities sourced from the Proquest Dissertation & Theses Database (plotted on the right axis).

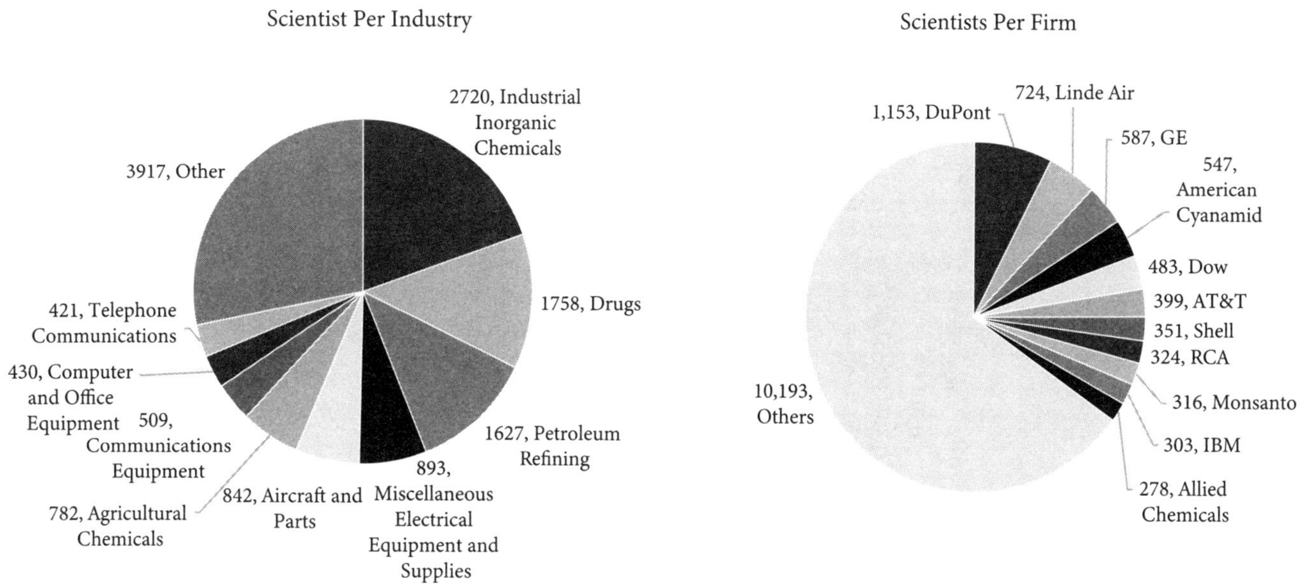

Figure 9.2 NRSTP Scientists' Employment (1964–1970)

Notes: The left pie chart takes the average number of scientists working for each 3-digit SIC industry from 1964, 1966, 1967, 1968, 1969 and 1970 National Register of Scientific and Technical Personnel (NRSTP) surveys. The right chart takes the average at the firm level.

to 1970, followed by the electrical industries (electrical equipment, communications and computers together employed 16 percent). The firm level distribution reflects the industry distribution, with DuPont employing the most scientists, followed by Linde Air and GE. Remarkably, the top ten firms employed 33 per cent of all NRSTP scientists during this period.

The changing nature of university research

Thanks to continued investments, American science, once relegated to catching up to the European "frontier" until the 1920s, established itself as a global leader in scientific research. Whereas U.S. institutions accounted for only 13 per cent of scientific Nobel laureates in the early 1900s, their share rose dramatically to reach 52 per cent in 1950–1954 and maintained a high level of 55–75 per cent through the latter half of the century. American universities expanded their scholarly output from approximately two thousand natural science and engineering publications in 1925 to forty-four thousand by 1970, representing a twenty-two-fold increase.[36] The dashed line in Figure 9.3 also shows that papers from Europe and Asia cite contemporary U.S. papers (i.e., those published up to five years prior) far more frequently: the share of American papers in their backward citations grew from under 20 per cent in 1939 to around 37 per cent in 1949. This share steadily grew, from an average of 35 per cent in the 1950s to 39 per cent in the 1960s.

The increased funding came with limited oversight. Given the nature of scientific inquiry, grants could not be designed as contracts with concrete deliverables. The principal mode of financing, which was at the Principal Investigator level, also encouraged scientists to explore their own curiosity rather than support a specific, overarching objective or "grand challenge," as in the years of the OSRD. In Bush's view, it was in such blue-sky research that public funding was needed most. As universities focused more on foundational research, their work became distinct from the more applied, mission-oriented research conducted in corporate labs and national laboratories. (For further discussion of mission-oriented research, see Chapter 13.)

The movement emphasising the pursuit of knowledge for its own sake has been a recurring theme in American educational history. Chapter 7

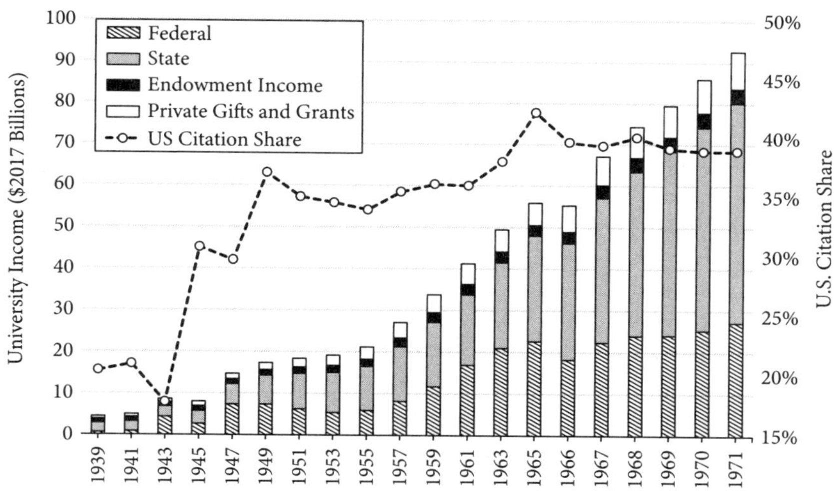

Figure 9.3 Expansion of the U.S. University Sector (1939–1971)

Notes: The stacked bar graph extends Figure 8.3 into 1971 and plots sources of revenue for the institutions of higher education in the United States. The dashed line graphs the share of citations made to U.S. authored publications from non-U.S. affiliated publications. "US Citation Share" is calculated by dividing total citations from European and Asian authors to U.S.-affiliated papers by total backward citations made by European and Asian authors. Backward citations up to five years prior to publication date are included. Citation and author affiliation data is sourced from the Dimensions database.

recounted the extent to which land grant colleges were focused on providing practical education to serve their surrounding industries. Even top institutions such as MIT instituted the Technology Plan as late as in the 1920s to pursue applied research directly relevant to industrial needs. Chapter 8 documents a parallel countermovement that traces its origins back to Rowland's 1883 "A Plea for Pure Science," which was inspired by the German research university.[37] As we further documented in this chapter, new institutions such as Caltech manifested this countermovement. The pendulum had also begun to swing back within established universities such as MIT, with G.N. Lewis (1912) and Arthur Noyes (1919) resigning from the institution, the replacement of Richard MacLaurin with physicist Karl Compton from Princeton, and the shutting down of individual industrial research programs. This resistance to mission-oriented research pre-World War II had its limits: universities were resource-constrained, beholden to state governments and regional industries for funding. Catering to the interests of these funders through relevant research and training was often a necessity, not a choice.

The postwar infusion of federal funding, however, fundamentally changed this dynamic. Much of the federal investment during this period—even that from mission-oriented agencies like the Department of Defense or the AEC—was focused on building human capital and supporting faculty-originated research. This federal support gradually distanced universities from the specific needs of corporations and business interests, allowing them to pursue more fundamental, curiosity-driven research.

We find evidence of this movement toward "Bohr's Quadrant" from American universities from the aggregate data.[38] Inventions as a whole were becoming even more reliant on science (measured by citations to the science and engineering literature): around 1.1 per cent of all patents in 1947 cite science; this number doubles to 2.0 per cent in 1957 and continues rising over the rest of the century (3.4 per cent in 1967; 5.0 per cent in 1977; 7.2 per cent in 1987). Moreover, this greater reliance is especially marked in "high-tech" inventions. Between 1947 and 1967, reliance on science grows over tenfold (from 1 per cent to 10.4 per cent) for breakthrough patents, those that are in the top 5 per cent of patent importance scores,[39] but only 2.7 times for non-breakthrough patents (from 1.1 per cent to 3.0 per cent). The increase during this period was distributed relatively evenly between chemicals, IT, the life sciences, and electrical engineering as seen in Figure 9.4, which extends Figure 8.1 from Chapter 8. Chemicals, electrical engineering, and computers and communications patents show a roughly twofold increase in the share of patents citing science between the 1940–1960 and 1960–1980 periods,[40] The increase for the life sciences is more modest 64 per cent, but in absolute terms, 23.1 per cent of all life science patents cite science in the 1960–1980 period, more than all other sectors.[41] Moreover, newly produced science during this period seems to be more "useful" for invention, suggesting a move toward "Pasteur's Quadrant" overall. Figure 9.5 shows that the share of papers cited by patents increases for both corporate and university authors.

However, this increase is more pronounced for corporate papers: while less than 2 per cent of papers during the 1920s in both sectors were cited by patents in the 1920s, this share jumps to 6 per cent for corporate papers, while it stays under 4 per cent for university papers. In fact, for most of the postwar period, only 2 per cent of university papers are cited by patents. This is consistent with our speculation that funding for university science through the principal investigator system (as opposed to mission-oriented, short-term projects such as the CMR) allowed academics the freedom to

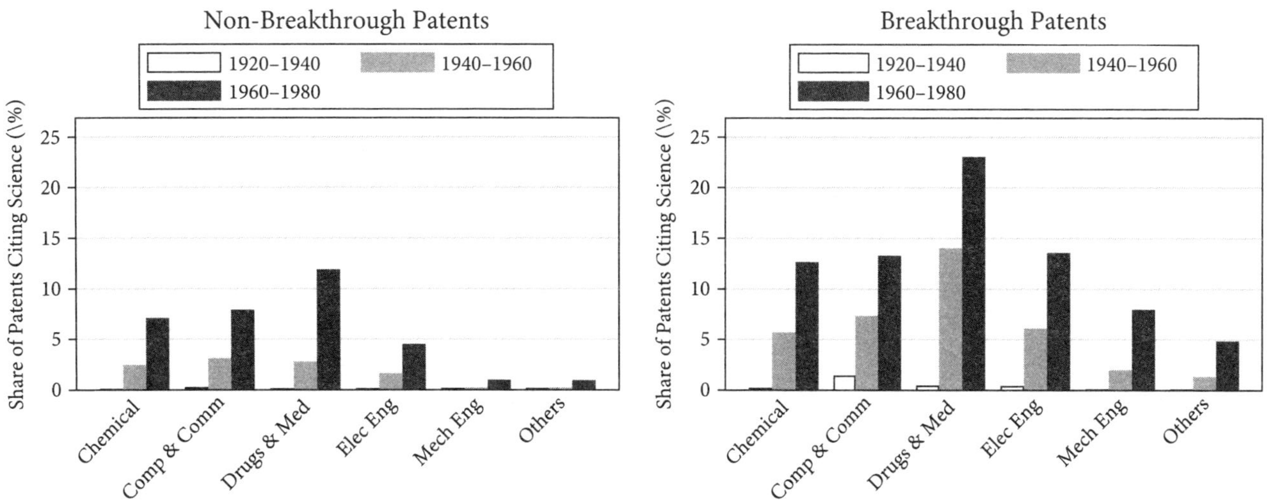

Figure 9.4 Patent Citations to Science, by Breakthrough Patent Status and Technology Category (1920–1980)

Notes: This plot extends Figure 8.1 into 1980. The right panel plots the percentage share of "breakthrough" patents that cite scientific articles for patents issued between 1900 and 1919 and 1920 and 1940, by NBER patent categories. The left panel plots the same for all other ("non-breakthrough") patents. Breakthrough patents are defined as those that are in the top 10 per cent of the importance measures from Kelly, Papanikolaou, Seru, and Taddy (2021)[42], where importance is calculated by dividing similarity with future patents (ten years after focal patent issuance) by similarity with past patents (five years before focal patent issuance) comparing patents granted in the same year.

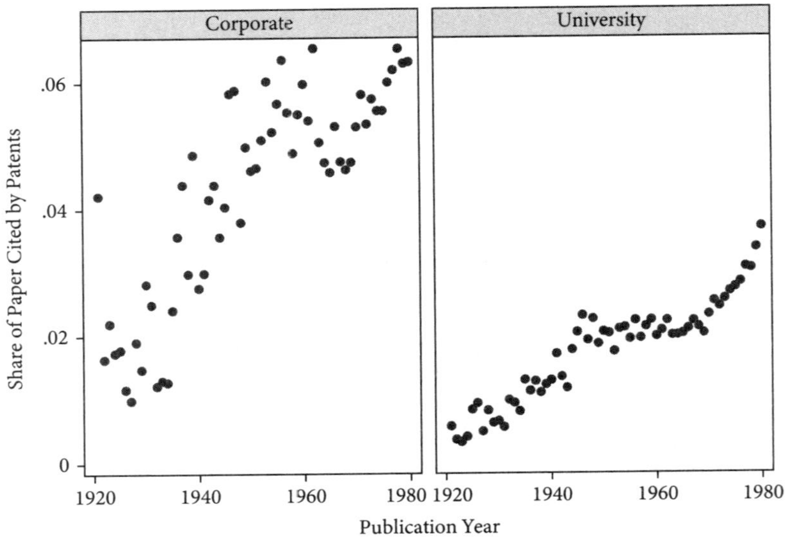

Figure 9.5 Share of Publications Cited by Patents, by Author Type (1920-1980)

Notes: The left plot divides the number of papers authored by corporate authors by total papers. The right plot shows the numbers for university authors. Author affiliations and type are sourced from the OpenAlex Database. Sample is limited to papers whose authors have a U.S. affiliation and granted patents from the USPTO.

explore more purely curiosity-inspired research in Bohr's Quadrant. In the next chapter, we show evidence that the need to absorb this new knowledge may have contributed to the postwar expansion of corporate research.

Federal demand for science-based innovations

During World War II, American policymakers employed demand-side interventions to foster corporate innovation. An expanded system of research contracts and defence procurement offered both direct support for foundational R&D and stable markets for advanced technologies. By reducing uncertainty about future demand, these programs especially incentivised firms at the scientific frontier (those that we term "Leader" firms in Chapter 10) to undertake ambitious technological projects. The Cold War sustained the imperative to maintain scientific and technological leadership.

The scale and scope of this federal commitment to technological advancement are illustrated in Figure 9.6, which tracks federal R&D obligations

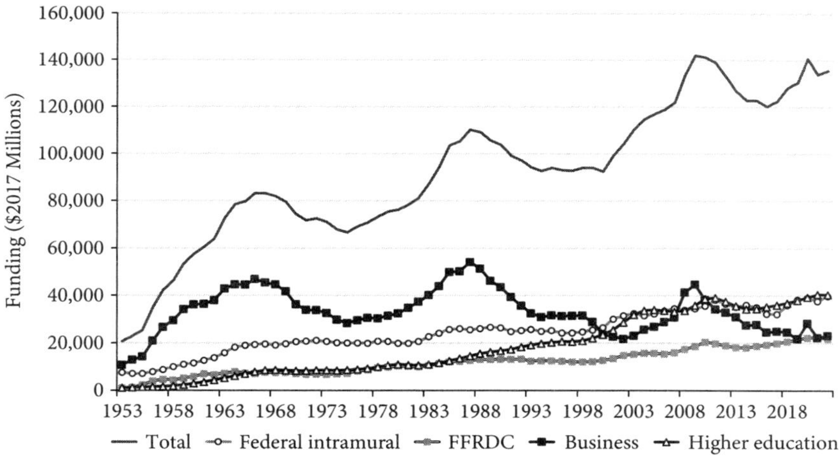

Figure 9.6 Federal Obligations for R&D, by Performer, 1953–2022

Notes: The figure illustrates federal R&D obligations distributed across five performing sectors: Total, Intramural, Industry, FFRDCs, and University. Intramural activities encompass both the administration costs of intramural R&D programs and extramural R&D procurements by federal personnel, as well as actual intramural research performance. FFRDCs include facilities administered by industry, universities, and non-profit organisations, with their funding levels reflecting changes due to the establishment of new centres, discontinuation of existing ones, and modifications in administrator classifications. Data is sourced from the National Center for Science and Engineering Statistics, Survey of Federal Funds for Research and Development. Dollar values are deflated to millions of 2017 dollars.

across different performing sectors from 1953 to 2022.[43] The data reveals a dramatic surge in total federal R&D obligations during the post-Sputnik period, with industry emerging as the largest nongovernmental performer. Federal funding to industry peaked in the mid-1960s at approximately $45 billion (in 2017 dollars), coinciding with the height of the Space Race and major defence initiatives such as the Minuteman Intercontinental Ballistic Missile program, the Polaris submarine-launched ballistic missile system, the development of advanced radar systems like SAGE (Semi-Automatic Ground Environment), and the early stages of the F-111 fighter-bomber project. While funding for industrial R&D fluctuated a bit, it remained a substantial component of federal R&D investment, typically exceeding funding to universities and FFRDCs (Federally Funded Research and Development Centers). Simply put, sustained federal investment provided crucial support for corporate research capabilities during the postwar period.

Defence procurement was especially important, creating both immediate demand and long-term incentives.[44] The most substantial expansion of defence research funding occurred in the late 1950s, when defence R&D expenditures more than doubled from $13.21 billion in 1953 to $40.22 billion in 1959.[45] The Korean War served as the primary impetus behind the U.S. military's embrace of high technology, as the services sought new weapons systems including jet-propelled fighters and bombers, nuclear-powered submarines, and experimental aircraft like the Dyna-Soar.

Throughout the 1960s, annual defence R&D hovered between $48 billion and $55 billion, exceeding non-defence R&D allocations. The Department of Defense strategically directed funds to multiple competing technologies supporting similar missions, thereby fostering innovation through competition both within military services and between defence contractors. Although the Vietnam War shifted some focus toward immediate operational needs, the "DOD's commitment to high technology almost regardless of cost remained on display."[46] By 1980, defence R&D stood at $43.32 billion, compared to nondefence R&D at $46.14 billion.

The impact of defence procurement on corporate research was both widespread and transformative. Among the 877 public firms operating an industrial laboratory in 1965, 356 (over 40 per cent) conducted research under government contracts. A notable illustration is the American Telephone and Telegraph Company (AT&T), home to one of the largest U.S. corporate labs. According to the Industrial Research Labs of America Directory (IRL) of 1965, Bell Labs employed 720 physicists, 535 mathematicians, 296 chemists, 2,589 electrical engineers, 419 mechanical engineers, 282 other engineers, 29 metallurgists, 411 other professionals, 4,051 technicians, and 4,929 additional lab staff. Its Bellcomm division worked exclusively for the federal government, focusing on space exploration, missile systems, propulsion technologies, and communications for NASA missions. Even within Bell Labs itself, 44.7 per cent of R&D activities were reported as government-funded in 1965. IBM received approximately $500 million—its largest contract in the 1950s—to build fifty-six SAGE computers, advancing digital computing and networking technologies that would later influence modern computer architectures.[47,48]

This "technological mobilisation" extended beyond defence into civilian space exploration, as NASA's Apollo Program directed $25.8 billion ($257 billion in 2020 dollars) in contracts to corporations between 1961 and 1972.[49] North American Aviation, later part of Rockwell International, received a contract of $3.7 billion to develop the Apollo Command and Service Module (CSM).[50] This engineering challenge required breakthrough innovations in thermal protection systems capable of withstanding reentry temperatures exceeding 5,000°F, the development of advanced life support systems for extended missions, and precision guidance computers with unprecedented reliability requirements.[51] The company also built Saturn V's second stage, which demanded novel solutions in large-scale cryogenic propulsion technology and structural materials capable of containing super-cooled liquid hydrogen and oxygen.[52]

The technological legacies of both ARPA and NASA highlight the critical relationship between federal funding and corporate innovation during this period. Through these programs, the federal government fulfilled a dual role: serving simultaneously as a research sponsor, providing financial resources for ambitious R&D initiatives, and as a lead customer, creating guaranteed markets for the resulting technologies. This dual function created a uniquely favourable environment that enabled leading firms to sustain ambitious basic research programs throughout the Golden Age, assuring that their technological developments would find both financial support and practical application in a willing buyer. (Chapter 13 is dedicated to analysing the relationship between procurement and mission-oriented innovation.)

Chapter takeaways

The Golden Age of American scientific research marked an unparalleled period of collaboration within the nation's innovation ecosystem. Universities, startups, large corporations, and the government coalesced to create a synergistic environment that advanced both scientific discovery and technological progress.

At the heart of this ecosystem were universities, which excelled in producing fundamental scientific knowledge and training highly skilled scientists and engineers. This intellectual capital made corporate investment in research not only viable but highly productive. Corporate laboratories, in turn, leveraged this talent and knowledge to focus on applied research, which often unearthed new scientific questions. These questions were fed back to universities, creating a virtuous cycle where curiosity-driven science and practical innovation advanced hand in hand.

The government played a pivotal role by funding research and serving as a key customer for advanced technologies. During the Cold War, federal funding priorities centred on achieving technological superiority rather than pursuing economic efficiency. This strategic focus reduced overlap with corporate objectives, allowing both sectors to operate in tandem without stifling private-sector innovation. The result was a cohesive system in which government procurement, academic discovery, and corporate application worked seamlessly to propel the United States to the forefront of global innovation. The next chapter contextualises the continued expansion of corporate research in this broader policy environment.

As we explore further in Chapter 11, this alignment began to shift, beginning in the 1980s. Universities increasingly commercialised their research, licensing their discoveries and spinning off entrepreneurial firms that allowed established companies to acquire prepackaged scientific advancements. While this market-based approach enabled faster commercialisation, it also diminished the incentives of established corporations to maintain internal research capabilities or engage deeply with basic science.

10

The Golden Age of Industrial Research

Introduction

The mid-twentieth century is often described as the "Golden Age" of American corporate R&D. While only a fifth of publicly listed firms in America that had patents operated an industrial lab in 1927, over 80 per cent of them would be operating one by 1956. New polymers, transistors and integrated circuits, software, and antibiotics originated in these labs. In the process, leading firms such as DuPont, AT&T, Xerox, GE, IBM, and Merck pushed the boundaries of science, on a par with the top academic departments in their respective fields. However, many more corporate labs were engaged in absorbing science rather than producing it, and an even larger share consisted of labs engaged in improving existing technology rather than searching for major innovations.

We revisit the postwar surge of corporate research by distinguishing among different types of firms and their labs. "Leaders" operated labs that were pushing the boundaries of science in the hope of generating breakthrough inventions. "Absorbers" invested in research to assimilate and use scientific advances from the public domain. Absorbers' inventions were often science-based, but the science used was rarely produced internally. "Followers" were concerned with improving existing products and processes rather than applying internally or externally produced science.[1] The first half of the chapter describes in greater detail this taxonomy, noting differences among these firms in their scientific output and the type of science they use: While both Leaders and Absorbers were more likely to use science in their inventions (relative to Followers), only Leaders used internal science. The development of laser science showcases the three distinct motives in more detail.

The second half of the chapter analyses how public policy contributed to the emergence of these research strategies. The third section shows how the supply-side forces reviewed in the previous chapter (university expansion, federal fellowships, and the migration of PhDs into industry) accentuated the distinctions between these types of firms. The final section examines the effect of federal policies on competition and procurement and shows how the government, as the buyer of first resort, encouraged research at Fairchild and RCA.

The uneven rise of corporate research

Between 1954 and 1970, the private sector doubled its employment of science and engineering doctorates, with numbers rising from 11,181 to 22,915.[2] Figure 10.1 shows that the proportion of patenting firms operating dedicated research laboratories more than doubled, growing from 38 per cent in 1940 to 83 per cent by 1956.[3]

Despite this expansion on the extensive margin, firms advancing the scientific frontier were few and far between. Rather, the corporate research programs established during this period were largely tasked with absorbing and translating knowledge from an ascendant U.S. academic sector. The "golden

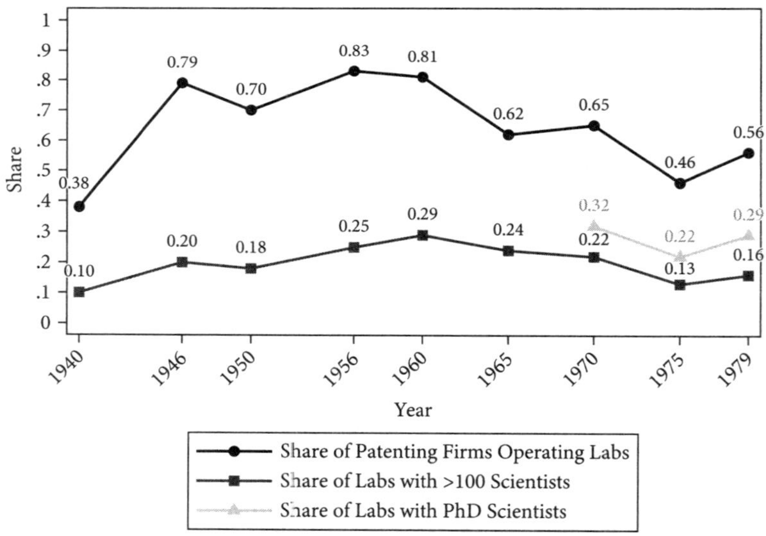

Figure 10.1 Share of Public Firms Operating Labs (1940–1979)

Notes: This figure is the first of two panels examining the growth of industrial research in our sample of public patenting firms from 1925 to 1980. We show three metrics related to industrial laboratories, with each dot representing a different edition of the Industrial Research Laboratory (IRL) directory: the share of firms operating labs (black line); the share of labs with more than 100 scientists (dark grey line); and the share of labs with PhD scientists (light grey line), available for select years after 1965.

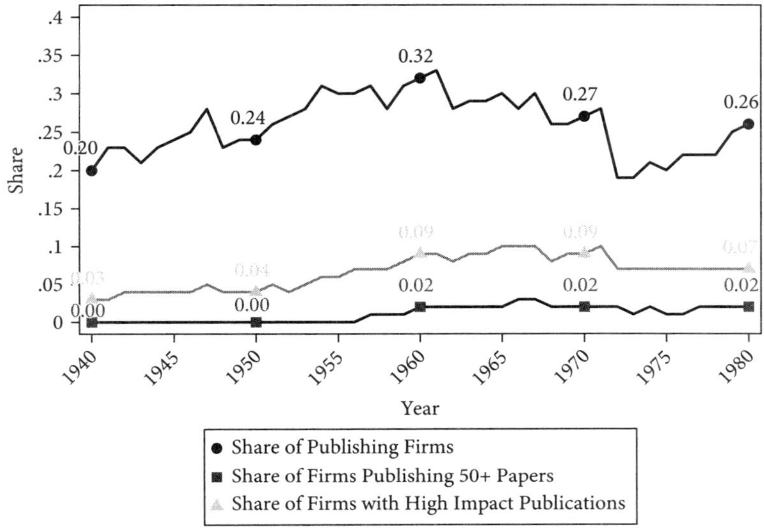

Figure 10.2 Share of Public Firms with Scientific Publications (1940–1980)

Notes: This figure is the second of two panels examining the growth of industrial research in our sample of patenting firms from 1925 to 1980. Here, we track corporate publication: the share of firms publishing in peer-reviewed journals (black line); the share of firms publishing fifty or more papers (dark grey line); and the share of firms producing high-impact publications (light grey line), defined as publications receiving forward citations in the top 10th percentile of their OECD subfield.

age of antibiotics" illustrates this focus on incremental, follow-on work by firms emulating landmark discoveries at universities. Pharmaceutical companies like Pfizer, Merck, and Eli Lilly systematically absorbed academic discoveries in microbiology from the academic successors of Florey and Chain (recounted in the previous chapter): chief among these was Selman Waksman.[4] In the process of discovering Streptomycin in 1943 (which would later earn him the Nobel Prize in Medicine in 1952), Waksman developed routine screening procedures[5] which inspired the establishment of large-scale antibiotic screening operations at most major pharma companies by the 1950s. Parke-Davis, for instance, funded work by Paul Burkholder at Yale to discover Chloromycetin (brought back from a soil sample in Venezuela). Lederle Laboratories hired Yellapragada Subbarow from Harvard University to lead a team that would discover Aureomycin.[6]

In contrast to this strategy geared toward tracking university advances, a handful of firms, such as AT&T and DuPont, maintained research programs that actively steered the direction of the latest research, partly because academic research still often lagged the frontier in polymers, computer science, and solid-state electronics. These "Leader" firms also greatly benefited from government procurement contracts for defence and space exploration, which created markets for products such as integrated circuits, computers, and diode lasers.

Bell Laboratories became the premier industrial research institution, making significant contributions to both basic science and technology. Their work in solid-state physics led to the transistor. Claude Shannon's mathematical theory of communication established the foundations for digital communication. The lab later expanded into quantum optics with maser and laser research and made contributions to cosmology by discovering cosmic microwave background radiation.

The laboratory's fundamental contributions were recognised through the 1956 Physics Prize awarded to Bardeen, Brattain, and Shockley for their 1947 invention of the transistor,[7] the 1978 Physics Prize shared by Penzias and Wilson for their 1965 discovery of cosmic microwave background radiation,[8] and the 1981 Prize to Schawlow for his contributions to lasers in 1958.[9] This remarkable clustering of Nobel-winning research, all of which was conducted within a roughly twenty-year period at a single corporate laboratory, underscores Bell Labs' unique position in the history of industrial research and exemplifies the profound integration of fundamental scientific inquiry with technological innovation.[10]

General Electric's (GE's) research laboratory demonstrated exceptional strengths across multiple scientific domains. Their breakthrough research in superconductivity, notably Giaever's work on electron tunnelling in superconductors,[11] advanced the fundamental understanding of quantum mechanics. GE's scientific excellence extended into computer science, recognised through Charles Bachman's 1973 Turing Award for pioneering work in database technology.[12] In applied research, GE achieved a significant milestone with the development of the first civilian nuclear power plant.[13]

IBM, meanwhile, emerged as a pioneer in computer science and information technology. The laboratory's theoretical contributions to computational methods, particularly the Fast Fourier Transform,[14] demonstrated IBM's ability to advance both mathematical foundations and practical applications. IBM's scientific preeminence was recognised through awards, with John Backus receiving the Turing Award in 1977 for developing FORTRAN and programming language theory,[15] and Kenneth E. Iverson being honoured in 1979 for his work on mathematical notation and programming languages.[16] IBM's development of the hard disk drive[17] represented a fundamental advance in digital data storage, while its work in cryptography[18] established essential principles for modern computer security.

Figure 10.3 underscores how corporate science during the Cold War managed to push the scientific frontier: the number of Nobel Prizes awarded to American corporate scientists rises from four right after World War II to eleven between 1965 and 1974. The number of Turing Award winners and National Medal of Science recipients at firms also peaks during this period, with twelve and seven laureates each. These frontier firms, however, were the exception rather than the norm. Nelson and Langlois's historical analysis of industrial innovation[19] demonstrates that even during periods of widespread R&D expansion, scientific production remained concentrated among a select group of firms. For instance, the prevalence of very large corporate labs, indicated by labs employing over one hundred scientists, reached 20 per cent by 1946 but then plateaued, fluctuating between 18 and 29 percent through the next three decades. Figure 10.2 confirms this pattern with corporate publications, showing that the share of firms publishing in scientific journals hovered around 25–30 percent throughout the period. The production of scientific knowledge also remained concentrated: only

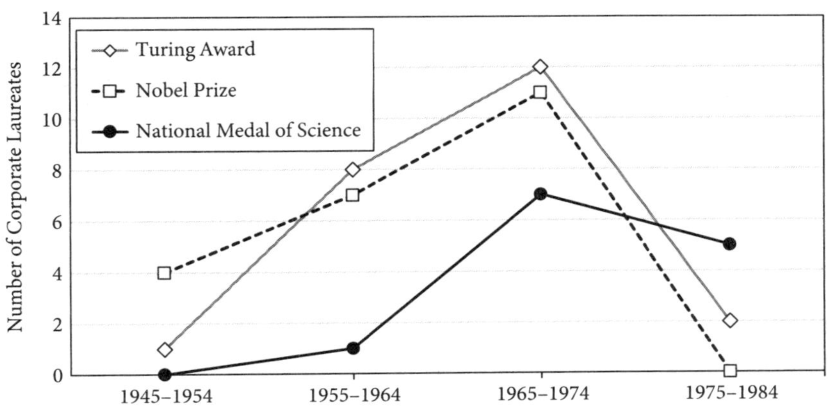

Figure 10.3 Prestigious Scientific Awards won by American Public Firms (1945–1985)

Notes: This figure counts the number of American corporate laureates of the Turing Award, Nobel Prizes in Physics, Chemistry and Medicine, and the National Medal of Science. The years denote when the paper credited with the achievement was published, and are binned into decades beginning from 1945.

2–4 percent of firms published fifty or more papers per year, while fewer than 10 percent produced a high-impact publication.

Figure 10.4 shows the strong concentration of scientific knowledge production: the top four firms, which owned 18 per cent of all corporate assets, employed 19 per cent of all industrial scientists, held 32 per cent of corporate patents, and accounted for 53 per cent of corporate publications. High-impact publications show an even greater concentration at 65 per cent. Strikingly, the top four firms accounted for all prestigious scientific awards given to corporate scientists.[20]

A larger group of firms established labs to absorb and translate outside knowledge.[21] These firms focused primarily on applying existing scientific knowledge from leading firms and universities. The vast majority of labs, however, focused on developing and improving existing products.

The case of Koppers Company is an example of a firm whose investments were focused on absorbing and applying external scientific knowledge. Despite averaging 413 scientists and substantial patenting (46 per year), Koppers had a modest annual rate of publications (2.64) from 1945 to 1980. Koppers's resources were primarily directed toward absorbing and applying existing science rather than producing new advances. In polymer science, a 1966 paper, "Axial Dispersion of Polymer Molecules in

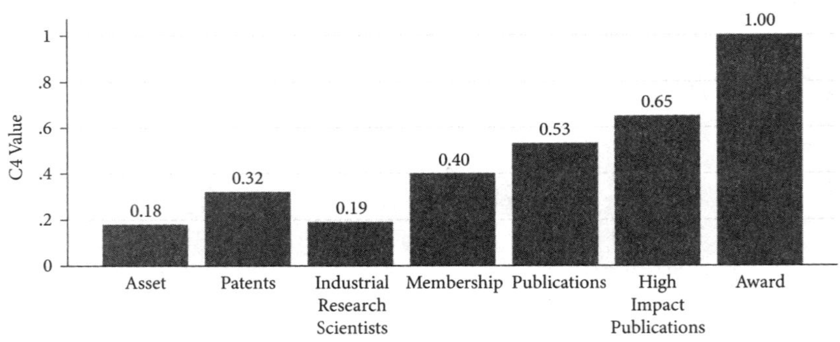

Figure 10.4 Four-Firm Concentration Ratio (C4), by Engagement with Science (1945–1980)

Notes: This figure presents the average C4 concentration ratios (share of top 4 firms) across different scientific and economic metrics for 1945–1980. For each metric, the C4 ratio is first calculated annually by identifying the share of the top 4 firms in that year, then averaged across all years in the sample period. "Membership" refers to the number of corporate scientists who are members of scientific and engineering societies. "High-Impact Publications" refers to the number of publications with forward citations in the top 10th percentile of their respective OECD subfield in a given year. "Award" refers to the scientific and engineering awards received by corporate scientists in Figure 10.3.

Gel Permeation Chromatography,"[22] is about refining and improving gel permeation chromatography. The authors adapt existing dispersion models from chemical engineering to correct chromatographic data to enable a more accurate polymer characterisation. Citation data confirms this applied orientation: the paper received eighty-eight citations predominantly from applied technical journals (e.g., twenty-three in *Journal of Applied Polymer Science*). The paper itself relies heavily on practical information sources, with five of fifteen of its references being private communications or technical data sheets. The authors emphasise practical necessity, stating their goal as addressing "an error for which correction is needed" in polymer analysis, to provide solutions directly usable by scientists and engineers.

The firm's patent filings also make clear that when they built upon science, they did so on scientific discoveries generated outside of the firm. For example, Koppers's patent "Production of benzophenones" (US 3403183A), assigned to researchers Elmer Dobrotz and Alfred Kolka from Pittsburgh in 1966, builds on scientific knowledge developed at nearby Pennsylvania State College. The patent adapts a scientific discovery on "Hydrogen Fluoride as a Condensing Agent," by Simons, Randall, and Archer published in the *Journal of the American Chemical Society*[23] in 1939 to improve manufacturing processes for benzophenones.

In the field of polymer chemistry, Koppers's patent "Self-extinguishing expandable polymers containing volatile hydrocarbon, organic bromide, and n-nitroso secondary amine" (US 3274133A) cites research by J. Eichhorn of Dow Chemical Company, published in *the Journal of Applied Polymer Science*. Eichhorn's work provides the scientific foundation that Koppers researchers adapted to develop improved flame-retardant polymer formulations. Similarly, in Koppers's 1951 patent, "Manufacture of Melamine" (US 2559617A), inventor Raymond Hartigan builds upon research by P. P. McClellan of American Cyanamid Company published in 1940.[24] Clearly, these inventions by Koppers rely on science, but they are based on older scientific discoveries by external researchers. By contrast, as we will show later, patents by Leaders typically cite their own scientific work as well.

The company's role as an Absorber rather than a Leader is further evidenced by its minimal presence in elite scientific achievements. It employed only two members of the American Association for the Advancement of Science, and its researchers earned no prestigious scientific awards. Collectively, these indicators suggest that while Koppers was highly skilled in applying established scientific principles to practical problems, it was not a significant producer of scientific discoveries.

The third, and oldest, function of corporate labs was development and testing.[25] The National Biscuit Company (Nabisco) provides a telling example of this "Follower" approach. Despite maintaining a large research centre in Fair Lawn, New Jersey, complete with pilot plants and machine shops, and a technical staff of 205 personnel (52 chemists, 30 mechanical engineers, and 94 technicians in 1960), the company's activities were confined to routine development and testing rather than research and invention.

Although Nabisco's lab reported that it dedicated 75 per cent of its effort to R&D and only 25 per cent to testing and experimentation in the 1965 Industrial Research Laboratories directory, closer examination reveals that these R&D activities were primarily routine product and process development. The company's 1960 Annual Report shows that its laboratories concentrated on practical manufacturing concerns, including mixing and baking techniques, ingredient handling, and packaging methods.[26] A typical project during this period involved flour milling technology at the company's mills in Toledo, Ohio; Carthage, Missouri; and Cheney, Washington, which produced over 80 per cent of the company's flour requirements.

The company's scientific and technical output from the 1940s to 1980s confirms this development-centric approach. Their publications in the *Journal of the Association of Official Agricultural Chemists International* were limited to routine quality control procedures, such as measuring sugar content and moisture levels in baked goods, and they required no advanced scientific knowledge. Technical studies such as "Correlation of Keeping Properties of Shortenings with Keeping Quality of Biscuits"[27] and "The Change in Thiamin Content of Breakfast Cereals during Cooking"[28] consisted mainly of routine testing procedures and little engagement with recent science. Similarly, "Report on Sugars in Baked Products" describes a method for determining invert sugar and sucrose in biscuits, a standard quality control procedure for a biscuit company.[29] This approach to the use of science recalls the earliest applications of science in U.S. industry reviewed in Chapters 6 and 7.

To gauge how common each type of firm (Leader, Absorber, or Follower) was during the period 1945–1980, we fed several measures of corporate science (including publications, lab employees, scientific society memberships and awards) into an ensemble of deep-learning model to cluster firms into three groups.

Table 10.1 Ensemble Classification Results

	1945–1965	1965–1980
% of Leader	0.69%	1.87%
% of Absorber	8.41%	14.20%
% of Follower	90.90%	83.93%

Notes: This table reports the proportion of firms classified into three categories—Leaders, Absorbers, and Followers—over different time periods from 1945 to 1980. The proportions are reported as percentages for each time period. All values are rounded to two decimal places. Details regarding its implementation are found in Arora, Belenzon, Suh, and Zhang (2025).

Table 10.1[30] shows that the vast majority of firms with labs were Followers, focusing on quality control, process improvements, and building on existing inventions. Another 8–15 per cent of the firms used their labs to apply external scientific discoveries to their inventions as well. A scant 1–2 per cent engaged in scientific discovery themselves. The table also suggests that the proportion of Absorbers and Leaders grew during the period, but their combined share remained below one-sixth of firms with corporate labs.

Public science and corporate R&D

The scale and orientation of corporate research were shaped by three forces: the expansion of universities, antitrust policy, and federally funded programs informed by World War II and accelerated by the Cold War. Federal support combined R&D contracts with large purchases of the resulting products. The principal beneficiaries of these policies were defence contractors and other scientifically advanced firms, the group we label Leaders. Leaders invested partly in response to government demand, partly to ward off antitrust scrutiny, but also to forestall rivals and maintain their position in the large and growing U.S. domestic market.

In addition to mission-oriented research, the government funded investigator-initiated research projects in universities, in part to increase the country's base of scientists and engineers. The scientific knowledge produced by universities was sufficiently distant from commercial applications that firms needed absorptive capacity to use university knowledge. As Rosenberg put it

> . . . knowledge is regarded by economists as being "on the shelf" and costlessly available to all comers once it has been produced. But . . . it frequently requires a substantial research capability to understand, interpret and to appraise knowledge that has been placed upon the shelf . . . . The cost of maintaining this capability is high, because it is likely to require a cadre of in-house scientists who can do these things. And, in order to maintain such a cadre, the firm must be willing to let them perform basic research. The most effective way to remain effectively plugged in to the scientific network is to be a participant in the research process. . . .basic research may be thought of as a ticket of admission to an information network."[31]

That is, growing university research encouraged firms whose inventions were reliant upon science to invest in internal research to absorb external scientific knowledge from universities. This set of firms includes both Leaders and Absorbers. A smaller subset, the Leaders, looked to internal research for breakthrough inventions as well. To support this narrative, we provide quantitative evidence that firms classified as Leaders and Absorbers produce inventions that rely on science. By contrast, inventions by Followers are much less reliant on science. We then show that Leaders were more likely to use their own science in inventions compared to Absorber firms. We illustrate the absorption and production of science through the history of the invention and development of laser technology in the 1960s.

The left subplot of Figure 10.5 compares the share of firms' patents citing external science (i.e., from universities or rivals). The share of patents of both Leaders and Absorbers that cite scientific publications is more than double that of Followers. This points to the absorption of university science as an important incentive for corporate labs in Leaders and Absorbers. The right subplot, on the other hand, shows that the use of internal science in inventions is highest for Leaders, more than double that of Absorbers. This suggests that Leader firms had an additional motive beyond "mere" absorption of outside knowledge. They were creating knowledge to be used directly in their inventions.

Why were Leader firms compelled to create their own science? One reason is that their inventions were on the technical frontier, as measured by patents that are the first in a new patent class, as well as by how different their patents are from prior patents. This motive to substitute for poor public science formed the impetus for the rise of industrial research before

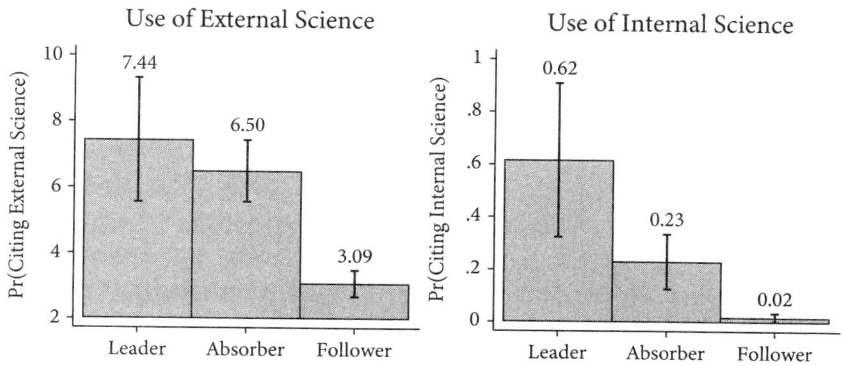

Figure 10.5 Share of Patents Citing Science, by Source of Science and Firm (1945–1980)

Notes: The left plot divides the number of firm patents citing scientific papers published outside of the focal firm by total firm patents and summarizes this number by Leader, Absorber, and Follower firm types. The right plot does the same for patent citations to scientific papers published by the focal firm. Capped spikes indicate 95% confidence intervals.

World War II, as surveyed in Chapter 7. Figure 10.6 shows that Leader firms produce around 7.2 times more patents that are first in a new patent class compared to Absorber firms (left plot). They also produce 7.6 times more breakthrough patents that are textually dissimilar to prior art but similar to subsequent patents. The differences hold even after we adjust for the number of patents as well as the industry to which the firm belonged. Producing novel, science-based inventions likely required Leaders to be on the relevant scientific frontier themselves, which in turn meant investing in pushing out the scientific frontier.

The absorption and production of laser science at firms

The invention and development of lasers shows both motives—translation and leadership—at play. As the acronym suggests, LASERs (Light Amplification by Stimulated Emission of Radiation) are devices that stimulate atoms to achieve coherent radiation in the infrared and visible ranges. An intense light source or electric current stimulates an active medium, such as a crystal, gas, or liquid mixed with dyes. The medium emits photons (light) that are amplified by bouncing back and forth inside a resonating chamber sealed off by reflective material. The idea for the laser was first conceived in its microwave-range predecessor, the Maser, which was invented in 1953 by

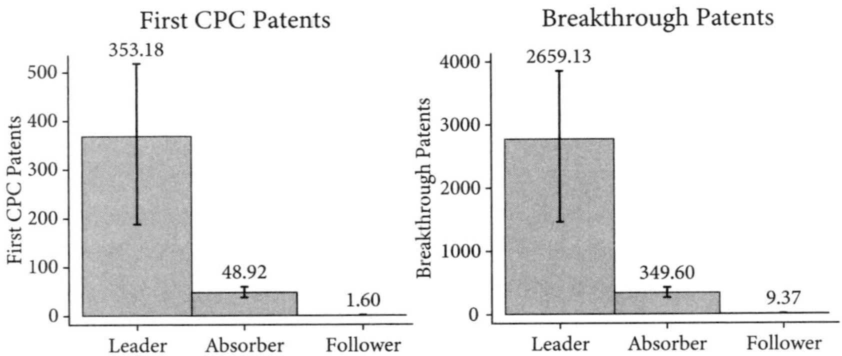

Figure 10.6 Technological Frontier, by Firm Type (1945–1980)

Notes: Left plot averages the number of inaugural CPC patents by firm type. Inaugural patents are the first patents ever granted in their respective CPC (Cooperative Patent Classification) classes. Right plot averages the number of breakthrough patents by firm type. "Breakthrough Patents" are patents in the top 20 per cent of importance measures from Kelly, Papanikolaou, Seru, and Taddy (2021).[32]

Charles Townes, a faculty member at Columbia, with support from the military's Joint Services Electronics Program. Townes then co-wrote a seminal paper with AT&T's Arthur Schawlow that conceived of the laser as a practical possibility.[33] It was also around this time that Gordon Gould, a graduate student at Columbia, coined the acronym LASER in a memo in 1957. The locus of early theoretical work on the laser, therefore, was squarely within academia.

Upon the publication of Schawlow and Townes's paper, an R&D race to build the first working laser ensued. Schawlow at Bell Labs, Gould at TRG, Thomas Maiman at Hughes Aircraft, Elias Snitzer at American Optical Company, and Peter Sorokin and Mirek Stevenson at IBM raced to build the first laser. Some of these firms, like Hughes and TRG, were defence contractors, while others, like AT&T and IBM, saw applications in communications. The first step was to absorb academic research. Townes was a consultant to Bell Labs, a tie formed during his wartime work at AT&T on radar bombing systems. Later, Gould was recruited to TRG (Technical Research Group), a defence contractor, which tried to absorb the latest academic developments in the field to prepare for a $999,000 contract with ARPA that was trying to augment its GLIPAR (Guide Line Identification Program for Anti-missile Research) programme.

However, after absorbing what was in the public domain, firms had to push the boundaries of science themselves. The key challenges were to find a suitable gain medium and a method for stimulating the atoms in the medium so that more atoms were in an "excited" state (also called population inversion) because lasing occurs when excited atoms return to their ground state.

Townes's approach at Columbia had focused on potassium gas as the primary gain medium. This research was funded by the Air Force's Office of Scientific Research, in the hope of improvements in air-to-air missile guidance systems. Some firms followed this university-initiated trajectory of using a gas-based gain medium. For instance, Ali Javan and John Sanders at Bell Labs used helium and neon gas. However, researchers at other firms chose other types of media. American Optical's Elias Snitzer, for instance, adopted glass fibres in light of his firm's expertise with the material. The IBM team experimented with solid uranium crystals in addition to calcium fluoride gas. Thomas Maiman at Hughes (who would win the race) used a ruby crystal and optical pumping via a camera flashlight. Neither the medium nor the pumping method was explored in the original Townes–Schawlow paper or Gould's notebook. Maiman's choice of ruby as the gain medium came from his prior work at Hughes Research Lab, building ruby masers for the Army Signal Corps. An early application of the ruby laser in 1961, barely a year after Maiman developed it in 1960, was to treat a retinal tumour for a patient at Columbia-Presbyterian Medical Center in New York City.[34]

The race to build the laser, therefore, required original research by corporations. Indeed, an analysis of the 1963 volume of the *Physics Abstracts*, a peer-reviewed academic journal, found that industrial scientists wrote 71 per cent of American-authored papers.[35] The recruitment of maser and laser academics into firms and the swift establishment of laser research programs at half a dozen competing firms show that the absorption of theoretical advances at universities was an important incentive for firms. At the same time, no one university could match the breadth and depth of firms that had prior experience dealing with the optical properties of glasses and solid crystals. Firms did not shy away from publishing their scientific discoveries, contributing to the pool of knowledge in the American innovation ecosystem.

Industrial research and market concentration

Similar to the leading firms of the interwar period, Leader firms in the Golden Age tended to be larger and to operate in concentrated industries. Figure 10.7 shows that Leader firms are more likely to operate in concentrated industries. We measure industry concentration using the share of industry assets held by the top 1 per cent of firms.[36] Industries are categorised into low concentration (0–25 per cent), medium concentration (25–75 per cent), and high concentration (75–100 per cent) based on the fraction of assets held by the top 1 per cent firms in the industry in a given year. In the vertical axis, the number of Leader firms is divided by total firms in a focal industry-year. The dots connected by a dashed line in Figure 10.7 show the average Leader share in each concentration category (Absorber firm shares are connected by solid lines). It shows that in concentrated industries, around 5 per cent of the firms in the industry are classified as Leaders, whereas in unconcentrated industries, only 1 per cent are Leaders.

The link between industry concentration and frontier-science investment reflects several forces. Firms that push the scientific frontier are usually large, naturally raising concentration. Spillovers add a second layer: knowledge leaks to rivals unless the innovator commands the downstream market. A dominant product position thus helps a Leader retain the gains from its breakthroughs.

The postwar period saw the emergence of giant corporations such as General Motors, AT&T, and IBM, which established commanding positions in their respective sectors. The resulting concentrations of these industries posed a tricky enforcement problem for the Department of Justice. AT&T, for example, maintained near-total control of telecommunications services and equipment manufacturing through its Bell System. Yet, it was also fulfilling its end of a "social bargain" whereby it would share and publish its scientific knowledge for the benefit of the broader scientific community. Although Bell Labs operated as a state-regulated monopoly, it also functioned as the nation's informal information-and-communications laboratory. Whether such "Leader" firms viewed their scientific output as part of a broader quid pro quo for market dominance remains uncertain. Tellingly, while the Department of Justice pressed the antitrust case that would end in AT&T's breakup, the company issued a seven-volume compendium of Bell Labs' advances in physics, materials science, electrical engineering, and chemistry—an implicit bid to show that its market power served the public good.[38]

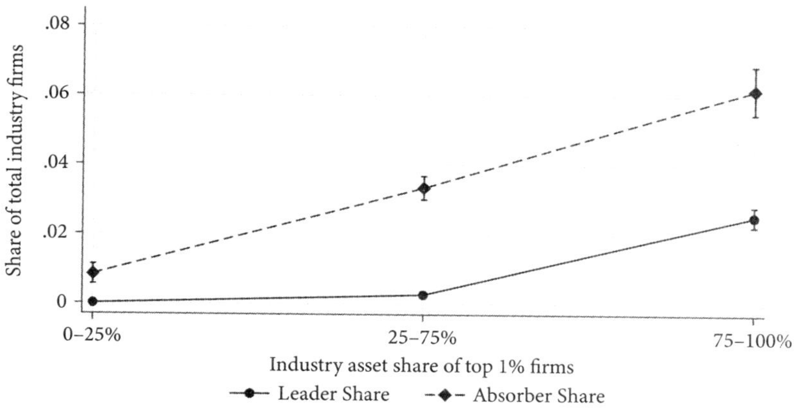

Figure 10.7 Comparison of Leader and Absorber Shares by Asset Concentration (1945–1980)

Notes: This figure examines the relationship between asset concentration and the prevalence of Leader and Absorber firms at the Bureau of Economic Analysis (BEA) Subsector level from 1945 to 1980. Industry-years are categorised by concentration percentiles (0–25%, 25–75%, 75–100%) defined as the asset share of the top 1% firms estimated from IRS Statistics of Income data by Kwon, Ma, and Zimmermann.[37] The points represent the average share of Leaders (connected by solid line) and Absorbers (dashed line) out of total firms in each industry-year, with 95% confidence intervals.

In practice, the tension between corporate "bigness" and the implicit social bargain was mediated by a series of consent decrees arising from landmark big-tech antitrust cases. In 1953, AT&T agreed to license its telecommunications patents royalty-free in exchange for maintaining its dominant market position.[39] A similar deal was signed by RCA in 1958 when it agreed to license its colour TV patents royalty-free to manufacturers in exchange for the Department of Justice dropping prosecution. In 1954, Kodak entered into an agreement whereby it made its colour photofinishing technology available to competitors. In 1956 IBM reached a similar settlement with antitrust regulators, agreeing to license its technology to rivals on reasonable-royalty terms while forgoing exclusive deals.

The consent decrees, in a sense, incentivised more sharing of scientific information in two ways. First, as patenting became a less viable appropriability mechanism, all four of these firms maintained defensive publication outlets. If knowledge around an invention could be made publicly available to the scientific community, the invention typically failed the novelty test at the Patent Office. The *Bell System Technical Journal*, the *IBM Technical Bulletin*, the *RCA Review*, and *Abridged Scientific Publications from Kodak Laboratories* all published findings from their respective labs. The grand bargain in the patent system is to grant a monopoly to an individual for making their invention publicly available. Arguably, the bargain implicitly struck in the Golden Age was to let "big tech" firms of their time maintain their dominant market positions in exchange for the provision of scientific knowledge to the broader innovation ecosystem.

Procurement policy

A pivotal shift from the interwar to the postwar innovation regime was the federal government's rise as a buyer of first resort for science-based innovation. Building on the Office of Scientific Research and Development (OSRD) and War Production Board (WPB) model, which linked upstream research with downstream procurement, the government kept this bundling strategy for major projects. Chapter 13 analyses recent procurement policy and its consequences for corporate R&D. It also develops the theoretical rationale for bundling R&D contracts with production contracts, showing why such bundling matters for upstream research, especially in vertically integrated firms. The discussion that follows takes that rationale as given.

The Space Race and Cold War procurement programs shaped not just technological innovation but also the structure of corporate R&D. Government contracts, designed to secure technological superiority over the Soviet Union, required strategic decisions about organising procurement. One of those decisions was whether to contract separately with specialised research firms for R&D and manufacturing companies for production or to bundle these functions into a single contract. In practice, American procurement practices favoured the latter approach, awarding contracts to firms that could handle both R&D and production. These contracts substantially bolstered research at many of the Leader firms. In some cases, R&D at these firms was primarily sustained by government R&D contracts and downstream procurement, as is true of Hughes (see Chapter 13), and to a lesser extent, RCA and Fairchild as well.

Figure 10.8 shows three types of government links. The first is patents with government interest clauses (left plot). Second, firms sometimes self-reported in surveys of industrial labs that they were involved in upstream government research contracts (middle plot). Third, downstream procurement participation can be measured by dividing the total defence contract values by sales (right plot). In all three cases, we find that Leaders are

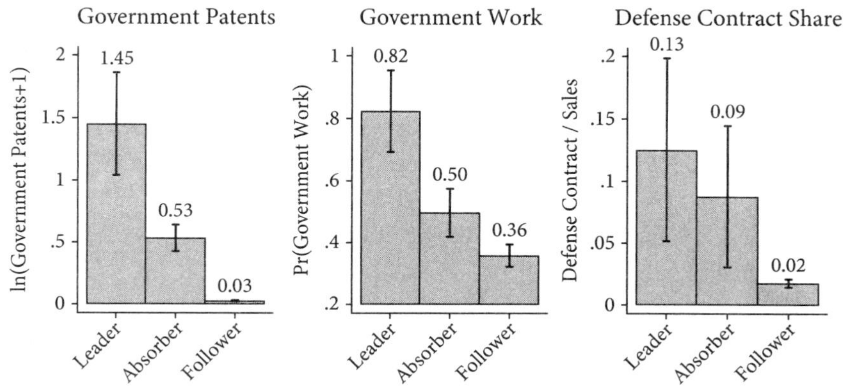

Figure 10.8 Corporate Engagement with Government Contracts, by Firm Type (1945–1980)

Notes: The three plots display averages and 95% confidence intervals for measures of corporate engagement with government procurement. "Government Patents" in the left plot refer to the number of firm patents licensed to or held by government entities. "Government work" is a dummy equal to one if the research facilities either fully or partially dedicated their research activities to government-sponsored projects, based on the 1965 Industrial Research Laboratories directory; and "Defense Contract Share" divides the dollar value of Department of Defense procurement contracts won by the focal firm by its sales. The middle plot limits the sample to firms that operate industrial laboratories only.

more likely to have upstream and downstream links to the government than Absorber firms (though the difference for defence contract shares is not statistically significant). Leaders have roughly three times as many patents with a government interest clause as Absorbers, who in turn have nearly 18 times that of Followers. Similarly, over 80 per cent of corporate labs from Leaders report government R&D contracts compared to only 50 per cent for Absorber labs and 36 per cent for Follower labs. Leaders report 13 per cent of sales coming from government procurement contracts compared to 9 per cent for Absorbers and only 2 per cent for Followers.

Fairchild Semiconductor

Fairchild Semiconductor illustrates that startups, too, could tap the federal procurement pipeline, provided they paired their breakthrough R&D with in-house manufacturing capability. Established in 1957, Fairchild's semiconductor division quickly became a key player in the semiconductor industry. One of the company's earliest semiconductor breakthroughs, the planar process, allowed for the reliable production of silicon transistors. This innovation positioned Fairchild to compete for government contracts. In 1960, Fairchild secured a contract for the Minuteman II missile program, which required advanced, reliable silicon transistors to guide intercontinental ballistic missiles (ICBMs). This $3 million contract was transformative, enabling Fairchild to invest heavily in production facilities and scale the planar process, which laid the groundwork for the commercial integrated circuit (IC) industry.

The development of ICs was one of Fairchild's major contributions to both military and commercial technology. In 1961, Fairchild won another key contract to supply ICs for NASA's Apollo Guidance Computer (AGC), which was part of the Apollo Program led by MIT's Instrumentation Laboratory. NASA needed compact, reliable electronics to ensure the precision required for manned lunar missions. The technical demands of the AGC forced Fairchild to innovate rapidly, pushing the limits of manufacturing capabilities by refining its planar process to improve production yields and component reliability. These innovations were essential for meeting NASA's stringent standards and provided Fairchild with the expertise needed to become a leader in semiconductor manufacturing.

By 1965, Fairchild Semiconductor had grown from a small startup into a manufacturing powerhouse, generating over $130 million in revenue, with defence and space contracts accounting for a significant portion of its business. The lessons Fairchild learned in meeting the demands of the Apollo Program, such as improving component reliability and refining production techniques, were instrumental in its later success in the commercial semiconductor market. By the late 1960s, Fairchild had become a key supplier to both military and commercial markets. In 1967, the company introduced the first commercial ICs, which found applications in products such as calculators, hearing aids, and early computers.

The structure of government procurement programs during the Cold War thus facilitated rapid technological progress but also reinforced a model of vertical integration. The government's preference for awarding bundled contracts to firms with both R&D and manufacturing capabilities created barriers for startups that wanted to specialise in either research or production. The focus on integration limited opportunities for firms that sought to specialise in specific parts of the value chain.

Radio Corporation of America

Radio Corporation of America (RCA) provides an example where federal R&D contracts directly sustained corporate R&D projects. Unlike Fairchild, which began with a nascent technology, RCA had nearly two decades of expertise in radio technology by the start of World War II. Established in 1919 as a trust for pooled patents on the then-emerging radio technology, RCA invested heavily in research to service existing patent licencees and to out-innovate potential rivals. Built during World War II, RCA's David Sarnoff Research Center (DSRC) produced research that led to television (Vladimir Zworykin), liquid crystal displays (George Heilmeier), blue-violet light-emitting diodes (Herbert Maruska), semiconductor lasers, and complementary metal-oxide-semiconductor, a dominant design for integrated circuits.

In its early years, a chief source of revenue for RCA was its patent licensing programme in radio and TV, and lab activities were primarily focused on servicing licensees and bolstering the patent position of the company.[40] This revenue source was abruptly curtailed in 1957, when an antitrust consent decree forced the firm to license its existing patents to competitors, royalty-free.[41] The successful launch of Sputnik, also in 1957, spurred federal interest in research that would help the United States gain an advantage over the Soviet Union in nuclear weapons systems, space missions, and solid-state electronics.[42] RCA made it lab policy to solicit more funding from the armed services, the National Bureau of Standards (NBS), the National Aeronautics and Space Administration (NASA), and the Advanced Research Projects Agency (ARPA). The Annual Research Report from the Lab in 1964 indicates that around 30 per cent of research was directly supported by government contracts.[43] Figure 10.9 shows that the expansion of scientific output from the lab (measured by the number of peer-reviewed scientific publications) was closely related to an expansion of aerospace and defence contracts during the 1960s. The gradual drop in government contracting share thereafter coincided with a sharp drop in scientific publishing in the 1970s.

Government contracts and procurement enabled RCA to start or sustain research projects that otherwise had no direct commercial prospects for the company. Research into thermoelectricity was first motivated by David Sarnoff's request that the lab produce an all-electric air conditioning unit in 1951. RCA was planning to diversify into household appliances and acquired

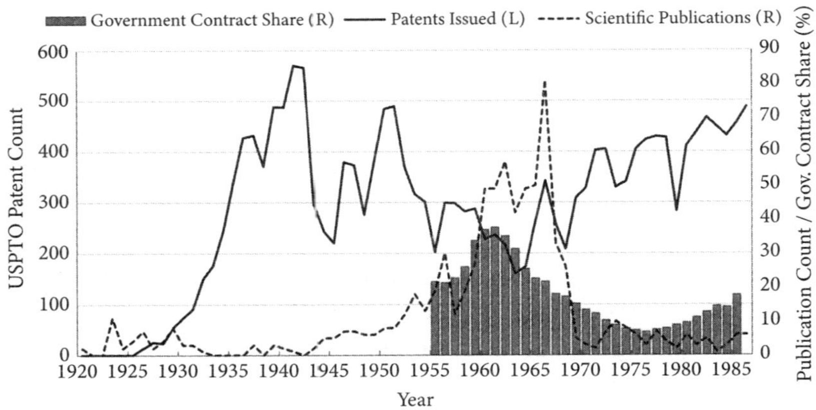

Figure 10.9 Patents and Scientific Publications by the Radio Corporation of America (1920–1986)

This figure plots the number of U.S. Patents (solid line) and scientific publications (broken line) that are attributed to RCA, along with the share of government contracts out of total revenues from 1955 to 1985 (grey bar). USPTO patent data is from Kogan, Papanikolaou, Seru and Stoffman (2017)[44]; publications are extracted from the Dimensions dataset; government sales data are available from 1955 and are sourced from Sobel (1986)[45] and Annual Reports sourced from Mergent Archives.

a 20 per cent stake in Whirlpool in 1955. Thermoelectric effects occur when electricity can be directly converted into heat (and vice versa). This direct energy conversion obviates the need for turbines in conventional power generators and coolants in air conditioners. RCA scientists experimented with bismuth telluride and germanium alloys to create working prototypes by 1956. However, the product could not compete with incumbent products, and the firm tried repurposing the technology for an all-electric refrigerator before exiting household appliances altogether by selling its Whirlpool stake in 1962.[46] However, thermoelectric research continued well into the 1970s, thanks to applications in space missions that required compact ways to generate electricity under extreme temperature conditions. Indeed, the 1962 research report states that "[a]lmost all of this [thermoelectric] work was done under Government contract," with an annual contract value of $4.5 million. The same report also mentions the possibility of manufacturing thermoelectric air conditioners for U.S. Navy submarines.

Semiconductor lasers offer another example where government funding sustained research that failed to be commercialised by RCA's product divisions. RCA labs began a laser research program immediately following the invention of Maiman's ruby laser and assumed a leading position in diode lasers, on a par with AT&T, General Electric, and MIT Lincoln Labs. Herbert Kroemer, for instance, won his Nobel Prize in Physics based on work on heterojunction lasers at RCA. The lab also pioneered work in reducing the operating temperature of diode lasers (a major technical bottleneck that reduced laser lifespan).[47] Lab scientists, therefore, proposed using semiconductor lasers in the firm's Videodisc project, but the proposal was rejected because the unit cost for laser pickups was too high.[48] RCA semiconductor lasers were thus used mainly in space and defence applications. For instance, the Gemini 7 mission used a diode laser transmitter manufactured by RCA, while the AIM-9 Sidewinder missile had a laser heat-seeking unit from RCA.[49,50]

Chapter takeaways

Often missed in accounts of pioneering firms is that most companies established research labs not to push the scientific frontier, but to absorb the expanding flow of university-generated knowledge made possible by growing federal support.[51] As startups began commercialising university science, and universities themselves sought industrial partners,[52] "translational corporate labs" lost their purpose, contributing to a broader shift among American firms away from industrial research in favour of development activities after the 1980s. Indeed, for a time, the labs spun out from their corporate parents, such as PARC, Sarnoff Labs, and Lucent, supplemented their budgets with contract research. SRI International, a large contract research organisation, later acquired Sarnoff (2011) and PARC (2023).[53] Between 1990 and 2019, for instance, American businesses reduced the share of their R&D budgets devoted to research from about 30 per cent to roughly 21 per cent.[54] However, even as most firms came to rely on this division of innovative labour with academia, some leading firms continued to invest in internal research, particularly where public science lagged the frontier.

America's post-1945 innovation ecosystem had three archetypes for corporate R&D labs: a handful of "Leaders" such as Bell Labs, GE, and IBM that produced frontier science; "Absorbers" like Koppers that translated outside discoveries; and "Followers" such as Nabisco that focused on routine development. Corporate labs borrowed academic norms—hiring PhDs, encouraging publication, running in-house journals—yet enjoyed industrial scale, interdisciplinary teams and long time horizons. This combination yielded breakthroughs (transistors, hard-disk drives, nylon) and spawned spinoff entrepreneurs who seeded regional innovation clusters such as Silicon Valley.

The laser narrative crystallises the system's symbiosis: university theory (Townes, Gould) met industrial execution at Bell, Hughes, IBM, and others, accelerated by military grants. Open information-sharing and varied corporate expertise allowed multiple media (ruby, HeNe gas, glass) to be tested in parallel, shortening the path from idea to application.

Federal money and university talent fed this ecosystem: GI-Bill-expanded PhD cohorts staffed labs, while defence and space contracts bundled R&D with guaranteed production orders. Cold War procurement favoured vertically integrated contractors, tying research to manufacturing, scaling new processes such as photolithography, and anchoring domestic supply chains. This structure catalysed the era's deep-tech progress but also narrowed opportunities for specialised R&D firms and locked the ecosystem into an integration-heavy model.

11
The Decline of Industrial Research

Introduction

Over the past four decades, the role of the American corporation in scientific progress has significantly changed. In the 1980s, roughly one-third of the average public firm's R&D budget was devoted to basic or applied research; today, barely one-fifth is.[1] The number of PhD scientists and engineers has continued to increase, yet the share of the nation's most elite researchers working for established companies has declined by more than half. Mirroring these trends, publication rates of industrial researchers have contracted even as patenting has surged.

Why did this transformation occur? The chapter examines a confluence of forces. Capital markets shortened managerial time horizons, spillovers made it easier for rivals to appropriate breakthroughs, and the dismantling of conglomerates narrowed the range of discoveries that firms could exploit internally. Global competition redirected managerial attention toward rapid commercialisation, while a more permissive antitrust climate allowed already-dominant firms to continue growing without the scientific ambition that once justified their scale. Simultaneously, mission-oriented government procurement waned, and thriving markets for technology made it cheaper to buy discoveries from universities and venture-backed startups than to generate them in-house.

The discussion proceeds in three stages. First, we document the magnitude and sectoral pattern of corporate withdrawal, drawing on data we have developed in the course of our research, national statistical accounts, and firm-level case studies. Second, we analyse the factors driving this transformation. Third, we examine the corporate laboratories that continue to operate today.

Corporate withdrawal from scientific research

By the 1970s, American firms with significant research labs began questioning their ability to profit from internal research, leading to the closing, downsizing, or reorientation of many corporate laboratories toward projects with nearer-term commercial prospects. Large corporations began to focus more on improving and marketing externally sourced inventions rather than investing in internal research. In some sectors, the loss of industrial research has significantly slowed the translation of scientific discoveries—now primarily produced in universities—into commercially applicable technologies.

The decline of industrial research is visible in trends in business R&D inputs and outputs. On both sides, we see a movement away from "R" and into "D" by publicly listed firms in America.

R&D inputs

Recall Figure 1.2 in Chapter 1: we used data from the National Science Foundation to show that the share of research (both basic and applied) in total R&D funded and performed by private business in the United States fell from about 28 per cent in 1985 to below 22 per cent in 2015. Other NSF data also show a significant drop in the share of research funded by business from the 1990s, despite an increase in the absolute amount of business R&D over the same period.

The shift away from research and towards development can also be seen in the number of PhD scientists employed by firms. Corporate employment of scientific talent has not diminished, but a smaller fraction is engaged in research. The grey bars in Figure 11.1 plot NSF data from the Survey of Doctorate Recipients (SDR) and show that the share of science and engineering doctorates working in industry stayed stable at 30–32 per cent between 1993 and 2013. However, when we limit the set to distinguished scientists, we see a steady decrease in the share working for corporations, as shown by the dashed lines. We consider a researcher to be distinguished if they are included in the AMWS directory. Inclusion in the AMWS is determined by an editorial board that gathers information from scientific and engineering societies, awards, and peer assessments. Approximately a quarter of all doctorate recipients are found in the AMWS directory.[2] The diamond-marked line in Figure 11.1 shows that the share of AMWS scientists working at

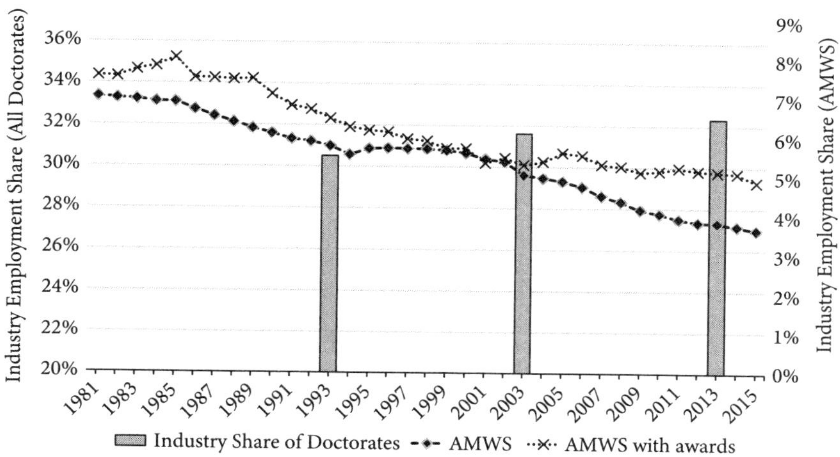

Figure 11.1 Employment of Distinguished Scientists by Industry

Notes: The bar graph plots the share of doctorates employed in industry (for-profit private organisations) from the 1993, 2003, and 2013 Survey of Doctorate Recipients (SDR). The line with × markers plots the share of scientists in the American Men & Women of Science (AMWS) directory with at least one award who work at a listed American firm. The line with diamond markers plots the same for AMWS scientists without awards. AMWS data from the 2005 to 2021 editions are used for this calculation.

a public firm approximately halved between 1980 and 2015. Limiting the sample to scientists with at least one award in the natural sciences (which comprise 1.65 per cent of the total sample of 202,115), we find the decline to hold (×-marked line). In sum, the changing composition of R&D expenditures and scientist employment points toward a retreat from industrial research.

R&D outputs

Data on R&D outputs paint a similar picture, with firms shifting resources from upstream research to downstream development. Figure 11.2 shows that, among corporations with at least $10 million of capitalised R&D expenses, scientific publications declined—from over twenty-five per company per year in 1980 to around thirteen in 2010, and then rose to about twenty by 2015. By contrast, patenting increased from around ten to over eighty patents per year during the same period. The average number of scientific publications per $1 million of R&D spending in real terms also declined from 1.00 articles between 1980 and 1985 to 0.43 articles between 2010 and 2015.[3]

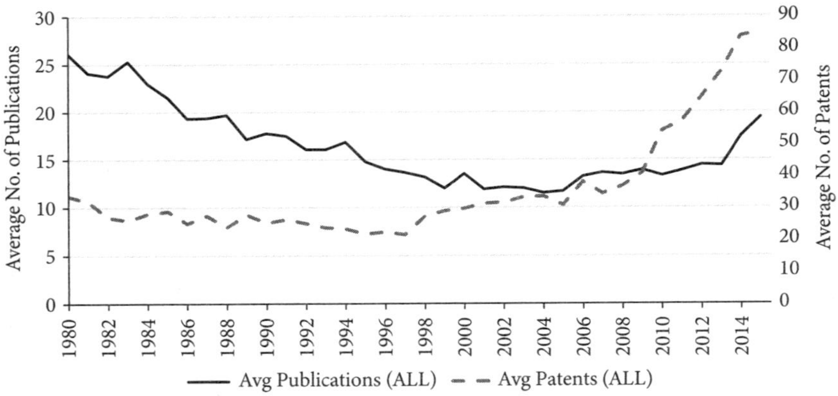

Figure 11.2 Scientific Publications and Patents by Compustat Firms (1980–2015, excluding life sciences)

Notes: This reproduces Figure 8 from Arora, Belenzon, Patacconi, and Suh (2020, hereafter ABPS).[4] The solid line represents the average number of publications in Clarivate Web of Science matched to Compustat firms with over $10 million of R&D Stock and in industry classes excluding the life sciences sector. The broken line represents the same for patents (details on matching procedure in Arora, Belenzon, and Sheer).[5]

While a portion of the decline in corporate publications can be attributed to the entry of firms that publish very little, incumbents with established research programs also markedly decreased their research. Among firms that did publish, the share that published more than ten articles per year dropped from 55.2 per cent in 1980 (111 out of 201 firms) to 29.8 per cent in 2015 (214 out of 717 firms).

The decline was evident even among the fastest-growing firms. For instance, U.S. public corporations whose sales grew by 100 per cent or more between 1980 and 1990 experienced an average drop of 20.6 scientific articles per year over that decade. Similarly, corporations that doubled in sales between 1990 and 2000 published 12.0 fewer articles over that decade, and publications dropped by 13.3 for the fastest-growing U.S. public firms between 2000 and 2010. In terms of research quality, the decline was most pronounced for highly cited papers and for papers published in high-impact scientific journals.[6]

The decline in corporate research was not confined to a particular industry. Figure 11.3 plots the ratio between the number of publications and the number of patents per firm for three sectors: life sciences, information and computer technology (ICT) and semiconductors. The ratio of publications to patents more than halved between 1980 and 2016 in both the

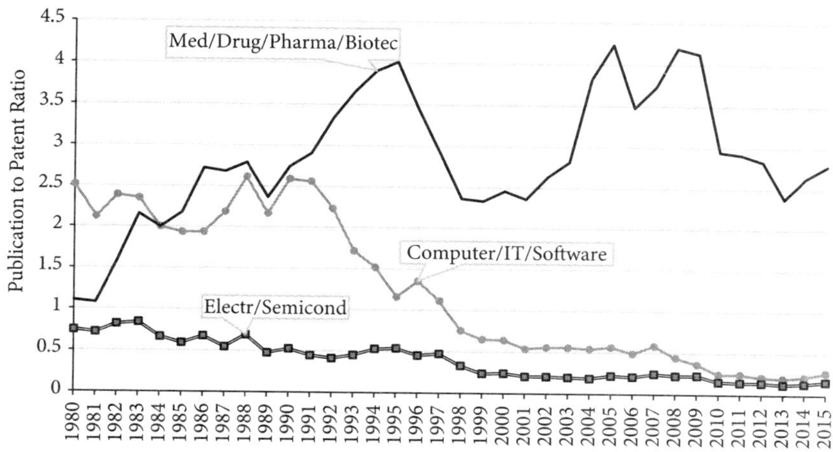

Figure 11.3 Ratio of Publications per Firm to Patents per Firm, by Industry (1980–2015)

Notes: This graph reproduces Figure 10 from ABPS (2020). The graph plots the ratio of publications to patents per firm in three industrial sectors. The number of publications per firm is calculated by matching publications in Clarivate Web of Science to Compustat firms with over $10 million of R&D Stock. The number of patents per firm is calculated by matching assignee names in EPO Patstat to the same firms.The Publication to Patent Ratio is calculated by dividing the number of publications per firm by the number of patents per firm.

computer/IT/software and electronics/semiconductor sectors. An exception to this pattern is found in the life sciences. The ratio of publications to patents grew from about one in the 1980s to between two and three in the 2010s in this sector.

Table 11.1 shows publication and patenting trends for the ten firms that published the most scientific articles in the 1980s, 1990s, 2000s, and 2010s. As expected, firms such as GE, Xerox, and AT&T exhibited some of the sharpest declines. GE saw a drop of 132 publications between the 1980s and 1990s (from 603 to 471), while Xerox's publications declined from 343 to 310. AT&T's publications declined sharply (by 73 per cent) from the 1990s to the 2000s, in line with the firm's restructuring efforts.[7] Also, IBM's publishing trend in the 1990s (a 9 per cent decline) contrasts with a doubling in patenting in the same period, consistent with the idea that IBM's pro-patent policies, introduced by James McGroddy in 1989, incentivised researchers to patent rather than publish research results.

Consistent with the pattern at the industry level, Table 11.1 shows that firms in the life sciences—such as Pharmacia, Lilly, Bristol Myers Squibb, Pfizer, and Amgen—significantly increased publications. In the case of Pfizer

Table 11.1 Changes in Publications and Patents by Top 10 Publishers for Each Decade from 1980 to 2015

Rank	Top 10 publishers in 1980–89	Publications Per Year				Patents Per Year			
		1980–1989	1990–1999	% Change	% Change (R&D Normalised)	1980–1989	1990–1999	% Change	% Change (R&D Normalised)
1	AT&T CORP	1,889	1,028	−46%	−58%	372	422	13%	−13%
2	INTL BUSINESS MACHINES CORP	1,612	1,929	20%	−16%	538	1,495	178%	96%
3	GENERAL ELECTRIC CO	603	471	−22%	−43%	908	876	−4%	−29%
4	DUPONT (E I) DE NEMOURS	600	762	27%	−25%	350	506	44%	−15%
5	EXXON MOBIL CORP	554	401	−28%	−23%	252	245	−3%	3%
6	XEROX CORP	343	310	−10%	−41%	271	718	165%	73%
7	PHARMACIA & UPJOHN INC	336	532	58%	−52%	101	56	−45%	−83%
8	CBS CORP -OLD	321	108	−66%	−47%	410	233	−43%	−11%
9	PHARMACIA CORP	302	383	27%	−43%	146	173	18%	−47%
10	ROCKWELL AUTOMATION	279	188	−33%	−63%	181	171	−6%	−49%

Rank	Top 10 publishers in 1990–1999	Publications Per Year				Patents Per Year			
		1990–1999	2000–2009	% Change	% Change (R&D Normalised)	1990–1999	2000–2009	% Change	% Change (R&D Normalised)
1	INTL BUSINESS MACHINES CORP	1,929	1,754	−9%	−21%	1,495	3,522	136%	104%
2	LUCENT TECHNOLOGIES INC	1,421	748	−47%	−9%	799	770	−4%	66%
3	AT&T CORP	1,028	279	−73%	119%	422	288	−32%	450%
4	DUPONT (E I) DE NEMOURS	762	423	−44%	−31%	506	475	-6%	17%
5	BRISTOL-MYERS SQUIBB CO	582	632	9%	−56%	135	158	17%	−53%
6	SCHERING-PLOUGH	565	557	−1%	−71%	99	111	11%	−67%
7	PHARMACIA & UPJOHN INC	532	merged with Pfizer (2003)	N/A	N/A	56	merged with Pfizer (2003)	N/A	N/A
8	LILLY (ELI) & CO	508	884	74%	−44%	138	97	−30%	−78%
9	ABBOTT LABORATORIES	474	600	26%	−48%	138	128	−7%	−62%
10	GENERAL ELECTRIC CO	471	762	62%	−11%	876	1,269	45%	−20%

continued

Table 11.1 *continued*

Rank	Top 10 publishers in 2000–2009	Publications Per Year				Patents Per Year			
		2000–2009	2010–2015	% Change	% Change (R&D Normalised)	2000–2009	2010–2015	% Change	% Change (R&D Normalised)
1	INTL BUSINESS MACHINES CORP	1,754	1,703	−3%	−11%	3,522	6,800	93%	76%
2	PFIZER INC	1,616	2,022	25%	19%	318	167	−47%	−50%
3	JOHNSON & JOHNSON	1,014	1,382	36%	-3%	378	781	106%	47%
4	LILLY (ELI) & CO	884	868	−2%	−33%	97	70	−28%	−51%
5	GENERAL ELECTRIC CO	762	997	31%	−23%	1,269	1,945	53%	−10%
6	LUCENT TECHNOLOGIES INC	748	merged with Alcatel (2006)	N/A	N/A	770	merged with Alcatel (2006)	N/A	N/A
7	MERCK & CO	648	866	34%	−36%	307	541	76%	−16%
8	BRISTOL-MYERS SQUIBB CO	632	844	34%	−4%	158	172	9%	−21%
9	INTEL CORP	625	702	12%	−44%	1,463	1,793	23%	−39%
10	ABBOTT LABORATORIES	600	568	−5%	−23%	128	532	316%	240%

Notes: This table replicates Table 2 from ABPS (2020) and describes the annual patenting and publication activities of Compustat firms that are the top publishers for each decade from 1980 to 2015 (1980–1989, 1990–1999, 2000–2009, 2010–2015). We divide the total number of publications by number of years in every decade for U.S.-headquartered firms in Compustat after matching them to the address information in each Web of Science article. After ranking the top 10 publishers each decade by publications per year (first column), we calculate the percentage change between the previous decade and the next decade (fourth column). We also divide the number of publications each year by $ million R&D spending and average over each decade for each firm. The percentage differences between each decade in this measure are presented in the sixth column. The same is done for patents from the seventh to tenth columns.

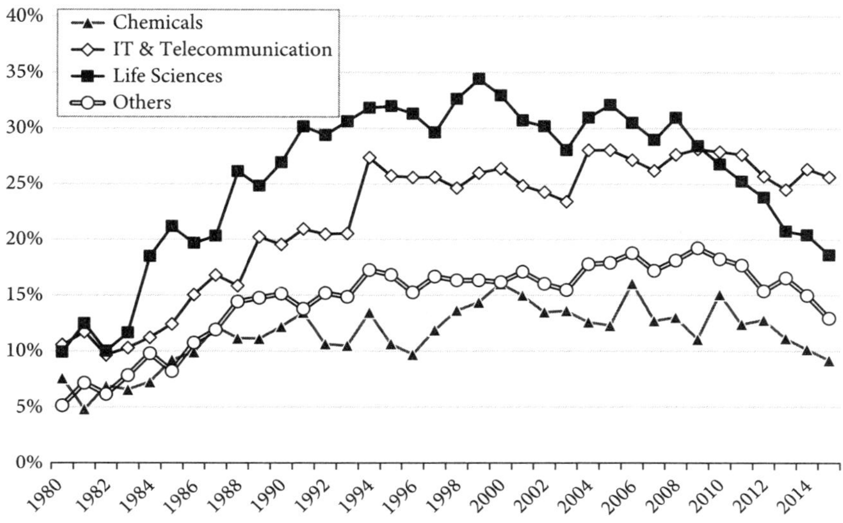

Figure 11.4 Share of Papers Cited by Patents, by Industry (1980–2015)
Notes: This graph plots the share of corporate papers in four industrial categories that are cited at least once by a U.S. patent within five years of publication. Data are sourced from the DISCERN database and combined with Marx and Fuegi (2020). The four industry categories are mapped from three-digit Standard Industrial Classification (SIC) codes using schema from Arora, Belenzon, and Sheer (2021).[8]

and Amgen in the 2000s, this increase in publishing kept up with changes in R&D expenditures. A key feature of the pharmaceutical industry during this period was its strong merger activity. However, increased consolidation is insufficient to explain changes in publishing behaviour. Other sectors of the economy that also experienced strong merger activity (such as computers and electronics) show a decline in publication-to-patent ratios as well.

Firms have also moved their research to be closer to application. Figure 11.4 shows that scientific publications of publicly listed firms are more likely to be cited by patents in the 2010s than in the 1980s. Interestingly, the increase is most pronounced in the life sciences, with over a fifth of publications being cited by U.S. patents after the 2000s, compared to only a tenth in the early 1980s. The increase for the ICT sector, which includes both semiconductor firms and software companies, is steadier, showing a twofold increase in patent citations received by their publications.

There are several reasons why firms in the life sciences bucked the trend of reduced scientific publications. First, upstream research is more commercially relevant in the life sciences than in other manufacturing sectors.

For example, an economy-wide survey of over three thousand corporate research labs in 1994 showed that 58 per cent of lab managers in the pharmaceutical sector reported that research conducted in academic or government labs suggested new project ideas, well above the average of 32 per cent for all manufacturing firms.[9] Second, patents are more effective in the drug industry than in other sectors. Relatedly, technology markets are very active in pharmaceuticals. As a result, returns to investments in research may be higher in the life sciences than in other sectors. Third, drugs require regulatory approval and scientific publications by demonstrating that the efficacy of new products can facilitate this process. Pharmaceutical products also require the cooperation of physicians who prescribe the products to patients. Scientific publications are one way of signalling quality, to convince physicians to prescribe the new drug.[10]

The fourth factor allowing life sciences firms to buck the secular decline in industrial research is the marked increase in federal funding for biomedical research through the NIH since the 1980s. Following the War on Cancer initiated by the Nixon administration and benefiting from the diversion of defence-related funding for the physical sciences after the Cold War, federal funding for biomedical research increased over fivefold, from $2.5 billion in

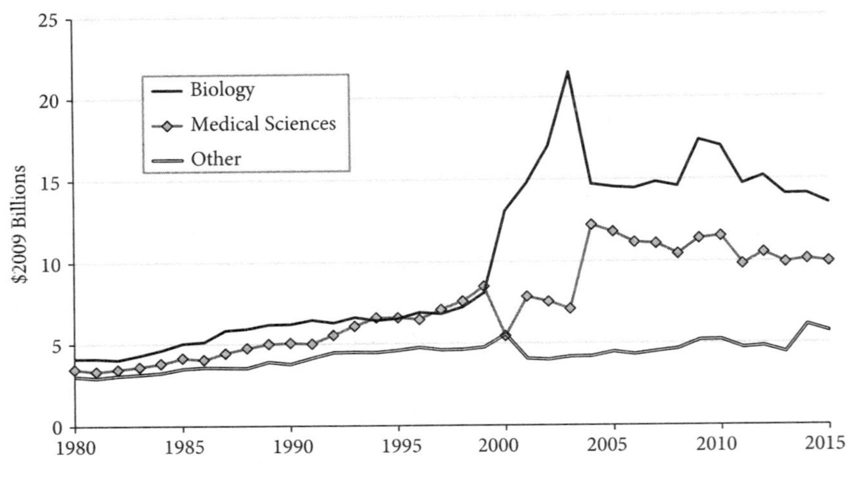

Figure 11.5 Federal Obligations by Selected Subfields (1980–2015)

Notes: This graph replicates Figure 4 in Merrill (2018) which uses data from the Federal Funds for Research and Development Data series (available from https://www.nsf.gov/statistics/srvyfedfunds/).[11] Biology excludes environmental sciences. Other includes chemicals, computer sciences, materials engineering, metallurgy, and electrical engineering.

1980 to $13.7 billion in 1998. Notably, the NIH budget nearly doubled over five years from 1998 to 2003, reaching just over $20 billion in 2003. In the early 1990s, "Big Science" projects in physics, such as the Superconducting Supercollider (SSC), were scuttled, whereas those in the life sciences, such as the Human Genome Project, received increased support from the government. Indeed, Figure 11.5 shows that this steep increase in federal funding for the life sciences has not been matched in other sectors such as chemistry, computer sciences, materials, and electrical engineering. This reallocation may have increased publication output by firms, not only those that made use of NIH funds, but also those that could freely access newly available public resources such as genome sequences, to increase research productivity. However, this confluence of factors was unique to the life sciences, which may explain why this sector has stood out among others.

Reshuffling research at IBM and DuPont

IBM: From moonshots to legacy technology

IBM is a prominent example of a firm that shifted research efforts from basic science toward applied science. Its research program has produced five Nobel laureates and has left a lasting mark on solid-state electronics, nanoscience, and mathematics. These laureates include Leo Esaki (Physics, 1973) for discovering electron tunneling in semiconductors; Gerd Binnig and Heinrich Rohrer (Physics, 1986) for inventing the scanning tunneling microscope; and Georg Bednorz and Alex Müller (Physics, 1987) for making advances in high-temperature superconductivity. As one of Intel's largest customers for silicon-based chips, IBM was motivated by the prospect of leapfrogging this dominant technology through alternative designs. One such alternative was the superconducting chip, also known as a Josephson junction, which operates by creating an energy gap between two superconductors separated by a thin barrier. First theorised in 1962 by Nobel Laureate Brian Josephson, IBM researchers had, by 1980, assembled an experimental electronic switch that delivered speeds 10 to 100 times faster than conventional semiconductor chips.

The underlying science was still to be developed when IBM first embarked on this project.[12] With an annual budget of $20 million, and about 120 personnel, the firm developed the science and won two back-to-back Nobel

Prizes in Physics: first for the scanning tunneling microscope (STM) in 1986 and the second for high-temperature superconductivity in 1987. The STM, developed by Gerd Binnig and Heinrich Rohrer at IBM Zurich in 1981, was the first microscope to allow atomic-scale imaging at the surface level. The STM allowed for lateral resolutions down to 0.1 nanometers (nm) that were superior to existing scanning electron microscopes. Unlike transmission electron microscopes (which provide images on a thinly sliced sample) that provided no vertical resolution, the STM provided vertical resolutions of up to 0.01 nm. This was a critical step in assessing imperfections that could affect the performance of the Josephson junction. Superconducting behaviour up until the 1980s was achievable only in extremely low temperatures approximating 0 Kelvin. These constraints were identified as one of the barriers to widespread adoption of superconducting computers. The discovery of a perovskite-based superconducting material in 1986, by Georg Bednorz and Alex Müller (both at IBM Zurich), broke the previous record by 12 degrees, superconducting at 35 Kelvin.

Benefits to the scientific community notwithstanding, the rapid advances in the legacy technology (i.e., in silicon) as well as the scientific and technical roadblocks to bringing a superconducting computer to market, were deemed prohibitively costly. This led the firm to abandon the project in 1983.[13]

Top managerial transitions around the turn of the decade also accelerated the move out of physics research that was considered farther from immediate application.[14] The first shift occurred as James McGroddy replaced John Armstrong as head of IBM Research. McGroddy emphasised that patents were a key instrument to appropriate returns from lab research. A new business development group was tasked with out-licensing patents to fund R&D expenditures. In McGroddy's words:

> Rewards [for IBM researchers] were given to "write and publish" and "write and file for patent." . . After becoming R&D head, [I] unilaterally set standards for the fraction of inventions that had to be "write and file" for rewards. At least [a] quarter or half had to be "write and file" now.[15]

In 1988, 82 per cent of invention disclosures were published, while only 18 per cent were patented; the numbers flipped by 1998 to only 15 per cent of invention disclosures being published, while 85 per cent were patented. Within ten years, the company had dramatically shifted the composition of its R&D efforts from a focus on upstream, basic science to applied, patentable research. Starting from the 1990s, IBM's research in the physics and material science shifted away from "leapfrog" projects such as superconducting computers to process innovations for semiconductor chips, such as the development of chemical-mechanical polishing, silicon-germanium transistors, and copper interconnects through the damascene process.[16] Furthermore, as seen in Figure 11.6, the firm shifted from the physical sciences (physics, engineering, and materials science) to computer science, which had more direct implications for its software business. Through the 1990s, IBM's computer science publications increased by 2.2 per cent per year, whereas its physics publications declined by 9 per centduring the same period.

IBM's shifting research priorities also had other effects: research expenditures were cut and many scientists left. Numbers from the AMWS directory show that IBM experienced a net outflow of prominent scientists in the 1990s, with an average of fourteen scientists leaving per year (Table 11.2). Of these, more than 60 per cent moved to academic institutions within

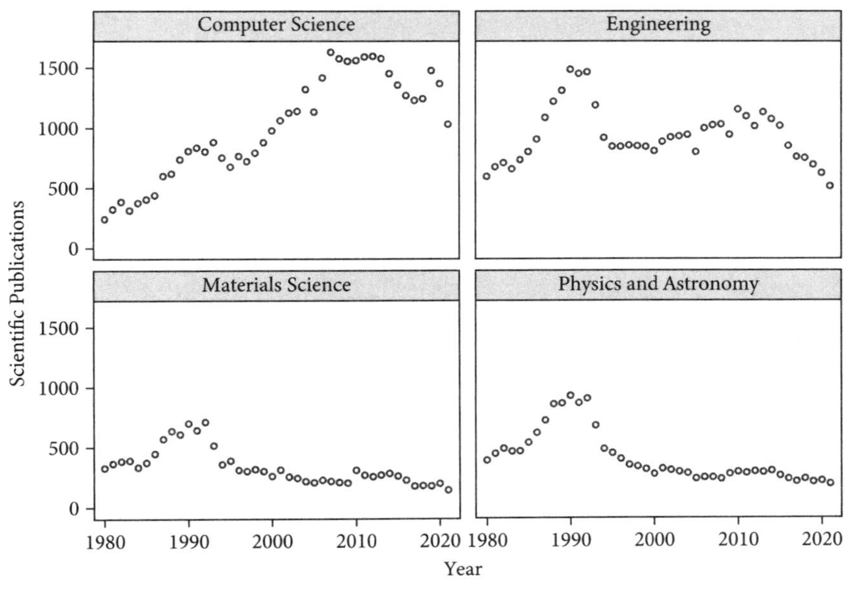

Figure 11.6 Publications at IBM by Scientific Field (1980–2020)

Notes: This graph plots the number of papers published by authors affiliated with IBM. Sample is limited to field where IBM publishes more than 100 papers per year between 1980 and 2020. Data are from the DISCERN database.[17]

Table 11.2 Net Outflow and Destination of IBM Scientists (1980–2019)

	AMWS Turnover (Averaged by Decade)			Destinations of Leavers (Total by Decade)		
	Outflow	Inflow	Net Outflow	Corporate	Public	University
1980–1989	60.4	78.0	−17.6	91	85	254
1990–1999	58.8	44.9	13.9	80	69	260
2000–2009	34.6	36.1	−1.5	37	28	161
2010–2019	22.4	18.7	3.7	22	14	117

Notes: The left three columns plot the yearly average number of scientists that enter IBM, exit IBM, and the difference between the two. The right three columns identify the destinations of scientists who exit IBM (those who retire or fail to find a job are dropped from the sample): "Corporate" refers to private firms, "Public" refers to government laboratories, and "University" refers to academic institutions. Scientist career data is sourced from the 2005–2021 editions of AMWS.

five years of leaving IBM. Overall, IBM shifted resources from research to development, with its remaining research efforts more narrowly focused on computer science, including quantum computing.

DuPont: Looking outside for new ideas

DuPont was in the vanguard that ushered in the "Golden Age" of industrial research, along with Kodak, AT&T, and General Electric. At its peak in 1980, DuPont employed around six thousand people in its labs, with an R&D budget exceeding a billion dollars supported by sales of about $30 billion. This represented a ten thousand-fold growth in R&D and a thousand-fold growth in sales since the early 1900s.[18] During the 1960s, DuPont researchers published more articles in the *Journal of the American Chemical Society* (JACS) than MIT and Caltech combined. However, starting in the 1970s, as its key products such as textiles and plastics matured, the firm began reducing its research intensity. Hounshell and Smith estimate that DuPont's R&D per sales decreased by half to 3.3 per cent during the 1970s.

Figure 11.7 shows DuPont's attempts to restructure through acquisitions. Attempting to diversify research avenues away from plastics and textiles, a life sciences program was launched in 1980, followed by joint ventures with existing pharmaceutical firms such as Merck in 1991.[19] However, with consolidation in the pharma sector and overseas competition intensifying in the textile business, the firm faced a tougher operating environment in the early 1990s. DuPont sold its pharma business to Bristol-Myers Squibb

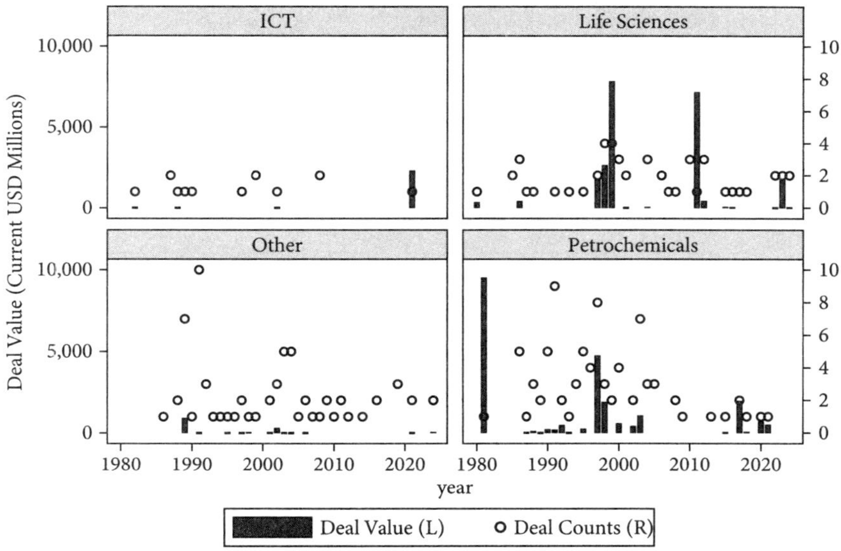

Figure 11.7 Acquisitions by DuPont, by Industry of the Target Firm (1980–2020)

Notes: The bar graphs (left axis) plot the total deal value of acquisitions completed by DuPont and its subsidiaries each year, sourced from SDC Platinum. The dot plots (right axis) present the number of companies acquired. The four industry categories are hand coded based on the Thomson Reuters Business Classification (TRBC) of the target company.

in 2001 and its textiles division to Koch industries.[20] The divestitures were part of a broader trend in the industry responding to calls for a narrower firm focus. Eastman Kodak had spun off the Eastman Chemical Company in 1994, while Monsanto had spun off its chemical business as Solutia in 1997 (which was later acquired by Eastman in 2012).[21] After divesting its pharmaceuticals business, the firm focused on its agro-biotechnology business by acquiring Pioneer Hi-Bred in 1999 for $7.7 billion. DuPont later also acquired Danisco, a Danish food enzyme company that discovered CRISPR CAS-9, for $7 billion in 2011. In the 1990s alone, the company had made forty-two acquisitions of petrochemical firms.

DuPont also strengthened and expanded its collaborations with universities. For instance, DuPont funded Harvard researchers who developed the OncoMouse, a genetically engineered mouse in 1983. The OncoMouse, designed to carry a gene that made it highly susceptible to cancer, quickly became a vital tool in cancer research. DuPont secured exclusive rights to market the OncoMouse, while Harvard retained the ability to use it for

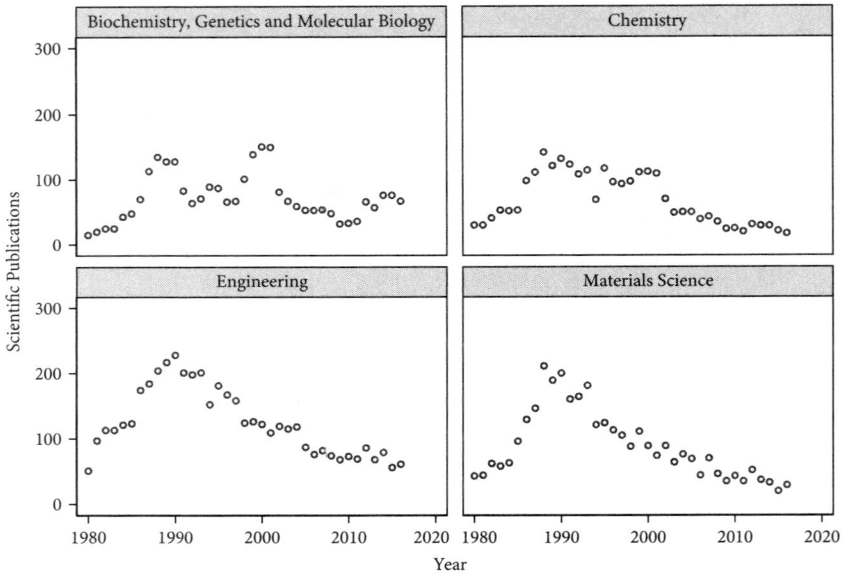

Figure 11.8 Publications at DuPont by Field (1980–2020)

Notes: This graph plots the number of papers published by authors affiliated with DuPont. Sample is limited to field where DuPont publishes more than fifty papers per year between 1980 and 2020. Data are from the DISCERN database.

academic research. This example also illustrates a broader trend in the innovation landscape: as corporations like DuPont move away from conducting basic research internally, they increasingly depend on universities to drive scientific discovery.

Lastly, DuPont started to increasingly prioritise projects with clear commercial potential over those oriented toward basic scientific inquiry. The "Apex" research process, implemented in 1998 at DuPont's Central Research & Development (CR&D) organisation, shifted the research focus from problems pursued by scientists to opportunities identified by business units. By 2002, more than 80 per cent of its R&D resources were closely aligned with the business units, according to Thomas Connelly, the Chief Science and Technology Officer at the time.[22] One veteran CR&D researcher, Andrew Feiring (who worked during 1974–2006 at the firm) recalled that "science became the loser" in the regime, as projects that did not clear a $100 million potential value threshold ceased to be pursued.[23] DuPont's output reflects this change: the number of first-authored journal articles by DuPont scientists plummeted from around 749 in 1994 to just 245 by 2015. At the

Table 11.3 Net Outflow and Destination of DuPont Scientists (1980–2019)

	AMWS Turnover (Averaged by Decade)			Destinations of Leavers (Total by Decade)		
	Outflow	Inflow	Net Outflow	Corporate	Public	University
1980–1989	73.7	85.2	−11.5	91	43	105
1990–1999	59.0	49.8	9.2	93	39	111
2000–2009	22.0	18.8	3.2	42	14	50
2010–2019	12.0	7.0	5.0	17	3	33

Notes: This table plots the difference between AMWS scientists leaving DuPont and those entering DuPont each year. See Table 11.2 for variable explanations.

same time, the company's patent filings with the U.S. Patent and Trademark Office soared, rising from approximately sixteen hundred in 1994 to nearly thirty-five hundred by 2012, highlighting a shift toward downstream development activities. Figure 11.8 shows that this withdrawal occurred relatively evenly across the firm's major scientific fields, though its renewed focus on agricultural-biology briefly broke this decline in the early 2000s (as seen in the uptick in publications for "Biochemistry, Genetics and Molecular Biology"). Table 11.3 shows that the company lost the most scientists (recorded in the AMWS) during the 1990s, with 9.2 scientists leaving per year. Similar to leavers from IBM, around half (46 per cent) found jobs at universities. While departures subsided in the 2000s, DuPont's hiring of prominent scientists also dropped 86 per cent from fifty per year in the 1990s down to seven per year in the 2010s.

This transition was further accelerated under the influence of activist investor Nelson Peltz, who pressured DuPont to prioritise shareholder value over long-term research endeavours. In response, DuPont made further cuts to its research operations, culminating in the dissolution of CR&D on January 4, 2016. The organisation was merged with DuPont's engineering division, signalling the end of an era.

Why have firms withdrawn from science?

There are several, nonmutually exclusive explanations for why corporations have withdrawn from science.

Short-termism of investors. One of the most common explanations for why firms are withdrawing from science is the short-termism of investors such as Peltz. Scientific discoveries take years, if not decades, before they reach commercialisation. Aggregate data linking the supply of scientific articles to industry-level productivity growth show a twenty-year lag.[24] Growing investor short-termism may thus help explain why firms find it more difficult to justify investments in long-term research. Indeed, recent results by Sampson and Shi show that investor short-termism may have increased.[25] The authors calculate U.S. public firms' "implied discount rate" (IDR) to measure the extent to which investors discount future cash flows, which has increased by 21 per cent from 1980 to 2013.

A follow-on study finds that firms facing more intense short-term pressures, as reflected in the relationship between their stock price and their dividend payments, are less likely to produce high-impact innovations.[26] That is, they produce fewer influential patents (measured by citations from follow-on patents) and fewer novel patents (measured by new terms introduced in the patent relative to prior patents). They also document that short-term pressures have increased over time. Consistent with this, they find that high-impact patents are increasingly concentrated in a smaller set of firms.

A recent study finds that firms targeted by activist investors were more likely to withdraw from research. They produced fewer articles following activism, especially in higher-impact journals. Pharmaceutical firms targeted by activist hedge funds shifted their R&D toward "me-too" drugs—compounds that are chemically close to existing molecules—and away from exploring novel compounds. The study concludes that hedge fund activism reorients corporate innovation away from research-oriented activity and toward more applied pursuits.[27]

Google illustrates the challenges that even highly innovative firms encounter in sustaining ambitious research programs. Under CFO Ruth Porat, a stronger emphasis on financial discipline and operational efficiency led to budget reductions and the termination of several initiatives, including Project Loon, which focused on delivering global internet access via high-altitude balloons, and Makani, which sought to generate renewable energy through airborne kites. Google X's robotics portfolio was also pared back. A prominent case was Boston Dynamics, acquired in 2013 and celebrated for developing advanced robots such as Atlas and Spot, which demonstrated exceptional mobility and dexterity. Yet by 2017, facing high development costs and limited commercial prospects, Google sold the company to SoftBank.

By contrast, Google adopted a different approach toward DeepMind. DeepMind, which has produced a series of groundbreaking scientific and technological advances such as AlphaZero and AlphaFold, has been consistently supported by Google despite heavy investments. For instance, in 2018 and 2019, DeepMind reported losses of $572 million and $649 million, respectively.[28] Founding DeepMind investor Humayun Sheikh told reporters in 2020 that the lab would have "probably failed" if Google had not bought it. The story of Google's autonomous driving project, now incorporated as Waymo, is similar.

One must be careful in interpreting claims about short-termism. While Google may have scaled back some research programs, it has also demonstrated a willingness to commit billions of dollars to projects it judges promising. At the same time, universities and startups are increasingly advancing early-stage research and bringing it closer to market, which makes it reasonable for established firms to focus on downstream development and commercialisation. What might look like short-termism can instead reflect a rational response to a shifting division of innovative labour. In any case, short-termism is at best only a small part of the broader story behind the decline of American industrial research. After all, investment in uncertain, long-horizon technologies—quantum computing, for instance—remains abundant. In what follows, we consider five additional explanations: (i) knowledge spillovers to competitors; (ii) a trend toward narrower firm scope; (iii) increasing firm scale; (iv) a shift in government procurement priorities; and (v) the rise of markets for technology.

Knowledge spillovers to competitors. The research output of industrial research labs often produces significant external benefits, sometimes benefiting rivals at the expense of the sponsoring firm. Xerox PARC's development of the personal computer is a well-known example. Xerox's Alto computer was the first of its kind with a graphical user interface (GUI) and an operating system featuring an office desktop metaphor that included folders, file icons, and windows, based on bitmap technology and controlled by a mouse pointer. The Alto preceded mass-market PCs by a decade and influenced subsequent iterations such as the Three Rivers PERQ, Apple Lisa and Macintosh, and Sun workstations. However, only two thousand Alto computers were produced for internal use. A follow-on product, the Xerox Star, failed commercially because of its high price. By learning from Xerox's prototypes, it was startups such as Apple and Microsoft that captured most of the returns from the personal computer and the GUI.

Another well-known example is large language models. OpenAI's success, as well as that of many other AI firms, owes a great deal to breakthroughs by Google researchers, most notably the introduction of the transformer in the landmark "attention" paper co-authored by scientists at Google Brain and Google Research.

Research spillovers have likely increased over time, as noted by former Bell Labs researcher, Andrew Odlyzko:

> Xerography was invented by Carlson in 1937, but it was only commercialised by Xerox in 1950. Furthermore, there was so little interest in this technology that during the few years surrounding commercialisation, Xerox was able to invent and patent a whole range of related techniques, while there was hardly any activity by other institutions. This enabled Xerox to monopolize the benefits of the new technology for over two decades. [. . . By contrast,] when Bednorz and Mueller announced their discovery of high-temperature superconductivity at the IBM Zurich lab in 1987, it took only a few weeks for groups at University of Houston, University of Alabama, Bell Labs, and other places to make important further discoveries. Thus even if high-temperature superconductivity had developed into a commercially significant field, IBM would have had to share the financial benefits with others who held patents that would have been crucial to developments of products.[29]

Investments in internal research tend to decline when knowledge spillovers benefit product-market competitors, as shown in a study we co-authored with Lia Sheer.[30] Evidence from patent citations supports this view: corporate rivals are increasingly able to build on the discoveries of others. In 1990, firms were just as likely to cite their own scientific publications as those of competitors. By 2015, however, citations by competitors had doubled relative to internal ones, underscoring the rapid diffusion of knowledge across organisational boundaries.[31] Thus, if such spillovers have indeed increased over the past four decades, they may help explain firms' growing reluctance to invest in scientific research.

Narrower firm scope. The last quarter of the twentieth century marked a retreat from the conglomerate model that had flourished in the 1960s. By the 1980s, a broad consensus had emerged that unrelated diversification across industries destroyed shareholder value. Empirical research in corporate finance reinforced this view by documenting a "conglomerate discount," showing that multi-division firms traded at lower market-to-book ratios (Tobin's Qs).[32] Divisions of conglomerates such as Beatrice, Textron, and General Electric were thus spun off and sold, as firms were urged to "stick to their knitting." Specialisation was justified on the grounds that it would sharpen managerial focus and enhance operational efficiency.

In a classic paper, however, Richard Nelson had emphasised the advantages of diversification for scientific discovery. He argued that conglomerates were best positioned to benefit from the uncertain outcomes of scientific research because "[a] broad technological base ensures that, whatever direction the path of research may take, the results are likely to be of value to the sponsoring firm."[33]

A narrowing of firm scope may thus have reduced the incentives of firms to invest in scientific research. GE Research Lab's support of Nick Holonyak's work in lasers and LEDs, for instance, would have been difficult to justify if the company had not expanded beyond the lamp market to produce semiconductors and computers. Similarly, Monsanto's investment in LEDs owed much to its expansion from a manufacturer of food additives to polymers and plastics. A key assumption in Nelson's framework is the absence of markets for technology: the sponsoring firm cannot appropriate the returns from science by licensing patents. Over the past three decades, however, markets for technology have grown vigorously. This may have softened the blow to basic research that would have accompanied a narrower firm focus. For instance, after their divestitures, Lucent (from AT&T), Sarnoff Corporation (from RCA), and PARC (from Xerox) all survived largely through licensing revenues and spinoffs from their research. Kodak, too, earned substantial income from its digital photography patents long after the decline of its consumer film business.

Increasing product market dominance. The post-1980 era saw the American economy reshaped by globalisation and a shift in antitrust enforcement. Expanding international markets and the ascendancy of the Chicago School of Antitrust Law together contributed to the growth in firm size (holding the number of divisions in a firm constant).

The rise of the Chicago School began in the 1960s with the work of George Stigler and Milton Friedman, culminating in the publication of Robert Bork's "Antitrust Paradox," which argued that consumer welfare—not market structure—should be the primary concern of regulators. Concentration of market power was therefore acceptable so long as it lowered consumer prices. This view gained traction with the Department of Justice's merger guidelines of 1982 and 1984, which adopted a more permissive stance toward corporate consolidation. The result was a wave of mergers and acquisitions in pursuit of scale and global competitiveness.

Globalisation reinforced this trend. Successive reductions in tariff and nontariff barriers expanded international markets. The conclusion of the Uruguay Round and the creation of the World Trade Organisation halved the average most-favoured-nation tariff for developed economies from around 6 per cent in 1995 to 3 per cent in 2000.[34] In the four decades since 1980, global trade volume has increased fivefold.[35] Larger foreign markets encouraged firms to scale rapidly, reinforcing consolidation.

As firms grew, their R&D expenditures rose in proportion, but as Cohen and Klepper noted, their R&D projects were more incremental because large firms extract greater value from a given invention applied to a greater output.[36] This conjecture was confirmed by later studies.

The liberalisation of global trade thus expanded the addressable market for American firms' innovations, making commercialisation of existing technology more lucrative than investment in new breakthroughs. Put differently, globalisation increased the rewards from development and deployment while reducing relative incentives for discovery. Supporting this view, a recent study shows that from 1980 to 2010, large firms exposed to tariff reductions disproportionately reduced the diversity of their patent portfolios and product lines, as well as their scientific publication intensity.[37] In sum, from the 1980s onward, globalisation and weaker antitrust enforcement resulted in firms with larger scale (within product markets) but narrower scope (across markets). This tilted corporate research toward product development and commercialisation, and away from science and discovery.

A shift in government procurement priorities. During the Cold War, the U.S. government served as the buyer of first resort for many deep-tech innovations. Research into the graphical user interface by Douglas Engelbart, Ivan Sutherland, and Alan Kay, for instance, was made possible through extensive funding from ARPA, the Air Force, and NASA. Carnegie Mellon's work in the 1970s and 1980s on applying artificial intelligence to speech recognition and autonomous driving was similarly supported by the Defense Advanced Research Projects Agency (DARPA). The government also played a foundational role in the development of key technologies: AT&T's transistor, used in proximity fuses for artillery shells during the Korean War, was first purchased by the military; the first laser, invented by

Ted Maiman at Hughes Aircraft, was built on a prior Army Signal Corps contract to manufacture masers; and early computers such as ENIAC (Electronic Numerical Integrator and Computer), EDVAC (Electronic Discrete Variable Automatic Computer), and UNIVAC (UNIVersal Automatic Computer) were built to support the Army's Ballistic Research Laboratory in calculating artillery tables (ENIAC and EDVAC) and the Census Bureau in processing population and economic data in the 1950s (UNIVAC).

What distinguished government funding during the Cold War was not only its scale but also its objectives. Policymakers prioritised impact and technical feasibility, seeking breakthroughs that could secure an advantage over the Soviet Union. With the Cold War's end and the decline of national security threats, however, procurement reforms shifted the focus toward cost discipline and increased representation of smaller firms in government contracts.

As discussed in greater detail in Chapter 13, this shift coincided with a reduction in government investment in innovative technologies and a growing reliance on commercially proven technologies. The share of R&D contracts, by value, in total government contracts fell from 13 per cent in 1980 to 8 per cent in 2020, while the share of commercial contracts, which resemble market transactions, increased to 27 per cent in 2020. Reforms such as the Federal Acquisition Streamlining Act of 1994 increased the share of competitive contracts from 43 per cent to 66 per cent over the same period. Winning a government contract now also requires less scientific capability: whereas 94 per cent of public firms contracting with the government published in the sciences in 1980, only 58 per cent did so in 2015.[38] By cutting investment in innovative technologies, the government arguably contributed to the decline in industrial research.

The rise of markets for technology. Starting in the 1980s, markets for technology expanded rapidly.[39] Science-based startups played a central role in this expansion. Many were founded by academic researchers seeking to commercialise their discoveries. For instance, CRISPR gene-editing technology, developed in part at the University of California, Berkeley, gave rise to multiple biotech startups aiming to revolutionise medicine. Startups also flourished in the information technology sector.

Corporations, in turn, embraced these burgeoning markets by forging closer ties with universities and startups. Pharmaceutical companies, as well as firms such as IBM and Google, partnered with academic institutions and spinoffs to secure early access to emerging technologies and talent.

These collaborations took a variety of forms, including licensing agreements, research alliances, minority equity stakes, and acquisitions. Stronger and more enforceable patent rights facilitated such transactions, making knowledge and inventions increasingly tradable assets.

The rise of markets for technology fundamentally altered the incentives of large firms to engage in in-house research. Firms could now source innovations externally rather than relying solely on internal R&D, weakening the rationale for maintaining large, vertically integrated research laboratories. As a result, some firms scaled back their internal research efforts, reallocating resources toward development and commercialisation of externally sourced innovations.

In conclusion, all of these factors contributed to the decline of industrial research. While such shifts may have enhanced efficiency by allowing large firms to focus on their comparative advantage in scaling and deployment, they also narrowed the scope of innovation, potentially curtailing the creation of future breakthroughs.

The modern corporate lab

Despite its overall decline, research continues in parts of corporate America. We have already noted the important exception of the life sciences. Beyond that, a handful of companies with a specialised industry focus have also sustained their commitment to R&D. Corning is a notable example: renowned for its long-term investments in materials science, the company has reaped major rewards multiple times, first with Pyrex, later with optical fibre, and most recently with Gorilla Glass, now ubiquitous in mobile devices.[40] In addition, large technology companies such as Google (now Alphabet) and Microsoft, along with well-capitalised startups including OpenAI and Anthropic, have poured vast resources into advancing and commercialising artificial intelligence. Compared to the large laboratories of the past, today's corporate labs display both continuity and change.

In terms of continuity, they remain centrally concerned with translation. Recall Andrew Odlyzko's observation, reported fully in Chapter 4 and based on twenty-six years of experience at Bell Labs and AT&T Labs, that "It was very important that Bell Labs had a connection to the market, and thereby to real problems." Google similarly emphasises the focus on real problems and applications: "in the terminology of Pasteur's Quadrant, we do 'use-inspired basic' and 'pure applied' [computer science] research."[41]

What has changed is the competitive pressure, which has made firms more open to alliances and acquisitions, more willing to license internal discoveries that could not be exploited internally, and more focused on speedy translation. The changes in IBM's research practices, discussed earlier in this chapter, reflect the emphasis on translation. David Tennenhouse, former vice president and director of research at Intel, also explicitly noted the need to compress the technology transfer process, relative to the traditional corporate lab model.[42] Echoing this, Google's Alfred Spector, Peter Norvig, and Slav Petrov write:

> By coupling research and development, our goal is to minimise or even eliminate the traditional technology transfer process, which has proven challenging at other companies. [. . .] Google's approach to research is iterative and usually involves writing production, or near-production, code from day one. Elaborate research prototypes are rarely created, since their development delays the launch of improved end-user services. Typically, a single team iteratively explores fundamental research ideas, develops and maintains the software, and helps operate the resulting Google services—all driven by real-world experience and concrete data. This long-term engagement serves to eliminate most risk to technology transfer from research to engineering.[43]

Demis Hassabis, CEO and co-founder of Google DeepMind and Isomorphic Labs, highlights a similar point:

> Another big thing that we do at DeepMind is to combine research and engineering at scale. [. . .] We have theory work and experimental work going on in tandem. [. . .] In fact, we created our own new specialist role, the research engineer, which has now been adopted by the industry.[44]

Evidence that companies are indeed accelerating the transfer of scientific knowledge from the lab to the business units comes from joint work with Lia Sheer, which shows that "internal use"—measured as the citation of a firm's scientific papers in its own patents—has been steadily rising, with marked acceleration in recent years. Note that "internal use" is equivalent to "internal translation" of in-house scientific research.

The imperative to more quickly translate research results into commercial applications and reduce costs has also induced corporate labs to open themselves more fully to the external research environment, as illustrated by

DuPont's effort to strengthen its collaborative ties to universities. Of course, openness must be balanced against the protection of valuable intellectual assets. DeepMind, for instance, has recently introduced a more restrictive vetting process that makes publication more difficult. Current and former employees report that papers disclosing innovations that could be exploited by competitors, or cast Google's products in a negative light, are subject to particular scrutiny. Among the changes is a six-month embargo on "strategic" papers in generative AI, with additional internal approvals required before publication.[45]

Companies can boost their labs' research capabilities not just by engaging in collaborations with external actors, but also by acquiring companies with distinctive scientific and technological capabilities. Much of the recent diversification of large American technology firms into related markets has been spurred by acquisitions. Companies internalise the competencies of their targets, then develop new products building on these capabilities. The strategy has sometimes been dubbed "acquire and develop."

In joint work with Nick Vikander, we have examined the determinants of the choice between acquisitions and alliances to build research capabilities.[46] Our theoretical model suggests that acquisitions are more likely to be selected for high-risk "moonshot" projects under conditions of intense technological competition. Integration offers stronger control and protection over critical knowledge assets, which is especially valuable in technically demanding domains where failure rates are high and the competition for scarce scientific and engineering talent is fierce.[47]

Interestingly, the model also shows that integration is under-provided in a market economy. Social welfare would increase if firms acquired more than they currently do. Mergers can benefit nonmerging firms: mergers result in higher investment than alliances, which boosts investment incentives in alliances because alliance partners are less concerned about knowledge leakage when they are successful. Thus, our analysis provides a novel rationale for antitrust authorities to be lenient on technology acquisitions. By allowing mergers to occur, authorities strengthen collaborative ties, not just within merging firms but also inside alliances.

Firms have also learned, often through costly experience, how to manage discoveries from their corporate labs when internal exploitation proves infeasible or undesirable. As discussed in Chapter 4, Xerox and its Palo Alto Research Center (PARC) developed many foundational technologies of the information age, including the first computer with a graphical user interface.

Yet it was primarily startups such as Apple and Microsoft that reaped the commercial rewards. Xerox and PARC became paradigmatic cases of missed opportunities, memorably chronicled in "Fumbling the Future: How Xerox Invented, Then Ignored, the First Personal Computer" by Smith and Alexander (1988).[48] Over time, however, large companies have developed systematic approaches to prevent their intellectual property from languishing like "Rembrandts in the attic."[49] Companies now are far more likely to license internally developed technologies. Xerox itself eventually instituted a series of initiatives to manage spinoffs from PARC. Because specifying research outputs is inherently uncertain, internal research often generates spillovers that are difficult to absorb within the parent organisation. Spinoffs can provide a mechanism for commercialising discoveries that do not align with a firm's core business. Henry Chesbrough's analysis of thirty-five Xerox spinoffs highlights the strategic tensions involved.[50] Xerox sought to balance financial returns with strategic benefits, often prioritising internal coordination over the independent financial performance of spinoffs, ultimately limiting the payoff from its research.

Other firms with large internal research labs also instituted programmes to profit from discoveries that could not be exploited internally by spinning them off as startups or licensing to others. Marshall Phelps, at IBM, is a case in point. Under his leadership, IBM's licensing revenues went from virtually nothing in the 1980s to well over $ 1 billion a year at their peak in the 1990s. Phelps thereafter moved to Microsoft Research, where he instituted a similar programme. In 2001, Phelps and Nathan Myhrvold co-founded Intellectual Ventures to acquire technologies from Microsoft and other firms and develop and license them to unlock their value.[51] Google X follows a similar strategy, where innovations that are promising but do not fit with Google's business are spun off into standalone ventures.[52] Of about thirty projects started at Google X by 2024, about half were absorbed by Google itself, implying the technology was used internally. One-sixth failed, and a similar fraction was spun out, with the remaining one-sixth continuing to be developed.

Chapter takeaways

The 1980s marked the beginning of a fundamental restructuring of the American innovation landscape. For much of the twentieth century, corporate laboratories such as DuPont Central Research, Bell Labs, IBM Research, and Xerox PARC had been engines of both science and technology. By the early 1980s, however, the scientific capabilities of large firms began to erode, and over the following decades the decline became unmistakable.

This broad shift reflected several underlying forces. The growing pressure of capital markets shortened managerial horizons, making it harder to justify large research laboratories when results might only arrive after decades. The problem was compounded by spillovers: knowledge created inside corporate labs was rapidly appropriated by rivals. At the same time, corporate scope narrowed. The wave of conglomerate breakups reduced firms' ability to absorb discoveries across a wide technological base, undermining the rationale for investing in upstream science. Globalisation and a more permissive antitrust climate further reinforced the trend. Expanding markets increased the returns to incremental innovation and commercialisation, while regulators allowed consolidation on the grounds of consumer welfare, encouraging scale without the scientific ambition that once justified it.

The policy environment also changed. Mission-oriented government procurement, which had underwritten the early transistor, lasers, and the first computers, waned after the Cold War. Cost discipline and competition rules reshaped contracting practices, reducing the government's willingness to act as the buyer of first resort for high-risk technologies. Finally, the rise of robust markets for technology meant that companies no longer needed to sustain broad internal research capabilities. Universities and startups increasingly provided a steady stream of patents and spinoffs that could be licensed or acquired. By the 2000s, nearly one-fifth of patents assigned to American firms were invented elsewhere, a dramatic increase over earlier decades.

The decline of industrial research was not uniform. Life sciences firms expanded their scientific output, supported by stronger patent protections, a vibrant market for licensing, and sustained growth in NIH funding. In these fields, scientific publications served a dual purpose, advancing knowledge while also signaling quality to regulators and physicians. But in chemicals, ICT, and semiconductors, the retreat was broad and sustained. DuPont's shuttering of its storied Central Research and Development division in 2016 marked the end of an era, but the erosion had begun long before, as the company shifted toward projects closely aligned with its business units and increasingly turned to universities for basic discovery.

Taken together, these changes amount to a deep transformation in the structure of American innovation. Large firms moved away from producing science-based inventions internally and increasingly turned to sourcing them from universities and startups. This shift created strengths: specialisation, faster experimentation, and more diverse entry. But it also created vulnerabilities, especially in areas where markets for technology do not function effectively, where scaling requires vast capital outlays, and where the coordination of complementary advances is essential. The decline of corporate research left gaps in the innovation ecosystem that universities and startups have struggled to fill.

The next chapter turns to this division of innovative labour itself and the way it now shapes the organisation of American innovation.

12
Filling the Void
Entrepreneurial Academics and Science-Based Startups

Introduction

As with all long-term historical processes, the decline of the large corporate lab was intertwined with, and evolved alongside, other significant changes in the innovation ecosystem. The post-1980s era witnessed the rapid development of a robust market for technology, wherein knowledge, patents, and innovations could be traded more easily. This market allowed universities and startups to monetise their intellectual property, while allowing large corporations to acquire external innovations rather than rely solely on in-house R&D. The shift fostered a collaborative ecosystem that broke down traditional silos between academia, startups, and corporations. However, it also contributed to the decline of corporate research, as internal R&D could more easily be substituted with external invention.

Several important institutional developments facilitated the growth of technology markets. The Bayh–Dole Act of 1980, which permits academic institutions to own patents resulting from publicly funded science, encouraged American universities to become more engaged in the commercialisation of their research. Various patent and administrative reforms, such as the creation in 1982 of a "pro-patent" Court of Appeals in the United States, strengthened intellectual property rights, promoting entrepreneurship and licensing activity. The widely successful initial public offerings (IPOs) of venture-backed Genentech in 1980, 3Com in 1984, and Sun Microsystems and Oracle in 1986 contributed to the growth of the venture capital (VC) industry in the United States.[1]

This chapter describes the organisations that have emerged in the aftermath of the decline of industrial research: entrepreneurial universities and their technology-transfer offices, science-based startups, venture capital and public funding mechanisms for small firms, university-industry collaborations and other types of collaborative mechanisms that are subsumed under the banner of open innovation. We assess how effective these organisations have been in spurring innovation and fostering growth across sectors.

The diminishing role of large firms in innovation

In the new innovation ecosystem that arose after 1980, the contribution of large companies to R&D declined. NSF data indicate that "mega" companies with more than ten thousand employees accounted for 73 per cent of nonfederally funded R&D in 1985. By 1998, this share had dropped to 54 per cent and to 51 per cent by 2008.[2] Recent research matching the universe of U.S. firms in the Census Bureau's Longitudinal Business Database to U.S. patents provides a consistent picture.[3] In the late 1970s, mega firms accounted for 58 per cent of patents and citations, 70 per cent of breakthroughs, and 89 per cent of monetary value. By the 2010s, their share of patents, citations, and value had fallen over 15 per cent, to 48, 49, and 72 per cent, respectively.[4] By contrast, the shares of patents, citations, and value by the smallest firms—those with fewer than twenty employees—have grown steadily over time, from 7, 8, and 6 per cent in the 1970s, to 10, 11, and 10 per cent, respectively, in the 2010s.

Patterns linking patenting and firm age further corroborate the analysis. Young firms (zero to ten years old) have a disproportionate share of high-impact patents, as measured by citations. In the 1990s, 2000s, and 2010s, young firms accounted for 15, 14, and 13 per cent of patents versus 19, 18, and 17 per cent of cites. In contrast, the oldest firms produce an increasingly lower share of high-impact patents. In the 1990s, they accounted for 74 per cent of granted patents, 67 per cent of citations, 68 per cent of breakthroughs, and 80 per cent of patent value. By the 2010s, however, their share of granted patents was 55 per cent, while their share of high-impact, breakthrough, and monetary value was 49, 48, and 58 per cent.

These findings are especially remarkable considering the growing size advantage of the largest American firms. The share of employment in mega firms, for instance, grew from 25 per cent in the 1970s to 28 per cent in the 2010s. The share of the smallest firms decreased from 22 per cent in the 1970s to 18 per cent in the 2010s.

A final indicator of the reduced contribution of large firms to innovation is the sharp drop in the share of Fortune 500 companies among the R&D 100 Awards winners. While 41 per cent of the awards went to Fortune 500 companies in 1971, only 6 per cent went to them in 2006.[5] Overall, the evidence strongly suggests that, over time, small firms and startups became a more potent source of technological invention.

Open innovation

Collaboration among different actors in an innovation ecosystem is part of a larger movement often labelled "open innovation." Open innovation is best thought of as a process-based view of the division of innovative labour. It rejects the traditional model of innovation in which companies rely solely on their internal resources to develop new products and services. Instead, technology and ideas can be sourced from a diverse array of external partners, including universities, startups, other firms, and even customers.[6]

A survey of innovation in American manufacturing firms reveals the extent of the reliance on external sources of ideas for innovation. Between 2007 and 2009, 49 per cent (of product innovators in American manufacturing) report that their most important new product had originated from an outside source, notably customers, suppliers and technology specialists (i.e., universities, independent inventors and R&D contractors). This implies that if external sources of innovation were not available, only about 9 per cent of the firms would innovate instead of 16 per cent.[7]

Open innovation enables firms to accelerate their innovation processes by leveraging the expertise and resources of external partners. Online platforms for crowdsourcing, open-source software communities, and innovation contests have become popular ways for companies to engage with a broad range of external contributors. Changes in intellectual property (IP) policy and management have also facilitated the rise of open innovation. In the open innovation model, companies are more willing to license their IP to others and to acquire external IP that can be integrated into their own offerings.

A famous example of open innovation is Procter & Gamble's (P&G) "Connect + Develop" programme, which was launched in 2000. Faced with stagnating growth, P&G decided to open up its innovation process to external partners, aiming to source 50 per cent of its innovations from outside the company. Company sources estimated that the programme doubled P&G's innovation success rate, and increased its R&D productivity by nearly 60 per cent.[8]

The software sector has perhaps been the most visibly transformed by open innovation, particularly through the rise of open-source software. Open-source projects, such as Linux, Android, and Apache, have revolutionised the software industry by enabling thousands of developers worldwide to contribute to and improve these platforms. Companies like IBM, Google, and Microsoft have embraced open-source software. For instance, Google's Android operating system, based on open-source software, has become the dominant mobile operating system globally, driving innovation in mobile applications and services while allowing device manufacturers to build on a common platform.

The emergence of new business models specialising in IP commercialisation also shaped the market for technology. Companies such as ARM in semiconductor design, Qualcomm in telecommunications, and UDC in OLED demonstrated that firms can succeed by focusing on innovation and licensing rather than manufacturing. ARM's ability to license its chip designs to manufacturers worldwide revolutionised the semiconductor industry, creating a blueprint for how technology could be monetised without traditional production capabilities.

Table 12.1 provides information on technology royalty and licence fee income by American corporations for 2002 and 2011.[9] American corporations reported $66.6 billion of income from licensing intellectual property in 2002 and $111.2 billion in 2011. The supporting IRS data show an annual growth of 11 per cent from 1994 to 2004, which outpaced average GDP growth (3.42 per cent) in the same period.[10] Figure 12.1 also shows that international IP trade steadily climbed since the early 1990s and experienced a 2.6-fold growth in exports between 2000 and 2015.

Patent reassignments between firms refer to the transfer of ownership rights of a patent from one legal entity to another. These transfers are recorded with patent offices such as the U.S. Patent and Trademark Office (USPTO) in the United States to update the public record of who controls the intellectual property. Patent reassignments constitute a key institutional mechanism through which open innovation is realised. Beyond direct patent sales, they frequently occur in the context of market transactions such as mergers and acquisitions, spinoffs, joint ventures, and certain forms of licensing that entail partial assignment of rights.

The number of transferred patents, as measured by reassignments between firms, rose substantially from around seven thousand cases per year to over twelve thousand cases per year between 1987 and 2014.[11] Figure 12.2

Table 12.1 U.S. Distribution of Technology Licensing Receipts by Sector for 2002 and 2011 (in Billions of Dollars)[12]

Sector	Licensing of IP Protected as Industrial Property (2002)	Technology Royalty and License Fee Income (2011)		
		Total	Tech and Ind Process	Software
Manufacturing	59.5	25.7	24.8	0.9
Wholesale, retail, transport	1	49.6	49.4	0.3
Information	1.9	27.7	2.1	25.6
Finance and insurance	0.2	1.6	1.3	0.3
Professional and bus. services	3	4.5	2	2.5
Other industries	1	1.2	1.1	0.1
Total	66.6	111.2	81	30.2

Notes: This table reproduces Table 1 from ABPS (2020). It shows the distribution of technology licensing receipts in the United States. The figures for 2002 are from Robbins (2009), Table 4.10. The figures for 2011 are from the Census Enterprise Statistics Program (ESP) 2011: "Table 3: Royalty and License Fee Income from Rights to Use Intellectual Property (Detail)." (Available from https://www.census.gov/econ/esp/historical.html)

shows that, as a share of total patents in force, traded patents jumped by 41 per cent (from 0.37 per cent to 0.52 per cent) during the same period.

Universities and the commercialisation of science

Several developments encouraged American universities to become more engaged in the commercial application of their scientific discoveries. These included the Bayh-Dole Act, the growth of the venture capital sector, and the Small Business Innovation Research (SBIR) programme.

The Bayh–Dole Patent and Trademark Amendments Act

An important transformation in the U.S. university system came with the Bayh–Dole Patent and Trademark Amendments Act of 1980. Prior to Bayh–Dole, inventions arising from federally funded research were owned by the government; by 1980, federal agencies had accumulated about 28,000

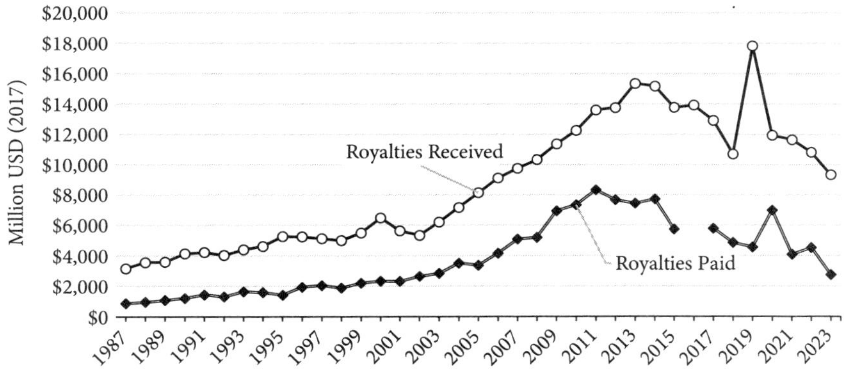

Figure 12.1 U.S. Trade in Royalties Generated from Industrial Processes with Unaffiliated Foreign Companies (1987–2023)

Notes: The line graphs plot the export (receipt) and import (payment) of royalties and licensing fees for intellectual property from 1987 to 2023. Data for 2006–2023 is downloaded from the Bureau of Economic Analysis's International Transactions, International Services, and International Investment Position Tables page (Table 2.3, "U.S. Trade in Services, by Country of Affiliation and by Type of Service"). Data for 1987–2005 are found in the NSF Science & Engineering indicators (appendix tables 60793 from 1993, 06-08 from 2006, 06-24 from 2008). Industrial processes (or manufacturing know-how) include patents and other proprietary inventions and technology. Affiliate refers to business enterprise located in one country directly or indirectly owned or controlled by an entity in another country. Controlling interest must equal ≥10% or more of its voting stock or its equivalent. All dollar figures are deflated to 2017.

patents, of which fewer than 5% had ever been licensed to industry.[13] The Bayh–Dole Act allowed universities to claim title to intellectual property from federally sponsored research and license it at their discretion. This seemingly simple change had enormous impact: universities, rather than the government, could negotiate licenses and partnerships, creating clearer incentives for commercialisation. Even before Bayh–Dole, some universities engaged in patenting and licensing (Caltech's Arnold Beckman famously commercialised a pH meter in 1934, forming National Technical Laboratories), but the legal uncertainty around federally funded innovations limited such activity. Bayh–Dole removed these barriers.

Specialised technology transfer offices (TTOs) spread rapidly across universities in the 1980s to manage the surge in patenting and licensing. Only twenty-five universities had dedicated TTOs around 1980, but by 1990 over two hundred institutions had established such offices. Early exemplars included Stanford University's Office of Technology Licensing (founded in 1970) and the University of California, Berkeley's office (1976). With Bayh–Dole in place, these offices aggressively stepped up efforts to patent

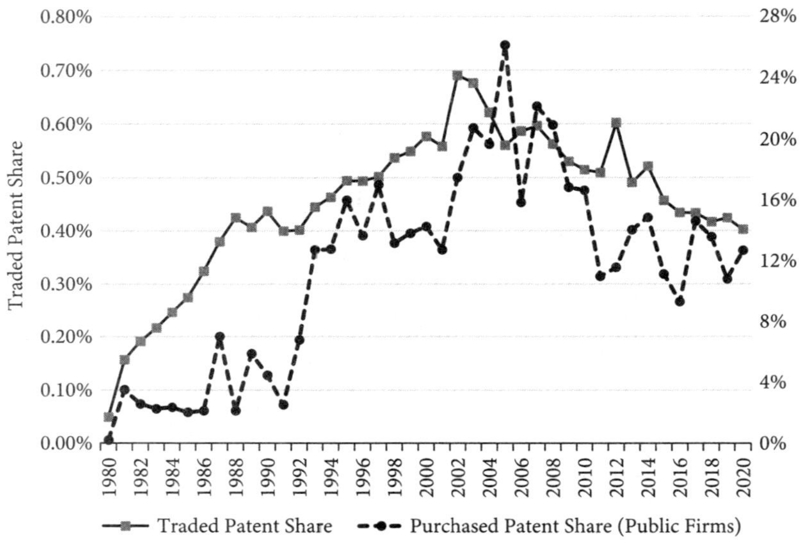

Figure 12.2 Patent Trade (1980–2020)

Notes: The solid line (left axis) divides the number of USPTO patents traded each year by the number of U.S. patents in force. Patent trade is identified by reassignments of ownership recorded in the USPTO Patent Assignment Dataset (details on cleaning this dataset to identify traded patents are available in Arora, Belenzon, and Suh (2022)).[14] The broken line (right axis) plots the average purchased patent share for U.S. headquartered patenting firms found in the DISCERN dataset. Purchased patent share for a firm is calculated by dividing the number of patents purchased by the number of patents granted to the firm each year. The purchase year of a patent is based on the date when the purchasing firm reports the change in ownership to the USPTO.

discoveries and market them to industry. Annual licensing revenues earned by U.S. universities climbed roughly 6.5 times in real terms, from $216 million in 1991 to $1.4 billion by 2004.[15] Patent output also surged. U.S. academic institutions increased their patent applications more than sevenfold from 1,335 to 9,462 during the same period.

Universities also became more efficient at translating research into patents: the number of patents per $1 billion of academic R&D almost doubled from 1975 to 1990 (from fifty-seven to ninety-six) according to Mowery and Ziedonis.[16] This growing propensity to patent suggests that more university discoveries were disclosed to the private sector, deepening a division of innovative labour. AUTM estimated that over forty-three hundred new companies were founded from university-developed inventions between 1980 and 2002.[17]

The growing market orientation of universities coincided with, and indeed partly stemmed from, a broader shift in research funding toward more applied purposes over the late twentieth century. In the early postwar decades, universities were seen primarily as centres of basic research and training, while industry and mission-oriented government labs handled much of the applied R&D. This began to change by the 1970s. A notable episode was the National Science Foundation's Research Applied to National Needs (RANN) program, launched in 1971. RANN was an ambitious federal effort to fund applied research in areas such as energy, environment, health, and urban problems—essentially, to harness academic science to solve practical national challenges. Between 1971 and 1977, NSF channelled almost half a billion dollars into RANN projects, a substantial amount, given that the NSF annual budget in 1972 was $622 million.[18,19,20] Although the program was terminated in 1977 amid concerns about whether the NSF was incurring mission creep by spreading its focus beyond basic research, RANN reflected a philosophical shift: government and society were increasingly looking to universities for innovation with impact. Future initiatives such as the SBIR program (launched in 1982, detailed later in this chapter), the National Institute of Standards and Technology's Advanced Technology Program (ATP, begun in 1990), and the Department of Energy's ARPA-E (2009) are some of the successors to the RANN initiative.

Finally, following the collapse of the Soviet Union and the end of the Cold War, defence research and procurement declined, which meant that industry, rather than the government, became the primary user of university research. Around the same time, the "War on Cancer" and other disease-specific initiatives greatly expanded the budgets of the National Institutes of Health (NIH), reinforcing the shift toward applied life science research. Indeed, from 1970 through 2003, NIH's research funding grew consistently and significantly faster than that of other science agencies. Congress doubled the NIH budget between 1998 and 2003, a boon that brought NIH annual funding to around $27 billion in 2003. By the mid-2000s, NIH alone accounted for roughly half of all U.S. nondefence research spending.[21]

Another consequence was cultural: faculty in many fields began to orient their work toward practical problems or at least to consider the "translation" of their discoveries as part of their professional role. Universities performed 56 per cent of the nation's basic research by 2008, but they also ramped up applied work, often in partnership with industry or through translational research centres. By the early twenty-first century, the divide between basic and applied research had softened, with concepts such as "Pasteur's Quadrant" (use-inspired basic research) and the "third mission" of universities becoming increasingly popular.

By the 1980s and 1990s, the collaboration between research universities and industry had created several important regional innovation ecosystems. Well-known examples include Silicon Valley around Stanford and UC Berkeley, Route 128 in Massachusetts around MIT and Harvard, and the Research Triangle around Duke and the University of North Carolina (UNC). In these regions, clusters of startups and large firms coalesced around universities, supported by venture capital. These ecosystems flourished through a self-reinforcing cycle: university labs generated talent and ideas; some of those ideas spun out into startups; successful ventures attracted more investment and inspired further entrepreneurship. Today, many university technology transfer offices actively support this model by offering incubator space, enabling entrepreneurial leaves for faculty, and accepting equity in lieu of royalties to better align with the startup pathway. According to the Association of University Technology Managers (AUTM), hundreds of university spin-off companies are formed each year across the U.S.; in 2018 alone, academic tech transfer generated nearly $3 billion in licensing revenue and launched over one thousand startups in North America.[22]

Based on a large-scale survey of Stanford alumni and staff, Chuck Eesley and William Miller estimated in 2018 that nearly forty thousand companies could trace their roots to Stanford. These companies created an estimated 5.4 million jobs and generated annual world revenues of $2.7 trillion. Eesley and Miller calculated that "[i]f these companies collectively formed an independent nation, its estimated economy would be the world's 10th largest."[23]

Figure 12.3 shows the trends in companies created to commercialise university inventions. The information comes from AUTM surveys and includes data on 329 universities from 1995 to 2015. The bars describe how many startups were based on technology licensed from universities. The number of startups formed using university inventions more than quadrupled, from less than two hundred in 1995 to more than nine hundred in 2015. A substantial fraction of these startups were also "local," meaning their primary place of business was the home state or province where the university licensing the invention was located.

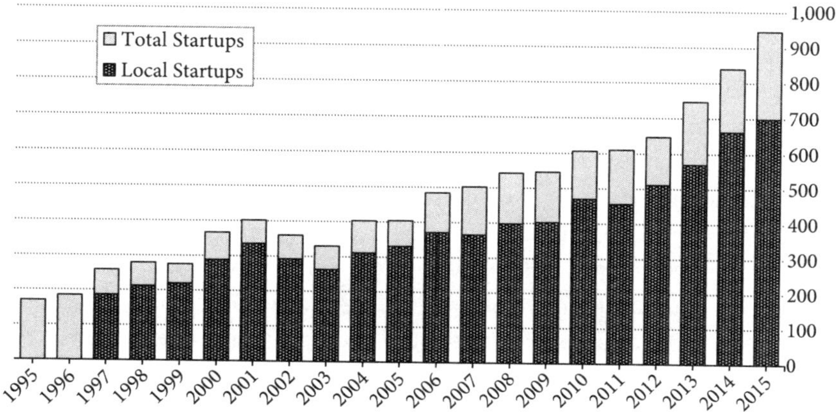

Figure 12.3 Start-ups Formed on University Inventions (1995–2015)

Notes: Data is summarised using TLO survey data from the Association of University Technology Managers (AUTM). The dataset is an unbalanced panel of 329 universities from 1995 to 2015. The grey bars plot the total number of startup companies that were founded on technology licensed from U.S. universities. The black patterned bars plot the number of such startups within the university's state.

University technology transfer offices

When universities began to own the intellectual property generated by their researchers, they established technology transfer offices (TTOs) to file for patents and identify potential licensees and buyers, although a few rely on external entities. For example, the Wisconsin Alumni Research Foundation (WARF), founded in 1925 to commercialise University of Wisconsin discoveries, is an independent foundation model of a tech transfer arm. By contrast, MIT's Technology Licensing Office and Stanford's Office of Technology Licensing (OTL) are internal units.

Despite structural differences, nearly all TTOs share common practices: universities typically require faculty inventors to assign intellectual property rights to the university in exchange for a share of any licensing income. Revenue-sharing formulas vary, but a common approach is to split net royalty income roughly one-third to the inventor, one-third to the inventor's academic department or laboratory, and one-third to the university.[24] University inventions are typically not big revenue earners, but the occasional big success can generate outsized returns. For example, Northwestern University reaped an estimated $700 million in royalties from a single drug (the painkiller Lyrica), and New York University's stake in the HIV/AIDS drug Remune earned it over $100 million.

Technology licensing revenues earned by universities reflect a combination of several factors: the overall R&D performed by the university, the share of medical research, and the efficacy of the TTO. Licensing of medical technologies accounts for the bulk of university TTO revenues, consistent with university medical research being closest to commercialisation. Universities with large medical schools, such as the University of California system, Duke, and Harvard earn about $100 million a year in licensing revenues.[25] However, roughly half of all U.S. tech transfer programs operate in the red, and even the most profitable offices rarely earn income exceeding 5 per cent of their university's research budget. Larger TTOs with experienced staff tend to secure more licences and startups than smaller, newer offices can.[26] This has spurred some universities to pool resources or form joint offices across institutions. In Europe, for instance, "strong hub" or consortium models have emerged where a central office serves multiple universities.

Generating revenue is not the sole purpose of university tech transfer. Indeed, many offices emphasise that their mission is to facilitate the utilisation of innovations, even if that means accepting modest financial returns. As MIT's long-time tech transfer director, Lita Nelsen, put it, "Impact, not income" is the guiding principle; getting a deal done to develop a technology is valued more than maximising the royalty.[27] MIT consistently ranks among the top universities for licensing income (around $30–$40 million per year in the early 2000s) and startup formation. MIT formalised its Technology Licensing Office (TLO) in 1986 and has encouraged faculty entrepreneurship for decades. Indeed, spinning off companies was common at MIT long before it was mainstream in academia. By the 2000s, MIT cultivated an extensive internal ecosystem for innovation: venture mentoring services, entrepreneurship centres and competitions (e.g., the MIT $100K Business Plan Contest), and streamlined licensing policies.

Established in 1970, Stanford's OTL was one of the first of its kind. It evaluates, markets, and licenses technology owned by Stanford University; its mission is to encourage effective technology transfer for the public benefit and generate income for teaching and research.[28] In 2024, it evaluated 541 new technologies, signed 114 new agreements (licences and options), and held equity in 23 new startups. Licensing revenue was $68.6 million; however, while more than a thousand technologies contributed to this sum, the lion's share, $43.7 million, came from just thirteen technologies.

The University of California (UC) system unites ten research campuses. From the late 1990s through the early 2000s the system collected about $100 million per year in royalties, more than any other academic institution at the time. A 2006 assessment of biotechnology patents ranked UC first nationwide; it received 723 U.S. biotech patents between 2000 and 2004. During the same time period, the campuses spun out roughly forty to fifty startups each year, second only to MIT.[29]

The American success with university technology commercialisation has inspired other advanced economies, though with varied approaches and results. In the United Kingdom, a government body, the National Research Development Corporation (later the British Technology Group, or BTG), held rights to many academic inventions and managed their commercialisation on behalf of universities. Starting in the mid-1980s, the UK adopted a similar approach to the Bayh–Dole philosophy, empowering individual universities to own and license their faculty inventions. The BTG was privatised, and universities like Cambridge, Oxford, and Imperial established in-house technology transfer offices during the late 1980s and 1990s. Today, virtually every major British university has a tech transfer office or affiliate company (e.g., Cambridge Enterprise, Oxford University Innovation) that handles patenting, licensing, and spinoff formation. The transition has borne fruit in the form of notable UK spinouts. For example, Cambridge University gave rise to ARM Holdings (mobile microprocessors) and Solexa (pioneering DNA sequencing technology), while Oxford's research led to Oxford Nanopore and the COVID-19 vaccine spinout Vaccitech.

Israel is often highlighted as a tech transfer success story. Israeli universities and institutes have long embraced commercialisation. The Weizmann Institute of Science established Yeda, one of the world's first dedicated technology transfer companies, in 1959. Its track record is remarkable: Yeda's licensing of the multiple sclerosis drug Copaxone (developed at Weizmann and commercialised by Teva Pharmaceuticals) has yielded an estimated $2 billion in royalties over the years. In recent years, Yeda has generated on the order of $50–$100 million per year in revenues, contributing roughly 10–20 per cent of the Weizmann Institute's operating budget. Hebrew University's Yissum (founded in 1964) handled the licensing deals for cherry tomato and cancer therapies; Technion's T3 office has spawned high-tech startups in fields such as cybersecurity and nanotech.

Israel's success can be attributed to a combination of factors. Strong government support in the form of R&D grants and incubator programs helped nurture academic spinoffs. Crucially, Israeli defence procurement provides a pull mechanism, particularly for Information and Communication Technology (ICT)-related inventions. Culturally, Israeli academia also values practical problem-solving and has fewer barriers between professors and industry. Many faculty serve in dual roles or take leaves to found companies. The result is an innovation ecosystem where the university is a central node feeding talent and IP into the startup sector. A distinctive feature of Israel's landscape is the large role played by foreign investment: Foreign funds accounted for over 75 per cent of total venture capital investments in 2023.[30]

Germany's and Norway's experiences provide cautionary tales. Both countries maintained a "Professor's Privilege" well into the twentieth century, which assigned intellectual property rights to faculty that originated inventions (rather than their universities). Around the early 2000s, Germany (2002) and Norway (2003) undertook reforms to align closer to the U.S. model and abolished this system, assigning IP ownership to universities for inventions arising from publicly funded research.[31] Yet, Hans Hvide and Benjamin Jones show that the rate of startups founded by university researchers in the Norwegian case fell by more than 50 per cent after the policy change.[32] By taking away scientists' ownership of their discoveries, the government may have inadvertently disincentivised entrepreneurial activity. In a study of the German reform, Sidonia von Ledebur and coauthors similarly showed that faculty patenting did not rise, though patent assignments to universities increased, suggesting a reassignment within academia rather than an aggregate increase in inventions.[33]

To examine the importance of individual monetary incentives, Ouellette and Tutt have studied policies on sharing royalty revenues with faculty in 152 universities. Universities differ in their policies, and, importantly, many universities have over time changed their policies.[34] They have found little evidence that increasing inventors' royalty share has a significant effect on the commercialisation of university discoveries. This does not imply that inventors' incentives are unimportant. Instead, academics may be motivated by more than simply royalty shares. The "gold-ribbon-puzzle" model contends that scientists are motivated by three factors: Gold, representing the financial gain from licensing proceeds, and equity stakes in startups; Ribbon, referring to the prestige gained from being recognised as innovators; and Puzzle, signifying the intellectual fulfilment from solving complex challenges. Henry Sauermann and Wes Cohen have analysed data on more than seventeen hundred PhD scientists and engineers from a nationally representative survey of doctoral recipients conducted by the National Science Foundation to probe the relationship between individuals' motives and their patenting output. They have found that intellectual challenge (Puzzle) and money (Gold) have a strong positive relationship with patenting.[35]

A few tentative lessons can be drawn from these examples. Clarifying intellectual property rights is important. Assigning them to the funder (e.g., the federal government, or government agencies, as in the UK before the 1980s) is probably a bad idea. These organisations are often bureaucratic and lack the expertise to deal with technology transactions. Assigning at least some intellectual property rights to the inventor (or "professor") seems necessary, as illustrated by the examples of Norway and perhaps Germany. However, a risk is that the inventor may not be interested in further developing and commercialising the technology. Commercialisation may also require additional resources from the university, such as graduate students, equipment, and broader business development support. Thus, assigning a share of the intellectual property rights to the university may be a reasonable compromise. Finally, a common policy response, namely, encouraging or creating investment funds may be less effective than is commonly believed. As Israel's example makes clear, capital is willing to travel quite far to match with good ideas. Lack of commercialisable ideas, rather than lack of capital, is often a more serious roadblock.

University–industry collaborations

After Bayh–Dole, Congress introduced additional tools to facilitate university–industry collaborations. The Federal Technology Transfer Act of 1986 amended the Stevenson–Wydler Act to authorise Cooperative Research and Development Agreements (CRADAs). A CRADA allows a federal laboratory to share staff, facilities, and know-how with a private firm. The firm may commercialise any resulting invention, while the government retains a royalty-free licence. In 1989 Congress extended the Act to contractor-run facilities such as the Department of Energy's national laboratories. Uptake was rapid: agencies signed hundreds of CRADAs in the late 1980s and early 1990s, and by 1995 the Department of Energy alone had executed more than one thousand agreements.

Other policy changes further smoothed collaboration: for example, the National Cooperative Research Act of 1984 reduced antitrust barriers by creating a "safe harbour" for firms engaging in joint R&D ventures, encouraging consortia that often included universities. In parallel, federal agencies like the NSF launched programs requiring or rewarding industry participation in academic research (e.g., NSF's Engineering Research Centers in the 1980s). Taken together, these post-1980 policy developments created a more permissive environment for universities and large firms to form research alliances and translate academic discoveries into commercial innovation.

One measurable outcome of these policy changes has been increased industry investment in academic research. Industry funding of university R&D, which had sunk to only a few percent in the 1970s, began rising in the 1980s. The corporate share of U.S. academic research funding grew from about 4.9 per cent in 1980 to a peak of 7.4 per cent in 1999. (In dollar terms, industry funding of university R&D rose by more than 70 per cent in just the first five years after Bayh–Dole.) The share declined in the 2000s, reaching 5.9 per cent by 2016.

The trend is also evident in the proliferation of formal research centres and contracts. Wes Cohen and colleagues estimate that there were 1,056 university–industry R&D centres in the United States in 1990. Although the first of these was apparently established in the 1880s, almost 60 per cent of them were formed between 1980 and 1989.[36] Moreover, the impetus for forming the centres for nearly three-quarters came from the university, typically from the faculty researchers. In 1990, these centres spent $2.9 billion in R&D, more than double the NSF's support for all academic R&D in the same year.[37] Government funding accounted for just under half of the funds for the centres (46%), while industry provided just under a third (31%) in 1990.

A recent high-profile partnership between IBM and MIT is a case in point. In 2017, IBM committed $250 million over ten years to establish the MIT–IBM Watson AI Lab, a joint research centre for artificial intelligence.[38] Billed as one of the largest long-term AI collaborations between academia and industry to date, this lab brought together over one hundred IBM researchers, MIT faculty, and students to advance AI algorithms, hardware, and applications.[39]

Intel's long-running partnership with UC Berkeley is another example. Intel has a history of embedding its research efforts in academic settings. In the 2000s, it operated an "Intel Research Network of University Labs," hosted at major universities, including an Intel lab on the Berkeley campus.[40] At Intel's Berkeley lab, company engineers worked side-by-side with Berkeley professors and students on emerging technologies such as wireless sensor networks and distributed computing. In an unusual move, Intel adopted an open intellectual property model for these labs, agreeing that any IP developed would be jointly owned and could be freely published. This openness meant that research would often be exploratory and precompetitive, focusing on long-term topics not immediately tied to Intel's product lines. Although Intel eventually transitioned from running on-campus labs to funding university research centres through grants, its deep ties with academia continued.[41] Intel continues to fund university research programs spanning from artificial intelligence to automation to the tune of about $100 million per year.[42]

In the life sciences, Pfizer and UCSF launched the Center for Therapeutic Innovation (CTI) at UCSF in 2010.[43] It is, effectively, a joint research hub where UCSF scientists and Pfizer researchers work side by side on early-stage drug development projects. Pfizer committed up to $85 million in funding and milestone payments to move academic biomedical discoveries more quickly toward clinical trials. A distinguishing feature of the Pfizer–UCSF collaboration is its openness and integration: Pfizer co-located a team on the UCSF campus, giving university investigators access to Pfizer's drug development experts and proprietary tools (such as compound libraries and screening technologies). Clear IP terms were established to avoid conflicts.

The relationship between Google and Stanford University highlights a different facet of university–industry collaboration. Google's own origins trace back to Stanford: the company's founders developed their search algorithm (PageRank) as Stanford graduate students and licensed the technology from the university. Google has maintained close connections with Stanford. The firm frequently sponsors research at Stanford in areas like computer science and biomedicine. For instance, Stanford's School of Medicine formed a collaborative initiative with Google to harness data science for health care, leveraging Google's cloud computing capabilities to analyse large biomedical datasets. The alliance has enabled Stanford to implement a clinical genomics service using Google's technology, dramatically accelerating data analysis for patient care.[44] More broadly, Google and Stanford engage in an ongoing exchange of talent and knowledge; Google hires many Stanford graduates and faculty (some faculty have taken senior roles at Google AI and have later

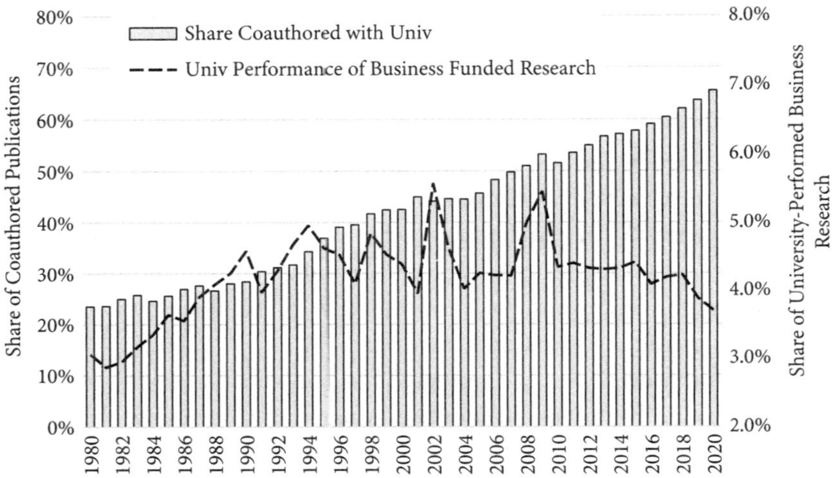

Figure 12.4 Research Collaboration between Corporations and Academia (1980–2020)

Notes: The bar graph plots the share of corporate papers co-authored with an academic institution. Corporate scientific papers are sourced from the DISCERN dataset.[45] Academic institutions are identified through author affiliations in the OpenAlex database. The dashed line divides the applied and basic research funded by businesses and performed by universities by the total business funding for research. Funding data is calculated from the *National Patterns of R&D Resources: 2021–22 Data Update, NSF 24-318* from the National Science Foundation.

returned to academia), and in turn, Google's campuses in Silicon Valley host Stanford interns and visiting researchers.

The trend of increasing university–industry collaboration is also captured in joint research outputs. Figure 12.4 indicates that co-authorship between university researchers and company scientists has risen markedly over time. The share of corporate publications with a university co-author increased from around 25 per cent in 1980 to nearly 66 per cent in 2020. The dashed line reflects research performed by universities for private business as a fraction of total business research. This share averaged at 3.5 per cent in the 1980s, rising to 4.5 per cent in the 1990s and holding thereafter: in the 2000s and 2010s, it averaged at 4.6 and 4.2 per cent, respectively. Overall, collaboration between university and industry has deepened, with greater co-authorships and more business-sponsored research at universities. This reflects three factors: the increasing reliance of invention on science; the decline in federal support for university research, except possibly in the life sciences; and the decline in internal research capacity in industry.

Collaboration between university and industry can also influence research direction. When large companies fund academic work, they can steer what gets studied. Industry scientists help frame research questions and pick projects that dovetail with commercial roadmaps: Dror Shvadron's dissertation research shows how firms shape scientific agendas when they publish their research.[46] Studying corporate-authored journal articles over a period of more than two decades, Shvadron shows that a firm's decision to place basic results in the public literature sparks a surge of follow-on papers by university and government scientists, whose findings are used to develop the firm's patents. In other words, companies can direct academic effort by seeding topics they deem strategic, letting publicly funded researchers extend the science before the firm re-absorbs it.

Venture capital

Venture capital (VC) plays an outsized role in funding innovation. While fewer than 0.5 per cent of new U.S. firms receive venture backing annually, these firms constitute nearly half of those that reach public markets.[47] In fields such as biotechnology, software, and electronics, many breakthrough products trace their origins to startups funded by venture capital. A canonical example is Genentech, founded in 1976 by UCSF biochemist Herbert Boyer and venture capitalist Robert Swanson to commercialise recombinant DNA methods. The company developed synthetic human insulin—a landmark biotech product—and proved the startup model viable in the life sciences.

The origins of the modern VC industry can be traced to the establishment of American Research & Development Corporation in 1946, although precursors already existed in the late nineteenth century. Significant growth, however, only occurred in the 1980s after regulatory changes allowed pension funds to invest in riskier assets. A crucial policy change occurred in 1979, when the U.S. Department of Labor reinterpreted the "prudent man" rule within the Employee Retirement Income Security Act (ERISA).[48] Originally, pension funds were constrained to invest only in low-risk assets. The reinterpretation allowed pension fund managers to consider portfolio diversification when evaluating risk, thereby legitimising small allocations to illiquid, higher-risk assets like venture capital. This regulatory clarification unleashed a wave of institutional investment into VC from corporate pension funds throughout the 1980s. The impact of this change was profound. Prominent firms such as Sequoia Capital and Kleiner Perkins, founded in the 1970s, gained access to more funds. By the 1990s, public pension funds, sovereign wealth funds, and university endowments had also entered the space.

This growth in venture capital arguably spurred technological progress. A study found that VC activity is associated with higher rates of patenting: a dollar of VC investment generates three to four times more patents than traditional corporate R&D spending.[49] Additionally, venture-backed firms were two to four times more likely to produce highly influential patents, measured by forward citations.[50] VC-backed startups grow faster and are more likely to go public.[51] VC-backed firms are also more R&D-intensive than their non-VC-backed peers. Among firms that went public between 1995 and 2018 and remained listed as of 2019, VC-backed companies accounted for 89 per cent of total R&D expenditures. VCs do more than channel investment. Their involvement often includes recruiting management talent, guiding product development, and facilitating business partnerships. VCs with a nonstop flight to their portfolio firms improved startup performance, emphasising the value of active, hands-on monitoring.[52]

Despite its impressive track record, venture capital has significant structural limitations that constrain its ability to support a broad spectrum of technological innovation. Most venture funds operate on a ten-year life cycle, with approximately five years allocated for making new investments and the remainder for "harvesting" returns through exits, such as IPOs or acquisitions. Therefore, venture capitalists gravitate toward companies that can demonstrate proof of concept, scale rapidly, and generate a liquidity event within that period. Technologies that require a decade or more of R&D or infrastructure development, such as novel battery chemistries, carbon capture systems, or next-generation semiconductors, often fall outside the VC investment model. As Roelof Botha, a partner at Sequoia Capital, put it:

> Our industry is still beholden to a rigid 10-year fund cycle pioneered in the 1970s. As chips shrank and software flew to the cloud, venture capital kept operating on the business equivalent of floppy disks.[53]

Lerner and Nanda provide evidence in support of a narrowing VC focus.[54] Between 1985 and 1989, hardware, materials, and energy startups accounted for about 42 per cent of VC investment in the United States, while software and service startups represented a similar share. By 2015–2019, the balance had dramatically shifted: software and digital services dominated VC portfolios, while investment in sectors such as clean energy, industrial hardware, and advanced materials became negligible. The share of funding in biopharmaceuticals and medical devices was unchanged. VC-backed innovation is similarly highly concentrated, with nearly half of all patents filed by venture-backed firms between 2008 and 2017 falling into just ten patent classes, mostly in software and information technology.

The analysis in Chapter 4 corroborates these broad patterns. There, we measured the translation of science into technology by the share of highly cited papers in a scientific field and year that are cited in a U.S. patent document. Figure 4.3 showed that the translational effort by VC-backed startups, which was increasing up to the 2000s, has since then plateaued. There is also considerable heterogeneity across scientific fields. As shown by Figure 4.4, translational efforts by VC-backed startups declined in the physical sciences (physics, chemistry, materials, engineering) and increased in the life sciences (biology and medicine) and computer science.

Honggi Lee, Matt Marx, and Lia Sheer systematically document these same trends.[55] They track VC-backed startups in the United States from 1995 to 2013 and find that over time VC-backed startups became less likely to cite scientific articles as prior art in their patents, less likely to publish scientific articles themselves, and less likely to have a PhD founder. They also show that VC funds invested more over time in IT (particularly, IT firms that are less science-intensive).

To sum up, VC-backed startups are unable to make up for the withdrawal of large firms from research, particularly outside the life sciences. VC investments are increasingly concentrated in software and digital services. Sectors such as hardware, materials, and energy, are receiving less funding.

The Small Business Innovation Research program

Several attempts have been made to fill the gaps left by venture capital. A moderately successful one is the Small Business Innovation Research (SBIR) programme. Established in 1982, with a current annual budget of about $3.5 billion, it awards research grants and contracts to small businesses "to support scientific excellence and technological innovation" that meet federal research needs.[56]

SBIR-backed firms show distinct patterns compared to venture capital (VC)-backed firms. A recent study, using a new dataset linking SBIR and VC funding to business growth, patenting, and federal contracting, found that SBIR-backed firms are more focused on innovation aligned with public sector needs.[57] They are 1.4 per cent more likely to survive year to year (off a base rate of 80 per cent), although they employ about two fewer workers and earn $360,000 less revenue per year compared to VC-backed peers. Despite these lower private market growth metrics, SBIR firms outperform in innovation-related outcomes: they produce three times as many patents, receive two times as many citations, and generate 20 per cent more breakthrough patents. For every patent produced by an SBIR recipient, up to three more are created by other firms benefiting from the shared knowledge. SBIR grantees make especially valuable contributions to "small parts of big networks": specific technological components (like sensors, measurement tools, and robotic arms) that play critical roles in larger systems such as defence platforms, health care networks, or energy infrastructure.[58] For example, SBIR firms developed key technologies for the F-35 fighter jet and the Mars Perseverance rover. In the medical and environmental sectors, SBIR-backed innovations such as wearable sensors and drone-mounted air quality monitors serve similar roles. SBIR firms have also provided solutions to global problems—such as clean cookstoves or water purification systems—that have limited private market appeal but high social value.

Many science-based startups use SBIR funds to develop prototypes or explore test applications and, if successful, they seek private investment thereafter. Sabrina Howell's study of SBIR grants by the Department of Energy finds that winning an early-stage grant approximately doubles the likelihood that a firm will receive subsequent venture capital funding.[59] Grant winners also produce more patents and are more likely to generate revenues. The effects are stronger for early-stage grants and for financially constrained firms, suggesting that the grants help overcome a lack of private funding. The study also provides evidence that it is the grant money itself—rather than government selection or certification—that drives these outcomes. Thus, SBIR and VC funding are often complements rather than substitutes. In some cases, SBIR may enable startups to complete critical proof-of-concept work that reduces investor uncertainty about the technology. However, given its relatively modest budget and the fact that a substantial share goes to established small businesses rather than startups, SBIR's overall impact on innovation gaps is likely to be modest.

Corporate venturing

In an open innovation ecosystem, large corporations not only engage with universities, but also collaborate with other firms and startups. The goal of these collaborations is often to bring startup ideas and technologies to market or commercialise them more widely. Collaboration can take many forms, from contractual alliances to equity joint ventures. Occasionally, collaborations give way to integration, as when an established company acquires its smaller partner.

One important type of collaborative arrangement is corporate venture capital (CVC). CVC refers to minority equity investments made by established firms in entrepreneurial ventures.[60] CVC agreements differ from alliances because in alliances, partners together pursue negotiated objectives. In corporate venturing, by contrast, the funded venture performs its activities to a very large extent independently of the investing firm.[61]

Reflecting these differences, established firms often manage alliances and CVC through distinct organisational units. For instance, Alphabet manages its venture investments through GV (formerly Google Ventures), which operates independently of its strategic business partnerships. Intel operates Intel Capital, a long-established CVC arm that invests in technologies aligned with its future innovation needs. An Arthur D. Little report claims that 52 per cent of Fortune 100 companies have established their own CVC arms. According to CB Insights, the majority of CVC activity is concentrated on early-stage ventures, with over 60 per cent of deal activity (in the past four to five years) focused on this area.[62] Established firms benefit from CVC investments because they provide a strategic "technology window" to monitor and learn from startup innovations.

Thus, corporate venturing offers a flexible and lower risk way to gain exposure to new technologies while retaining the option to deepen engagement later through acquisitions, licensing, or R&D partnerships.[63]

Thomas Chemmanur and his colleagues have found that entrepreneurial firms backed by CVC are significantly more innovative than those backed by venture capital. In addition, they produce more patents, and their patents are of higher quality, as measured by future citations.[64] Chemmanur and colleagues suggest two possible reasons for this gap. First, they document that entrepreneurial ventures that operate close to the industrial expertise of the CVC's parent company are more innovative. Second, they show that CVCs are more failure-tolerant than VCs, which may give entrepreneurial ventures more time to pursue risky but potentially breakthrough innovations.

Universities and the retreat of corporate science

Has the expansion of universities contributed to the withdrawal of large corporations from scientific research? The relationship between universities and corporate R&D involves mechanisms that can either be complementary or competitive. Universities, in addition to producing scientific knowledge, also train future researchers and increasingly produce inventions and startups. Universities contribute to the foundational scientific knowledge that can boost the productivity of corporate inventors. Along with research, universities also produce researchers. Corporations can employ them in their labs. Firms can undertake more ambitious and complex R&D projects with the assurance that they have the necessary expertise. On the other hand, at any given point in time, universities also compete with corporate labs for talent, as the recent exodus of AI researchers shows only too well.[65] The commercialisation of university inventions also introduces the possibility of a substitution dynamic. Companies may choose to buy externally developed technologies from universities instead of relying on internal invention alone. This can reduce the incentives for companies to invest in their own research.

In the late nineteenth and early twentieth centuries, inventions were not science-based, and, to a large extent, companies relied upon the market for technology (Chapter 7). As inventions became more science-based, companies invested in internal research (Chapter 8). As university research expanded, the growing supply of scientists and engineers bolstered industrial research efforts. University discoveries also fed industrial research (Chapters 9 and 10). In the late twentieth century, however, universities increasingly expanded into translational research, particularly in fields such as medicine, as shown in this chapter. Burgeoning supplies of human capital fueled startups, which became significant sources of invention, often substituting for industrial research within corporations.

The net effect of the expansion of universities on industrial research is therefore nuanced and contingent on the size of the university research sector, the stock of scientists and researchers, the share of science-based industries in the economy, and the effectiveness of markets for technology. It is difficult to analyse all these variables at once. One of our recent studies examines the interplay between university inventions and human capital supply.[66] Corporate labs initially grew by hiring university-trained scientists, but then withered as universities and startups increased their inventions. Markets for technology provided most of the large firms' inventions both early on and in later periods. The reason, however, was different. Early on, technology markets were thin, but setting up a large corporate lab was prohibitively expensive due to lack of human capital. Over time, hiring scientists became relatively cheap, but technology markets became even more attractive. An interesting implication of our analysis is that the U.S. economy may have transitioned from a situation where corporate investment in internal research was socially excessive (from the 1950s to the 1970s) to a situation where internal research is now underfunded (from the 1980s).

Chapter takeaways

This chapter examined how institutions such as universities and startups have increased their presence in the U.S. innovation ecosystem. Key legislative reforms, notably the Bayh–Dole Act of 1980, allowed universities to claim ownership of inventions derived from federally funded research, catalysing a wave of academic entrepreneurship. Technology transfer offices were established across universities to manage patenting and licensing activities, particularly in the life sciences.

Open innovation strategies for established firms, such as corporate partnerships with startups, academic alliances, and corporate venture capital, also became more widespread over this time period. Universities started working more closely with industry, leading to shared research, infrastructure, and talent.

The rise of startups, often born in university labs and supported by venture capital or government programs, represents an important feature of the current ecosystem. Regulatory changes in the late twentieth century enabled institutional investors to invest in venture capital funds. While VC-backed firms are very innovative, over time, VC investments became increasingly concentrated in a narrow set of sectors such as software, digital services, and biotech, with less attention to hardware, energy, and materials science startups.

As previously discussed, further efforts are needed to strengthen the various components of the innovation ecosystem. The chapters that follow will detail how.

13
The Government as a Buyer of Innovation

Introduction

Most discussions of the government's role in technology emphasise two policy levers: funding and regulation. Funding instruments, including federal grants to universities, agency research budgets (e.g., NSF, NIH), and Research and Development (R&D) tax credits, provide the capital that converts ideas into experiments. Regulatory instruments, such as patent law, antitrust policy, and safety and environmental standards, shape who can profit from an invention, how and when rivals may enter a market, and what safeguards innovators must satisfy.

What is often underemphasised is a third, potentially even more powerful tool: the government as an early user (and buyer) of innovative products. When the government acts as an early customer of knowledge-intensive products or services, it can do far more than subsidise discovery. It can create demand when none exists, set performance targets that stretch the state of the art, and signal to private investors that an unproven technology may be worth the risk. Consider the Apollo program. During the 1960s, NASA bought the majority of the United States' output of integrated circuits, driving manufacturers to improve quality years before private-sector demand could have done so.[1]

A similar pattern occurred with the first GPS satellites and stealth technology during the Cold War, and with mRNA vaccines during the COVID-19 pandemic. In each case, government procurement pulled ideas out of laboratories and into mass production, bridging the gap between invention and adoption. Recall from the earlier chapters that every deep-tech venture must juggle two risks: One is the technical risk of meeting performance targets; the other is the commercial risk of finding buyers. When a government agency commissions the first run of advanced chips, space launch vehicles, or ultra-efficient solar cells, the commercial risk is partly mitigated. Agencies act as early customers, provide user feedback, and often finance iterative redesign. In this way, procurement fills the demand gap that would otherwise stall many deep-tech ventures.

In the mid-twentieth century, government procurement created integrated supply chains spanning universities, startups, and large corporations, which private markets alone could not emulate. The retreat of large industrial laboratories discussed in Chapter 11 coincided with procurement reforms that favoured cost savings and commercial off-the-shelf solutions over ambitious, mission-driven development.

This chapter examines how procurement has shaped industrial research and how that influence has waned as government priorities shifted from technological superiority to economic efficiency. It concludes with signs of a reversal, with initiatives such as NASA's Artemis program pointing to a renewed willingness to use demand policies to steer innovation.

Size and scope of government procurement

The total value of procurement contracts for goods and services awarded by the U.S. government rose from $446 billion in 2014 to $755 billion in 2024. Figure 13.1 decomposes this total value into two components: Research and Development (R&D) contracts and production contracts. It also shows, by way of comparison, the value of project grants and cooperative agreements awarded to businesses (hereafter 'grants' for short).[2]

Both R&D contracts and grants are instruments that the government can use to spur innovation. R&D contracts fund the development of new technologies or prototypes for specific government needs. The government specifies requirements, deliverables, and deadlines, and can direct work during the project. Payments are tied to milestones and deliverables. R&D grants differ in both purpose and structure. They are assistance awards intended to advance science or technology in the public interest. Grants are typically awarded through competitive peer review, with light oversight, and with the flexibility to adapt the research plan as results emerge. Success is defined in terms of knowledge generated rather than the delivery of an operational system. Grants are a "push" mechanism, seeding high-risk, early-stage research that may later feed into contracts.

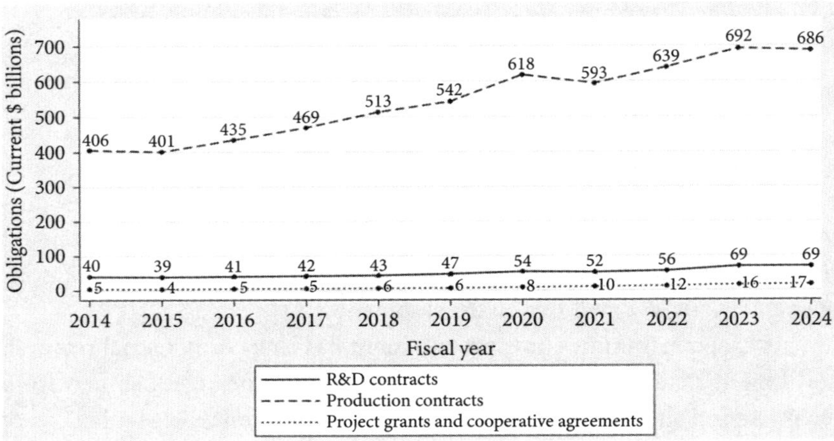

Figure 13.1 Value of Procurement Contracts and Grants Awarded to Businesses (2014–2024)

Notes: This figure plots the value of procurement contracts (R&D contracts and production contracts) awarded to businesses during 2014–2024 (in current $ billions). It also plots the value of project grants and cooperative agreements awarded to businesses during the same period.

R&D contracts dwarf grants in value. As shown in Figure 13.1, over the past decade, businesses have received four to ten times more R&D contracts than grants each year. In 2024, for instance, $69 billion was allocated to R&D contracts, while only $17 billion was allocated to grants.

Although R&D-related procurement remains largely defence-oriented, multiple civilian agencies also use R&D contracts. In 2024, roughly 64 per cent of the $69 billion in R&D-related contract obligations came from the Department of Defense. The rest was spread across agencies such as NASA ($10.97 billion), Health and Human Services ($6.54 billion), the Department of Energy ($3.61 billion), the General Services Administration ($1.76 billion), the Department of Transportation ($0.62 billion), and the Department of Homeland Security ($0.35 billion).

Production contracts come into play once a technology has been proven and the government elects to acquire it. At this stage, requirements are tightly specified. These contracts are the principal mechanism for turning prototypes into operational assets—whether for aircraft, satellites, or new vaccines. They can be awarded competitively or sole-sourced to the original developer. Production contracts account for the vast majority of federal procurement.

Guaranteed demand and the crowding-in of private investment in Research and Development

Research and Development (R&D) contracts provide explicit incentives to perform R&D by setting stretch performance targets that exceed the current state of the art. Given high technical uncertainty, these contracts frequently use reimbursement arrangements, such as cost-plus-fixed-fee or cost-plus-incentive, that shift most of the risk to the government. However, unlike grants, R&D contracts not only subsidise R&D (a supply-side effect) but also signal future demand (a demand-side effect). Successful performance may lead to lucrative follow-on production contracts. This creates an implicit incentive. Anticipating these sales, firms frequently co-invest alongside public funding to increase R&D success and secure lucrative follow-on contracts. These incentives favour large, vertically integrated contractors capable of carrying designs from development through production.

Recent work by Belenzon and Cioaca provides a systematic analysis of guaranteed demand: the implicit promise that innovative products developed by successful R&D contractors will be purchased, yielding profits to the R&D contractor.[3] Using a comprehensive dataset covering $4.2 trillion in procurement contracts and 4,520 U.S. publicly traded firms, they show that firms increase their own R&D investment when they win R&D contracts. Each additional $10 million in federal R&D contracts raises firms' own R&D expenditures by $5.3 million, increases publications by corporate scientists by 3 per cent, and boosts the employment of prominent researchers by 12 per cent. However, R&D contracts do not lead firms to increase patenting, which suggests that the guaranteed demand mechanism operates mostly for upstream research that is otherwise difficult to appropriate or contract upon.

The Belenzon–Cioaca study also finds that only large, vertically integrated firms are likely to co-invest private funds in R&D in connection with R&D contracts. This crowding-in of private R&D is consistent with the idea that the benefits from bundled R&D and production contracts accrue mostly to firms with significant in-house production capabilities. Smaller firms without such capabilities appear instead to have weaker incentives to co-invest.

The procurement of the Human Landing System (HLS), which will take humans back to the Moon, provides an illustration of the crowding-in effect. In April 2020, the National Aeronautics and Space Administration (NASA) awarded $1 billion in R&D contracts to SpaceX, Blue Origin, and Dynetics to start development of the HLS over ten months. A year later, NASA awarded a single $2.9 billion R&D contract to SpaceX to continue HLS development. Blue Origin and Dynetics protested this decision but lost. In July 2021, Blue Origin offered to invest up to $2 billion in company-funded R&D to remain in the HLS R&D competition. It did so to improve its chances of winning the R&D race, with the strong possibility of billions in future government demand. While NASA did not respond to Blue Origin's offer, the agency did award it an R&D contract worth up to $3.4 billion in May 2023 for developing a second HLS.

Blue Origin's example is not unprecedented. In January 1975, DARPA issued contracts to McDonnell Douglas and Northrop to design a stealthy manned aircraft. Lockheed requested permission to proceed without compensation (and hence without having to share the rights to its technology). DARPA Director George Heilmeier granted this request and allowed Lockheed into the study under a $1 contract. The Experimental Survivable Testbed was the precursor to the F-117 Nighthawk, the world's first operational stealth aircraft.[4] In 2025, Anthropic offered Claude for Enterprise and Claude for Government to all three branches of government, including federal civilian executive branch agencies, as well as legislative and judiciary branches of government, for $1.[5] Though undoubtedly motivated by a fear of getting locked out of the government market, it is perhaps not a coincidence that the DoD awarded Anthropic a two-year prototype contract worth up to $200 million.[6] These examples illustrate the point that firms invest in R&D when they expect downstream rewards, making explicit the kind of strategic calculation that is typically unobservable in procurement data.

A follow-up study estimates the private returns to federal research and development contracts, using stock market reactions to contract award announcements.[7] The private value is related to the obligated value of future noncompetitive product contracts, which represent expected revenue. Because share prices embed investors' forecasts of a firm's profitability, a research award should lift the stock if investors anticipate follow-on production orders. Three results from the study stand out. First, the average increase in market value after a research contract award equals nineteen times the contract's maximum revenue, but the returns are highly skewed: Large gains accrue to a small subset of firms. Second, the private returns are higher for large, vertically integrated companies, echoing earlier evidence that crowding-in is strongest for big firms. Third, the expected value of future noncompetitive product contracts explains most of the private value attached to a research award, with the effect clearest among large, vertically integrated firms. Together, these findings show that guaranteed demand (noncompetitively awarded product contracts to firms succeeding at R&D contracts), rather than upfront payment for R&D, drives the private returns to government-focused innovation. They also show that those returns are concentrated among a few large firms.

Government procurement as a venue for startup experimentation

Procurement also supports high-tech startups, not just large, vertically integrated firms. In 2019 alone, startups received $2.1 billion in R&D contracts, $7.7 billion in venture capital investment, and $2 billion in federal grants. R&D contracts serve a dual role: supporting technological exploration and facilitating market testing. Contrary to the perception of the federal government as a monolithic buyer, 734 distinct contracting offices across thirty-three agencies awarded R&D contracts in 2019, each with its own specialised needs. These agencies act as sophisticated "lead users," co-developing products with startups, setting technical standards, and creating markets for emerging technologies.

Larisa Cioaca's analysis of the National Establishment Time Series (NETS) Hitech Database (1989–2019) shows that fewer than 2 per cent of the nearly six million startups received venture capital or government procurement contracts in their first decade.[8] Of these, nearly five times as many firms secured government contracts (1.59 per cent) than venture capital (0.36 per cent), and only 0.04 per cent of startups accessed both funding streams. These findings suggest that venture capital and government procurement operate as distinct funding mechanisms for U.S. high-tech startups. Using a panel of 106,462 U.S. startups founded between 1989 and 2019, including 16,983 that won at least one federal R&D award, Cioaca shows that the dollar volume of contracts (roughly $42 billion in total) has little additional explanatory power for subsequent firm outcomes such as employment growth, sales, or the probability of exit via IPO or successful acquisition. What matters is breadth: startups that transact with a larger number of distinct government contracting offices experience faster headcount expansion, higher revenue, and a greater likelihood of a successful exit. In other words, it is the diversity of agency relationships, not the aggregate funding level, that appears to unlock scale and market traction for deep-tech ventures.

The evolution of Amprius—a battery technology startup spun out of Stanford University—illustrates Cioaca's thesis that targeted government procurement can address the dual uncertainties of technology and market demand confronting deep-tech startups. After Stanford professor Yi Cui and his graduate student developed an innovative silicon nanowire anode for lithium-ion batteries in 2007, Amprius faced considerable early-stage hurdles. The firm had to scale its novel nanostructured materials from laboratory prototypes to mass-manufacturable battery cells, an undertaking with significant technical uncertainty. On the commercial side, Amprius struggled with identifying and securing initial markets for its promising but unproven battery technology.

In this environment, federal agencies played a critical role not only as early customers, but also by providing diverse procurement opportunities, thereby simultaneously reducing technological and market uncertainty. Initially, the Department of Commerce awarded Amprius a crucial $3 million Technology Innovation Program grant in 2009, specifically targeting the challenge of scaling up manufacturing processes for its silicon nanowire technology. However, it was NASA and the Department of Defense that most clearly demonstrated the government's unique advantage: the broad variety of specialised applications it could offer. NASA commissioned Amprius to deliver advanced battery cells for deep-space exploration, setting demanding specifications such as a 50 per cent reduction in battery mass alongside rigorous safety and performance standards. This structured procurement not only defined clear technological milestones but also validated Amprius's technology under highly specialised and demanding conditions.

The Department of Defense also offered a broad set of targeted procurement opportunities, with more than ten projects spread across different agencies. From 2021 to 2023, the Army Manufacturing Technology program (ManTech) put roughly $3 million into rugged, lightweight battery cells for gear that soldiers can wear and required tests such as nail penetration for safety. In parallel, the Army Rapid Capabilities and Critical Technologies Office (RCCTO) asked Amprius for cells with almost double the current energy density for military drones. In 2024, the Army xTech-Prime competition granted Amprius $1.9 million to build batteries that are ultra-lightweight, once again setting demanding technical milestones.

This early strategic intervention produced substantial commercial payoffs. In 2022, Amprius successfully went public through a Special Purpose Acquisition Company merger. Its batteries now power Airbus's high-altitude pseudosatellite platforms, commercial drones, and electric aviation prototypes. Government procurement did more than supply early financing. The portfolio of projects stretched across many agencies, each with its own technical goal. That diversity let Amprius experiment, gather feedback, and identify the most promising applications.

Examples such as Biomason (biocement), the Universal Display Corporation (UDC; OLED display), and Solid Power (energy storage) from Chapter 3 illustrate the same point. Government procurement delivers two demand attributes, depth and scope, that seldom appear together in private markets. Depth means large multiyear orders from single buyers such as the Department of Defense or NASA: these commitments cut revenue uncertainty and raise the expected payoff from upstream R&D inside integrated manufacturers. Scope reflects the varied missions of federal agencies; it provides a portfolio of early use cases that lets resource-limited startups iterate, pivot, and discover product-market fit without bearing the full cost of failure. Policy must preserve both qualities. A diverse set of programs exposes emerging technologies to many real-world applications early, sharpening their readiness for commercial markets. At the same time, Cioaca's analysis uncovers a critical trade-off: while engagement with numerous government clients fosters greater technological refinement and market validation, it may also divert resources and managerial attention from focusing on the most promising commercial market opportunity.

Corporate research at Hughes Research Labs

Hughes Aircraft and its network of laboratories show how government procurement sustained corporate research over decades. What began as a small division of Howard Hughes's business empire grew rapidly during World War II and the Cold War through military contracts. Procurement at Hughes contributed to advances in quantum electronics, atomic timekeeping, plasma and ion optics, semiconductor physics, and infrared detection. Contracts provided both the resources and scientific challenges that guided discovery.

Hughes grew from a wartime shop into a Cold War electronics firm by winning Air Force, Navy, and Army contracts for radars and guided missiles. By the 1950s, it was a major supplier of air-to-air missiles. The scale of government procurement support was large. Between fiscal years 1966 and 1975 Hughes signed more than eleven thousand defence contracts, averaging about one thousand per year and peaking at over fifteen hundred by 1975. The Air Force accounted for nearly half the value, and the Navy for about one-third, with the Army and other agencies making up the rest.

To consolidate and strengthen its research efforts, the company established Hughes Research Laboratories (HRL) at Malibu in 1960. Procurement at Hughes became a source of risk capital for industrial research. Federal rules allowed contractors to recover Independent Research and Development (IR&D) costs as allowable overhead. This meant companies like Hughes could fund exploratory projects that were not tied directly to existing contracts, using procurement revenue to support scientific work adjacent to mission needs.

Laboratory directories from the time confirm how procurement built scientific capacity inside Hughes. In 1950, the Hughes Aircraft Research and Development Laboratories listed 70 physicists, 8 mathematicians, 331 engineers, and 5 chemists. By 1956, after the buildup of Air Force and Navy programs, the labs reported 1,169 engineers, 190 physicists, and 32 mathematicians. Their research by then spanned radar, missile systems, antennas, electron tubes, and semiconductors—the scientific foundations of interceptor radars, missile seekers, and air defence networks.

The scientific publication records of individual scientists reinforce the procurement–science relationship. Robert G. Wilson, for instance, was a prolific scientist at Hughes Research Laboratories with more than 180 publications. He earned his PhD in electronics and nuclear physics from Ohio State University in 1961 and joined HRL in 1963. His research covered ion implantation, semiconductor devices and integrated circuits, electron and ion emission from surfaces, scanning acoustic microscopy, and low-energy nuclear physics. These topics mapped directly to the needs of military programs for reliable, radiation-tolerant electronics in radar, guidance, and space systems. The military and aerospace contexts were central. Defence and space systems demanded electronics that would not fail under radiation, vibration, or extreme temperatures. Procurement contracts from DARPA and the National Bureau of Standards funded Wilson's projects specifically to meet these needs. But solving them required deeper scientific knowledge.

Wilson's research, for instance, contributed to a better understanding of how ions enter, move through, and change a crystal, and of how those changes can be controlled. By studying ion channelling, defect creation, annealing, and dopant activation, Wilson answered fundamental physics questions that had broad scientific and technological value. His work produced reliable, radiation-hardened devices for satellites, radars, and missiles, while at the same time advancing general scientific understanding that benefitted the entire semiconductor industry.

Hughes researchers also pushed gallium arsenide (GaAs) physics. Paul T. Greiling's team, using molecular-beam epitaxy, produced some of the first high-electron-mobility transistors in the early 1980s.[9] Their work clarified how electrons move at material boundaries and how quantum effects can be harnessed for ultrafast switching. Earlier studies by R. Hunsperger and R. Baron documented how GaAs responded differently from silicon under ion implantation, requiring new theories of defect behaviour. Together, this research established GaAs as a material central to ultrafast digital circuits supported by DARPA's Microwave and Millimeter Wave Monolithic Integrated Circuits program.

One of the most celebrated scientific advances made at HRL was the invention of the first working laser in 1960. Physicist Theodore H. Maiman and colleagues built a device using a synthetic ruby crystal and a photographic flash lamp to achieve light amplification by stimulated emission of radiation. This was the first time coherent light had ever been generated from a solid medium.

The link to procurement was strong. During the late 1950s, the U.S. military and DARPA had been funding "optical maser" research because of its potential in weapons, secure communications, and rangefinders. Hughes Aircraft approved Maiman's project with about $50,000 of overhead research funds. Once demonstrated, the ruby laser was tied to a U.S. Army program for laser rangefinders. Within a few years, Hughes was producing rangefinders for tanks and other systems, and laser technology became central to U.S. defence electronics.

Another research area at HRL involved atomic clocks. Navy requirements for secure communications and navigation sustained a program at HRL devoted to more precise timekeeping. In the 1960s, HRL built hydrogen maser clocks. A maser clock is an atomic timekeeper that relies on the resonance of hydrogen atoms to generate an exceptionally stable signal. Unlike mechanical or quartz clocks, which drift because their physical components wear or fluctuate, a maser clock ties measurement to a constant atomic process. This made it one of the first devices able to maintain accuracy within a few billionths of a second per day, a breakthrough that supported secure communications, navigation, and later GPS.

A follow-on "subcompact" maser program extended this line of work into new territory. The prevailing view at the time was that miniaturisation would inevitably reduce stability because more frequent wall collisions and environmental disturbances would overwhelm the atomic signal. Some sources of error, such as random quantum noise, cannot be removed, but many others, including wall interactions, cavity losses, and thermal drift, can be reduced through careful design and deeper physical understanding. In the mid-1980s, Robert R. Hayes and Harry T. M. Wang at HRL reported a "Q-enhanced" active maser with electronic cavity stabilisation.[10] Hayes and Wang showed that a hydrogen maser could operate near its fundamental noise limits even in compact form. This shifted the science of clock design: accuracy was no longer a matter of size and isolation but of mastering the physical mechanisms that sustain resonance and coherence.

To sum up, federal procurement at Hughes linked mission needs to unresolved scientific questions. Demanding performance targets required answers at the frontiers of physics and materials. Contracts supplied both risk capital and a market willing to pay for discovery. The result was a stream of breakthroughs that extended far beyond defence needs. Procurement at Hughes did not just accelerate engineering; it advanced science because mission performance required it.

The reforms in the 1990s: Balancing technological leadership with economic efficiency

Mission-oriented procurement occurs when government agencies buy goods and services with the explicit purpose of advancing a mission, such as space exploration, national security, or pandemic response. Because missions often involve formidable technological challenges (e.g., landing on the Moon), they frequently spur technological progress that spills over to other sectors of the economy.

History bears witness to these innovation spillovers. In the wake of Sputnik's launch, the United States' space procurement financed breakthroughs in rocketry, materials, telecommunications, and computing. NASA's early bulk purchases of integrated circuits drove down unit costs and accelerated the rise of the semiconductor industry. DARPA contracts aimed at secure communication produced packet-switching protocols that formed the backbone of the internet, and similar defence funding supported the first global positioning satellites and early unmanned aerial systems. More recently, advance-purchase commitments for Covid-19 vaccines eliminated scale-up risk before regulatory approval, facilitating the development of mRNA technologies for cancer and rare-disease therapies.

Procurement systems, however, adapt when the strategic landscape changes. During the Cold War, the Pentagon relied on bundled contracts that combined research, development, and production. This structure weakened cost discipline because a single firm controlled both design and manufacturing. It was tolerated at the time because of the perceived military needs and because part of the objective was the development of domestic scientific and technological capabilities. After the Soviet Union collapsed, defence procurement shifted markedly. The priority placed on mission-oriented innovation diminished, and cost considerations became more important: contracts were separated into distinct stages, competitive tenders became standard practice, and agencies were encouraged to buy commercial off-the-shelf (COTS) solutions whenever feasible.

This shift was institutionalised through key legislative reforms, notably the Federal Acquisition Streamlining Act (FASA) of 1994 and the Clinger–Cohen Act of 1996.[11] The underlying logic was that market-based competition would drive down costs, reduce inefficiencies, and increase transparency in government spending. A wave of defence firm consolidations followed, changing the R&D landscape. Northrop Corporation acquired Grumman Corporation to form Northrop Grumman (1994). Lockheed Corporation and Martin Marietta merged to form Lockheed Martin (1995). Boeing acquired McDonnell Douglas (1997), while Raytheon acquired parts of Hughes Aircraft's defence operations from General Motors (1997).

The Clinger–Cohen Act of 1996 further entrenched these changes. Initially focused on information technology (IT) procurement, the Act required agencies to prioritise commercial IT solutions and introduced performance-based contracting, where firms were paid based on outcomes rather than costs. This approach created incentives for firms to deliver results quickly but discouraged long-term R&D investments. Instead of multiyear, high-risk contracts for large R&D projects, firms faced shorter contracts with more accountability for performance, including cost reduction.

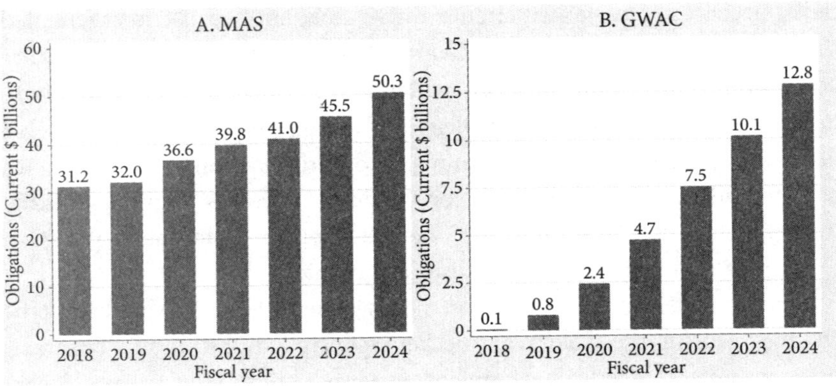

Figure 13.2 Multiple Award Schedule (MAS) and Government-Wide Acquisition Contract (GWAC) Program Spending (2018–2024)

Notes: This figure plots the value of procurement contract obligations made via Multiple Award Schedules (MAS, Panel A) and three Government-Wide Acquisition Contracts (GWACs, Panel B; includes 8A Stars III, Alliant 2, and VETS 2) during fiscal years 2018–2024. Data are from the General Services Administration's Agency Financial Reports for 2020–2024 and GWAC dashboard.[12]

Another key reform was the introduction of contracting arrangements such as the Multiple Award Schedule (MAS) and Government-Wide Acquisition Contracts (GWACs). MAS allowed federal agencies to purchase commercial products and services through prenegotiated contracts. Agencies could purchase "off-the-shelf" solutions from a fixed list of suppliers, rather than long-term R&D partnerships with firms. As shown in Figure 13.2, MAS procurement spending rose from $31.2 billion in fiscal year 2018 to $50.3 billion in 2024, reflecting the growing reliance on commercial solutions. As a share of total procurement, MAS spending rose from 5.60 per cent in 2018 to 6.66 per cent in 2024. GWACs are pre-competed multi-agency contracts for IT and other services (e.g., hardware, software, services, cybersecurity, cloud, and systems integration). These reforms reduced the use of custom R&D contracts. An unwanted outcome was that suppliers had lower incentives to innovate for the government. Instead, existing commercial technology was adapted and improved.

Another unintended effect of these reforms was to reduce the ability of the U.S. government to coordinate national innovation priorities. Firms had to compete for small, discrete contracts rather than develop customised, cutting-edge technologies. The role of the Department of Defense (DoD), in particular, was curtailed. During the Cold War, the DoD had a significant

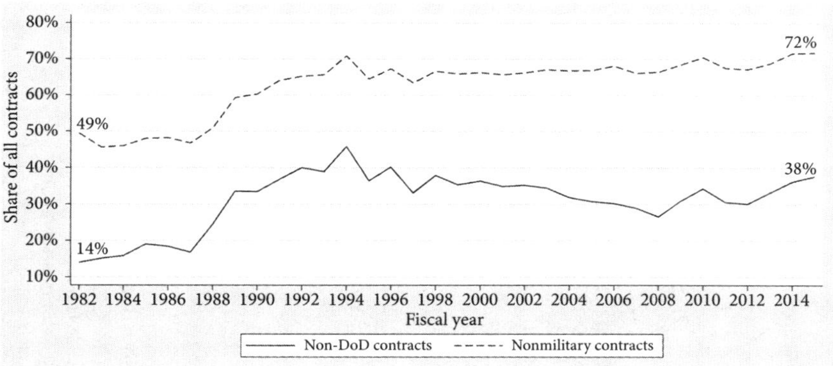

Figure 13.3 Share of Non-DoD and Nonmilitary Procurement Contracts (1982–2015)

Notes: This figure plots the shares of federal procurement contract dollars awarded by other agencies than the Department of Defense (solid line) and for nonmilitary purposes (dotted line), respectively, in all the procurement contract dollars obligated by federal agencies over time.

influence over the direction of industrial research, steering it toward strategic areas such as semiconductors, aerospace, and information technology.[13] After the Cold War, procurement decisions were more widely distributed across contracting offices within federal agencies.[14] Each purchasing office pursued its own operational objectives, leading to fragmented and inconsistent funding for long-term R&D. As Cioaca's results indicate, the more decentralised procurement system was beneficial to startups. However, it likely discouraged long-term research.

Military products and services today no longer dominate federal procurement. The share of the DoD in all federal procurement dollars declined from 86 per cent in 1982 to 62 per cent in 2015, as shown in Figure 13.3. At the same time, the share of military products and services in all DoD procurement dollars declined from 64 per cent in 1980 to 45 per cent in 2015. Finally, the reforms in the 1980s and 1990s progressively decoupled R&D contracts from production, weakening the guaranteed demand effects discussed in the previous section.

Figure 13.4, reproduced from Belenzon and Cioaca (2025), illustrates several important trends. Starting from about 1994, the year marking the passage of the Federal Acquisition Streamlining Act, the relative importance of R&D contracts declined (Panel A), while the relative importance of commercial contracts surged (Panel B). Commercial contracts are those awarded using simplified acquisition procedures resembling commercial

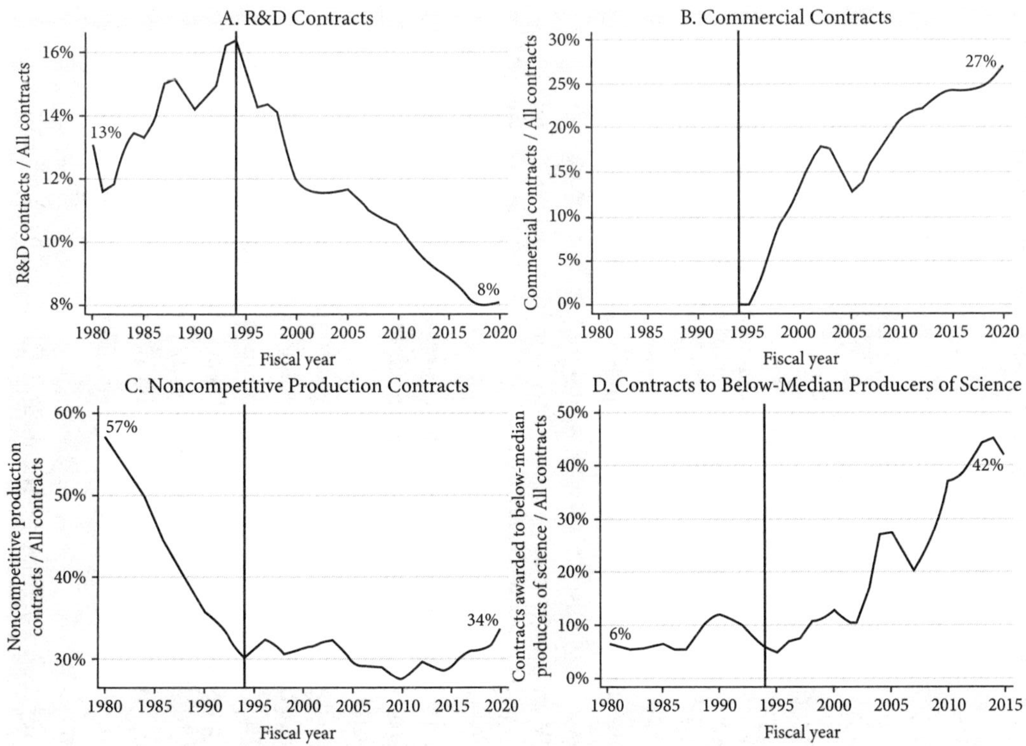

Figure 13.4 Trends in the Composition of Procurement Contracts Over Time (1980–2020)

Notes: This figure shows changes in the nature and composition of government procurement contracts over time. Panel A plots the share of R&D contract dollars in all contracts. Panel B shows the share of commercial contract dollars in all contracts, where commercial contracts are those awarded using simplified requirements designed to resemble transactions in commercial markets. Panel C plots the share of noncompetitive production contract dollars in all contracts. Panel D shows the share of contract dollars awarded to firms that do not make significant investments in upstream research—whose annual publications divided by their annual sales is below the industry median value. The vertical lines mark the passage of the Federal Acquisition Streamlining Act of 1994.

market transactions. Quantitatively, the share of R&D contract dollars in all contracts fell from 13 per cent in 1980 to 8 per cent in 2020, while the share of commercial contract dollars increased to 27 per cent in 2020 (Panel B).

Panel C also shows that the share of noncompetitive production contract dollars decreased from 57 per cent in 1980 to 34 per cent in 2020, driven by policy changes such as the Competition in Contracting Act of 1984. Panel D further shows that winning a large procurement contract today is much less likely to be tied with the possession of strong scientific capabilities than in the past. The share of contract dollars to firms that do not make significant investment in research increased from 6 per cent in 1980 to 42 per cent in 2015. This suggests that government agencies, not just investors in large public firms,[15] began to place a lower value on scientific capabilities.

Taken together, this evidence strongly suggests that the guaranteed demand mechanism has weakened in recent decades. By decoupling R&D contracts from subsequent production orders, the government reduced firms' incentives to invest in scientific research.

Back to mission-oriented procurement

In the 1990s, after the collapse of the Soviet Union, military technological leadership became less important to policymakers, while cost considerations rose in prominence. Now, the clock appears to be turning back. Amid mounting global tensions, particularly the rise of a more assertive China, military priorities are once again at the forefront of policymakers' agendas. This development is spurring a renewed interest in industrial policy and mission-oriented procurement.

CHIPS and Science Act

Signed into law in 2022, the CHIPS and Science Act (often shortened to "CHIPS Act") authorised federal investment of roughly $280 billion in U.S. science and technology capabilities, with about $52.7 billion targeted specifically to revitalise the domestic semiconductor ecosystem. On the supply side, the Act provided $39 billion in direct subsidies to spur construction of chip fabrication plants and related facilities in the United States, along with a 25 per cent investment tax credit to encourage purchases of semiconductor manufacturing equipment. Another $11 billion (through the Commerce Department) is devoted to chip research, development, and workforce training programs. The Act also established collaborative structures to guide innovation. Foremost is the National Semiconductor Technology Center (NSTC). Backed by $2 billion in initial funding, the NSTC is expected to bring together industry, academia, and government agencies to coordinate R&D and prototyping of advanced chips.

The CHIPS Act created a CHIPS for America Defense Fund of $2 billion over five years to spur the development of secure and specialised chips for national security uses.[16] This fund is complemented by the "Microelectronics Commons" program for lab-to-fab prototyping to support a pipeline of domestically produced microchips for the U.S. military. This is in the spirit of earlier policies which combine procurement and R&D contracts: the government is organising and guaranteeing a market for domestically produced chips for defence and security applications.

However, compared to earlier programs, there are important differences. Other than custom chips for the military, the government is not the primary customer. Moreover, large as the funding authorised might appear, it is a tiny fraction of the American semiconductor sales of about $180 billion. It may well be that its primary impact will take the form of the location of fabrication facilities in the United States and some specialised defence-related chips.

Artemis and the return of space procurement

NASA's Artemis initiative arguably provides a better example of recent mission-oriented procurement. Unlike semiconductor chips, the government remains the buyer of first resort for space exploration. The mission is also clear: to establish a long-term presence on the Moon. Compared to the 1950s and 1960s, the supply of private capital is much greater, and so are the technical capabilities in the private sector. Accordingly, the initiative differs from the Apollo program in important ways, but it retains the key aspects: the use of R&D contracts to seed innovation and procurement contracts to "pull" innovation, and attention to the different elements required for the mission.

Transporting crew from lunar orbit to the surface is the most capital-intensive element of Artemis. Rather than building the vehicle internally, NASA launched the Human Landing System as a multi-stage commercial competition. Phase 1 funded three firms to produce preliminary designs. NASA's $2.9 billion award to SpaceX is designed as a firm fixed price contract, with payment released only after defined technical milestones such as cryogenic propellant transfer, an uncrewed lunar demonstration, and environmental qualification. The agreement commits NASA to purchasing one crewed landing mission once the demonstration is successful, providing SpaceX with a guaranteed buyer while limiting federal exposure if milestones are missed.

Sustained operations in lunar orbit require propulsion capabilities beyond the chemical thrusters used during Apollo. Artemis addresses this by serving as an anchor customer for advanced electric drives. The Gateway outpost's power and propulsion element must deliver 50 kilowatts of continuous thrust, roughly three times the output of any previous solar electric spacecraft. NASA awarded Maxar Technologies a $375 million firm fixed price contract with milestone-based payments tied to solar array deployment, Hall thruster qualification, and full system integration, with Maxar assuming cost and schedule risk.

The agreement also commits NASA to purchase and launch the completed module in 2026. This combination of milestone-based cash flow and a guaranteed final sale reduces revenue uncertainty, enabling Maxar to raise private capital and secure suppliers for large Hall thrusters, high-voltage power processors, and lightweight radiators. Retaining intellectual property rights allows Maxar to market the subsystem for applications such as commercial satellite servicing, deep space tugs, and geostationary station keeping. NASA's orders create anchor demand that accelerates investment, learning, and domestic supply chain development for high power electric propulsion, an enabling technology for the broader space economy.

Long-duration lunar surface operations require advances in three interconnected systems: life support hardware capable of extended operation without resupply; pressurised habitats able to withstand micrometeoroids and cosmic radiation; and extravehicular suits designed for mobility in abrasive lunar dust. Under Artemis, NASA specifies performance requirements, shares operational expertise, and purchases services from industry, rather than designing and owning the equipment outright.

The new spacesuit contracts illustrate this approach. NASA conducted an open competition and selected Axiom Space and Collins Aerospace under an indefinite delivery, indefinite quantity framework with a ceiling of approximately $3.5 billion. Payments are tied to technical milestones such as pressure shell testing, thermal vacuum demonstrations, and integrated trials in simulated lunar dust. Hardware ownership remains with the companies, allowing them to adapt designs for commercial markets.

Similar arrangements are emerging for lunar habitats and closed-loop recycling systems for water and oxygen. NASA defines outcome targets for volume, radiation protection, and autonomous operation, and invites firms to propose solutions. Concepts under review include inflatable modules and three-dimensional printed structures. Contracts combine milestone payments with options for procurement contracts on follow-on services, enabling a transition from short-term demonstrations to sustained base operations.

This service purchase strategy reduces financial risk for NASA while creating a pathway for industry to scale production and move down the cost curve. Government demand allows firms such as Axiom and Collins to spread engineering costs across multiple customers, while suppliers of components from composite joints to radiation-hardened avionics gain confidence to invest in capacity.

In summary, Artemis matches Apollo in scale and ambition. Whereas Apollo relied on cost plus contracts and single prime contractors, Artemis employs fixed price, milestone-based awards with multiple competing providers for each critical system, reflecting the greater technical capabilities in the private sector and the greater supply of private capital. However, for each critical component, purchase arrangements ensure recurring revenue once capabilities are proven, encouraging substantial private investment. More than twenty-seven hundred American companies are participating, revitalising capabilities in propulsion, avionics, and life support.[17]

The technological advances fostered by Artemis have potential applications well beyond the space sector. High-power electric propulsion, advanced robotics, autonomous navigation systems, and durable life support technologies could find markets in commercial satellite services, aviation, maritime operations, remote mining, and other civilian industries. In this sense, Artemis may also serve as an instrument for industrial policy, although that is ancillary to its primary mission.

Lessons from mission-oriented procurement

As is evident from the discussion above, mission-oriented procurement has historically delivered significant social and technological benefits. By tying public funding to concrete missions, governments have stimulated research and engineering that have often spilled over well beyond the original objectives. Advances in areas such as atomic clocks, GPS, and integrated circuits illustrate how government demand accelerated fundamental science. A key mechanism underpinning these outcomes is guaranteed demand: when agencies credibly commit to purchasing successful innovations, they not only lower commercial risk, but also crowd in private investment in R&D, particularly by large, vertically integrated firms with the capacity to see programs through from research to production.

David Mowery, Richard Nelson, and Ben Martin have argued that the most valuable public procurement often targets knowledge and techniques that are at some distance from commercial application but are nonetheless important for future problem-solving.[18] These projects involve "research focused on overcoming specific roadblocks to the development of new or improved technologies, where the success of particular efforts is highly uncertain. [They may also] involve the design, development, and testing of prototypes of new technologies." This is precisely translational research as defined in this book.

Compared with supply-side policies such as grants or loans, demand-side measures can provide stronger discipline and incentives. Whereas firms may treat grants as windfalls without clear obligations, procurement requires the delivery of workable prototypes or systems. In this regard, subsidies for clean energy companies under the Obama administration drew criticism. Observers argued that loan and grant programs—such as those extended to the battery startup A123—were far less effective in fostering viable businesses than purchase incentives, which directly stimulated market demand.

A key advantage of mission-oriented procurement is its focus on narrowly defined and concrete goals. Unlike traditional industrial policy, which often pursues diffuse objectives such as job creation or supply-chain security, missions concentrate attention on products that the government would itself use—for example, developing a radar-evading bomber or a COVID-19 vaccine. This enhances the prospect of downstream government purchases from successful R&D.

The governance of mission-oriented programs must strike a balance between decentralisation and coordination. Diversity in contracting offices and agency missions can expose emerging technologies to multiple use cases, thereby enhancing technological refinement and market discovery, as Larisa Cioaca's research shows. At the same time, long-term strategic priorities require centralised coordination to ensure stable funding and coherent direction. In the context of energy R&D policy, Mowery, Nelson, and Martin note the following:

> A considerable amount of decentralization is desirable or even essential in an energy R&D program that spans such a diverse array of technologies, industries, countries, users, and applications, and which involves such a wide range of activities. Nonetheless, a centralized administrative structure for setting broad priorities, monitoring overall progress, and evaluating performance is a necessary complement to a decentralized program structure.[19]

Problems with mission-oriented procurement must be acknowledged. Beyond delays and cost overruns, missions themselves can be mis-specified. A case in point is the development of the Predator and Reaper drones in the 1990s and 2000s. The procurement process prioritised performance over production scale, resulting in highly sophisticated but costly systems optimised for counter-terrorism rather than large-scale conflict with a near-peer adversary. In hindsight, this left the United States with a fleet ill-suited to an era increasingly defined by mass, low-cost drones.

The credibility of government commitments is also paramount. The mechanism of guaranteed demand discussed in this chapter rests on an implicit promise to reward successful R&D. Such a promise is most credible when the government is buying for its own use and when the objectives of the contract are aligned with the mission. In democracies, this requires broad political consensus on the mission. A recurring weakness of U.S. policy, particularly in sectors such as energy, has been the instability of program goals and funding. When support is perceived as fleeting rather than sustained, it discourages long-term private investment.

Lastly, in public R&D programs, user interests should not be allowed to dominate program design and priorities. Drawing on the case of agricultural research in the United States, Mowery, Nelson, and Martin argue that when established firms exert excessive influence over the agenda, R&D efforts tend to concentrate on incremental improvements to existing technologies rather than on more radical innovations. Applied to mission-oriented procurement, this underscores how important it is for the government to act not only as buyer but also as user of new technologies. When the government itself is the user, the tendency of private firms to prioritise the short term is reduced; the likelihood that the program will yield breakthrough innovations is correspondingly higher.

Chapter takeaways

The chapter argues that any serious account of American technological leadership must give due weight to the federal government's role as an early and technically demanding customer. When the federal government purchases the first wave of still unproven technologies, such as microchips for the Apollo missions, GPS satellites during the Cold War, or mRNA vaccines in 2020, it does more than subsidise research and development. It guarantees a market, absorbs high failure rates, compresses learning curves, and links universities, startups, and established firms into new dynamic ecosystems.

Historical evidence shows that federal demand pull was a decisive force in the postwar electronics boom. In the 1960s, NASA bought most of the integrated circuits produced in the United States, and the Department of Defense placed purchase orders for guidance computers, radar processors, and other systems that engineers had not yet learned to mass produce. These advanced commitments pushed radical concepts out of university and corporate laboratories and into high-volume fabrication years before consumer markets could have supported such investment. By coupling upstream research support with production contracts, the government drew private laboratories into projects that would otherwise have been prohibitively risky.

Legislative changes in the 1990s reversed much of this model. The Federal Acquisition Streamlining Act and the Clinger–Cohen Act shifted procurement toward cost efficiency and commercial off-the-shelf goods, separating research and development competitions from production awards and sharply reducing the share of noncompetitive contracts with guaranteed demand. As a result, contracts went increasingly to firms with little in-house scientific capacity. Their share of federal dollars rose from 6 per cent in 1980 to 42 per cent in 2015, while the overall share of research and development contracts in federal purchasing fell to 8 per cent. The retreat from bundled, mission-oriented procurement coincided with the decline of Bell Labs-style corporate laboratories and with firms' shift toward shorter-term, market-ready research. Recent programs, such as NASA's Artemis, represent a partial return to mission-oriented procurement, which will advance frontier technologies, including advanced chips, reusable rockets, and quantum computers. Such mission-aligned procurement is an important part of reinvigorating deep-tech innovation in America.

14
What Is to Be Done
Rethinking Innovation Policy

Introduction

The American innovation system has done well, but its triumphs have also laid bare its frailties. This chapter examines the policy tools that might bolster the system. There are no silver bullets. Still, there are several things worth trying. Encouraging industrial research, experimenting with fresh modes of funding for university-based science and fledgling ventures, and strengthening the entrepreneurial ecosystem all hold promise. No single approach guarantees success, but together they may improve the odds of translating new knowledge into valuable innovations.

Protecting industrial research is a priority. It is essential to renew the social compact with firms that commit significant resources to advancing science. Companies that contribute meaningfully to scientific progress should be rewarded with regulatory forbearance. This tailored approach acknowledges the broader societal value of businesses that genuinely push scientific frontiers, distinguishing them from those that merely leverage their heft to dominate markets.

A vibrant startup sector is equally vital to America's innovation engine. Startups need not just investment but also a deeper pool of potential acquirers. Because most young firms end up being bought by larger producers, the level of rivalry among buyers determines how much value the startup (and its investors) can capture. This is especially true in deep-tech fields, where the path from concept to product is long and uncertain. The smaller pool of potential acquirers erodes entrepreneurs' bargaining power. That, in turn, saps risk-taking and discourages investment in high-stakes ventures. Robust competition among incumbents, by contrast, spurs innovation, helps startups secure fair valuations, and gives new ideas a real chance to become marketable breakthroughs.

The government also has a critical role to play. On the supply side, public investment in universities, research institutions, and foundational grants keeps fresh ideas flowing. Universities will probably remain the main wellspring of research, aided by agencies such as the NIH, NSF, DoD, and DoE. Yet it is worth experimenting with new ways of funding and conducting research. Private initiatives, such as those by the Rockefeller Foundation, the Howard Hughes Medical Institute, and the Sloan Foundation, and newer ones, such as Schmidt Futures and the Chan-Zuckerberg foundation and others can offer useful lessons. In the public sphere, there is much to learn from highly focused research outfits like Bolt, Beranek, and Newman (BBN) and the mission-driven efforts at the Defense Advanced Research Projects Agency (DARPA). On the demand side, innovation procurement programmes can create markets for emerging technologies, encouraging businesses to invest in innovation.

Renewing the social compact with market leaders

Both Joseph Schumpeter and Karl Marx recognised the deep connection between innovation and capitalism. Marx's *Das Kapital* is a veritable paean to capitalism's capacity to drive innovation. Schumpeter's theory of creative destruction highlights how entrepreneurs continuously reshape the productive landscape by introducing new goods and services, opening new markets, and transforming production methods. Marx also noted that this transformative process leads to larger manufacturing plants and firms, resulting in market concentration and power.

> The battle of competition is fought by the cheapening of commodities. The cheapness of commodities depends, caeteris paribus, on the productiveness of labour, and this on the scale of production. [. . .] Every new accumulation, in its turn, becomes the means of new accumulation. The concentration of wealth in the hands of a few individual capitalists [...] is the key to all subsequent economic development. Capital, Vol I, Chapter 25.[1]

Similarly, Schumpeter observed that successful innovators attract investment and grow, gaining market power as a result of their innovations. This market power serves both as a reward for innovation and as an incentive for further innovation, encouraging others to emulate and potentially displace the original innovator. Schumpeter presciently connected large firms and technological progress when he noted that (some) large firms would be able to ward off competitors because they had developed the ability to manage innovation, hitherto a chaotic and unpredictable process.[2] As he put it, "Technological progress is increasingly becoming the business of teams of trained specialists who turn out what is required and make it work in predictable ways." By the 1940s, Schumpeter had grasped the idea that industrial research had become the motive force of technological progress.

Indeed, a key theme running throughout the present volume is the special role of industrial research. Since the 1980s, America has experienced a significant decline in corporate research, which is crucial for many breakthrough innovations and is irreplaceable by universities and startups alone. American technological and scientific leadership, particularly in deep-tech, heavily relies on corporate research. Unfortunately, only a few companies, like IBM, Microsoft, and Alphabet, continue to invest substantially in research. They do so despite the challenges of managing long-term projects within for-profit corporations accountable to shareholders. These companies, which are carrying on the legacy bequeathed by GE, DuPont, Kodak, and Xerox, face significant government scrutiny over market dominance, much as their predecessors once did.

The special place of industrial research in the innovation ecosystem

AT&T, once a regulated monopoly that produced numerous Nobel Laureates, demonstrates the research strengths large corporations can bring to bear. Its investments in Bell Labs arose partly from a "social compact" designed to justify its market dominance to regulators, one that went well beyond perfecting telephony or boosting profits. In exchange for regulatory forbearance, AT&T channelled substantial resources into Bell Labs, not merely to refine its core business but also to pursue scientific breakthroughs, including those with significant national security implications.

Bell Labs' military work covered a wide range of projects.[3] During World War II, it played a central role in developing advanced radar systems that greatly enhanced the Allies' detection capabilities. Later on, it led efforts to create the Nike family of anti-aircraft and anti-ballistic missile systems, a mainstay of America's Cold War defences. Bell Labs also made key advances in secure communications by pioneering encrypted transmission and new switching technologies. In the postwar era, it made further strides in laser and optical systems for military applications, from targeting apparatuses to secure signal transmission.

Beyond its work in defence, Bell Labs was far more than a typical corporate R&D wing. It became a crucible of innovation, attracting some of the most brilliant researchers of its time. Their achievements ranged from inventing the transistor—catalysing modern electronics—to expanding our understanding of the Big Bang, and from creating the UNIX operating system to laying the groundwork for the internet and today's computing landscape.[4] This legacy underscores how, under the right conditions, large firms can serve as exceptional engines of discovery and societal progress.

The social compact with AT&T started to weaken during the second half of the twentieth century, culminating in its ultimate breakup in 1984. The divestiture stemmed from efforts to promote competition in telecommunications. MCI Communications' 1974 antitrust lawsuit against AT&T triggered a parallel one by the U.S. Justice Department. In 1982, a settlement led to AT&T's breakup in 1984. The company divested its local operations into seven Regional Bell Operating Companies (RBOCs), while retaining long-distance services, equipment manufacturing, and Bell Labs. Bell Labs was later spun off as a separate company, Lucent Technologies, in 1996. After facing financial difficulties in the early 2000s, Bell Labs merged with Alcatel and was later acquired by Nokia in 2006. By 2007, Bell Labs' role as a leading centre for scientific research had been largely dismantled, with much of its talent and resources dispersed.[5]

The breakup may have spurred lower prices, improved services, and accelerated technological advancement. A study by Watzinger and Schnitzer in 2020 provides a detailed analysis of the breakup's impact on innovation. These authors found a substantial increase in patenting activity, with more than seventy additional patents per year, representing a 60 per cent increase in innovation output.[6] The quality, not just the quantity, of patenting increased as well. This surge in patenting was not limited to former AT&T entities but also involved inventions from other firms in the telecommunications industry.

However, the breakup also reduced the scientific capability of AT&T's Bell Labs. Before the breakup, Bell Labs scientists had been awarded seven Nobel Prizes for groundbreaking work, including developing the transistor and for discovering cosmic microwave background radiation and the fractional

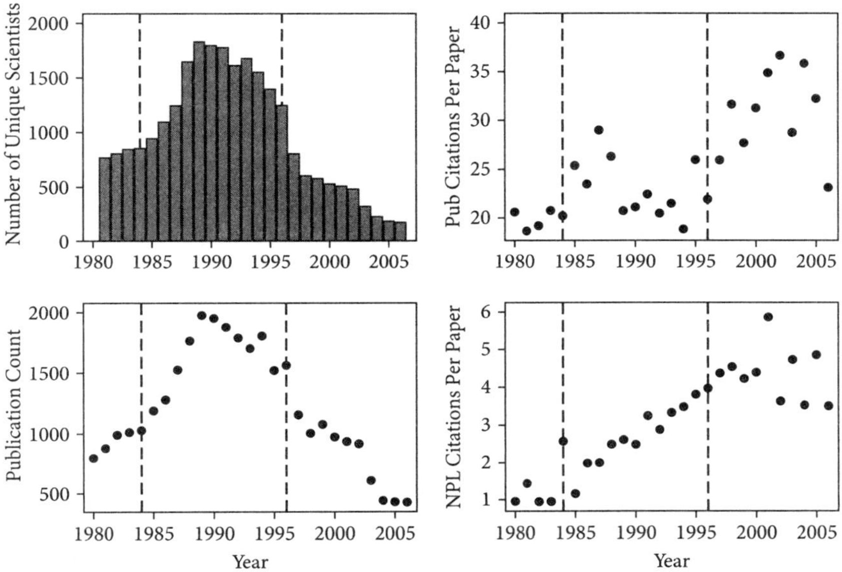

Figure 14.1 Publications by AT&T Bell Labs (1980–2006)

Notes: The top left plot counts the number of unique scientists listing Bell Labs as their affiliation each year in peer-reviewed science and engineering publications. The bottom left plot counts the number of publications from Bell Labs. The top right plot divides ten-year forward citations received from publications by number of publications. The bottom right plot divides 10-year forward citations received from patents (i.e., NPL citations) by number of publications. Bell Labs publications are sourced from the DISCERN dataset. Forward publication citations are sourced from Dimensions, while NPL citations are sourced from Marx & Fuegi (2020).[7]

quantum Hall effect. In 1969 alone, the company introduced UNIX, the first tunable high-powered infrared laser, superconducting alloys, and one of the earliest text-to-speech programs. The postbreakup era saw a noticeable decline in high-impact scientific achievements. The focus of the newly formed entities shifted towards commercially driven R&D, which, while leading to increased patenting activity, did not produce the same level of breakthrough scientific discoveries. The top left histogram from Figure 14.1 shows that the number of unique authors bearing a Bell Labs affiliation dropped steadily shortly after the 1984 breakup: after a peak of around 1,835 scientists in 1989, the number more than halved to 810 when the lab was spun out of the parent company as Lucent Technologies in 1996. By the time the lab was sold to the French telecoms giant Alcatel in 2006, the lab recorded 180 unique authors. The total number of publications by Bell Labs (in the bottom left subgraph) follows a similar trend, with a steady decline

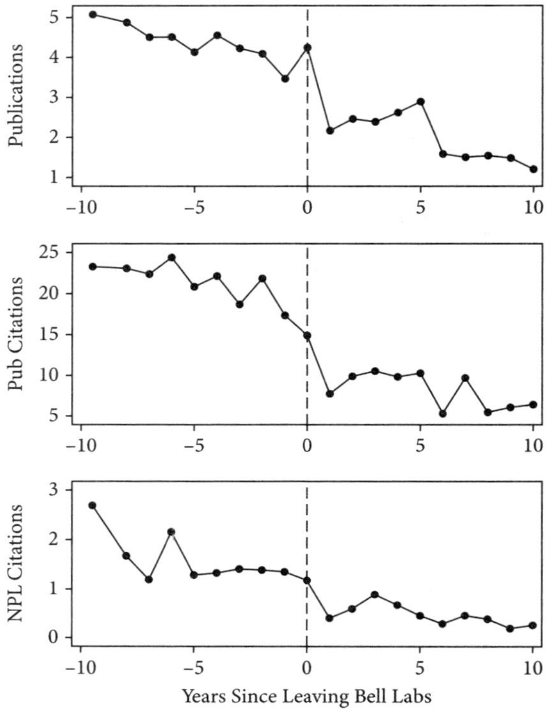

Figure 14.2 Publications by Bell Lab Alums Before and After Lucent Divestiture (1996)

Notes: The plots graph the scientific output of Bell Labs scientists 10 years before and after leaving the lab. The top plot shows the number of yearly publications per scientist; the mid plot shows total forward publication citations received by yearly publications per scientist; the bottom plot shows total patent citations received by yearly publications per scientist. Publication and patent citations are counted up to ten years post publication. The sample is limited to scientists that leave the company since 1996 (the year of the spinoff as Lucent Technologies). We focus on scientists with more than twenty publications with Bell Labs, and who have published for more than five years with the organisation. The observation window runs until 2015. Bell Lab publications are identified through the DISCERN dataset; future publications of Bell alums are collected through Dimensions; NPL citations are sourced from Marx & Fuegi (2020).[8]

since the late 1980s. The scientific recognition received by Bell publications also suffered (top right plot), with the gains made in the 1980s erased by the mid-1990s. After the Lucent spinoff in 1997, the firm recovered some of its scientific prestige (in the 2000s, it averaged around thirty forward citations per publication), though total publication output was smaller, at around seven hundred publications per year. Most notably, the lab steadily shifted toward applied research, as measured by patent citations received by paper: the bottom right plot shows that the average Non Patent Literature (NPL) citations received by a Bell Labs paper effectively quintupled from the 1980s to the 2000s at a continuous pace throughout. Therefore, while the breakup was associated with greater innovation in the broader ecosystem, it came at the cost of less fundamental science at AT&T itself, for which there was no ready substitute.

Is it possible that there were inefficiencies at Bell Labs that kept the whole from being greater than the sum of its scientists? Figure 14.2 finds no support for this claim in the bibliographic data. Focusing on 393 Bell Labs alumni who left the company in 1996 or after, we find that leaving the lab is associated with publications dropping by more than half (from 4.5 publications per year to 1.9), as seen in the top subplot.[9] Total forward citations (mid-subplot) from papers dropped even more starkly (by close to 60 per cent, from twenty-two citations per year before leaving down to eight after leaving the Labs). Patent citations to papers (bottom subplot) declined the steepest (by around 73 per cent) from around 1.7 citations per year down to 0.45 citations per year. In terms of the quantity and quality of scientific work produced, the demise of Bell Labs was a significant loss.

The breakup of AT&T is not without precedent. IG Farben, the largest chemical company in Germany, was formed in 1925 through the merger of several major German chemical firms. IG Farben combined centralised administration with decentralised production and research, maintaining at least twenty-five research laboratories across Germany. This structure allowed IG Farben to dominate the German organics, plastics, and explosives industries, making significant contributions such as synthetic fuel and rubber from coal and pioneering research in high-pressure chemistry, pharmaceuticals, and synthetic fibres. IG Farben accounted for nearly 6 per cent of all patents by German inventors, three times AT&T's share of US patents.[10]

The constituent firms of IG Farben had been known for their scientific achievements. These included early synthetic dyes (following Perkin's serendipitous discovery in 1856 in London), the development of sulfonamides (the first antibiotics), and advances in synthetic rubber. They earned Nobel Prizes for four of their scientists. Richard Willstätter received the Nobel Prize in Chemistry in 1915 for his research on plant pigments, particularly chlorophyll. Carl Bosch and Friedrich Bergius were awarded the

Nobel Prize in Chemistry in 1931 for their contributions to high-pressure chemistry. Gerhard Domagk won the Nobel Prize in Physiology or Medicine in 1939 for his discovery of the antibacterial effects of prontosil, the first of the sulfonamide antibiotics.

During World War II, IG Farben was crucial to the German war effort, supplying essential materials such as synthetic fuels and rubber. The company was dismantled after the war because it was deeply involved in war crimes, including the use of forced labour from concentration camps and the production of Zyklon B, the pesticide used in gas chambers. The breakup, formalised in 1952, resulted in the creation of three major successor companies—BASF, Bayer, and Hoechst—along with a dozen smaller firms. Bayer and Hoechst continued to excel in pharmaceuticals and fine chemicals, while BASF focused on bulk chemicals, plastics, and synthetic fibres.

The breakup of IG Farben led to increased competition within the chemical industry. Patenting rose mainly among firms outside the IG Farben group. Two mechanisms could explain this pattern. The breakup may have intensified competition and spurred innovation by other domestic companies. It may also have increased research output at the successor firms, with spillovers that lifted patenting by their rivals. These channels are not mutually exclusive. The evidence, as analysed by Felix Poege, points to knowledge spillovers as an important channel. Complicating the story, however, during this period, the production of plastics and synthetic fibres switched from coal-based inputs to those derived from petroleum. Much of the technology for the latter was developed by American firms.[11] It is therefore difficult to arrive at definitive conclusions.[12]

IBM offers a more modern example as described in Chapter 11. After World War II, the firm launched a sustained research program, beginning with the Watson Lab at Columbia and expanding into an independent research division in 1956. Its scientists went on to win five Nobel Prizes in Physics—Leo Esaki (1973) for tunneling in semiconductors; Gerd Binnig and Heinrich Rohrer (1986) for the scanning tunneling microscope; and J. Georg Bednorz and K. Alex Müller (1987) for high-temperature superconductivity. IBM researchers also shaped computer science: John Backus (FORTRAN, 1977), Ken Iverson (APL, 1979), Edgar Codd (relational databases, 1981), and John Cocke (RISC computing, 1987), each receiving Turing Awards. This tradition endures in IBM's current work on artificial intelligence and quantum computing.

IBM's inventions were also more reliant on science and built upon more recent technology. Bhaskarbhatla and Hegde report that relative to industry peers such as Texas Instruments, Intel, Kodak, HP, and Motorola, IBM patents cited a greater share of scientific publications and also built on more recent prior art.[13] IBM researchers are credited with several important technological advances, including the floppy disk, the hard disk drive, the magnetic stripe card, the relational database, the Fortran programming language, Dynamic Random Access Memory (DRAM), and copper wiring in semiconductors. Perhaps not coincidentally, IBM had faced an antitrust lawsuit for its dominance of tabulating machines. In 1969, IBM again faced an antitrust case, one that would last thirteen years before it was dismissed. Bhaskarbhatla and Hegde, using interviews and systematic statistical analysis, document that by the mid-1980s, IBM reoriented its R&D towards projects with more immediate commercial applications, dramatically increasing its patenting. Cause and effect are difficult to sort out, but there is no denying the association between the period when IBM is alleged to have exercised market power and its significant contribution to advancing physics, computer science, and electrical engineering.

Microsoft is another example. In the late 1990s and early 2000s, Microsoft faced major antitrust litigation from the U.S. Department of Justice regarding its actions to preserve its dominant position in desktop operating systems and productivity software. Over the same period, Microsoft made significant investments in research. Established in 1991, Microsoft Research advanced fields such as natural language processing, machine learning, and computer vision, laying the groundwork for many current AI applications. Fortunately, Microsoft was not dismantled, allowing it to continue investing in advancing science, including the development of quantum computing.

The vexed question of market power

The relationship between market concentration and innovation is a complicated one, and a very large literature has reached a variety of conflicting conclusions. The mixed evidence is consistent with ambiguous theory. Given its complexity and nuance, policy responses must proceed on a case-by-case basis.[14] Policies that aim to restrict firm size and market power cannot be mechanically applied, lest they destroy the golden goose of industrial research. Crucially, it is not just about money: big firms have organisational capabilities that are difficult to replicate elsewhere. Once dismantled, these capabilities are hard to rebuild.

A recent study analysed how the formation and dissolution of cartels are related to patenting. It found that cartelisation increases the quantity, quality, and range of patenting, especially by firms that are part of the cartel.[15] Interestingly, firms in the same industry, but not part of the cartel, also increase patenting when the industry is cartelised and decrease after the cartel is dissolved, but the changes are much smaller. In other words, there is an important interdependence: outcomes turn not on market power alone, but on whether the firm that holds it also has the scientific and technical capabilities to advance the technology.

On the one hand, large and profitable enterprises may have the resources to fund speculative research projects. For instance, a recent paper shows that pharmaceutical firms tend to invest windfall profits in novel (and riskier) innovations.[16] On the other hand, their very dominance can invite abuses, curb competition, and, paradoxically, limit the very innovation that such resources might otherwise foster.

A further worry is that dominant players retard innovation by hoarding talent and stifling competition. Some acquire upstart rivals, only to shelve the newly acquired technology or discontinue competing products. This phenomenon, known as a "killer acquisition," undercuts the principle of creative destruction. In the life sciences, research by Cunningham, Ederer, and Ma shows that roughly 5 per cent of acquisitions involve larger firms discontinuing projects that threaten their existing product lines.[17] Similarly, Kamepalli, Rajan, and Zingales have argued that incumbents create a "kill zone" around their platform that makes entry of competitors unprofitable.[18] John Haltiwanger and colleagues have documented a decline in the rate at which new firms have been started in the United States since the late 1970s, a shift that some observers attribute to the growing power of incumbent giants.[19] However, more recent evidence suggests that a resurgence has occurred since 2020.[20]

The spectre of market power extends beyond economics to poison politics. Deep-pocketed corporations can influence regulations and policymaking through lobbying, augmenting their position further. This can foster a self-reinforcing cycle in which firms that wield outsized power shape the environment to entrench their dominance, leaving smaller rivals at a structural disadvantage. On the other hand, some of these firms contribute meaningfully to scientific and technological advances. Restricting their market power too aggressively might inadvertently stifle research that yields substantial societal benefits.

We argue for a more refined approach, one that distinguishes between companies that invest in significant scientific research and those that merely leverage market dominance without fostering discovery. Rather than reflexively dismantle large firms or resort to across-the-board antitrust crackdowns, regulators should exercise discretion. In some cases, well-financed businesses may be the only ones capable of funding billion-dollar research initiatives. Conversely, unchecked consolidation risks fewer potential buyers for startups, hurting innovation.[21]

The Department of Justice's (DOJ's) scrutiny of Google highlights the complexity of lumping all tech giants together. Even as Google was being sued by the DOJ, two of Google's researchers, Demis Hassabis and John Jumper, won the Nobel Prize for a protein-structure breakthrough that emerged from DeepMind's machine-learning work. Though Google's technological contributions, including advances in AI and quantum computing, differ markedly from Apple's focus on product design or Amazon's emphasis on operational efficiency, regulators often treat them alike.

None of this implies lax enforcement. To the contrary, it is the enforcement that makes forbearance valuable. DuPont invested in internal research after an antitrust suit in 1913 convinced management that the path to future growth lay in entering new markets through innovation rather than the acquisition of existing producers. Kodak, Standard Oil, Xerox, and many others explicitly considered antitrust in their decision to invest in internal research.[22] In short, antitrust policy must look beyond short-term consumer interests to the wider societal good. Pricing alone cannot capture a firm's overall impact. Regulators instead need to judge how large firms contribute to science, technology, and public needs, from national security to clean energy. A careful, case-by-case approach can separate companies that drive scientific progress from those merely extracting rents.

Improving the startup ecosystem in deep-tech

While industrial research by large corporations is an important component of a healthy innovation ecosystem, it is not enough. The second leg of the tripod, an innovative and vibrant startup sector, is also necessary. While software and biotech startup ventures have flourished, deep-tech startups have often struggled. Research by Honggi Lee, Matt Marx, and Lia Sheer cited in Chapter 4 bears this out. They show that the share of science-based startups with venture capital (VC) in the United States declined between 1995 and 2013. Newly funded high-tech ventures are less likely to cite scientific articles as prior art in their patents. Similar declines are evident in the share of VC-backed startups that publish scientific articles and those that have a PhD founder.

Facilitating value creation: New venture models beyond "spray and pray"

A great strength of the American innovation ecosystem is that it facilitates startup formation and growth. Nowhere is this advantage more evident than in the provision of risk capital. The United States has a vibrant venture capital industry that is willing to bet on companies with little collateral, no sales, and sometimes not even a product. But the current venture-financing model, so well suited to digital startups, where the biggest uncertainty is customer demand rather than technological feasibility, may not cope with the long horizons that deep-tech requires. Resolving uncertainty about demand—how popular a product might be and how to reach its customers—is the main challenge for software and digital startups, and venture funding is typically geared to that purpose. Because human tastes are notoriously difficult to predict, venture capitalists have adopted a "home-run" approach in which a single spectacular success must pay for many misfires. Speed is paramount: VC funds usually last only a decade. Yet haste can mean prematurely discarding potentially viable ideas. In pushing for quick resolutions, venture capitalists may inadvertently drive promising startups into failure.

The much-lauded Lean-Startup model is a case in point. Its emphasis on rapidly testing a "minimum viable product" is equivalent to conducting a test with a high false negative but a very low false positive rate: If potential customers are satisfied with the minimal feature product, it is highly likely that the product will gain widespread favour. However, the converse is not true. If a substantial fraction of early customers dislikes the minimal feature product, this does not imply that a more fully developed product would not find favour. This problem becomes more acute for deep-tech innovations, where the performance and unit cost may depend significantly on the scale of adoption, as illustrated by the discussion of new materials in Chapter 4.

HighTechXL in Eindhoven is an interesting attempt to advance deep-tech startups. It sources ideas from prestigious research organisations, including European Organization for Nuclear Research, the Netherlands Organisation for Applied Scientific Research (TNO), and the European Space Agency (ESA). HighTechXL also brings together scientists, engineers, investors, and business strategists to scrutinise each technology's potential applications. For each selected technology, HighTechXL assembles a team and provides early-stage support. In 2022 HighTechXL helped establish a €100m DeepTechXL fund, from a large Dutch pension fund, ASML, Philips, the Brabant Development Company, the Dutch government, and several family offices. Many of these institutions also participate in the Eindhoven Startup Alliance, which provides new companies with access to IP lawyers, specialised manufacturing know-how, and connections to potential customers and suppliers. Some startups from HighTechXL have successfully raised follow-on funding. Accerion, which developed locational technology for robots and autonomous vehicles, was acquired in 2025 shortly after its seed round of funding by a German industrial equipment manufacturer. This model for deep-tech startups is still in its infancy, and it is too early to judge its effectiveness.

Some favour East Asian, government-based financing models, such as China's National Integrated Circuit Fund. Launched in 2014 with an initial war chest of $50 billion, it is designed to strengthen China's semiconductor industry. Its goal is not quick returns but industrial sovereignty. By providing patient capital to domestic firms like the Semiconductor Manufacturing International Corporation (SMIC), the fund enables companies to build multibillion-dollar fabrication plants and pursue the development of next-generation chips. Singapore's Economic Development Board Investments (EDBI) co-invests in startups working on AI, advanced manufacturing, and health care technologies.

These financing models are obviously different from the VC model, which requires not only a healthy return on investment but also a rapid return *of* investment. The former is challenging for deep-tech startups, but so is the latter. The two problems are related, particularly because a commonly used measure of return, namely, the internal rate of return (IRR), is sensitive to how quickly the returns are realised. Even so, it is helpful to keep the two problems separate, especially because many discussions of "patient" capital tend to confound the two and, additionally, confound private returns with social returns.

Deep-tech ventures may need to be subsidised if the social returns exceed the private payoff, but they frequently also need financing arrangements with longer duration, where the return *of* investment happens in the form of return on investment, at least in part. Few investors in startups currently seek such arrangements, but perhaps more could. University endowments, philanthropies, and family offices may consider financing startups that offer a return through a dividend-like mechanism.

Eric Gilliam, among others, has suggested exploring alternative venture models such as revenue-based financing, where startups secure capital and repay it via a fixed percentage of future revenues.[23] This model can align investor-startup incentives over a longer horizon. Unlike the current "boom or bust" model, it would likely result in fewer homeruns and more singles, but also fewer strikeouts. Scale-up would be slower, and many startups are likely to operate for a longer period before reaching a liquidity event - going public or getting acquired. Some may not even reach the necessary scale for a public company and may remain private, albeit profitable.[24]

Some key differences with the current software-oriented VC model include the following.

- Lower outright failure—The standard VC model assumes high failure rates and seeks to offset failures with a few big successes in relatively short time. Given the longer time required and lower value capture, viable deep-tech investments must have lower rates of outright failure. Stated as a baseball metaphor, deep-tech financing has to be about a higher batting average by hitting more singles rather than swinging for the fences. This implies that investments have to be more selective, and perhaps the underlying technology needs to be more mature before institutional investment. In turn, this would require potential investors to understand the science and be familiar with the scientists through prior interactions with universities and researchers. R&D contracts and agreements with potential buyers would be very useful in this respect.
- Startup founders may have to go beyond developing technology and build companies. Insofar as returns will take longer and some may be in the form of dividends from profits, deep-tech founders may have to be prepared to build companies, not simply develop products. This implies that deep-tech startups will need the managerial capabilities required to develop both the technology and the company itself.

- Investors have to be willing to accept returns and invested capital in the form of dividends from operating profits rather than sale of shares to a strategic investor (acquisition) or retail investors (IPO). In turn, this would require more patient investors rather than the ten-year fund term typical of venture capital. Potentially, this creates opportunities for established firms to source promising technology by acting as strategic investors in deep-tech startups.

Not surprisingly, few institutional investors have attempted this, and fewer still have succeeded. One early example is Calm Funds, launched by Tyler Tringas, which has not yet succeeded despite strenuous efforts.[25] It may well be that the venture investor model is ill-suited for deep-tech ventures.[26] Consider First Solar, a leader in thin-film photovoltaic technology for solar power. When it was founded in 1999, most investors considered solar energy to be unreliable and unprofitable. However, some patient investors, including family offices and impact funds, recognised a greater potential: significant returns if solar production costs could be lowered through innovation. First Solar concentrated on developing a new production technique: thin-film photovoltaic (PV) technology, which was less expensive to produce than conventional silicon-based panels. Early backers faced years of uncertainty, as scaling up production necessitated costly infrastructure, and subsidies for solar energy were politically unstable. Nevertheless, First Solar remained committed. Today, the company is one of the largest solar manufacturers globally, and its technology has played a crucial role in accelerating the worldwide transition to renewable energy.

It is noteworthy that a serial science-entrepreneur, Harold McMaster, co-founded First Solar. McMaster had previously founded companies such as Permaglass (which commercialised his process for producing curved glass for appliances, TV sets, and automotive applications) and Glasstech (which pioneered the production of high-strength tempered glass for skyscrapers, automobiles, and other applications).[27] In both cases, the companies were set up to generate positive cash flow, not just demonstrate the potential of the technology.

Revenues can also facilitate debt financing. Unlike traditional bank loans, which require immediate repayment schedules, development bank loans are structured to reflect the long timelines required for R&D-heavy ventures. CATL, China's world-leading battery manufacturer, used loans from the China Development Bank to fund its gigafactories and support R&D on lithium-sulfur and solid-state batteries. Another example is the U.S. Department of Energy's Loan Program Office (LPO), which benefited Tesla and QuantumScape.

Government contracting, akin to what Bolt, Beranek, and Newman (BBN) Technologies pioneered, is another option. BBN was a famed contract research firm during the Cold War that made significant contributions to the ARPANET, the precursor to the modern internet. Deep-tech startups can work on R&D projects for agencies like DARPA or the Department of Energy, establishing an immediate funding pipeline and validating their technology's potential. Many deep-tech startups, including Biomason, UDC, and Solid Power, discussed in Chapter 3, benefited from such contracts. These contracts not only bolster financial stability but also lend credibility, making follow-on investment more likely.

Enhancing value capture

Deep-tech startups can flourish if supported in their ability not just to create value but also to capture a meaningful share of that value. Given that most startups ultimately realise returns through acquisition, their value capture potential critically hinges upon the number of viable acquirers, the startups' capability to commercialise and scale their technologies independently, and the terms and timing of their financing. Startups are especially vulnerable when the pool of potential acquirers is limited to a few large incumbents. These dominant firms can use their market position to delay acquisition or reduce valuations. Encouraging robust competition within product markets can mitigate these vulnerabilities. Outright prohibitions on acquisitions would be counterproductive. On the other hand, regulators should keep a close eye on large-scale mergers and acquisitions, which could reduce the pool of potential acquirers.

Equally important is easing the "road to commercialisation." Creating prototypes and scaling production often demands extensive R&D facilities and compliance with complex regulatory requirements. Contract development and manufacturing organisations (CDMOs), widely used in sectors such as biopharma, can significantly ease these burdens. Companies like Lonza, ThermoFisher, Catalent, WuXi, and Fuji already provide crucial support services, enabling startups to scale innovations without building costly infrastructure from scratch. Similarly, battery ventures have benefited substantially from specialised contract manufacturers. In the United States, this sector grew to over $5 billion in 2023, with companies including Rose Batteries, Ttek Assemblies, Johnson Controls, Valmet Automotive, and smaller specialists like GUS Technologies. For example, Echion Technologies has leveraged GUS's manufacturing expertise to commercialise its innovative niobium-based, fast-charging battery materials.[28]

The U.S. government has launched programs that convert fixed manufacturing costs into variable, on-demand production capacity by offering shared foundries, pilot lines, and test beds. These platforms let firms validate processes, generate early data, and adjust designs before committing major capital. By lowering the cost of initial experimentation, they make deep-tech investments more attractive to early investors and improve value capture by strengthening the startup's bargaining position with future commercialisation partners.

The Advanced Research on Integrated Energy Systems (ARIES) platform at the U.S. National Renewable Energy Laboratory (NREL) offers a 1.25-MW electrolyzer, 600-kg hydrogen storage, and a 3.7-MW integrated cooling system. At its Flatirons Campus, researchers have access to a flexible power grid, equipment to connect and control different sections of that grid, and a system for producing and storing hydrogen.[29] NREL also has accelerators and incubators for startups. For instance, Antora, a startup focused on decarbonising industry by converting low-cost, intermittent renewable electricity into reliable industrial energy, got its thermophotovoltaic (TPV) cells from NREL in 2018. This was especially valuable because Antora itself lacked this capability. As Tarun Narain from Antora put it, "If we didn't have NREL and we had to figure it (TPV cell) out ourselves, we'd probably still be figuring it out."[30]

Materials discovery also struggles with the high cost of experimentation. The Materials Project is a free, open-access database hosted by Lawrence Berkeley National Laboratory which provides computed properties of materials using density functional theory; it contains data on more than one hundred fifty thousand compounds, including about thirty-four thousand predicted to be thermodynamically stable and around twenty-three thousand that have been experimentally observed. Argonne National Lab's Polybot uses machine learning to explore nearly a million processing combinations for the production of high-quality polymer films.[31]

Biological manufacturing innovation often stalls because safe laboratory space is scarce and expensive. Biosecurity requirements add further costs and regulatory burdens.[32] The NSF is investing $75 million to establish five biofoundries, which are integrated facilities that combine advances in biological sciences with automation, high-throughput measurement, integrated data acquisition and analysis, and artificial intelligence.[33]

Another policy initiative, Manufacturing USA, aims at helping startups manufacture their inventions. PowerAmerica, one of the Manufacturing USA institutes based at North Carolina State University (NCSU), helped establish the first "open" SiC chip foundry in the United States at X-FAB's Lubbock, Texas site. An open foundry sells wafer-fabrication services to many fabless firms, lowering entry barriers and minimum efficient scale for startups that design SiC power devices. The Commercial Leap Ahead for Wide-Bandgap Semiconductors (CLAWS) hub at NC State operates a "fab-in-a-lab" facility to speed the development of new devices made from materials that can handle very high voltages. These projects fund small-scale production runs and include partners such as NASA, the Naval Research Laboratory, General Electric, and Lockheed Martin.[34] These programs are still new, and their long-run impact is unknown. Nonetheless, these are welcome experiments for encouraging deep-tech startups.

In summary, the division of innovative labour creates distinct vulnerabilities for deep-tech startups, given their reliance on market access from established firms. Addressing these challenges involves public infrastructure to lower experimentation costs and streamline commercialisation pathways, and foster competitive markets for acquisition.

Rethinking the production of scientific knowledge

We also need to improve how the production of new knowledge is funded and organised. Universities are, and will likely remain, a primary source of useful knowledge. The public debate has highlighted two problems with university research. First, some believe that too much of university research is incremental. The second problem is that university research is typically nascent, insufficiently developed for commercial application.

Encouraging novel research

The NIH's annual budget in 2024 was $47 billion, and it is the largest funder of biomedical research. For several years there has been growing concern that NIH-funded research is too incremental. The difficulties that Katalin Kariko faced in obtaining grant funding for her work on applying mRNA for the treatment of human diseases are by now well documented. A chance encounter with Drew Weissman in 1997 led her to switch the focus from treating strokes and cerebral diseases to vaccines, supported by an existing NIH grant to Weissman which, however, had nothing to do with mRNA. A study by Franzoni, Stephan, and Veugelers found that obtaining grants remained difficult for Kariko. A 2007 grant application by Kariko was rejected in part because it was insufficiently novel![35] The same study also shows that conservatism is not limited to the NIH, but extends to other funding agencies, in Europe and the United States as well. The conservatism was not limited to funding. Their Nobel Prize-winning research was rejected by several journals before finally being published in 2005.

Packalen and Bhattacharya have studied the extent to which NIH supports the exploration of new ideas and how this has changed over time.[36] Their analysis covers more than 24 million research articles in the MEDLINE database. Using the Unified Medical Language System (UMLS) metathesaurus to classify the ideas explored in the articles, they measure the vintage of the idea by the year the idea first emerged. They find that of the papers published until 2010 by U.S.-based scientists, NIH-funded papers explore newer ideas than the papers without NIH support, but mostly for basic research rather than clinical purposes, and largely because NSF funds research in newer subfields. Most importantly, they find that the NIH's share of papers that build on the most recent advances has declined over time. They conclude that there is an apparent increase in conservatism despite NIH initiatives to increase funding for innovative projects. They attribute this conservatism to the nature of the NIH grant review process as well as the composition of the grant applications it receives.

It is natural that the attitudes of funding agencies, which rely upon peer evaluations to decide what to fund, should be closely related to the research strategies individual researchers choose. The available evidence bears this relation out.[37] For instance, Foster, Rzhetsky, and Evans (2015) found that research that explores previously unexplored chemical relationships is more likely to "fail" but, if the research succeeds, is more likely to make a breakthrough.[38] Indeed, papers that report highly innovative chemical combinations receive, on average, 22 per cent more citations than "repeat" papers that reuse known combinations. Papers with moderately innovative combinations perform even better, earning about 30 per cent more citations than repeat papers. Wang, Veugelers, and Stephan (2017) measure novelty by examining whether a published paper is the first to combine scientific knowledge components, proxied by referenced journals.[39] They find that novel papers have a higher mean and higher variance in citations received and that the citations take longer to accrue, both of which are consistent with novelty being riskier. Azoulay and Greenblatt find that of more than 100,000 R01 grants (the most frequent type of NIH grant) between 1980 and 2015, riskier grants were renewed at markedly lower rates than less risky ones, especially in novel areas of research and for novice investigators.[40] A plausible conclusion is that the greater rewards from risky research may be outweighed by the higher cost in the form of lower probability of successful grant applications and slower and more uncertain recognition in the form of accrued citations.

Why is novel research less likely to be funded? Hard data are scarce, but plausible explanations abound. Some fault program officers at funding agencies, who fear the higher failure rate that comes with bolder ideas. Others point to bibliometric-based evaluations, which reward citations that often take time to accrue, penalising unconventional research. Career-conscious scholars, particularly those in "soft-money" positions dependent on grants, may sensibly avoid riskier paths and instead opt for safe, incremental projects. Disciplinary boundaries draw criticism, too: they can disadvantage interdisciplinary proposals in peer review. Danielle Li finds that reviewers assessing NIH submissions favour work closer to their own expertise.[41] Still others highlight the absence of a "portfolio" strategy among funding bodies. Just as investors can reduce overall risk by holding a portfolio of individually risky assets, so also could funding agencies. This implies evaluating the portfolio of funded projects, not just the individual projects on their own.

Funding novel research

What might be done? No single solution is likely to work. One option is to reduce the weight placed on bibliometric scores when evaluating both researchers and research proposals. Another is to tweak assessment procedures so that exceptionally strong ratings matter more than the overall average. A long-standing idea is to fund people, not projects. Katalin Karikó's breakthrough mRNA work, for instance, was made possible by grants controlled by Drew Weissman, a senior scientist whose secure funding allowed him to take risks on ventures not fully outlined in the original proposal. This flexibility can be crucial in nurturing the most transformative ideas.

There is some evidence that expanding how research is funded could be beneficial. During the recent COVID crisis, Patrick Collison, Silvana Konermann, and Tyler Cowen started a program called Fast Grants, under the auspices of the Mercatus Center at George Mason University.[42] Throughout 2020, Fast Grants disbursed $50 million through 260 grants. Grant applications could be completed in minutes, and decisions took days rather than the months that NIH grants required. Fast Grants claimed successes such as an accurate, saliva-based COVID-19 test, successful clinical trials for a generic drug which might reduce COVID-19 hospitalisation rates by 40 per cent, and significant research into long COVID. Over two-thirds of the recipients claimed they would never have been funded without Fast Grants.

Philanthropies

Philanthropic gifts have long been seen as a means to fill gaps in scientific research, but this perspective understates their transformative impact. Unlike corporate or government funding, philanthropies can do much more than finance individual projects. They can create new organisational structures, fund bold, long-term initiatives, and facilitate forms of research that would otherwise be impossible under traditional funding regimes.

The Howard Hughes Medical Institute (HHMI) is one of the largest philanthropies funding research in the life sciences. In 2021, HHMI had an endowment of over $22 billion. The Howard Hughes Program funds researchers rather than projects. Selection is based on the quality of the researcher and the proposed research, and funding lasts for seven years. Azoulay, Graff Zivin, and Manso conclude that the selection criteria and longer funding periods are associated with more novel and riskier research.[43] They find that HHMI investigators produce more hits and more flops, as measured by citations received, compared with the NIH investigators.

There are several newer efforts as well. The ARC Institute resembles HHMI. Founded in 2021, with an endowment of over $650 million, it funds a number of promising researchers from Stanford, UC Berkeley, and UC San Francisco, mostly in life sciences, and typically early in their professional careers. Unlike HHMI, the program also envisages providing dedicated lab space and an engineering and technology infrastructure. The Chan-Zuckerberg Biohub similarly supports researchers, providing unrestricted support for five-year periods. It tries to build communities by also providing research infrastructure such as the Human Cell Atlas, which seeks to map every cell in the human body. The Allen Institute for Brain Science, founded with a $100 million gift from Paul Allen in 2003, aimed to create a complete map of the human brain. Over two decades later, the Allen Brain Atlas remains one of the most widely used datasets in neuroscience, underpinning discoveries in Alzheimer's disease, neurodegeneration, and cognitive science. Similarly, Eric and Wendy Schmidt's $25 million donation to Princeton University in 2009 funded projects aimed at converting sunlight into fuel. This transformative but speculative area of research falls outside the risk appetite of VCs. By providing multiyear, flexible support, the Schmidts helped Princeton pursue fundamental advances in solar fuels without constant pressure for commercialisation.

While HHMI and ARC are explicitly designed to change how science is conducted, other philanthropically funded organisations have achieved similar results more indirectly. The Rockefeller Foundation, for instance, played a pivotal role in establishing molecular biology as a distinct scientific field. Through strategic grants and investments in interdisciplinary research, the foundation created entirely new branches of science that did not exist before. As documented by Eric Gilliam in his essay, "Scientific Branch-Creation: How the Rockefeller Foundation Helped Bootstrap the Field of Molecular Biology," the foundation did not just fund experiments—it built a new research infrastructure.[44] By financing equipment like electron microscopes and underwriting research centres at places like the University of Chicago, Rockefeller created the institutional foundation for an entire field of science. Michael Waldrop argues that DARPA program managers such as J. C. R. Licklider played a similar role in establishing the modern discipline of Computer Science.[45]

New types of research organisations

In response to the changing landscape of research funding, there are also new types of research organisations, which combine elements of startups, academic research centres, and contract research organisations. Among these new models is Arcadia Science, a biotechnology company funded by OpenAI co-founder Sam Altman and crypto entrepreneur Jed McCaleb. Unlike most biotech firms, which tend to focus on near-term applications, Arcadia emphasises foundational research and openly publishes its findings. In that sense, it behaves more like a university department than a conventional startup, even though it is structured as a for-profit entity. By straddling the line between academic openness and corporate agility, Arcadia aims to encourage bolder experiments that standard grant mechanisms may not support, while maintaining the option to spin off commercial products when discoveries prove viable.

Another such venture is Arena BioWorks, launched in 2024 by a co-founder of the Broad Institute. A for-profit organisation, Arena invests in early-stage, high-risk exploration, then spins off separate companies once a discovery shows clear potential for market application. By maintaining full ownership of its research agenda and reinvesting proceeds from successful spinoffs, Arena aims to become financially self-sustaining. This differs from typical VC-funded ventures in allowing projects the flexibility to mature at their own pace, free from the constraints of tight investment timelines or narrowly defined project goals.

The Topos Institute is different from most of the other organisations mentioned earlier. Founded as a nonprofit in 2019 by mathematicians and computer scientists in Berkeley, it is a nonprofit research institute dedicated to advancing fundamental mathematical sciences and translating them into practical tools for the public good. It conducts fundamental research in category theory, but it also translates this research into open-source software tools and libraries, typically for encouraging collaboration across scientific domains (such as atmospheric scientists and oceanographers). It is funded by a combination of philanthropic gifts and research contracts, mostly from the U.S. Air Force. In a recent interview with Gilliam, Topos's CEO, Brendan Fong (a computer science PhD from Oxford University) explained how Topos was different from both universities and startups.

> Our core advantage over a university is that we can be user- and impact-driven. Our core advantage over a start-up is that we can tackle deep technical risk.... One thing that cannot be done in a university setting is, I think, build and maintain technologies for the long term.... Relatedly, another way we differ from a university is being intensely collaborative and team-driven. To me, the incentive structures of academia are entirely individual. Postdocs, tenure, awards, all go to individuals for individual success.... With that system, it can be difficult to find and maintain generative collaborations that lead to core breakthroughs.

> What separates us from start-ups? We're driven by producing public goods — as long as we can find the funding. We don't orient ourselves around what's best for investors.[46]

Some of these funding models and the new types of research organisations may fail. After all, the Mellon Institute was started in Pittsburgh as a problem-oriented research institute for chemical and allied industries. Despite some successful innovations by its researchers, the Mellon Institute ultimately failed to prosper as an independent contract research institute, in part because there were not enough technologically sophisticated customers. Nonetheless, it demonstrated the value of industrial research to companies.

Therefore, even the failures may prove to be useful inasmuch as they nudge American universities themselves to adapt. The process is likely to be slow and protracted, just as it was when American universities were encouraged to invest in research during the interwar period, by the Rockefeller Foundation and other philanthropies, and then by World War II and the subsequent Cold War. The other aspect of these alternative types of research organisations is the importance of diversity. Even experiments that work are unlikely to do so across the board. Different domains and types of problems are likely to require different solutions. Finding this out requires institutional experiments. America excels above all others in its scale and scope of institutional innovation.

Increasing the impact of research

Recent political events have brought to the fore a conversation that has simmered for some time now, namely, the societal impact of universities and, specifically, of university research.

Assessing the economic impact of university research is notoriously challenging. Academic research frequently produces knowledge that is too preliminary for immediate commercial exploitation. Indeed, we found in recent work that except in the life sciences, scientific discoveries by university researchers rarely affect R&D by established companies, unless these insights are further developed.[47] However, the same study also shows that universities significantly enhance industry innovation indirectly by supplying highly skilled science and engineering PhDs. An earlier survey of industrial R&D labs from the 1990s by Wes Cohen, Richard Nelson, and John Walsh also found consistent results.[48] Except in pharmaceuticals, semiconductors, and communication (the high-tech sectors of that period), respondents typically reported that fewer than a third of their R&D projects used university research at all. The most important sources of university research were materials science and computer science, arguably the most applied of the scientific disciplines. Thus, the primary economic contribution of universities may lie not just in specific discoveries themselves, but in the human capital they cultivate. University and government labs were rated as important sources of information for initiating or completing R&D projects by fewer than a third of the labs, ranking below sources such as internal operations, customers, suppliers, and joint ventures, and even competitors for project initiation. The pharmaceuticals sector was an outlier there as well, with a much higher reported importance of university labs.

It also follows that attempts to reform university research, such as making university research more "relevant," must also contend with the problem of the education and training function of the university. In particular, simplistic prescriptions often run the danger of impairing this very important benefit of university research.

Bridging the gap between university science and commercial impact

Turning promising university research into scalable commercial technologies remains essential. Achieving this goal requires more than increased funding for universities. Effective technology transfer mechanisms, strengthened incentives for university–industry collaboration, and supportive commercialisation ecosystems are critical. Yet, the top 100 universities around the world produce fewer than ten thousand patents per year.[49] American universities, in spite of their increased participation in inventions noted in Chapter 12, were granted just under eight thousand patents in 2024, a modest number considering the scale of academic research in the United States.[50] However, the logic of specialisation implies that it would be naive to expect much more without compromising the main function of universities.

The nascent nature of university knowledge reflects a division of labour, of specialisation based on comparative advantage. Curiosity-driven research into the mysteries of nature complements the educational and training function that is unique to universities. As such, it is neither surprising nor particularly undesirable if what universities produce does not appear to be immediately applicable. The gulf between the abstract knowledge produced in universities and that required by industry is a long-standing phenomenon. Indeed, as discussed in Chapters 8 and 10, corporate labs were founded precisely because university research could not deliver the type of knowledge and inventions the leading companies of the day required.

Some have argued that university researchers should be pushed to be more "relevant" to local and national economic needs. Indeed, in recent years, the NIH itself has appeared to stress the importance of clear research goals with obvious practical applications in awarding grants.[51] Notice, however, that doing so cuts against the other goal of encouraging novel rather than incremental science. As also discussed earlier, high-risk projects tend to be more open-ended and unpredictable, and thus they are heavily penalised if the evaluation process requires likely outcomes that can be translated into practical, public benefits. Narrow, incremental projects, on the other hand, have more predictable results.

Consider the discovery of DNA as the basis of genetic inheritance. Up until Oswald Avery showed otherwise, it was believed that cellular proteins were the basis of inherited biological traits. Avery had studied the pneumococcus bacterium, responsible for most cases of pneumonia, and discovered that some strains of the bacterium, which lacked a polysaccharide shell, were easily destroyed by the body's immune system. In a series of experiments in 1944, Avery, Colin MacLeod, and Maclyn McCarty showed that the bacterial strain without the polysaccharide shell would develop the shell when placed with a bacterial strain with the shell, even when the latter were dead, their proteins removed, and their RNA degraded. However, when the DNA of the bacterial strain with the shell was degraded, they could not induce the development of polysaccharide shell in bacterial strains lacking the shell. Their discovery launched the modern era of molecular biology and genetics. Peter Medawar called this "the most interesting and portentous biological experiment of the 20th century."[52] The Nobel Laureate Joshua Lederberg called it "the pivotal discovery of 20th-century biology."[53]

These experiments by Avery, undertaken in the midst of a World War, might have appeared to a review panel as tangentially related, if at all, to the objective of reducing pneumococcal infections. Its practical benefits would be years in the coming. The successful production of penicillin and other antibiotics was more immediately useful. Yet, arguably, Avery's work was of greater long-run significance, even from a narrow practical viewpoint. Forcing researchers to become more "relevant" would deepen the problem, making the research more incremental, with little to show for it in terms of industrial uptake.

The Bayh–Dole Act (mentioned in Chapters 11 and 12), was passed with the intention of facilitating the commercialisation of university research. The Act allowed universities to claim title on intellectual property arising from federally funded research. There are several different, albeit complementary, views on the rationale for the reform. In one view, the absence of property rights left university discoveries as orphans. No one had the incentive to develop it without some type of exclusivity. A second view was that the researchers needed the allure of profits, underpinned by patent protection, to develop promising discoveries into useful innovations. There is some evidence for both views. However, as discussed in Chapter 12, there is no doubt that American universities became more eager to find commercial applications for their research after the 1970s.[54]

Passage of the Act coincided with a marked increase in university patenting and licensing. An *Economist* article dubbed it the "Golden Goose" of innovation.[55] The apparent success led other countries to follow suit and assign property rights to the university. Although many believe that Bayh–Dole increased the flow of economically useful technology from universities, substantiating this position is not straightforward, as David Mowery and colleagues conclude from their analysis of the patenting and licensing behaviour of the University of California, Columbia University, and Stanford University.[56] They note that Bayh–Dole more or less coincided with an increase in biomedical research (which is more readily commercially applicable, particularly after the breakthroughs in genetics and molecular biology), and legal changes that allowed the patenting of life forms. Each of these developments would also be expected to increase university patenting and licensing. Indeed, the bulk of TTO revenues are from licensing (typically for drugs), rather than proceeds from the sale of equity in startups founded on university technology.

What should policymakers learn from all this? First, clarifying the ownership of the intellectual property created is important to facilitate the follow-on work of translation and commercialisation. In most instances, they are assigned to universities, but as discussed in Chapter 12, perhaps they could go to individual researchers.[57] In 2010, the U.S. National Academy of Sciences commissioned an extensive review of the Bayh–Dole Act. The final report contained six findings and fifteen recommendations.[58] These findings suggest that assigning ownership of inventions to universities (or even perhaps university inventors themselves) is superior to letting the government retain ownership, but effective commercialisation requires effort and initiative by the researchers themselves. Beyond that, reducing bureaucratic frictions is important. Many of the Committee's recommendations were about improving the functioning of university tech transfer offices and reducing transaction costs by standardising procedures and license terms to expedite startup formation.[59]

Cyclotron Road, an initiative at the Lawrence Livermore Labs, represents a different approach to improving the translation of university science.[60] This programme provides funding and support to help scientists bring their ideas to market. In partnership with a nonprofit, Activate, it provides two-year fellowships and research support to prospective scientist-founders. Started in 2016, with philanthropic support from Schmidt Futures, the programme appears to be filling an important niche. Companies by Cyclotron Road founders have raised more than $3 billion in follow-on funding since the programme started.[61] The UK's Advanced Research and Invention Agency (ARIA) recruited Ilan Gur, the founder of Activate and Cyclotron Road, as its founding CEO in 2022. ARIA is following DARPA's playbook by choosing eight scientists to allocate up to £50 million each, in the hope that a high-risk, high-reward approach to research funding will deliver results that benefit UK society and fuel economic growth. [62]

Unbundling the university?

Instead of finding ways to make university research novel and relevant and transfer university discoveries to the market more efficiently, some commentators have taken a different approach, namely, removing universities from the task of developing technology altogether. For instance, Ben Reinhardt at Speculative Technologies has called for "unbundling" the research university by removing applied research from universities altogether.[63] Reinhardt makes a persuasive case that the university research model is poorly suited for mission-oriented research. As he puts it, "Academia's core structures and incentives revolve around education and scientific inquiry, not building useful technologies."

It is worth noting that Reinhardt's critique is aimed at the deep-tech related parts of university research. However, the lion's share of university research is in life sciences. Academic medical centres can be seen as collections of university-affiliated, Focused Research Organisations (FROs), closely connected to the end users. Academic medical centres are typically associated with teaching hospitals, closing the loop between scientific discoveries, the development of new treatments, and the testing of new cures.

In other words, in the life sciences, the nascent nature of university knowledge appears to be less of a problem for its application, in part because universities have affiliated organisations that can readily absorb and apply the knowledge. But in some sectors, academic research is too distant from its economic applications. These sectors, which have a very substantial overlap with deep-tech, face greater challenges. It is here that FROs may be of greater value.

It is certainly true that university labs are unlikely to develop a new material that can be transitioned to industry in order to create an effective robot, or, apparently, even a world-class large language model. But this limitation is broadly understood. With some exceptions, such as Carnegie Mellon University's Robotics Institute, American universities are not designed to yield solutions to societal challenges, at least not directly. For that, more focused and coordinated efforts are required, to which university scientists may contribute.

Proposals to establish such FROs have attracted attention as a way to tackle large-scale scientific challenges. One advocate is Convergent Research, which has spun off multiple FROs: E11 Bio is creating tools to map the brain's wiring; Cultivarum builds open-source resources for studying novel microbes; PIT aims to expand proteomic analysis a hundredfold; Lean FRO pursues automated theorem proving and verification software; and [C]Worthy devises methods to sequester carbon dioxide in ocean environments.[64] Although the name is new, the concept of an application-focused research institution is not. Across the globe, well-funded laboratories—like America's National Labs, Germany's Max Planck Institutes, Australia's Commonwealth Scientific and Industrial Research Organisation (CSIRO), and the UK's Central Research Laboratory (CSL)—have yielded transformative innovations. Likewise, more narrowly focused examples such as the UK's Laboratory for Molecular Biology and the NIH's in-house scientist teams have made significant scientific contributions.

Another proposal envisages the creation of X-labs, each with an annual budget of $10 million to $50 million per year. Drawing inspiration from initiatives such as the Allen Brain Atlas and Arc Institute, the proposed X-Labs would fund a portfolio of independent research organisations, not restricted to universities, with long-term missions — some in fundamental science, others on building critical tools and infrastructure, with only the most successful renewed. These labs would be hubs for high-risk, high-reward research in basic science in fields such as biotechnology, materials science, next-generation energy, and chronic disease research that university-imposed structures and private markets are not well suited to solve.[65]

Promising though these proposals may be, it is not time to give up on the American research university, which, for all its seeming inefficiencies, nurtures a complementary relationship between experimentation and training. Part of the reason universities thrive is that they produce methods, tools, and skilled graduates, rather than market-ready inventions. Zvi Griliches's analysis of hybrid corn famously captured this insight, describing it as "the invention of a method of inventing."[66] As Cohen, Nelson, and Walsh noted in their 2002 study, the ultimate commercial value often comes from applying techniques refined in academia.[67] Further research supports this viewpoint: Sampat and Lichtenberg (2011) demonstrate that universities were directly responsible for only 10 per cent of drugs developed between 1988 and 2005, but indirectly influenced two-thirds of them.[68] Cockburn and Henderson find similar results, implying that real value emerges from cumulative knowledge and well-trained scientists, rather than from blockbuster inventions alone.[69]

Reinhardt acknowledges the importance of training but points out that training researchers and developing technology are at odds. Indeed, tools and technologies that emerge from university labs often need substantial refinement before they can be put to use, much as Alexander Fleming's penicillin mould needed systematic follow-on characterisation and purification by Florey and Chain (ironically enough, both were university researchers).

Reinhardt's critique also spotlights the lack of diversity among leading research universities themselves. It would certainly be good if universities differed more from each other in how they organise research and training. In the country's early years, poly-lithic institutions such as MIT and Carnegie Tech, classical universities like Harvard and Yale, land-grant colleges such as Michigan and Berkeley, and research-heavy newcomers modelled on

German universities, like Johns Hopkins, Chicago, and Caltech, did things differently. Over time, debate, rivalry, and a steady stream of postwar federal research support encouraged these different strands to converge into the modern American research university.

It may be time to de-converge. Competition among universities, coupled with a lack of visionary leadership, has led universities to become too similar. It has also trickled down to individual incentives for researchers, resulting in an ever-growing number of scientific journals being flooded with incremental research. Collectively, universities may ponder how to change academic norms to reduce the flood of incremental publications. Farsighted university leaders (and their rich benefactors) ought also to consider how they can differentiate themselves horizontally, not simply vertically, in terms of being better at generating breakthroughs. We need more institutions like the Robotics Institute at Carnegie Mellon University, which gave us the Mars Rover and contributed to advances in speech recognition and text mining, as well as self-driving cars. Other than perhaps medical schools, the Robotics Institute remains more the exception than the rule for academic departments.

Yet abrupt or short-sighted overhauls could undercut an institution that remains the envy of the world. American universities attract global talent and serve as a potent source of "soft" power. They also anchor a system that, despite its shortcomings in turning lab discoveries into commercial hits, has seldom been surpassed. To paraphrase Winston Churchill, this research-university model might be the worst arrangement for organising science, except for all the alternatives that have been tried from time to time.

Chapter takeaways

Since the 1980s, industrial research has declined. Today, few companies invest at levels necessary to sustain long-term, high-risk research. Managing such long-term projects within profit-driven firms poses substantial challenges. While companies like IBM, Microsoft, and Google have maintained internal research units, they increasingly face regulatory scrutiny regarding their market dominance, complicating their ability to pursue ambitious, long-term innovation agendas. Industrial research must be protected and nurtured.

However, corporate labs are unlikely to fully reclaim their earlier prominence, even under a more favourable social compact. Universities are likely to remain vital sources of new scientific ideas for the foreseeable future. Sustaining university research and establishing effective pathways for translating academic discoveries into commercial technologies is critical, especially for deep-tech sectors.

This calls for innovative approaches. Focused Research Organisations, which blend aspects of academic labs and startup accelerators, are potentially worthwhile additions to the innovation ecosystem. Ongoing private and public initiatives to explore better ways of funding and organising research are valuable and should be encouraged. Philanthropies can experiment with supporting nascent technologies and new organisational forms. Grant-making can be improved to discourage incremental research and promote novelty. However, any changes to the university structure must preserve the vital complementarity between university research and education that has been invaluable thus far.

15
Concluding Thoughts

In the mid-twentieth century, the United States relied on large corporate research labs to integrate science, engineering, and manufacturing. As those labs declined, the country turned to a fragmented mix of universities, startups, and corporations, supported by government grant funding of R&D and procurement innovation programs. This arrangement has produced successes in fields like biopharmaceuticals, where large firms provide scale and patient capital, but it has struggled in deep-tech sectors such as advanced batteries, semiconductors, and clean energy hardware that require long timelines and heavy investment. As a result, many discoveries made in U.S. labs are commercialised elsewhere.

The weakness lies in the translational layer—the institutions that connect research to production. Two major policy prescriptions flow from this diagnosis. First, we call for renewing the social compact with large firms that still invest in scientific research: in exchange for the privileges that come with scale and regulatory tolerance, they should recommit to long-term R&D and more open knowledge sharing. Regulators can take these contributions into account when awarding contracts or weighing antitrust actions. Second, we argue for strengthening institutions that support the division of innovative labour. Policymakers can help by providing deep-tech startups access to shared equipment and expert support early, before large capital is sunk. Ready access to test beds, pilot lines, and regulatory guidance lets deep-tech startups validate designs quickly and improves their negotiating position with downstream commercialisation partners later on. Universities, national labs, and focused research organisations have a potentially useful part in such arrangements.

Policy imperatives: Strengthening the translational infrastructure

Strengthening the translation layer requires renewing the social compact with market leaders, reimagining the role of universities in the division of innovative labour, reinvigorating government as a buyer of breakthrough innovations, and trying out new types of focused research organisations.

Renew compacts with R&D-intensive firms

In practice, today's tech giants and other leading firms should be encouraged to invest more boldly in research that benefits the broader ecosystem. Historically, Bell Labs existed in part because AT&T's monopoly status came with an understanding that it would serve the national interest through scientific research and knowledge sharing. A modern compact could be lighter-touch but follow the spirit: for example, regulators and policymakers might explicitly consider a firm's research contributions and knowledge-sharing efforts as factors when crafting antitrust approaches or awarding government contracts. The goal is a public–private partnership model where, in exchange for regulatory or policy forbearance, companies take on responsibility for sustaining critical innovation capabilities. We should seek a balance that holds big firms accountable not just for market power, but also for their contributions to the nation's science and technology base.

Reimagine the role of universities, specialisation, and the missing middle

The story of American innovation in the past several decades has rested on specialisation. Universities generate frontier knowledge and train the next generation of researchers. Firms take on the work of translating that knowledge into marketable products. For much of the twentieth century, corporate laboratories filled the middle space, integrating science, engineering, and production. Their decline has exposed the structural gap between discovery and deployment. The problem is not that universities produce too little that is "relevant," but that the institutions once responsible for carrying nascent ideas into industry have eroded. The United States therefore confronts a missing middle in its innovation system.

One way forward is for universities to act as neutral conveners. Instead of treating commercialisation as a series of sequential handoffs, universities could assemble the full range of actors that shape whether a technology advances: suppliers of materials and equipment, regulatory agencies, downstream firms, and early customers. Because universities are not direct competitors, they can provide a neutral platform for collaboration that firms would struggle to create on their own.

Fulfilling such a role requires more than convening meetings. It demands physical infrastructure that lowers the cost of experimentation. Deep-tech ventures are most fragile when the cost of generating the first credible data is high. Universities can host shared pilot lines, demonstration labs, and testbeds that function as public goods. By opening these facilities to startups, small firms, and regulators, universities make it possible to validate designs, test manufacturability, and establish compliance pathways without requiring each entrant to build its own costly infrastructure. The benefits are visible in existing experiments: the "fab-in-a-lab" at NC State enables small companies to fabricate silicon carbide chips without investing in full foundries; the University of Illinois' bioprocessing laboratory allows new ventures to scale fermentation beyond the bench but short of commercial plants. These examples hint at a larger possibility: a distributed network of open facilities anchored in universities, each specialising in a strategic domain (batteries, advanced polymers, biomanufacturing, or carbon capture) and linked through common data and safety standards. Such a network would not replace industry's role in scaling production but would de-risk early stages, crowding in private capital that now hesitates to engage.

This model is not entirely new. Japan's Ministry of International Trade and Industry once organised consortia that brought multiple companies together to solve LED process challenges; more recently, university-based hubs such as the wide-bandgap semiconductor facility at North Carolina State have played a similar role. The difference is that these activities remain scattered and underfunded. A broader reimagining would place universities at the centre of coordinated, value-chain consortia around emerging technologies.

To support this agenda, universities may need to experiment with new organisational forms. Current incentive systems reward publications and grants, leaving translational work undervalued. It would be a mistake to force all faculty into the same mould, but universities could create parallel tracks that legitimise applied contributions. The Robotics Institute at Carnegie Mellon University offers a possible roadmap. Graduate curricula could be broadened to include exposure to manufacturability, standards, and quality control, ensuring that students leave fluent in the language of both science and scale-up. Initiatives like Cyclotron Road and Activate already illustrate how structured fellowships can help researchers bridge the divide between the lab and the market.

None of this will be simple, and the risks are real. Shared facilities may be captured by large firms. Translational metrics may be gamed. A focus on applied work may erode the space for curiosity-driven research that remains the university's core strength. These dangers can be managed, but only with safeguards. Translational entities should be institutionally separated from tenure decisions. Access to shared facilities should be transparently governed, with reserved capacity for small firms. Evaluations should focus on ecosystem outcomes rather than patent counts or licensing income. Above all, organisational diversity should be preserved. Some universities will continue to focus on fundamental research, others will become regional anchors, and a few will specialise as national hubs for scale-up. The system will be strongest if it remains plural.

The broader point is not that universities need to become commercial entities, nor that they should be asked to solve every bottleneck in the innovation process. Rather, their strength lies in knowledge creation and training. But their relevance in the American innovation system will increasingly depend on their ability to reduce the costs of translation for others. Other institutions, such as national labs and focused research organisations discussed in Chapter 14, may also be useful. The stakes are high. Deep-tech sectors demand new institutional arrangements. Some universities, national labs, and focused research organisations, supported by thoughtful federal policy, could be at the heart of those arrangements.

Revive mission-oriented procurement innovation programs

In the 1960s, NASA and the Air Force paid premium prices for early microchips, purchasing about 60 per cent of all chips made in the United States and thereby pushing costs from more than thirty dollars per unit to about one dollar in less than a decade. Reviving mission-oriented procurement programmes means more than romanticising the Apollo programme or the Manhattan Project; it means using government buying power to pull into the market, at scale, technologies for which the government will act as a buyer of the first resort.

Implications for deep-tech startups

Founders of deep-tech ventures face an unforgiving landscape. They must mitigate uncertainty as early and as cheaply as possible, and they must secure downstream partners before making large investments in translational research to avoid hold-up once the technology is ready.

The most effective deep-tech entrepreneurs often behave in what might be called a Smithian rather than a purely Schumpeterian fashion. They do not expect to displace incumbents; instead, they specialise and forge alliances across the value chain. This networked approach is better suited to sectors where complementary assets, including manufacturing capacity, distribution channels, and regulatory expertise, are held by established players. For established players, deep-tech startups are important sources of the technology needed to expand and extend their business. Philips built its LED leadership not by growing a new business from scratch but by integrating smaller firms and licensing arrangements. These are Smithian strategies: the startup focuses on its comparative advantage in translational research and captures value by linking with others early rather than attempting to internalise every function.

Grants, public R&D programmes, and procurement competitions provide a way for startups to validate key assumptions about the venture. Alliances with incumbents embed the technology within existing production and distribution networks. This combination converts the classic Schumpeterian gamble of replacing existing producers with innovative entrants into a Smithian process of expanding and recombining specialised capabilities.

Epilogue

We have argued that the strength of the American innovation system rests on its institutional diversity. Universities generate frontier research, startups convert discoveries into prototypes, and established firms scale products for the market. Industrial research anchors this specialised system.

The decline of corporate research labs has exposed weaknesses that need to be shored up.

The United States is rich in ideas; translating them into economic value is the challenge. Our future is determined not by how much we invest in science and technology alone, but by the institutions and policies we create to harness such investments. Climate change, the risks of war, geopolitical instability, and emerging health threats demand new tools to combat them. These tools will not emerge from scientific discovery in isolation; they depend on how we organise research, encourage its translation, and scale up solutions. The ideas in this book suggest a way forward: renewing the social compact with large research-intensive firms, experimenting with new ways of supporting science, strengthening the entrepreneurial ecosystem, and using government procurement strategically to reinvent prosperity.

Notes

Chapter 1

1 Robert J. Gordon. *The Rise and Fall of American Growth: The U.S. Standard of Living since the Civil War.* Princeton Economic History of the Western World. Princeton, NJ: Princeton University Press, 2016.

2 Benjamin F. Jones. "The Burden of Knowledge and the 'Death of the Renaissance Man': Is Innovation Getting Harder?" *The Review of Economic Studies* 76.1 (2009), pp. 283–317.

3 Michael Park, Erin Leahey, and Russell J. Funk. "Papers and Patents Are Becoming Less Disruptive over Time." *Nature* 613.7942 (2023), pp. 138–144. https://www.nature.com/articles/s41586-022-05543-x (visited on August 27, 2024).

4 Moore's Law is the empirical observation, made by Intel's co-founder Gordon Moore, that the number of transistors on a microchip doubles approximately every two years, leading to exponential growth in computing power.

5 Nicholas Bloom, Charles I. Jones, John Van Reenen, and Michael Webb. "Are Ideas Getting Harder to Find?" *American Economic Review* 110.4 (April 2020), pp. 1104–1144. https://www.aeaweb.org/articles?id=10.1257/aer.20180338 (visited on June 7, 2025).

6 Julian M. Alston and Philip G. Pardey. "Are Ideas Really Getting Harder to Find?" *Staff Papers* 320517 (April 2022). https://ideas.repec.org//p/ags/umaesp/320517.html (visited on June 7, 2025).

7 Indeed, James Bessen and colleagues find that the private returns to corporate R&D rose between 1977 and 2018. See Yoshiki Ando, James E. Bessen, and Xiupeng Wang. *The Rising Returns to R&D: Ideas Are Not Getting Harder to Find.* May 5, 2025. https://papers.ssrn.com/abstract=5242171 (visited on June 7, 2025). Pre-published.

8 G. Anderson and F. Moris. *Federally Funded R&D Declines as a Share of GDP and Total R&D.* NSF 23-339. Alexandria, VA: National Science Foundation, 2023. https://ncses.nsf.gov/pubs/nsf23339/ (visited on Sepember 9, 2024).

9 National Center for Science and Engineering Statistics (NCSES). *National Patterns of R&D Resources: 2021–22 Data Update.* NSF 24-318. Alexandria, VA: National Science Foundation, 2024.

10 NCSES; see n. 8.

11 Park, Leahey, and Funk; see n. 3, p. 141.

12 Vincent Holst, Andres Algaba, Floriano Tori, Sylvia Wenmackers, and Vincent Ginis. *Dataset Artefacts Are the Hidden Drivers of the Declining Disruptiveness in Science.* February 7, 2024. http://arxiv.org/abs/2402.14583 (visited on August 27, 2024). Pre-published.

13 An Zeng, Ying Fan, Zengru Di, Yougui Wang, and Shlomo Havlin. *Disruptive Papers in Science Are Losing Impact.* May 5, 2023. http://arxiv.org/abs/2305.03589 (visited on June 7, 2025). Pre-published; Nan Deng, Xifeng Gu, Ying Fan, Shlomo Havlin, and An Zeng. "The Critical Role of Persistent Disruption in Advancing Science." *Nature Computational Science* (May 20, 2025), pp. 1–10. https://www.nature.com/articles/s43588-025-00808-7 (visited on June 8, 2025).

14 Jeffrey T. Macher, Christian Rutzer, and Rolf Weder. "Is There a Secular Decline in Disruptive Patents? Correcting for Measurement Bias." *Research Policy* 53.5 (2024), p. 104992.

15 James D. Wells. "Prof. von Jolly's 1878 Prediction of the End of Theoretical Physics as Reported by Max Planck." (March 6, 2016). http://deepblue.lib.umich.edu/handle/2027.42/163719 (visited on June 8, 2025).

16 Albert A. Michelson. "Entry in the Annual Register of the University of Chicago." *The Annual Register of the University of Chicago.* Chicago: University of Chicago Press, 1896, p. 159.

17 Peter Brian Medawar. *Pluto's Republic.* Oxford: Oxford University Press, 1982, p. 29.

18 Florenta Teodoridis. "Understanding Team Knowledge Production: The Interrelated Roles of Technology and Expertise." *Management Science* 64.8 (September 2018), pp. 3625–3648. https://pubsonline.informs.org/doi/10.1287/mnsc.2017.2789 (visited on November 17, 2022).

19 Microsoft Research. *AI Meets Materials Discovery: The Vision behind MatterGen and MatterSim*. June 2025. https://www.microsoft.com/en-us/research/story/ai-meets-materials-discovery/.

20 Chan Kim. "From Research to Development: How Globalization Shapes Corporate Innovation." 2024. https://sites.google.com/view/chankimecon/home; Wesley M. Cohen and Steven Klepper. "A Reprise of Size and R & D." *The Economic Journal* 106.437 (1996), pp. 925–951.

21 Ando, Bessen, and Wang; see n. 6.

22 Holst, Algaba, Tori, Wenmackers, and Ginis; see n. 11.

23 Matt Marx and Aaron Fuegi. "Reliance on Science: Worldwide Front-Page Patent Citations to Scientific Articles." *Strategic Management Journal* 41.9 (2020), pp. 1572–1594.

24 Formally, the CD measure is defined as $\frac{N_F - N_B}{N_F + N_B + N_R}$ where N_F refers to papers that cite the focal paper but none of its references; N_B refers to papers that cite both the focal paper and at least one of its references; and N_R refers to papers that do not cite the focal paper but at least one of its references. We use data made available by Holst, Algaba, Tori, Wenmackers, and Ginis (see n. 11) that corrects for the bias introduced by papers with zero backward citations. The data is available for papers published until 2010. We use CD_5, which calculates disruption measures based on forward citations received up to five years after publication.

25 Paul A. David. "The Dynamo and the Computer: An Historical Perspective on the Modern Productivity Paradox." *The American Economic Review* 80.2 (1990), pp. 355–361.

26 Nathan Rosenberg. "Science, Technology and Society." *Rivista Internazionale di Scienze Sociali* 104.4 (1996), pp. 479–496.

27 U.S. Department of Agriculture, Agricultural Research Service. *The Rescue of Penicillin: How USDA Lab Strains Made Wartime Production Possible*. USDA ARS Timeline Feature. 2023. https://www.ars.usda.gov/oc/timeline/penicillin/.

28 Donald E. Stokes. *Pasteur's Quadrant : Basic Science and Technological Innovation*. Washington, DC: Brookings Institution Press, 1997.

29 Based on the count of firms reporting operating an industrial lab in survey data from National Research Council. *Industrial Research Laboratories of the United States, Including Consulting Research Laboratories*. RR Bowker Company, 1920; Industrial Research Laboratories of the United States, Including Consulting Research Laboratories. 10th ed. Washington, DC: National Academy of Sciences–National Research Council, 1960.

30 Davisson was the second American industrial scientist to win the award (after GE's Irving Langmuir).

31 Filippo Mezzanotti and Timothy Simcoe. *Innovation and Appropriability: Revisiting the Role of Intellectual Property*. July 2023. https://www.nber.org/papers/w31428 (visited on November 19, 2024). Pre-published.

32 Ashish Arora, Sharon Belenzon, and Andrea Patacconi. "The Decline of Science in Corporate R&D." *Strategic Management Journal* 39.1 (2018), pp. 3–32; Ashish Arora, Sharon Belenzon, and Lia Sheer. "Knowledge Spillovers and Corporate Investment in Scientific Research." *American Economic Review* 111.3 (2021), pp. 871–898.

33 Rafael A. Corredoira, Brent D. Goldfarb, and Yuan Shi. "Federal Funding and the Rate and Direction of Inventive Activity." *Research Policy* 47.9 (November 1, 2018), pp. 1777–1800. https://www.sciencedirect.com/science/article/pii/S0048733318301549 (visited on December 1, 2022).

34 Katalin Karikó, Michael Buckstein, Houping Ni, and Drew Weissman. "Suppression of RNA Recognition by Toll-like Receptors: The Impact of Nucleoside Modification and the Evolutionary Origin of RNA." *Immunity* 23.2 (August 1, 2005), pp. 165–175. https://www.cell.com/immunity/abstract/S1074-7613(05)00211-6 (visited on June 8, 2025).

35 National Center for Science and Engineering Statistics (NSF). *University Technology Licenses or License Options Executed, by Company Characteristic: 2009, 2014, and 2019 (Table INV-2)*. Science and Engineering Indicators 2022, Knowledge Transfer Indicators. 2022. https://ncses.nsf.gov/pubs/nsb20224/assets/knowledge-transfer-indicators-making-information-available/tables/nsb20224-tabinv-002.pdf.

36 Wesley M. Cohen and Daniel A. Levinthal. "Innovation and Learning: The Two Faces of R & D." *The Economic Journal* 99.397 (1989), pp. 569–596.

37 Ashish Arora, Sharon Belenzon, Larisa C. Cioaca, Lia Sheer, and Hansen Zhang. *The Effect of Public Science on Corporate R&D*. November 2023. https://www.nber.org/papers/w31899 (visited on August 19, 2024). Pre-published.

Chapter 2

1 Robert M. Solow. "A Contribution to the Theory of Economic Growth." *The Quarterly Journal of Economics* 70.1 (1956), pp. 65–94. https://www.jstor.org/stable/1884513 (visited on June 8, 2025).

2 Paul M. Romer. "Endogenous Technological Change." *Journal of Political Economy* 98.5 (1990), S71–S102. https://www.jstor.org/stable/2937632 (visited on June 6, 2025).

3 Philippe Aghion and Peter Howitt. "A Model of Growth Through Creative Destruction." *Econometrica* 60.2 (1992), pp. 323–351. https://www.jstor.org/stable/2951599 (visited on June 8, 2025).

4 Joseph A. Schumpeter. *Capitalism, Socialism, and Democracy*. New York: Harper, 1950 pp. 82–83.

5 Adam B. Jaffe, Manuel Trajtenberg, and Rebecca Henderson. "Geographic Localization of Knowledge Spillovers as Evidenced by Patent Citations." *The Quarterly Journal of Economics* 108.3 (1993), pp. 577–598.

6 Evgenii Fadeev. *Creative Construction: Knowledge Sharing and Cooperation between Firms*. Working paper, Duke University Fuqua School of Business, 2023.

7 Stefano Breschi and Francesco Lissoni. "Mobility of Skilled Workers and Co-Invention Networks: An Anatomy of Localized Knowledge Flows." *Journal of Economic Geography* 9.4 (July 1, 2009), pp. 439–468. https://doi.org/10.1093/jeg/lbp008 (visited on June 8, 2025).

8 Hannah Beech. "Apple Used China to Make a Profit. What China Got in Return Is Scarier." *The New York Times* (May 15, 2025). https://www.nytimes.com/2025/05/15/books/review/apple-in-china-patrick-mcgee.html.

9 Kwanghui Lim. "The Many Faces of Absorptive Capacity: Spillovers of Copper Interconnect Technology for Semiconductor Chips". *Industrial and Corporate Change* 18.6 (Dec. 1, 2009), pp. 1249–1284. https://doi.org/10.1093/icc/dtp044 (visited on June 8, 2025), pp. 1272–1273.

10 C. Freeman. "Chemical Process Plant: Innovation and the World Market." *National Institute Economic Review* 45 (August 1968), pp. 29–51. https://www.cambridge.org/core/journals/national-institute-economic-review/article/chemical-process-plant-innovation-and-the-world-market/29CF88A4ED837BEFCF58410C351ECD95 (visited on June 8, 2025).

11 Gary Saxonhouse. "A Tale of Japanese Technological Diffusion in the Meiji Period." *The Journal of Economic History* 34.1 (March 1974), pp. 149–165. https://www.cambridge.org/core/journals/journal-of-economic-history/article/tale-of-japanese-technological-diffusion-in-the-meiji-period/143E2B5FB648FB248D39466183375288 (visited on June 8, 2025), at p. 162.

12 Nathan Rosenberg. "Capital Goods, Technology, and Economic Growth." *Oxford Economic Papers* 15.3 (1963), pp. 217–227. https://www.jstor.org/stable/2661716 (visited on June 8, 2025), at p. 218.

13 Ashish Arora and Marco Ceccagnoli. "Patent Protection, Complementary Assets, and Firms' Incentives for Technology Licensing." *Management Science* 52.2 (Febuary 2006), pp. 293–308. https://pubsonline.informs.org/doi/10.1287/mnsc.1050.0437 (visited on August 19, 2025).

14 S. Aydin Ozden and P. Khashabi. "Patent Remedies and Technology Licensing: Evidence from a Supreme Court Decision." *Strategic Management Journal* 44.9 (2023), pp. 2311–2338.

15 Colleen V. Chien and Mark A. Lemley. "Patent Holdup, the ITC, and the Public Interest." *Chicago Law Review* 98.1 (2012), pp. 1–45.

16 Arqué-Castells, P. and Spulber, D.F., 2022. Measuring the private and social returns to R&D: Unintended spillovers versus technology markets. Journal of Political Economy, 130(7), pp. 1860–1918.

17 Yael V. Hochberg, Carlos J. Serrano, and Rosemarie H. Ziedonis. "Patent Collateral, Investor Commitment, and the Market for Venture Lending". *Journal of Financial Economics* 130.1 (Oct. 1, 2018), pp. 74–94. https://www.sciencedirect.com/science/article/pii/S0304405X1830151X (visited on June 8, 2025).

18 Carlos J. Serrano. "Estimating the Gains from Trade in the Market for Patent Rights". *International Economic Review* 59.4 (2018), pp. 1877–1904. https://onlinelibrary.wiley.com/doi/abs/10.1111/iere.12338 (visited on June 8, 2025).

[19] Allyn A. Young. "Increasing Returns and Economic Progress." *The Economic Journal* 38.152 (December 1, 1928), pp. 527–542. https://doi.org/10.2307/2224097 (visited on June 8, 2025); Roy H. Grieve and Ramesh Chandra. "Putting the Record Straight: Adam Smith, Allyn Young and the Division of Labour." 2006. Discussion paper. Department of Economics. University of Strathclyde. Glasgow.

[20] Ashish Arora, Sharon Belenzon, and Jungkyu Suh. "Science and the Market for Technology." *Management Science* 68.10 (October 2022), pp. 7176–7201. https://pubsonline.informs.org/doi/full/10.1287/mnsc.2021.4268 (visited on March 4, 2023).

[21] Gary P. Pisano. *Science Business: The Promise, the Reality, and the Future of Biotech*. Cambridge, MA: Harvard Business Press, 2006.

[22] Steven Klepper. *Experimental Capitalism: The Nanoeconomics of American High-Tech Industries*. Princeton, NJ: Princeton University Press, 2015.

[23] Daniel Clery. "Debate Erupts around Microsoft's Blockbuster Quantum Computing Claims." *Science* (March 19, 2025). https://www.science.org/content/article/debate-erupts-around-microsofts-blockbuster-quantum-computing-claims.

[24] Chris Metinko. "Quantum Computing Hits New Venture Dollar Highmark." *Crunchbase News* (March 12, 2025). https://news.crunchbase.com/ai/quantum-startup-venture-highmark-february-2025-quera-softbank/.

[25] Adam B. Jaffe and Josh Lerner. *Innovation and Its Discontents: How Our Broken Patent System Is Endangering Innovation and Progress, and What to Do about It*. Princeton, NJ: Princeton University Press, 2004. https://press.princeton.edu/books/paperback/9780691127941/innovation-and-its-discontents; Adam B. Jaffe and Josh Lerner. "Reinventing Public R&D: Patent Policy and the Commercialization of National Laboratory Technologies." *The RAND Journal of Economics* 32.1 (2001), pp. 167–198. https://www.jstor.org/stable/2696403 (visited on June 8, 2025).

[26] Kenneth J. Arrow. "Classificatory Notes on the Production and Transmission of Technological Knowledge." *The American Economic Review* 59.2 (1969), pp. 29–35. https://www.jstor.org/stable/1823650 (visited on June 8, 2025).

[27] Aneesh Datar, Mario Daniele Amore, and Andrea Fosfuri. "Strategic Patent Disclosure: Unraveling the Influence of Temporal Preferences." *Strategic Organization* (December 13, 2024). https://doi.org/10.1177/14761270241299756 (visited on June 8, 2025); Nancy Kong, Uwe Dulleck, Adam B. Jaffe, Shupeng Sun, and Sowmya Vajjala. "Linguistic Metrics for Patent Disclosure: Evidence from University versus Corporate Patents." *Research Policy* 52.2 (March 1, 2023), p. 104670. https://www.sciencedirect.com/science/article/pii/S0048733322001913 (visited on June 8, 2025); Arora, Belenzon, and Suh, "Science and the Market for Technology"; see n. 20.

[28] Min Ouyang, Jin-Lin Huang, Chin Li Cheung, and Charles M. Lieber. "Energy Gaps in 'Metallic' Single-Walled Carbon Nanotubes." *Science* 292.5517 (April 27, 2001), pp. 702–705. https://www.science.org/doi/10.1126/science.1058853 (visited on June 8, 2025).

[29] Matteo Tranchero. "Data-Driven Search and the Birth of Theory: Evidence from Genome-Wide Association Studies." 2025. https://www.matteotranchero.com/research.html.

[30] Carver Mead and Lynn Conway. *Introduction to VLSI Systems*. Reading, MA: Addison-Wesley, 1980.

[31] Anthony S. Travis, Willem J. Hornix, Robert Bud, and Henk van den Belt. "Why Monopoly Failed: The Rise and Fall of Société La Fuchsine." *The British Journal for the History of Science* 25.1 (March 1992), pp. 45–63. https://www.cambridge.org/core/journals/british-journal-for-the-history-of-science/article/why-monopoly-failed-the-rise-and-fall-of-societe-la-fuchsine/EF3B924A1445571B1045A50CCC09626C (visited on June 8, 2025).

[32] Arora, Belenzon, and Suh, "Science and the Market for Technology"; see n. 20.

[33] Bikard, M., 2018. Made in academia: The effect of institutional origin on inventors' attention to science. Organization Science, 29(5), pp. 818–836.

[34] Ramon Lecuona Torras. "Adjust the Mirror: The Pioneering Role of Firms That Develop Products and General Purpose Technologies in Introducing Architectural Innovations." 2017 Unpublished working paper. Fuqua School of Business. Duke University.

[35] Jon Gertner. *The Idea Factory: Bell Labs and the Great Age of American Innovation*. New York: Penguin, 2013.

[36] Daniel Holbrook, Wesley M. Cohen, David A. Hounshell, and Steven Klepper. "The Nature, Sources, and Consequences of Firm Differences in the Early History of the Semiconductor Industry." *Strategic Management Journal* 21 (October 11, 2000), pp. 1017–1041.

37 Nathan Rosenberg and L. E. Birdzell, Jr. *How the West Grew Rich: The Economic Transformation of the Industrial World.* New York: Basic Books, 2008; Nathan Rosenberg. "Economic Experiments." *Industrial and Corporate Change* 1.1 (1992), pp. 181–203. https://academic.oup.com/icc/article-abstract/1/1/181/753648 (visited on August 14, 2024).

38 Lu Hong and Scott E. Page. "Groups of Diverse Problem Solvers Can Outperform Groups of High-Ability Problem Solvers." *Proceedings of the National Academy of Sciences* 101.46 (Nov. 16, 2004), pp. 16385–16389. https://www.pnas.org/doi/10.1073/pnas.0403723101 (visited on September 5, 2025); Wesley M. Cohen and Steven Klepper. "The Tradeoff between Firm Size and Diversity in the Pursuit of Technological Progress." *Small Business Economics* 4.1 (March 1, 1992), pp. 1–14. https://doi.org/10.1007/BF00402211.

39 Ashish Arora, Sharique Hasan, and William D. Miles. *If You Had One Shot: Scale and Herding in Innovation Experiments.* April 2025. https://www.nber.org/papers/w33682 (visited on May 21, 2025). Pre-published.

40 Young; see n. 19; George J Stigler. "The Division of Labor Is Limited by the Extent of the Market." *Journal of Political Economy* 59.3 (1951), pp. 185–193.

41 In Stigler's words, "Young industries are often strangers to the established economic system. They require new kinds or qualities of materials and hence make their own; they must overcome technical problems in the use of their products and cannot wait for potential users to overcome them; they must persuade customers to abandon other commodities and find no specialised merchants to undertake this task." Stigler, see n. 41, p. 190.

42 Alfred D. (Alfred Dupont) Chandler. Scale and Scope: *The Dynamics of Industrial Capitalism.* Cambridge, MA: Belknap Press of Harvard University, 1990.

43 Nathan Rosenberg. "Technological Change in the Machine Tool Industry, 1840–1910." *The Journal of Economic History* 23.4 (December 1963), pp. 414–443. https://www.cambridge.org/core/journals/journal-of-economic-history/article/technological-change-in-the-machine-tool-industry-18401910/BC2D1F693FDAB12D327897FF86F6B4FF (visited on June 8, 2025).

44 Rosenberg, "Technological Change in the Machine Tool Industry, 1840–1910"; see n. 44, p. 424.

45 T. F. Bresnahan and A. Gambardella. "The Division of Inventive Labor and the Extent of the Market." *General Purpose Technologies and Economic Growth.* Ed. by Elhanan Helpman. MIT Press, 1998, pp. 253–281.

46 Michael Ewens, Ramana Nanda, and Matthew Rhodes-Kropf. "Cost of Experimentation and the Evolution of Venture Capital." *Journal of Financial Economics* 128.3 (June 1, 2018), pp. 422–442.

47 Ashish Arora, Andrea Fosfuri, and Alfonso Gambardella. "Specialized Technology Suppliers, International Spillovers and Investment: Evidence from the Chemical Industry." *Journal of Development Economics* 65.1 (2001), pp. 31–54.

48 Ashish Arora, William B Vogt, and Ji Woong Yoon. "Is the Division of Labor Limited by the Extent of the Market?: Evidence from the Chemical Industry." *Industrial and Corporate Change* 18.5 (2009), pp. 785–806.

49 Roman Jurowetzki, Daniel Hain, Juan Mateos-Garcia, and Konstantinos Stathoulopoulos. *The Privatization of AI Research(-Ers): Causes and Potential Consequences—From University-Industry Interaction to Public Research Brain-Drain?* February 15, 2021. http://arxiv.org/abs/2102.01648 (visited on June 8, 2025). Pre-published.

50 Michael Gofman and Zhao Jin. "Artificial Intelligence, Education, and Entrepreneurship." *The Journal of Finance* 79.1 (2024), pp. 631–667. https://onlinelibrary.wiley.com/doi/abs/10.1111/jofi.13302 (visited on June 8, 2025).

Chapter 3

1 Josh Lerner and Ramana Nanda. "Venture Capital's Role in Financing Innovation: What We Know and How Much We Still Need to Learn." *Journal of Economic Perspectives* 34.3 (2020), pp. 237–61.

2 Neela Narain. "Institutions and Incentives in R&D Finance." PhD thesis. Harvard University, 2025.

3 Ron Adner and Rahul Kapoor. "Value Creation in Innovation Ecosystems: How the Structure of Technological Interdependence Affects Firm Performance in New Technology Generations." *Strategic Management Journal* 31.3 (2010), pp. 306–333.

4 North Carolina Biotechnology Center. *Biomason Raises $65 million to Advance Biocement Technology*. NCBiotech News. February 28, 2022. https://www.ncbiotech.org/news/biomason-raises-65-million-advance-biocement-technology; International Business Forum (IBF). *Development Projects: A More Sustainable Development*. IBF Sustainability Website. 2025. https://www.ibf.dk/en/Sustainability/A-more-sustainable-development/Development-projects/.

5 John Maraganore. "Reflections on Alnylam." *Nature Biotechnology* 40.5 (May 2022), pp. 641–650. https://www.nature.com/articles/s41587-022-01304-3 (visited on June 8, 2025).

6 Benjamin Reinhardt. *Getting Materials out of the Lab*. May 2024. https://worksinprogress.co/issue/getting-materials-out-of-the-lab/.

7 Reinhardt; see n. 6.

8 Nathan Rosenberg. *Inside the Black Box: Technology and Economics*. Cambridge, UK: Cambridge University Press, 1982.

9 Nicola Clark. *The Airbus Saga: Crossed Wires and a Multibillion-Euro Delay*. December 11, 2006. https://www.nytimes.com/2006/12/11/business/worldbusiness/11iht-airbus.3860198.html.

10 Ashish Arora, Andrea Fosfuri, and Thomas Rønde. "The Missing Middle: Value Capture in the Market for Startups." *Research Policy* 53.3 (2024), p. 104958.

11 Philippe Soussan, Arnaud de la Tour, and Nicolas Harlé. *A Framework for Deep-tech Collaboration*. Boston Consulting Group article, Perspectives. April 4, 2017. https://www.bcg.com/publications/2017/digital-joint-venture-alliances-framework-deep-tech-collaboration.

12 Roger Masclans. "Science, Startups, and the Problem of Value Capture." 2025. https://rogermasclans.github.io/.

13 Florian Ederer and Bruno Pellegrino. "The Great Start-up Sellout and the Rise of Oligopoly." *AEA Papers and Proceedings* 113 (May 2023), pp. 274–278.

14 Ashish Arora, Andrea Fosfuri, and Thomas Rønde. "Waiting for the Payday? The Market for Startups and the Timing of Entrepreneurial Exit." *Management Science* 67.3 (March 2021), pp. 1453–1467.

15 Lerner and Nanda; see n. 1; Michael Ewens, Ramana Nanda, and Matthew Rhodes-Kropf. "Cost of Experimentation and the Evolution of Venture Capital." *Journal of Financial Economics* 128.3 (June 1, 2018), pp. 422–442.

16 Katie Fehrenbacher. "A Biofuel Dream Gone Bad." *Fortune* (December 15, 2015).

17 Sunset HQ. *What Happened to KiOR & Why Did It Fail?* January 24, 2025. https://www.sunsethq.com/blog/why-did-kior-fail.

18 Robert Dailey. *Lilly Settles Contract Dispute with Emisphere for $18 million*. September 28, 2007. https://www.patentdocs.org/2007/09/lilly-settles-c.html.

19 Solon Moreira, Thomas Maximilian Klueter, and Aman Asija. "Market for Technology 2.0? Reassessing the Role of Complementary Assets on Licensing Decisions." *Research Policy* 52.7 (2023), p. 104779.

20 Energy Information Administration data show that in 1962, the United States produced around 2.45 Terawatts of energy, of which only 2.15 Megawatts was from solar.

21 This historical discussion heavily borrows from Susan Walsh Sanderson and Kenneth L. Simons. "Light Emitting Diodes and the Lighting Revolution: The Emergence of a Solid-State Lighting Industry." *Research Policy* 43.10 (December 1, 2014), pp. 1730–1746 and Bob Johnstone. *Brilliant!: Shuji Nakamura and the Revolution in Lighting Technology*. Amherst, NY: Prometheus Books, 2007.

22 Hayashi had invented the first room temperature diode laser together with Morton Panish at Bell Labs in 1970.

23 https://archive.nytimes.com/bits.blogs.nytimes.com/2008/09/26/the-10-million-light-bulb/

24 Chapter 10 contains a detailed case study on the laser.

25 Interview by the authors with a DOE administrator during the 2011 L-Prize (September 2023).

26 The tacitness and fuzziness of key discoveries also cultivated fertile ground for patent disputes: Nichia sued Toyoda Gosei for its use of LEDs in automotive parts in 1996 (Toyoda Gosei countersued). Nichia followed these with suits against Cree, Epistar, Everlight and Seoul Semiconductor starting from 1999. Countersuits by Cree, most notably, weakened Nichia's position, since the North Carolina company's technology was based on an earlier GaN patent licensed from Boston University. Similar to other technical areas that rely on solid-state electronics (such as chip manufacturing), most firms agreed to a broad cross-licensing agreement by 2002.

27 Nathan Rosenberg. "Factors Affecting the Diffusion of Technology." *Explorations in Economic History* 10.1 (September 1, 1972), pp. 3–33.

28 C. W. Tang and S. A. VanSlyke. "Organic Electroluminescent Diodes." *Applied Physics Letters* 51.12 (September 21, 1987), pp. 913–915.

29 Grand View Research, Inc. *OLED Market Size, Share, Growth & Trends Report, 2030.* 2025. https://www.grandviewresearch.com/industry-analysis/oled-marketreport.

30 Since 2002, UDC worked on a series of DOE-funded projects to improve the basic performance of OLED lighting. See U.S. Department of Energy, Building Technologies Office. *SSL R&D Program Impacts—Universal Display Corporation (UDC).* December 2016. https://www.energy.gov/node/1175691/.

31 USAspending.gov. *Federal Grant to Universal Display Corporation (UEI: C884TD4KG1F6).* https://www.usaspending.gov/award/ASST_NON_DESC0002122_8900/.

32 U.S. Department of Energy, Building Technologies Office; see n. 29, p. 1.

33 M. A. Fusella, R. Saramak, R. Bushati, V. M. Menon, M. S. Weaver, N. J. Thompson, and J. J. Brown. "Plasmonic Enhancement of Stability and Brightness in Organic Light-Emitting Devices." *Nature* 585.7825 (2020), pp. 379–382.

34 UDC's CTO, Julia Brown, is a fellow of the Institute of Electrical and Electronics Engineers (IEEE) and the National Academy of Engineering. M. S. Weaver, Vice President of PHOLED R&D, has published over seventy publications and conference proceedings while at UDC, and over one hundred patents. Similarly, Michael Hack, its Vice President of Development, has nearly seventy-five publications listed in Google Scholar, and over eighty U.S. patents.

35 George C. Cromer and Orville C. Cromer. "Early Electric Automobiles." *Encyclopaedia Britannica.* Encyclopaedia Britannica, Inc., 2025. https://www.britannica.com/technology/automobile/Early-electric-automobiles.

36 Henry Sanderson. *Volt Rush: The Winners and Losers in the Race to Go Green.* New York: Simon and Schuster, 2022.

37 This analogy is borrowed from James Morton Turner. *Charged: A History of Batteries and Lessons for a Clean Energy Future.* Ed. by Paul S. Sutter and Paul S. Sutter. University of Washington Press, December 31, 2022.

38 Charles J. Murray. "Who Really Invented the Rechargeable Lithium-Ion Battery?": *IEEE Spectrum* (July 30, 2023). https://spectrum.ieee.org/lithium-ion-battery-2662487214 (visited on January 21, 2025).

39 For an excellent discussion of innovation in battery technology, on which the rest of this section is based, see Brian Potter, 2024, How We Got the Lithium-ion Battery. Available from https://www.construction-physics.com/p/how-we-got-the-lithium-ion-battery.

40 See the Global EV Outlook 2024 by the International Energy Agency (IEA). Available from https://www.iea.org/reports/global-ev-outlook-2024/trends-in-electric-vehicle-batteries.

41 See, for example, Wikipedia contributors. *A123 Systems.* https://en.wikipedia.org/wiki/A123_Systems.

42 Murray; see n. 37.

43 TS2 Tech. *QuantumScape 2025: Latest News, Solid-State Battery Breakthroughs, Financials & Outlook.* June 27, 2025. https://ts2.tech/en/quantumscape-2025-latestnews-solid-state-battery-breakthroughs-financials-outlook/.

44 Solid Power Inc. *Our History: From DARPA Spin-out to Solid-state Battery Pioneer.* Company website. 2025. https://www.solidpowerbattery.com/about/history/default.aspx.

Chapter 4

1 We use the terms "industrial research" and "corporate research" interchangeably to refer to research in large corporations, distinct from research by startups.

2 Ashish Arora, Sharon Belenzon, Larisa Cioaca, Lia Sheer, Hyunmoh Shin, and Dror Shvadron. *DISCERN 2.0: Duke Innovation & Scientific Enterprises Research Network.* Zenodo, 2024. https://doi.org/10.5281/zenodo.3594642.

3 Zihang Lin, Yian Yin, Lu Liu, and Dashun Wang. "SciSciNet: A Large-Scale Open Data Lake for the Science of Science Research." *Scientific Data* 10.1 (June 1, 2023), p. 315. https://www.nature.com/articles/s41597-023-02198-9 (visited on September 6, 2024).

4 Joshua Lerner. *The Architecture of Innovation : The Economics of Creative Organizations.* Oxford: Oxford University Press, 2012.

5 Samuel Kortum and Josh Lerner. "Assessing the Contribution of Venture Capital to Innovation." *The RAND Journal of Economics* 31.4 (2000), pp. 674–692.
6 Mike Ewens and Matt Marx. "Firm Age and Invention: An Open-Access Dataset." 2024.
7 Lin, Yin, Liu, and Wang; see n. 3.
8 Josh Lerner. "The Narrowing Ambitions of Venture Capital." *MIT Technology Review* (September 6, 2012). https://www.technologyreview.com/2012/09/06/18640/the-narrowing-ambitions-of-venture-capital/.
9 Benjamin Gaddy, Varun Sivaram, and Francis O'Sullivan. *Venture Capital and Cleantech: The Wrong Model for Clean Energy Innovation.* Cambridge, MA: MIT Energy Initiative, 2016. https://energy.mit.edu/research/venture-capital-and-cleantech/.
10 Honggi Lee, Matt Marx, and Lia Sheer. "The Changing Role of Scientific Discovery in VC-backed Startups in the U.S. Innovation Ecosystem." Unpublished working paper. Tel Aviv University. 2025.
11 Arora, Belenzon, Cioaca, Sheer, Shin, and Shvadron; see n. 2.
12 Ewens and Marx; see n. 6.
13 Lin, Yin, Liu, and Wang; see n. 3.
14 Di Tang. *Climate Tech's Evolution: The Maturation to a Competitive, Returns-focused Thematic Investment Sector.* Insight article, Cambridge Associates. February 2023. Unpublished working paper. Tel Aviv University. 2025. https://www.cambridgeassociates.com/insight/climate-techs-evolution/.
15 Ewens and Marx; see n. 6.
16 Arora, Belenzon, Cioaca, Sheer, Shin, and Shvadron; see n. 2.
17 Lin, Yin, Liu, and Wang; see n. 3.
18 Michaël Bikard. "Made in Academia: The Effect of Institutional Origin on Inventors' Attention to Science." *Organization Science* 29.5 (June 20, 2018), pp. 818–836.
19 Letter to the *Wall Street Journal*, available at http://www.dtc.umn.edu/~odlyzko/misc/wsj-bell-labs-20120326. Accessed February 18, 2019.
20 Eric Gilliam of *Freaktakes* characterises this as granting researchers "a long leash but a narrow fence" for exploration. See Eric Gilliam. *How Did Places like Bell Labs Know How to Ask the Right Questions?* FreakTakes (Substack) blog. April 20, 2023. https://www.freaktakes.com/p/how-did-places-like-bell-labs-know.
21 David F Noble. *America by Design: Science, Technology, and the Rise of Corporate Capitalism.* 588. Oxford University Press, USA, 1979, p. 119.
22 Philipp Hartmann and Joachim Henkel. "The Rise of Corporate Science in AI." Working Paper. Technical University of Munich, 2019.
23 Voxel51. *NeurIPS 2023 and the State of AI Research.* December 8, 2023. https://voxel51.com/blog/neurips-2023-and-the-state-of-ai-research.
24 Nur Ahmed, Muntasir Wahed, and Neil C. Thompson. "The Growing Influence of Industry in AI Research." *Science* 379.6635 (March 3, 2023), pp. 884–886.
25 Ashish Vaswani, Noam Shazeer, Niki Parmar, Jakob Uszkoreit, Llion Jones, Aidan N. Gomez, Lukasz Kaiser, and Illia Polosukhin. *Attention Is All You Need.* August 1, 2023. http://arxiv.org/abs/1706.03762 (visited on September 9, 2024). Pre-published.
26 Steven Klepper. *Experimental Capitalism: The Nanoeconomics of American High-Tech Industries.* Princeton, NJ: Princeton University Press, 2015.
27 Bob Metcalfe. "Where the Future Came from." *The Wall Street Journal* (March 17, 2012). https://www.wsj.com/articles/SB10001424052970204781804577271442604380350.
28 Jason Dedrick and Kenneth L. Kraemer. "Who Captures Value from Science-based Innovation? The Distribution of Benefits from GMR in the Hard Disk Drive Industry." *Research Policy* 44.8 (2015), pp. 1615–1628.
29 Cited on page 1623 of Dedrick and Kraemer; see n. 29.
30 Seagate itself was founded by Al Shugart, a senior engineering manager at IBM, after a stint at Memorex, and a startup. See Henry Chesbrough. "Arrested Development: The Experience of European Hard Disk Drive Firms in Comparison with US and Japanese Firms." *Journal of Evolutionary Economics* 9.3 (1999), pp. 287–329.
31 The study is available at https://www.belfercenter.org/critical-emerging-tech-index and draws on a comprehensive set of indicators, including levels of private investment and public funding (in absolute U.S. dollars), high-impact publications, R&D personnel counts, and patents. Some metrics are sector-specific: in AI, for instance, algorithms, computing power, and data metrics are also included.

32 See also K. F. Lee. (2018). *AI superpowers: China, Silicon Valley, and the new world order.* Boston: Houghton Mifflin Harcourt.

33 See fDi Intelligence, "China's universities outpace US peers amid tech competition," April 30 2025, https://www.fdiintelligence.com/content/d0a58f39-0ed0-4b58-8c51-477133b6d9e1.

34 *Financial Times*, "China's innovation paradox," October 19, 2025, https://www.ft.com/content/b44458cc-03fd-46a1-b003-b7a097419e66.

35 Chapter 3 goes into further detail about Maruska's project. Even the concept of active matrix technology, which would allow for pixels to be controlled on thin films, was invented by Bernard Lechner at RCA and prototyped at Westinghouse in 1974. The Westinghouse team realised the active matrix concept on a thin-film transistor (TFT), adding the other piece of the puzzle necessary for a TFT-LCD display. See Wikipedia contributors. *Active Matrix.* Wikipedia, The Free Encyclopedia. 2025. https://en.wikipedia.org/wiki/Active_matrix.

36 Margaret B. W. Graham. *The Business of Research: RCA and the VideoDisc.* Cambridge, UK: Cambridge University Press, 1988.

37 For more detail on the story of RCA research, please see Chapter 10.

38 Henry Kressel. "Lessons from the Corporate Labs: Technological Competition in a Changing Business Environment." *American Affairs* 8.1 (2024), pp. 53–69. https://americanaffairsjournal.org/2024/02/lessons-from-the-corporate-labs-technological-compet ition-in-a-changing-business-environment/.

39 China's electric vertical take-off and landing (eVTOL) aircraft sector is the most advanced in the world, thanks to dominance in battery production and China's supportive regulation. Indeed, Beijing designated the low-altitude economy, which covers both manned and unmanned activities up to 1,000 metres, as a strategically emerging sector. See, e.g., the *Financial Times*, "China's flying car start-ups take their case to the skies," September 18, 2025, https://www.ft.com/content/181b631b-a84a-4e4d-b2b2-69ff81de551c.

40 Global EV Outlook 2024. Available at https://www.iea.org/reports/global-ev-outlook-2024.

41 See https://www.iea.org/reports/energy-technology-perspectives-2024.

42 Kyle Chan, "China's overlapping tech-industrial ecosystems," High Capacity, https://www.high-capacity.com/p/chinas-overlapping-tech-industrial.

43 See Kyle Chan, "How China Uses Foreign Firms to Turbocharge Its Industries," High Capacity, https://www.high-capacity.com/p/how-china-uses-foreign-firms-to-turbocharge.

44 This discussion is based on Huckman, R. S., & MacCormack, A. D. (2009). BYD Company, Ltd. HBS Case, 9-606-139.

45 See the *Financial Times*, "How BYD caught up with Tesla in the global EV race," July 15, 2025, https://www.ft.com/content/81f97fd3-c889-46af-990c-051d32821102.

46 Unni Pillai. "The Origins of the Tools Suppliers in the Semiconductor Industry." *Business History* 65.6 (2023), pp. 959–982.

47 R. Henderson and I. Cockburn. "Measuring Competence? Exploring Firm Effects in Pharmaceutical Research." *Strategic Management Journal* 15 (1994), pp. 63–84.

48 Chris Miller. *Chip War: The Fight for the World's Most Critical Technology.* New York: Scribner, 2022, p. 184.

49 Miller; see n. 49, Chapter 32.

50 Pillai; see n. 47.

51 Hartmann and Henkel; see n. 23.

52 Nicholas A. Pairolero, Alexander V. Giczy, Gerard Torres, Tisa Islam Erana, Mark A. Finlayson, and Andrew A. Toole. "The Artificial Intelligence Patent Dataset (AIPD) 2023 Update." *The Journal of Technology Transfer* (February 22, 2025). https://doi.org/10.1007/s10961-025-10189-8 (visited on August 27, 2025).

53 https://itif.org/publications/2024/09/09/how-innovative-is-china-in-quantum/

54 Martin Giles. "Quantum Computers: We'd Have More Quantum Computers If It Weren't so Hard to Find the Damn Cables." *MIT Technology Review* (2019-01-17, 2019). https://www.technologyreview.com/2019/01/17/137811/quantum-computers-component-shortage/.

Chapter 5

1 John F. Kennedy. *Address at Rice University on the Nation's Space Effort.* John F. Kennedy Presidential Library and Museum. 1962-09-12, 1962. https://www.jfklibrary.org/learn/about-jfk/historic-speeches/address-at-rice-university-on-the-nations-space-effort (visited on August 7, 2025).

2 Joel Mokyr. *The Gifts of Athena: Historical Origins of the Knowledge Economy*. Princeton, NJ: Princeton University Press, 2002.
3 Herbert A. Simon. *The Sciences of the Artificial*. 3rd ed. Cambridge, MA: MIT Press, 1996.
4 As such, inventions in our taxonomy are necessarily technical.
5 Mokyr, *The Gifts of Athena: Historical Origins of the Knowledge Economy*; see n. 2.
6 Donald Fleming. "Latent Heat and the Invention of the Watt Engine." Isis 43.1 (1952), pp. 3–5.
7 Richard R. Nelson. "The Economics of Invention: A Survey of the Literature." *The Journal of Business* 32.2 (1959), pp. 101–127, at p. 105.
8 The actual mass ratio of hydrogen to oxygen is closer to 6:1 because the rocket engine performs an incomplete combustion.
9 https://esa.int/navipedia/index.php/GPS_Space_Segment
10 The literature on innovative search employs a cartographic analogy—science converts a "local search" for innovation toward a "global search." See Lee Fleming and Olav Sorenson. "Science as a Map in Technological Search." *Strategic Management Journal* 25.8–9 (2004), pp. 909–928.
11 Stefano Comino, Alberto Galasso, and Clara Graziano. "Market Power and Patent Strategies: Evidence from Renaissance Venice." *The Journal of Industrial Economics* 68.2 (2020), pp. 226–269. https://onlinelibrary.wiley.com/doi/abs/10.1111/joie.12223 (visited on August 11, 2025).
12 Daniel Garber. "Physics and Foundations." *The Cambridge History of Science, Volume 3: Early Modern Science*. Ed. by Katharine Park and Lorraine Daston. Cambridge, UK: Cambridge University Press, 2006, pp. 21–69.
13 Garber; see n. 10, p. 26.
14 The tetrahedron, cube, octahedron, dodecahedron, and icosahedron. Given the shapes of these regular solids, the orbits were also posited to be perfectly circular.
15 The Latin title translates to "New Organon," deliberately invoking Aristotle's logical treatise *Organon*.
16 Francis Bacon. *Novum Organum*. Ed. by Thomas Fowler. Oxford: Clarendon Press, 1620, Book I, Aphorism 110.
17 Bacon, *Novum Organum*; see n. 14, Book I, Aphorism 109.
18 Francis Bacon. *New Atlantis*. Ed. by Fulton H. Anderson. Indianapolis: Bobbs-Merrill, 1627.
19 Peter Mathias. *The First Industrial Nation: An Economic History of Britain, 1700–1914*. 1st ed. London: Methuen, 1983, p. 124.
20 Mathias, see n. 17, p. 125.
21 W. Walker Hanlon. "The Rise of the Engineer: Inventing the Professional Inventor during the Industrial Revolution." *The Economic Journal* 135.670 (August 1, 2025), pp. 1749–1781.
22 Joel Mokyr. *A Culture of Growth: The Origins of the Modern Economy*. Princeton, NJ: Princeton University Press, 2016.
23 Mokyr, *The Gifts of Athena: Historical Origins of the Knowledge Economy*; see n. 2, Chapter 2.
24 Wikipedia contributors. *Joseph von Fraunhofer. Wikipedia*. 2025. https://en.wikipedia.org/wiki/Joseph_von_Fraunhofer.
25 Mathias, see n. 17, pp. 124–125.

Chapter 6

1 N. F. R. Crafts and C. K. Harley. "Output Growth and the British Industrial Revolution: A Restatement of the Crafts-Harley View." *The Economic History Review* 45.4 (1992), pp. 703–730.
2 Gregory Clark. *A Farewell to Alms: A Brief Economic History of the World (The Princeton Economic History of the Western World)*. Princeton, NJ: Princeton University Press, 2008, p. xii, pp. 240–242.
3 As J. B. West notes "On investigating the pump, Watt recognised that one of the problems was that the cylinder was cooled during each down stroke of the piston as the steam was condensed. Therefore its temperature changed greatly with each cycle.... In addition he was surprised at the amount of water that was necessary to condense the steam. He then asked Black whether the amount of heat required to make steam was much greater than the heat required to raise water to its boiling point. Black realised that the key to this question was the latent heat of vaporisation, which he had shown to be very large. The upshot was that Watt decided to choose another design that did not involve heating and cooling the power cylinder." See John B. West. "Joseph

Black, Carbon Dioxide, Latent Heat, and the Beginnings of the Discovery of the Respiratory Gases." *American Journal of Physiology —Lung Cellular and Molecular Physiology* 307.1 (June 2014), pp. L1–L5.

4 This is a familiar pattern in which diffusion starts slowly, accelerates sharply once adoption reaches a critical mass, and eventually levels off as the market saturates.

5 Our account of the development of nylon is based chiefly on Chapter 13 of David Hounshell and John Kenly Smith Jr. *Science and Corporate Strategy: DuPont R&D, 1902–1980.* Cambridge, UK: Cambridge University Press, 1988.

6 Abby Callard. *Stocking Series Part 1: Wartime Rationing and Nylon Riots.* November 5, 2010. https://www.smithsonianmag.com/arts-culture/stocking-series-part-1-wartime-rationing-and-nylon-riots-25391066/.

7 The linear model is attributed to Vannevar Bush, the director of the U.S. Office of Scientific Research and Development during World War II and the architect of the postwar federal scientific establishment. See Vannevar Bush. "Science: The Endless Frontier." *Transactions of the Kansas Academy of Science (1903–)* 48.3 (1945), pp. 231–264, For more details, see Chapter 9 of the present volume.

8 Nathan Rosenberg. "Science, Technology and Society." *Rivista Internazionale di Scienze Sociali* 104.4 (1996), pp. 479–496, p. 484.

9 Chapter 3, Grace Rogers Cooper. *The Sewing Machine: Its Invention and Development.* 2nd, revised and expanded. Washington, D.C.: Smithsonian Institution Press, 1976, pp. ix, 238.

10 The Hopkin Thomas Project. *Chapter 3: The Boulton & Watt Engine.* The Hopkin Thomas Project (online monograph). 2011. https://www.thehopkinthomasproject.com/TheHopkinThomasProject/TimeLine/Wales/Steam/JamesWatt/Kelly/Watt.htm.

11 This was a tactic that Charles Martin Hall would later employ in the early days of Alcoa to seed early demand for aluminium. The Pittsburgh Reduction Company (as Alcoa was then known) entered the cookware market by developing a rust-proof aluminium teakettle in 1895 and aluminium foil in 1910. In 1916, it opened the aerospace market for its product by casting engines for the Wright brothers in 1903, and developing an aluminium alloy, the 2017-T4. See George David Smith. *From Monopoly to Competition: The Transformations of Alcoa, 1888–1986.* Cambridge, UK: Cambridge University Press, 2003; Alcoa Corporation. *Our History: A Legacy of Innovation.* Company website. 2025. https://www.alcoa.com/global/en/who-we-are/history.

12 The Hopkin Thomas Project; see n. 10.

13 Stephenson Steam Railway. *The Dawn of the Railways and the Role of the Stephensons.* 2024. https://stephensonsteamrailway.org.uk/the-dawn-of-the-railways.

14 Steven W. Usselman. "Patents, Engineering Professionals, and the Pipelines of Innovation: The Internalization of Technical Discovery by Nineteenth-Century American Railroads". *Learning by Doing in Markets, Firms, and Countries.* Ed. by Naomi R. Lamoreaux, Daniel M. G. Raff, and Peter Temin. Chicago: University of Chicago Press, 1999, pp. 61–102.

15 Steven W. Usselman. *Regulating Railroad Innovation: Business, Technology, and Politics in America, 1840–1920.* Cambridge: Cambridge University Press, 2002, pp. xviii, 368, p. 134.

16 Wikipedia contributors. *Westinghouse Air Brake Company.* Wikipedia, The Free Encyclopedia. Wikimedia Foundation, 2025. https://en.wikipedia.org/wiki/Westinghouse_Air_Brake_Company.

17 The Guardian. *Lingering Taste of Liebig's Cube.* June 19, 1999. https://www.theguardian.com/business/1999/jun/19/8; Wikipedia contributors. Liebig's Extract of Meat Company. Wikipedia, The Free Encyclopedia. 2025. https://en.wikipedia.org/wiki/Liebig%27s_Extract_of_Meat_Company.

18 Wikipedia contributors. *Bessemer Process.* Wikipedia, The Free Encyclopedia. Wikimedia Foundation, 2025. https://en.wikipedia.org/wiki/Bessemer_process.

19 Vaclav Smil. *Creating and Transforming the Twentieth Century, Revised and Expanded: Technical Innovations and Their Lasting Impact.* Oxford: Oxford University Press, 2025.

20 Ragnhild Lundström. *Alfred Nobel's Dynamite Companies.* Nobel Prize website. 2015. https://www.nobelprize.org/alfred-nobel/alfred-nobels-dynamite-companies/.

21 David S. Landes. *Unbound Prometheus : Technological Change and Industrial Development in Western Europe from 1750 to the Present.* West Nyack, NJ: Cambridge University Press, 2003, p. 272.

22 Wikipedia contributors. *Leblanc Process.* Wikipedia, The Free Encyclopedia. 2025. https://en.wikipedia.org/wiki/Leblanc_process.

23 Friedrich, Bretislav. 2016. "How Did the Tree of Knowledge Get Its Blossom? The Rise of Physical and Theoretical Chemistry, with an Eye on Berlin and Leipzig." Angewandte Chemie (International Ed. in English) 55 (18): 5378–92. https://doi.org/10.1002/anie.201509260.

24 Ernst Homburg. "The Emergence of Research Laboratories in the Dyestuffs Industry, 1870–1900." *The British Journal for the History of Science* 25.1 (1992), pp. 91–111, p. 95.

25 Homburg; see n. 23, p. 98.

26 Homburg; see n. 23, p. 101.

27 Terry Shinn. "The Genesis of French Industrial Research 1880–1940." *Sociology of Science* 19.3 (June 1, 1980), pp. 607–640.

28 Shinn; see n. 26, p. 145.

29 Paul A David. "The Dynamo and the Computer: An Historical Perspective on the Modern Productivity Paradox." *The American Economic Review* 80.2 (1990), pp. 355–361.

30 Brush's firm would later be absorbed by General Electric: Engineering and Technology History Wiki contributors. *Charles F. Brush*. 2020. https://ethw.org/Charles_F._Brush.

31 Western Union licensed Gray's patents, and operated telephone systems in competition with AT&T. A subsequent agreement with AT&T resulted in Western Union ceding the telephone business to AT&T in return for the latter staying out of telegraphy.

32 The transition was a long one, stretching well into the interwar period, but the seeds for corporate research were sown at the turn of the century.

33 Guglielmo Marconi's invention of wireless telegraphy and Walter Nernst's lamps were notable exceptions, which will be discussed in Chapter 8.

34 Alfred D. Chandler Jr. *The Visible Hand*. Cambridge, MA: Harvard University Press, 1993.

Chapter 7

1 Nathan Rosenberg and Richard Nelson. "The Roles of Universities in the Advance of Industrial Technology." Richard Rosenbloom and William Spencer. *Engines of Innovation: U.S. Industrial Research at the End of an Era*. Cambridge, MA: Harvard Business School Press, 1996.

2 U.S. Census Bureau. *The Fourth of July: The Nation's Population Then and Now*. Facts for Features (Census Newsroom). July 2025. https://www.census.gov/newsroom/facts-for-features/2025/fourth-of-july.html.

3 Miguel Urquiola. *Markets, Minds, and Money: Why America Leads the World in University Research*. Cambridge, MA: Harvard University Press, 2020, p. 35.

4 Urquiola; see n. 3.

5 Harvard University and Charles W. Eliot. *Addresses at the Inauguration of Charles William Eliot as President of Harvard College, Tuesday, October 19, 1869*. p. 48. Cambridge, MA: Sever and Francis, 1869. https://www.loc.gov/item/07004015/.

6 American Chemical Society. *Wallace Carothers and the Development of Nylon*. ACS National Historic Chemical Landmark webpage. 1995. https://www.acs.org/education/whatischemistry/landmarks/carotherspolymers.html.

7 Emily J. Levine. *Allies and Rivals: German-American Exchange and the Rise of the Modern Research University*. Chicago: University of Chicago Press, 2021, p. 72.

8 We gather data on all individuals who received a doctoral education between 1880 and 1925 by compiling scientist biographies from the 1906, 1910, 1921, and 1927 editions of *American Men of Science*.

9 History of Science at Williams contributors. *Chapter 1: The Sciences and the Curriculum*. N.d. https://sites.williams.edu/history-of-science-at-williams/chapter-1/.

10 Walter Rüegg, ed. *A History of the University in Europe, Volume 4: Universities since 1945*. Cambridge, UK: Cambridge University Press, 2011.

11 *MIT Undergraduate Physics Education History*. MIT Physics Education Group, 2024. https://peg.mit.edu/mit-physics-education-history/; Larry Hardesty. *The Birth of Electrical Engineering*. MIT News, 2011. https://news.mit.edu/2011/timeline-eecs-0309.

12 S. Warren. "A Century of Energy." *Sooner Magazine* 39.3 (2019).

13 *Colorado School of Mines History Timeline*. Colorado School of Mines Library Guides, 2024. https://libguides.mines.edu/Mines-History-Timeline.

14 Leonard S. Reich. *The Making of American Industrial Research : Science and Business at GE and Bell, 1876–1926*. Cambridge, UK: Cambridge University Press, 1985. xvi, 309 p. p. 8.

15 Charles Riborg Mann. *A Study of Engineering Education*. Bulletin No. 11. New York: Carnegie Foundation for the Advancement of Teaching, 1918. https://www.nationalsoftskills.org/wp-content/uploads/2025/03/Mann-1918-Study_of_Engineering_Educ.pdf, p. 7.

16 Earle D. Ross. *Democracy's College: The Land-grant Movement in the Formative Stage*. Ames: Iowa State College Press, 1942.

17 On the rise of elite American research universities, see Urquiola, n. 3; Roger L. Geiger. *To Advance Knowledge : The Growth of American Research Universities, 1900–1940*. New York: Oxford University Press, 1986.

18 Philip J. Pauly. *Controlling Life: Jacques Loeb and the Engineering Ideal in Biology*. New York: Oxford University Press, 1987; David Cahan. *Helmholtz: A Life in Science*. Chicago: University of Chicago Press, 2019, p. 463. Helmholtz's lecture tour in the United States was received with great fanfare during the International Electrical Congress of 1893 in Chicago (See Chapter 29).

19 Geiger; see n. 23.

20 Urquiola; see n. 3, p. 19.

21 Morton Keller and Phyllis Keller. *Making Harvard Modern: The Rise of America's University*. New York: Oxford University Press, 2001, p. 40.

22 Robert E. Kohler. *Partners in Science: Foundations and Natural Scientists, 1900–1945*. Chicago: University of Chicago Press, 1991.

23 Kevles. "Physics, Mathematics, and Chemistry Communities". *The Organization of Knowledge in Modern America, 1860–1920*. Ed. by Alexandra Oleson and John Voss. Baltimore: Johns Hopkins University Press, 1979, pp. 139–172.

24 Eric Gilliam notes that between 1954 and 1965, fifteen of the eighteen Nobel Prizes given out for molecular biology were supported by Rockefeller Foundation. Even more striking is that they were funded, average over nineteen years in advance of winning the prize. https://www.freaktakes.com/p/a-report-on-scientific-branch-creation.

25 Daniel J. Kevles. *The Physicists: The History of a Scientific Community in Modern America*.

26 Kevles, "Physics, Mathematics, and Chemistry Communities." *The Organization of Knowledge in Modern America, 1860–1920*. Ed. by Alexandra Oleson and John Voss. Baltimore: Johns Hopkins University Press, 1979, pp. 139–172, at p. 170.

27 Data from Angus Maddison, who estimates U.S. GDP in 1870 as $98,374 million in 1870 and $517,383 in 1913 (denominated in 1990 dollars). Per capita GDP for the two periods are estimated as $2,445 and $5,301 (Tables A1-b, A1-c.) See Angus Maddison. *The World Economy: A Millennial Perspective*. Development Centre Studies. Paris: Development Centre of the Organisation for Economic Co-operation and Development, 2001.

28 Jeremy Atack and Fred Bateman. "Manufacturing." *Historical Statistics of the United States, Millennial Edition on Line*. Ed. by Susan B. Carter, Scott Sigmund Gartner, Michael R. Haines, Alan L. Olmstead, Richard Sutch, and Gavin Wright. New York: Cambridge University Press, 2006, pp. 4-573–4-578, Chapter Dd: Manufacturing.

29 Alfred D Chandler Jr. *The Visible Hand*. Cambridge, MA: Harvard University Press, 1993; David A. Hounshell. *From the American System to Mass Production, 1800–1932: The Development of Manufacturing Technology in the United States*. Baltimore: Johns Hopkins University Press, 1984.

30 David Nasaw. *Andrew Carnegie*. New York: Penguin Press, 2006.

31 Wesley M. Cohen and Steven Klepper. "A Reprise of Size and R & D." *The Economic Journal* 106.437 (1996), pp. 925–951.

32 Milton L. Hoefle. "The Early History of Parke-Davis and Company." *Bulletin for the History of Chemistry* 25.1 (2000), pp. 28–34.

33 On ties between Parke-Davis and the University of Michigan, see B. Achilladelis. "Innovation in the Pharmaceutical Industry." *Pharmaceutical Innovation: Revolutionizing Human Health*. Ed. by R. Landau, B. Achilladelis, and A. Scriabine. Vol. 2. Philadelphia: Chemical Heritage Foundation, 1999, pp. 1–74.

34 Encyclopædia Britannica. *S.v. "J. P. Morgan."* 2025. https://www.britannica.com/money/J-P-Morgan.

35 Vincent P. Carosso and Rose C. Carosso. *The Morgans: Private International Bankers, 1854–1913*. Cambridge, MA: Harvard University Press, 1987, Chapter 7.

36 U.S. Office of Management and Budget. *Historical Tables.* In *Budget of the United States Government.* Executive Office of the President, Office of Management and Budget, 2025. https://www.whitehouse.gov/omb/information-resources/budget/historical-tables/, Table 1.1.

37 Carosso and Carosso; see n. 43, Chapter 13.

38 Ida M. Tarbell. *The History of the Standard Oil Company.* New York: McClure, Phillips & Co., 1904.

39 *Sherman Antitrust Act of 1890. 26 Stat. 209, ch. 647, §1. 1890.* https://www.law.cornell.edu/uscode/text/15/1.

40 Miller Center of Public Affairs, University of Virginia. *William Taft: Domestic Affairs.* N.d. https://millercenter.org/president/taft/domestic-affairs.

41 Frasch was a chemist and a prolific inventor of over sixty patents. He co-founded Empire Oil, during which time he also developed his process for removing sulphur from kerosene. The process was further developed in 1886 when Standard Oil acquired Frasch's equity in Empire Oil. See Wikipedia contributors. *Imperial Oil—Wikipedia, the Free Encyclopedia.* 2025. https://en.wikipedia.org/wiki/Imperial_Oil; Wikipedia contributors. *Herman Frasch—Wikipedia, the Free Encyclopedia.* 2025. https://en.wikipedia.org/wiki/Herman_Frasch.

42 F. M. Scherer. *Technological Innovation and Monopolization.* 2006. https://www.justice.gov/archives/atr/technological-innovation-and-monopolization.

43 Note, though, that the contributions of Standard to science were less clear-cut than those of AT&T, DuPont, or GE. Scherer cites a Bureau of Corporations study showing that crude and refined product prices dropped most between 1866 and 1872 before Standard's consolidation. The same study showed that Standard's unit costs were roughly similar to those of its rivals. Scherer also cites Jacob Schmookler's patent data suggesting that Standard's hegemony between 1870 and 1910 coincided with a lull in petroleum patenting growth. Scherer; see n. 50; Brief for Defendants on the Facts, United States v. Standard Oil Company (New Jersey), et al. 1910.

44 Louis D. Brandeis. *Other People's Money and How the Bankers Use It.* New York: Frederick A. Stokes Company, 1914, Chapter 8.

45 (*United States v. E. I. DuPont de Nemours & Co.* 1953), pages 217 and 233.

46 Naomi R. Lamoreaux and Kenneth L. Sokoloff. "Inventors, Firms, and the Market for Technology in the Late Nineteenth and Early Twentieth Centuries." *Learning by Doing in Markets, Firms, and Countries.* Ed. by Naomi R. Lamoreaux, Daniel M. G. Raff, and Peter Temin. Chicago: University of Chicago Press, 1999, pp. 19–60.

47 United States Constitution. *Article I, Section 8, Clause 8: The Intellectual Property Clause.* 1787. https://constitution.congress.gov/browse/essay/artI-S8-C8-1/ALDE_00013060/.

48 Gordon M. Winder. "Before the Corporation and Mass Production: The Licensing Regime in the Manufacture of North American Harvesting Machinery, 1830–1910." *Annals of the Association of American Geographers* 85.3 (1995), pp. 521–552.

49 B. Zorina Khan and Kenneth L. Sokoloff. "History Lessons: The Early Development of Intellectual Property Institutions in the United States." *Journal of Economic Perspectives* 15.3 (2001), pp. 233–246.

50 Lamoreaux and Sokoloff; see n. 54.

51 Khan and Sokoloff; see n. 57, p. 241.

52 Cited in Lamoreaux and Sokoloff; see n. 54, p. 42, fn. 29.

53 Lamoreaux and Sokoloff; see n. 54; Eric S. Hintz. "The Post-Heroic Generation: American Independent Inventors, 1900—1950." *Enterprise & Society* 12.4 (2011), pp. 732–748.

54 Tom Nicholas. "The Role of Independent Invention in US Technological Development, 1880–1930." *The Journal of Economic History* (2010), pp. 57–82.

Chapter 8

1 Nathan Rosenberg. "The Direction of Technological Change: Inducement Mechanisms and Focusing Devices." *Economic Development and Cultural Change* 18 (1, Part 1, 1969), pp. 1–24, at p. 84.

2 This chapter is primarily based on Ashish Arora, Sharon Belenzon, Konstantin Kosenko, Jungkyu Suh, and Yishay Yafeh. "The Rise of Scientific Research in Corporate America." *Organization Science* (2024).

3 Breakthrough patents are patents in the top decile of the "importance" measure from Bryan Kelly, Dimitris Papanikolaou, Amit Seru, and Matt Taddy. "Measuring Technological

Innovation over the Long Run." *American Economic Review: Insights* 3.3 (2021), pp. 303–320. The authors define importance as the ratio between ten-year forward similarity to other patents and five-year backward similarity. Patents with an importance higher than 90 per cent of patents awarded in the same year are designated as breakthrough patents.

4 George Wise. *Willis R. Whitney, General Electric, and the Origins of US Industrial Research.* Columbia University Press, 1985.

5 Angus Maddison. "A Comparison of Levels of GDP Per Capita in Developed and Developing Countries, 1700–1980." *The Journal of Economic History* 43.1 (1983), pp. 27–41.

6 Arora, Belenzon, Kosenko, Suh, and Yafeh; see n. 2.

7 Kelly, Papanikolaou, Seru, and Taddy; see n. 3.

8 Matt Marx and Aaron Fuegi. "Reliance on Science: Worldwide Front-Page Patent Citations to Scientific Articles." *Strategic Management Journal* (2020).

9 Bronwyn H Hall, Adam B Jaffe, and Manuel Trajtenberg. *The NBER Patent Citation Data File: Lessons, Insights and Methodological Tools.* National Bureau of Economic Research, 2001.

10 John W Servos. "Changing Partners: The Mellon Institute, Private Industry, and the Federal Patron." *Technology and Culture* 35.2 (1994), pp. 221–257, p. 223.

11 David C Mowery. "The Relationship between Intrafirm and Contractual Forms of Industrial Research in American Manufacturing, 1900–1940." *Explorations in Economic History* 20.4 (1983), pp. 351–374.

12 Roger L. Geiger. *To Advance Knowledge: The Growth of American Research Universities, 1900-1940.* New York: Oxford University Press, 1986, p. 179.

13 Ashish Arora. "Patents, Licensing, and Market Structure in the Chemical Industry." *Research Policy* 26.4 (December 1, 1997), pp. 391–403. https://www.sciencedirect.com/science/article/pii/S0048733397000140 (visited on 06/14/2025), p. 393.

14 W. Rupert (William Rupert) Maclaurin. *Invention and Innovation in the Radio Industry.* Massachusetts Institute of Technology. Studies of Innovation. New York: Macmillan, 1949.

15 "To Rule the Waves: Britain's Cable Empire and the Making of "Maxwell's Equations." *Imperial Science: Cable Telegraphy and Electrical Physics in the Victorian British Empire.* Ed. by Bruce J. Hunt. Science in History. Cambridge, UK: Cambridge University Press, 2021, pp. 216–271.

16 Frederick E. Terman. "A Brief History of Electrical Engineering Education." *Proceedings of the IEEE* 64.9 (1976), pp. 1399–1407.

17 Arora, Belenzon, Kosenko, Suh, and Yafeh; see n. 2, p. 1470.

18 Michaël Bikard. "Made in Academia: The Effect of Institutional Origin on Inventors' Attention to Science." *Organization Science* 29.5 (June 20, 2018), pp. 818–836.

19 A. Hunter Dupree. *Science in the Federal Government: A History of Policies and Activities to 1940. Three Centuries of Science in America.* Cambridge, MA: Belknap Press of Harvard University Press, 1957.

20 Thomas D. Snyder. *120 Years of American Education: A Statistical Portrait.* Collingdale, PA: DIANE Publishing, 1993.

21 Roger L. Geiger. *Knowledge and Money : Research Universities and the Paradox of the Marketplace.* Stanford, CA: Stanford University Press, 2004; Robert V. Bruce. *The Launching of Modern American Science, 1846-1876.* New York: Knopf, Distributed by Random House, 1987.

22 Snyder; see n. 20.

23 National Research Council. *Research: A National Resource : II. Industrial Research.* Washington, DC: The National Academies Press, 1938. https://www.nap.edu/catalog/20233/research-a-national-resource-ii-industrial-research.

24 David Hounshell and John Kenley Smith Jr. *Science and Corporate Strategy : DuPont R&D, 1902–1980.* Cambridge, UK: Cambridge University Press, 1988, p. 612.

25 Maclaurin; see n. 14, p. 158.

26 National Research Council (US), Research Information Service. *Industrial Research Laboratories of the United States, Including Consulting Research Laboratories.* RR Bowker Company, 1931.

27 We manually searched for firms in the entries of the 1927 (999 firms), 1931 (1,620 firms), 1933 (1,562 firms), 1938 (1,769 firms), and 1940 (2,264 firms) surveys.

28 We thank Petra Moser for supplying detailed data on the 1921 edition of AMS.

29 Naomi R. Lamoreaux and Kenneth L. Sokoloff. "Inventors, Firms, and the Market for Technology in the Late Nineteenth and Early Twentieth Centuries." *Learning by Doing in Markets, Firms, and Countries.* Ed. by Naomi R. Lamoreaux, Daniel M. G. Raff, and Peter Temin.

Chicago: University of Chicago Press, 1999, pp. 19–60; David Mowery and Nathan Rosenberg. *Paths of Innovation : Technological Change in 20th-Century America*. New York: Cambridge University Press, 1998.

30 Hall, Jaffe, and Trajtenberg; see n. 7.

31 T. D. Lockwood, on the "Duties of the patent department," AT&T, 1885 as cited in Lamoreaux and Sokoloff; see n. 29.

32 Leonard S Reich. *The Making of American Industrial Research : Science and Business at GE and Bell, 1876–1926*. Cambridge, UK: Cambridge University Press, 1985. xvi, 309 p., p. 193.

33 Hounshell and Smith; see n. 24.

34 Hounshell and Smith; see n. 24, p. 223.

35 Wise; see n. 8.

36 Reich; see n. 32.

37 Jon Gertner. *The Idea Factory: Bell Labs and the Great Age of American Innovation*. New York: Penguin, 2013.

38 Specifically, they replaced the tantalum filaments with more reliable oxide-coated cathodes and eliminated the blue haze issue. These improvements transformed the Audion into a reliable amplifier.

39 These are GE, AT&T, Westinghouse, RCA, and Kodak.

40 Kelly, Papanikolaou, Seru, and Taddy; see n. 3.

41 Joseph Alois Schumpeter. *Business Cycles*. Vol. 1. New York: McGraw-Hill, 1939.

42 Kenneth Arrow. "Economic Welfare and the Allocation of Resources for Invention." *The Rate and Direction of Inventive Activity: Economic and Social Factors*. Princeton, NJ: Princeton University Press, 1962, pp. 609–626.

43 David F Noble. *America by Design: Science, Technology, and the Rise of Corporate Capitalism*. 588. New York: Oxford University Press, 1979, pp. 120–121.

44 Gertner; see n. 37, p. 29.

45 Henry Augustus Rowland. "A Plea for Pure Science." *Science* 2.29 (1883), pp. 242–250; Ronald Kline. "Construing 'Technology' as 'Applied Science': Public Rhetoric of Scientists and Engineers in the United States, 1880–1945." *Isis* 86.2 (1995), pp. 194–221.

46 Geiger, *To Advance Knowledge: The Growth of American Research Universities, 1900–1940*, see n. 12.

47 Reich, see n. 32, p. 111.

48 Augustin Cerveaux. "Taming the Microworld: DuPont and the Interwar Rise of Fundamental Industrial Research." *Technology and Culture* 54.2 (2013), pp. 262–288.

49 Peter Galison and Bruce William Hevly. *Big Science: The Growth of Large-Scale Research*. Stanford, CA: Stanford University Press, 1992, Chapter 1.

50 Thomas C. Lassman. "Industrial Research Transformed: Edward Condon at the Westinghouse Electric and Manufacturing Company, 1935–1942." *Technology and Culture* 44.2 (2003), pp. 306–339.

51 Miguel Urquiola. *Markets, Minds, and Money: Why America Leads the World in University Research*. Cambridge, MA: Harvard University Press, 2020.

52 Jeffrey L Furman and Megan MacGarvie. "Academic Collaboration and Organizational Innovation: The Development of Research Capabilities in the US Pharmaceutical Industry, 1927–1946." *Industrial and Corporate Change* 18.5 (2009), pp. 929–961.

53 Ramana Nanda and Tom Nicholas. "Did Bank Distress Stifle Innovation during the Great Depression?" *Journal of Financial Economics* 114.2 (November 1, 2014), pp. 273–292.

54 Tania Babina, Asaf Bernstein, and Filippo Mezzanotti. "Financial Disruptions and the Organization of Innovation: Evidence from the Great Depression." *The Review of Financial Studies* 36.11 (November 1, 2023), pp. 4271–4317.

55 Lamoreaux and Sokoloff; see n. 29; Eric S. Hintz. "The Post-Heroic Generation: American Independent Inventors, 1900–1950." *Enterprise & Society* 12.4 (2011), pp. 732–748.

56 Alexander J Field. "The Most Technologically Progressive Decade of the Century." *American Economic Review* 93.4 (2003), pp. 1399–1413; Kelly, Papanikolaou, Seru, and Taddy; see n. 3.

57 Hugh Davis Graham and Nancy Diamond. *The Rise of American Research Universities: Elites and Challengers in the Postwar Era*. Baltimore: Johns Hopkins University Press, 1997; Henry Etzkowitz. *MIT and the Rise of Entrepreneurial Science*. Routledge Studies in Global Competition; 12. London; Routledge, 2002.

Chapter 9

1 This chapter draws materials from Ashish Arora, Sharon Belenzon, Jungkyu Suh, and Hansen Zhang. *The Rise of Absorptive Research in Corporate America: 1945–1980*. NBER Working Paper 33713. Cambridge, MA: National Bureau of Economic Research, 2025. https://www.nber.org/papers/w33713.

2 The Tizard mission was a British delegation of scientists and engineers that transferred radar technology (among others) to their U.S. counterparts. Wikipedia contributors. *Tizard Mission—Wikipedia, the Free Encyclopedia*. 2025. https://en.wikipedia.org/wiki/Tizard_Mission.

3 Daniel P. Gross and Maria P. Roche. *Coordinated R&D Programs and the Creation of New Industries*. October 1, 2024. https://papers.ssrn.com/abstract=5052658 (visited on June 27, 2025). Pre-published, p. 12.

4 National Inventors Hall of Fame. *Percy L. Spencer—High-Efficiency Magnetron*. 2025. https://www.invent.org/inductees/percy-l-spencer; Raytheon Technologies. *How Radars Tell the Tech Story of Raytheon Company*. 2022. https://www.rtx.com/news/2022/06/28/how-radars-tell-the-tech-story-of-the-raytheon-company; Spencer Lab. *Read-dig: A History of Reading/Editing in Spencer Lab*. Archived webpage via Internet Archive (AOL Members). 2005. https://web.archive.org/web/20050306112532/http://members.aol.com/spencerlab/history/readdig.htm.

5 *Fortune Magazine*. "RADAR—the Industry." *Fortune* 32.4 (1945), p. 146, As cited in Gross & Roche 2024.

6 Gross and Roche; see n. 3.

7 *Fortune Magazine*; see n. 5.

8 Cameron D. Collier. "Tiny Miracle—the Proximity Fuze." *Naval History* 13.4 (August 1999), pp. 43–45. https://www.usni.org/magazines/naval-history-magazine/1999/august/tiny-miracle-proximity-fuze.

9 This was also thanks to Percy Spencer's work in 1938. Mark P. D. Burgess. *Raytheon Part One: From Transistor to Spacistor (Transistor History)*. 2009. https://sites.google.com/site/transistorhistory/Home/us-semiconductor-manufacturers/raytheon-partone-2.

10 Mark P. D. Burgess. *Raytheon Part One: Semiconductor Research and Development at Raytheon*. Google Sites. 2010. https://sites.google.com/site/transistorhistory/Home/us-semiconductor-manufacturers/raytheon-part-one-2.

11 D. D. Jackson. *VT Proximity Fuze Manufacturers of World War Two*. 2021. https://usautoindustryworldwartwo.com/vtproximityfuze.htm; Edward A. Sharpe. SMECC. *Radio Proximity Fuzes*. N.d. http://www.smecc.org/radio_proximity_fuzes.htm.

12 Daniel P. Gross and Bhaven N. Sampat. *The Therapeutic Consequences of the War: World War II and the 20th-Century Expansion of Biomedicine*. February 2025. https://www.nber.org/papers/w33457 (visited on March 21, 2025). Pre-published.

13 Gross and Sampat, *The Therapeutic Consequences of the War*; see n. 12, p. 35.

14 Gross and Sampat, *The Therapeutic Consequences of the War*; see n. 12, p. 32.

15 Arthur Daemmrich. "Synthesis by Microbes or Chemists? Pharmaceutical Research and Manufacturing in the Antibiotic Era." *History and Technology* 25.3 (2009), pp. 237–256.

16 The USSR also ran a similar program, named Operation Osoaviakhim.

17 Vannevar Bush. "Science: The Endless Frontier." *Transactions of the Kansas Academy of Science (1903–)* 48.3 (1945), pp. 231–264.

18 Roger L. Geiger. *Research and Relevant Knowledge : American Research Universities since World War II*. New York: Oxford University Press, 1993, pp. 15–18.

19 Angela N. H. Creager. *Life Atomic: Radioisotopes in Biology and Medicine*. Chicago: University of Chicago Press, 2013.

20 In 1974, the AEC was dissolved, and its functions were split between two new agencies: the Energy Research and Development Administration (ERDA) and the U.S. Nuclear Regulatory Commission (NRC). ERDA continued the AEC's work on nuclear energy research and development, becoming part of the Department of Energy (DOE) in 1977, which today oversees national energy policy and research efforts. The NRC was established to regulate the nuclear industry, with a mandate to ensure the safe use of radioactive materials for civilian purposes. This includes licensing nuclear power plants, managing radioactive waste and regulating nuclear materials in medicine, industry, and research. The NRC's oversight has been essential in maintaining nuclear safety and advancing peaceful applications of nuclear technology. See

Terrence R. Fehner and Jack M. Holl. *Department of Energy, 1977–1994: A Summary History.* Washington, D.C.: U.S. Department of Energy, History Division, 1994. https://www.energy.gov/sites/prod/files/2017/09/f36/DOE%201977-1994%20A%20Summary%20History_0.pdf.

21 U.S. Congress. *Public Law 588: An Act to Establish an Office of Naval Research in the Department of the Navy; to Plan, Foster, and Encourage Scientific Research.* 79th Congress, 2nd Session, 60 Stat. 779. 1946. https://www.nre.navy.mil/media/document/public-law-588.

22 Harvey M. Sapolsky. *Science and the Navy: The History of the Office of Naval Research.* Princeton, NJ: Princeton University Press, 1990.

23 National Aeronautics and Space Administration. *110 Years Ago: The National Advisory Committee for Aeronautics Founded.* NASA History Feature. 2025. https://www.nasa.gov/history/110-years-ago-the-national-advisory-committee-for-aeronauticsfounded/.

24 Walter A. McDougall. *The Heavens and the Earth: A Political History of the Space Age.* New York: Basic Books, 1985; National Aeronautics and Space Administration. *NACA to NASA to Now: The Frontiers of Air and Space in the American Century.* Washington, D.C.: NASA History Division, 2008.

25 DARPA (Defense Advanced Research Projects Agency). *Stealth Aircraft.* June 2020. https://www.darpa.mil/news/features/stealth.

26 Peter J. Westwick. *Stealth: The Secret Contest to Invent Invisible Aircraft.* New York: Oxford University Press, 2020, p. 272.

27 The Rockefeller Foundation played a crucial part during this early period, providing substantial financial resources to combat infectious diseases. By 1951, when the Foundation ended its thirty-seven- year program, it had expended 94 million dollars. By this time, malaria and hookworm had disappeared from the southern United States, and a revolutionary yellow fever vaccine had been developed in the Foundation's laboratories by Max Theiler in 1937.

28 Office of NIH History and Stetten Museum. *A Short History of the National Institutes of Health.* National Institutes of Health, 2025. https://history.nih.gov/display/history/A+Short+History+of+the+National+Institutes+of+Health (visited on 01/07/2025).

29 Daniel P. Gross and Bhaven N. Sampat. "America, Jump-Started: World War II R&D and the Takeoff of the US Innovation System." *American Economic Review* 113.12 (2023), pp. 3323–3356.

30 Justin Stambaugh. "Overview of High-Power and Wideband Radar Technology Development at MIT Lincoln Laboratory." *Remote Sensing* 16.9 (2024), p. 1530. https://www.mdpi.com/2072-4292/16/9/1530; M. D. Fagen. *Technology in Support of National Security: MIT Lincoln Laboratory.* Lexington, MA: MIT Lincoln Laboratory, 1978. https://www.ll.mit.edu/sites/default/files/other/doc/2018-04/MIT_Lincoln_Laboratory_history_book.pdf (visited on January 9, 2025); MIT Lincoln Laboratory. *History of MIT Lincoln Laboratory.* 2025. https://www.ll.mit.edu/about/history (visited on March 13, 2025).

31 Jet Propulsion Laboratory. *History of the Jet Propulsion Laboratory.* 2025. https://www.jpl.nasa.gov/who-we-are/history (visited on January 7, 2025); Kent C. Redmond and Thomas M. Smith. *JPL and the American Space Program: A History of the Jet Propulsion Laboratory.* New Haven, CT: Yale University Press, 1983.

32 Lawrence Livermore National Laboratory. *Our History.* 2025. https://www.llnl.gov/about/history (visited on January 16, 2025); Lawrence Livermore National Laboratory. *Our History.* 2025. https://www.llnl.gov/purpose/history/1970s (visited on January 16, 2025).

33 Wikipedia contributors. *G.I. Bill.* 2025. https://en.wikipedia.org/wiki/G.I._Bill.

34 Wikipedia contributors. *National Defense Education Act.* 2025. https://en.wikipedia.org/wiki/National_Defense_Education_Act.

35 Pierre Azoulay, William Greenblatt, and Misty L. Heggeness. "Long-Term Effects from Early Exposure to Research: Evidence from the NIH 'yellow Berets.'" *International Journal of Population Data Science* 3.5 (2018). https://doi.org/10.23889/ijpds.v3i5.1070; Ethan Smith. "From the Annals of NIH History: Yellow Berets to Nobel Laureates—the Vietnam War and Nih's Clinical Associates Program." *The NIH Catalyst* 29.2 (March–April 2021). https://irp.nih.gov/catalyst/29/2/from-the-annals-of-nih-history.

36 Publication data were collected from Web of Science and Dimensions databases using the Organisation for Economic Co-Operation and Development's Frascati Manual 2015 classification system. We included publications in the fields of Natural Sciences, Engineering and Technology, Medical and Health Sciences, and Agricultural Sciences, while excluding Social Sciences and the Humanities. The dataset was further refined to include only publications affiliated with U.S. universities. The Frascati Manual, available at https://www.oecd.org/en/publications/2015/10/frascati-manual-2015_g1g57dcb.html, provides standardised

classifications for research activities, and it has been maintained by the OECD's National Experts on Science and Technology Indicators (NESTI) Group since 1963.

37 Specifically, the Humboldtian research university envisioned itself as a centre of fundamental research driven by intellectual curiosity, advocating for the autonomy of researchers to explore topics without the pressure of immediate practical applications.

38 "Bohr's Quadrant" refers to the type of research that is inspired by curiosity but not by usefulness. This contrasts with "Edison's Quadrant," which is inspired by usefulness but not curiosity; "Pasteur's Quadrant" is inspired by both. The quadrants were first introduced by Donald E. Stokes. *Pasteur's Quadrant: Basic Science and Technological Innovation.* Washington, D.C.: Brookings Institution Press, 1997.

39 Bryan Kelly, Dimitris Papanikolaou, Amit Seru, and Matt Taddy. "Measuring Technological Innovation over the Long Run." *American Economic Review: Insights* 3.3 (2021), pp. 303–320.

40 12.7 per cent vs 5.7 per cent for Chemicals, 13.6 per cent vs 6.9 per cent for electrical engineering 13.3 per cent vs 7.4 per cent for computers and communications.

41 This share jumps even further to 52 per cent in the 1980–2000 period.

42 Kelly, Papanikolaou, Seru, and Taddy; see n. 41.

43 Obligations represent federal financial commitments through both grants and contracts, including amounts for orders placed, contracts awarded, services received, and similar transactions during a given period.

44 David C Mowery. "Defense-Related R&D as a Model for "Grand Challenges"' Technology Policies." *Research Policy* 41.10 (2012), pp. 1703–1715; David C. Mowery. "Military R&D and Innovation." *Handbook of the Economics of Innovation.* Vol. 2. Elsevier, 2010, pp. 1219–1256.

45 American Association for the Advancement of Science. *Historical Trends in Federal R&D: Defense and Nondefense R&D Outlays, 1953–2023.* American Association for the Advancement of Science, 2022. https://www.aaas.org/programs/r-d-budget-and-policy/historical-trends-federal-rd (visited on August 1, 2024).

46 John Alic. *Trillions for Military Technology: How the Pentagon Innovates and Why It Costs so Much.* New York: Springer, 2007.

47 Emerson W. Pugh. *Building IBM: Shaping an Industry and Its Technology.* Cambridge, MA: MIT Press, 2009.

48 The Semi-Automatic Ground Environment (SAGE) air defence system represented one of the era's most ambitious computing initiatives, with costs exceeding those of the Manhattan Project. See Kent C. Redmond and Thomas M Smith. *From Whirlwind to MITRE: The R&D Story of the SAGE Air Defense Computer.* Cambridge, MA: MIT Press, 2000.

49 Casey Dreier. "An Improved Cost Analysis of the Apollo Program." *Space Policy* 60 (2022); Richard W. Orloff. Apollo by the numbers: A statistical reference (NASA SP-2000-4029). Washington, DC: National Aeronautics and Space Administration, p. 20 (2000).

50 https://en.wikipedia.org/wiki/Apollo_command_and_service_module/

51 Courtney G. Brooks, James M. Grimwood, and Loyd S. Swenson, Jr. *Chariots for Apollo: A History of Manned Lunar Spacecraft.* NASA SP-4205. Washington, D.C.: National Aeronautics and Space Administration, Scientific and Technical Information Branch, 1979.

52 Roger E. Bilstein. *Stages to Saturn: A Technological History of the Apollo/Saturn Launch Vehicle.* Bilstein, R.E., 1996. Stages to Saturn: A Technological History of the Apollo/Saturn Launch Vehicles (Vol. 4206). US Government Printing Office.

Chapter 10

1 This chapter is primarily based on Ashish Arora, Sharon Belenzon, Jungkyu Suh, and Hansen Zhang. *The Rise of Absorptive Research in Corporate America: 1945–1980.* NBER Working Paper 33713. Cambridge, MA: National Bureau of Economic Research, 2025. https://www.nber.org/papers/w33713.

2 Figure 9.1 in the previous chapter.

3 Our panel consists of 2,904 patenting firms from the CRSP database of listed U.S. firms spanning the years 1940 to 1980.

4 Jeho Lee. "Innovation and Strategic Divergence: An Empirical Study of the US Pharmaceutical Industry from 1920 to 1960." *Management Science* 49.2 (2003), pp. 143–159, p. 146.

5 Dubbed the "Waksman Platform," this method involved large arrays of soil samples screened in parallel. Streptomycin itself was dug up from a soil sample on a New Jersey farm. See Kim Lewis. "Recover the Lost Art of Drug Discovery." *Nature* 485.7399 (May 2012), pp. 439–440. https://www.nature.com/articles/485439a (visited on September 22, 2025).

6 Chloromycetin was used to treat typhus, meningitis, and rickettsial diseases. Aureomycin was used to treat pneumonia, typhus, and trachoma. See Chapter 2, Robert Burlingham. *The Odyssey of Modern Drug Research*. Kalamazoo, MI: Upjohn Company, 1951.

7 John Bardeen and Walter H. Brattain. "The Transistor, a Semi-Conductor Triode." *Physical Review* 74.2 (1948), pp. 230–231.

8 Arno A. Penzias and Robert W. Wilson. "A Measurement of Excess Antenna Temperature at 4080 Mc/s." *The Astrophysical Journal* 142 (1965), pp. 419–421.

9 Arthur L. Schawlow and Charles H Townes. "Infrared and Optical Masers." *Physical Review* 112.6 (1958), p. 1940.

10 Jon Gertner. *The Idea Factory: Bell Labs and the Great Age of American Innovation*. New York: Penguin Press, 2012; Richard R. Nelson. "The Link between Science and Invention: The Case of the Transistor." *The Rate and Direction of Inventive Activity: Economic and Social Factors* (1962), pp. 549–583.

11 Ivar Giaever. "Energy Gap in Superconductors Measured by Electron Tunneling." *Physical Review Letters* 5.4 (1960), pp. 147–148.

12 Thomas Haigh. *Charles W. Bachman*. Association for Computing Machinery, 1973. https://amturing.acm.org/award_winners/bachman_9385610.cfm (visited on August 17, 2024).

13 GE Vernova. *Large Boiling Water Reactors*. GE Hitachi Nuclear Energy, 2024. https://www.gevernova.com/nuclear/carbon-free-power/large-reactors (visited on August 13, 2024).

14 James W. Cooley and John W. Tukey. "An Algorithm for the Machine Calculation of Complex Fourier Series." *Mathematics of Computation* 19.90 (1965), pp. 297–301.

15 Grady Booch. *John Backus*. Association for Computing Machinery, 1977. https://amturing.acm.org/award_winners/backus_0703524.cfm (visited on August 17, 2024).

16 Keith Smillie. *Kenneth E. Iverson*. Association for Computing Machinery, 1979. https://amturing.acm.org/award_winners/iverson_9147499.cfm (visited on August 17, 2024).

17 T. Noyes and W. E. Dickinson. "Engineering Design of a Magnetic-Disk Random-Access Memory." *Proceedings of the Western Joint Computer Conference*. American Institute of Electrical Engineers, February 1956, pp. 42–44.

18 Horst Feistel. *Cryptographic Coding for Data-Bank Privacy*. Research Report RC-2827. IBM Thomas J. Watson Research Center, 1973.

19 Richard R. Nelson and Richard N. Langlois. "Industrial Innovation Policy: Lessons from American History." *Science* 219.4586 (1983), pp. 814–818.

20 We analyse recipients of the Nobel Prizes, the National Medals of Science, and Turing Awards.

21 Wesley M. Cohen and Daniel A. Levinthal. "Innovation and Learning: The Two Faces of R&D." *The Economic Journal* 99.397 (1989), pp. 569–596.

22 M. Hess and R. F. Kratz. "Axial Dispersion of Polymer Molecules in Gel Permeation Chromatography." *Journal of Polymer Science Part A-2: Polymer Physics* 4.5 (1966), pp. 731–743.

23 J. H. Simons, D. I. Randall, and S. Archer. "Hydrogen Fluoride as a Condensing Agent. VII. The Acylation of Aromatic Compounds." *Journal of the American Chemical Society* 61.7 (1939), pp. 1795–1796.

24 P. P. Mccellan. "Melamine Preparation." *Industrial & Engineering Chemistry* 32.9 (1940), pp. 1181–1186.

25 David Mowery and Nathan Rosenberg. *Paths of Innovation : Technological Change in 20th-Century America*. Cambridge, MA: Cambridge University Press, 1998.

26 *National Biscuit Company (Nabisco) Annual Reports*. 1960. https://archive.org/details/nationalbiscuitcompanynabiscoannualreports/nationalbiscuit1960/ (visited on December 21, 2024).

27 M.R.D.J. Maveety. "Correlation of Keeping Properties of Shortening with Keeping Quality of Biscuits." *Quartermaster Corps Manual, Committee on Food Research, Subsistence Research and Development Laboratory, Deterioration of Fats and Oils* (1945), p. 136.

28 E. G. White, M. Murray, and D. J. Maveety. "The Change in Thiamin Content of Breakfast Cereals during Cooking." *Journal of the American Dietetic Association* 22.2 (1946), pp. 770–771.

29 R. P. Smith. "Report on Sugars in Baked Products." *Journal of Association of Official Agricultural Chemists* 35.3 (August 1, 1952), pp. 682–686.

30 Arora, Belenzon, Suh, and Zhang; see n. 1.

31 Nathan Rosenberg. "Why Do Firms Do Basic Research (with Their Own Money)?": *Research Policy* 19.2 (1990), pp. 165–174, p. 170.

32 Bryan Kelly, Dimitris Papanikolaou, Amit Seru, and Matt Taddy. "Measuring Technological Innovation over the Long Run." *American Economic Review: Insights* 3.3 (2021), pp. 303–320.
33 Schawlow and Townes; see n. 9.
34 New York-Presbyterian. *It Happened Here: The Ruby Laser.* March 30, 2017. https://healthmatters.nyp.org/ruby-laser/.
35 Joan Lisa. Bromberg. *Fusion: Science, Politics, and the Invention of a New Energy Source.* Cambridge, MA: MIT Press, 1982, p. 98.
36 The variables are derived from IRS Statistics of Income data and were obtained through Spencer Y Kwon, Yueran Ma, and Kaspar Zimmermann. "100 Years of Rising Corporate Concentration." *American Economic Review* 114.7 (2024), pp. 2111–2140. The asset shares are calculated for BEA subsectors, which are similar to two-digit SICs.
37 Kwon, Ma, and Zimmermann; see n. 36.
38 M. D. Fagen, ed. *A History of Engineering and Science in the Bell System, Volume 1: The Early Years (1875–1925).* New York: Bell Telephone Laboratories, 1975.
39 Martin Watzinger, Thomas A. Fackler, Markus Nagler, and Monika Schnitzer. "How Antitrust Enforcement Can Spur Innovation: Bell Labs and the 1956 Consent Decree." *American Economic Journal: Economic Policy* 12.4 (November 2020), pp. 328–359. https://www.aeaweb.org/articles?id=10.1257/pol.20190086 (visited on December 23, 2024).
40 Margaret B. W. Graham. *The Business of Research: RCA and the VideoDisc.* Cambridge, MA: Cambridge University Press, 1988. 274 pp.
41 Hyungsub Choi. "The Boundaries of Industrial Research: Making Transistors at RCA, 1948–1960." *Technology and Culture* 48.4 (2007), pp. 758–782.
42 Office of Management and Budget. *Historical Tables—OMB —the White House.* Washington, D.C.: The White House, 2025. https://www.whitehouse.gov/omb/informationresources/budget/historical-tables/, Total federal outlays on defence hovered around 60 percent during this period.
43 RCA Laboratories. *Annual Research Report Collections, RCA David Sarnoff Research Center, David Sarnoff Library Digital Archive (Accession AVD.2464.001).* Hagley Museum & Library, Wilmington, DEL 19807.
44 Leonid Kogan, Dimitris Papanikolaou, Amit Seru, and Noah Stoffman. "Technological Innovation, Resource Allocation, and Growth." *The Quarterly Journal of Economics* 132.2 (2017), pp. 665–712.
45 Robert Sobel. *RCA.* New York: Stein and Day, 1986.
46 Alfred D. Chandler. *Inventing the Electronic Century: The Epic Story of the Consumer Electronics and Computer Industries, With a New Preface.* Harvard Studies in Business History. Cambridge, MA: Harvard University Press, 2005. p. 35.
47 A. H. Guenther, H. R. Kressel, and W. F. Krupke. "Epiloge: The Laser Now and in the Future." *The Laser in America, 1950–1970.* Cambridge, MA: MIT Press, 1991, pp. 228–248.
48 The Videodisc was a Capacitance Electronic Disc that used a needle to read audiovisual information. During the 1970s, it was the largest research project at the labs, and it consumed approximately half of all lab resources. Its launch in 1981 failed against competing products by Japanese VCR manufacturers. The concept proposal to use lasers as data pickups was later commercialised by Philips and Sony in their invention of the optical Compact Disc (CD). See Graham, n. 40.
49 Michael Ettenberg. *First-Hand:Apple, RCA and the Visionaries.* Engineering and Technology History Wiki (ETHW). 2015. https://ethw.org/First-Hand:Apple,_RCA_and_the_Visionaries (visited on June 16, 2023).
50 Corroborated through individual interviews with Henry Kressel, vice president of solid-state research at RCA labs.
51 Philip E. Auerswald and Lewis M. E. Branscomb. "Reflections on Mansfield, Technological Complexity, and the 'Golden Age' of US Corporate R&D." *The Journal of Technology Transfer* 30 (2004), pp. 139–157; Wesley M. Cohen and Daniel A. Levinthal. "Absorptive Capacity: A New Perspective on Learning and Innovation." *Administrative Science Quarterly* 35.1 (1990), pp. 128–152; Rosenberg; see n. 31.
52 Ashish Arora, Andrea Fosfuri, and Alfonso Gambardella. "Markets for Technology and Their Implications for Corporate Strategy". *Industrial and Corporate Change* 10.2 (2001), pp. 419–451; Ashish Arora, Andrea Fosfuri, and Alfonso Gambardella. *Markets for Technology: The Economics of Innovation and Corporate Strategy.* MIT Press, 2004; Ashish Arora, Sharon

Belenzon, Andrea Patacconi, and Jungkyu Suh. "The Changing Structure of American Innovation: Some Cautionary Remarks for Economic Growth." *Innovation Policy and the Economy* 20.1 (2020), pp. 39–93; Ashish Arora, Sharon Belenzon, and Jungkyu Suh. "Science and the Market for Technology." *Management Science* 68.10 (2022), pp. 7176–7201.

53 Wikipedia contributors. *SRI International.* Wikipedia, 2025. https://en.wikipedia.org/wiki/SRI_International.

54 Ashish Arora, Sharon Belenzon, Larisa C Cioaca, Lia Sheer, and Hansen Zhang. "The Effect of Public Science on Corporate R&D". Working Paper Series 31899 (November 2023). http://www.nber.org/papers/w31899; National Science Foundation. *Business Research and Development and Innovation: 2019.* 2019. https://ncses.nsf.gov/pubs/nsf22343 (visited on January 21, 2025); Mark Boroush. *National Patterns of R&D Resources: 2018–19 Data Update.* 2021. https://ncses.nsf.gov/pubs/nsf21325 (visited on May 6, 2024); Ashish Arora, Sharon Belenzon, and Andrea Patacconi. "The Decline of Science in Corporate R&D." *Strategic Management Journal* 39.1 (2018), pp. 3–32.

Chapter 11

1 Ashish Arora, Sharon Belenzon, Andrea Patacconi, and Jungkyu Suh. "The Changing Structure of American Innovation: Some Cautionary Remarks for Economic Growth." *Innovation Policy and the Economy* 20.1 (2020), pp. 39–93.

2 462,870 doctorates are found in the NSF's Survey of Doctorate Recipients in 1993, of which 119,140 are listed in AMWS. In 2013, SDR recorded 720,800 active doctorates; AMWS listed 188,666.

3 R&D spending has been deflated to 2017 using the Federal Reserve Economic Database.

4 Arora et al.; see n 1.

5 Ashish Arora, Sharon Belenzon, and Lia Sheer. "Back to Basics: Why Do Firms Invest in Research?" (February 2017). http://www.nber.org/papers/w23187 (visited on February 20, 2019).

6 Calculations based on data we compiled on Compustat firms matched to Clarivate Web of Science and EPO Patstat.

7 However, AT&T's R&D budget fell even more drastically, from $4,083 million in 1995 to $640 million in 1996, when it spun off Bell Labs to Lucent Technologies. As a result, AT&T's papers normalised by R&D expenditures rose.

8 Ashish Arora, Sharon Belenzon, and Lia Sheer. "Knowledge Spillovers and Corporate Investment in Scientific Research." *American Economic Review* 111.3 (2021), pp. 871–898.

9 Wesley M. Cohen, Richard R. Nelson, and John P. Walsh. "Links and Impacts: The Influence of Public Research on Industrial R&D." *Management Science* 48.1 (2002), pp. 1–23.

10 Pierre Azoulay. "Do Pharmaceutical Sales Respond to Scientific Evidence?". *Journal of Economics & Management Strategy* 11.4 (2002), pp. 551–594; Diana Hicks. "Published Papers, Tacit Competencies and Corporate Management of the Public/Private Character of Knowledge." *Industrial and Corporate Change* 4.2 (1995), pp. 401–424.

11 Stephen A. Merrill. *Righting the Research Imbalance.* The Center for Innovation Policy at Duke Law, 2018. https://law.duke.edu/sites/default/files/centers/cip/CIPWhite-Paper_Righting-the-Research-Imbalance.pdf.

12 Cyrus C. M. Mody. "The Diverse Ecology of Electronic Materials." *Cahiers François Viète* III-2 (III-2 June 1, 2017), pp. 217–241.

13 The firm's assessment was based on two internal "extendibility studies" that assessed the competitiveness of a potential Josephson junction chip against various silicon-based chips. IBM's conclusions have been vindicated, as superconducting computers have yet to find widespread market adoption.

14 Ajay Bhaskarabhatla and Deepak Hegde. "An Organizational Perspective on Patenting and Open Innovation." *Organization Science* 25.6 (2014), pp. 1744–1763.

15 McGroddy interview (2011) as quoted in Bhaskarabhatla and Hegde; see n. 14.

16 Ross Knox Bassett. *To the Digital Age: Research Labs, Start-up Companies, and the Rise of MOS Technology.* Johns Hopkins Studies in the History of Technology. Baltimore: Johns Hopkins University Press, 2002.

17 Ashish Arora, Sharon Belenzon, Larisa Cioaca, Lia Sheer, Hyunmoh Shin, and Dror Shvadron. *DISCERN 2.0: Duke Innovation & SCientific Enterprises Research Network.* Zenodo, 2024. https://doi.org/10.5281/zenodo.3594642.

[18] David Hounshell and John Kenly Smith, Jr. *Science and Corporate Strategy: DuPont R&D, 1902–1980*. Cambridge, UK: Cambridge University Press, 1988, p. 9.

[19] DuPont Merck focused on medical imaging products such as Cardiolite, a heart-imaging agent that is the best-selling radiopharmaceutical; Quadramet for palliation of bone pain; and Miraluma, a breast imaging agent based on Cardiolite. The company also developed ultrasound contrast agents such as DMP-115, in collaboration with ImaRx Pharmaceutical of Tucson. The radiopharmaceuticals business contributes about one-third of DuPont Merck's earnings, according to the company. See Diagnostic Imaging Staff. "DuPont to Buy out Merck Stake in Pharmaceutical Joint Venture." *Diagnostic Imaging* (May 27, 1998). https://www.diagnosticimaging.com/view/dupont-buy-out-merck-stake-pharmaceutical-joint-venture

[20] Institutional Investor Staff. "Former Chemical Giant DuPont Attempts to Reinvent Itself Once More." *Institutional Investor* (June 13, 2024). https://www.institutionalinvestor.com/article/2bsup25m3wdeka2j3vchs/portfolio/former-chemical-giant-dupont-attempts-to-reinvent-itself-once-more.

[21] See, for instance, Ashish Arora and Alfonso Gambardella. "Evolution of Industry Structure in the Chemical Industry." *Chemicals and Long-term Economic Growth: Insights from the Chemical Industry*. Ed. by Ashish Arora, Ralph Landau, and Nathan Rosenberg. New York: John Wiley & Sons, 1998, pp. 379–413.

[22] Marc S. Reisch. "DuPont Gets an Overhaul." *Chemical & Engineering News* 80.15 (April 15, 2002), pp. 22–27.

[23] Alexander H. Tullo. "Why DuPont Shrunk Its Central Research Unit." *Chemical & Engineering News* (January 21, 2016). https://cen.acs.org/articles/94/i4/DuPont-Shrunk-Central-Research-Unit.html (visited on January 20, 2025).

[24] James D. Adams. "Fundamental Stocks of Knowledge and Productivity Growth." *Journal of Political Economy* 98.4 (1990), pp. 673–702.

[25] Rachelle C. Sampson and Yuan Shi. "Are U.S. Firms Becoming More Short-Term Oriented? Evidence of Shifting Firm Time Horizons from Implied Discount Rates, 1980–2013." *Strategic Management Journal* 44.1 (2023), pp. 231–263. https://onlinelibrary.wiley.com/doi/abs/10.1002/smj.3158 (visited on October 19, 2024).

[26] Yuan Shi, Rachelle C. Sampson, Brent Goldfarb, and Rafael A. Corredoira. *The Changing Nature of Firm R&D: Short-termism & Influential Innovation in US Firms*. March 18, 2022. Pre-published.

[27] Elia Ferracuti, Kevin Standridge, and Rahul Vashishtha. "Hedge Fund Activism and the Retreat from Corporate Science." 2025.

[28] In 2023, DeepMind reported a modest profit. However, its revenue of nearly $2 billion was from performing R&D for Alphabet.

[29] The quote is from Andrew Odlyzko. "The Decline of Unfettered Research." Unpublished, University of Minnesota, *http://www.dtc.umn.edu/~odlyzko/doc/decline.txt* (1995).

[30] Arora, Belenzon, and Sheer "Knowledge Spillovers and Corporate Investment in Scientific Research"; see n. 8.

[31] Arora, Belenzon, and Sheer. "Knowledge Spillovers and Corporate Investment in Scientific Research"; see n. 8.

[32] Larry H. P. Lang and René M. Stulz. "Tobin's q, Corporate Diversification, and Firm Performance." *Journal of Political Economy* 102.6 (1994), pp. 1248–1280; Philip G. Berger and Eli Ofek. "Diversification's Effect on Firm Value." *Journal of Financial Economics*. Symposium on Corporate Focus 37.1 (January 1, 1995), pp. 39–65.

[33] Richard R Nelson. "The Simple Economics of Basic Scientific Research." *Journal of Political Economy* 67.3 (1959), pp. 297–306.

[34] Federica Coelli, Andreas Moxnes, and Karen Helene Ulltveit-Moe. "Better, Faster, Stronger: Global Innovation and Trade Liberalization." *The Review of Economics and Statistics* 104.2 (March 1, 2022), pp. 205–216.

[35] World Trade Organization. *Evolution of Trade under the WTO*. https://www.wto.org/english/res_e/statis_e/trade_evolution_e/evolution_trade_wto_e.htm.

[36] Wesley M. Cohen and Steven Klepper. "A Reprise of Size and R&D." *The Economic Journal* 106.437 (1996), pp. 925–951; Ashish Arora, Wesley Cohen, Honggi Lee, and Divya Sebastian. "Invention Value, Inventive Capability and the Large Firm Advantage." *Research Policy* 52.1 (January 1, 2023), p. 104650.

37 Chan Kim. "From Research to Development: How Globalization Shapes Corporate Innovation," 2024.
38 Sharon Belenzon and Larisa Cioaca. "Guaranteed Demand and Corporate R&D." *Management Science* (August 6, 2025).
39 We examine these developments in greater detail in the following chapter.
40 Gino Cattani. "Preadaptation, Firm Heterogeneity, and Technological Performance: A Study on the Evolution of Fiber Optics, 1970–1995." *Organization Science* 16.6 (December 2005), pp. 563–580; Gino Cattani. "Technological Pre-Adaptation, Speciation, and Emergence of New Technologies: How Corning Invented and Developed Fiber Optics." *Industrial and Corporate Change* 15.2 (April 1, 2006), pp. 285–318.
41 Alfred Spector, Peter Norvig, and Slav Petrov. "Google's Hybrid Approach to Research." *Communications of the ACM* 55.7 (2012), pp. 34–37.
42 David Tennenhouse. "Intel's Open Collaborative Model of Industry-University Research." *Research-Technology Management* 47.4 (2004), pp. 19–26.
43 See above note.
44 Demis Hassabis. "DeepMind: From Games to Scientific Discovery." *Research-Technology Management* 64.6 (2021), pp. 18–23.
45 *Financial Times*. "DeepMind Slows down Research Releases to Keep Competitive Edge in AI Race." *Financial Times* (Sept. 22, 2025). https://www.ft.com/content/2ee1ffde-008e-4ea4-861b-24f15b25cf54.
46 Andrea Patacconi and Nick Vikander. *Organizing for Moonshots*. SSRN Working Paper. 2025. https://papers.ssrn.com/sol3/papers.cfm?abstract_id=5257044.
47 For evidence on how HP Labs protects its knowledge internally, see also Karen Elliott, Andrea Patacconi, Joseph Swierzbinski, and Julian Williams. "Knowledge Protection in Firms: A Conceptual Framework and Evidence from HP Labs." *European Management Review* 16.1 (2019), pp. 179–193.
48 Douglas K. Smith and Robert C. Alexander. *Fumbling the Future: How Xerox Invented, Then Ignored, the First Personal Computer*. New York: William Morrow, 1988.
49 The metaphor is drawn from Rivette and Kline's 2000 book, which compares underused IP assets to valuable art left forgotten in storage. See Kevin G. Rivette and David Kline. *Rembrandts in the Attic: Unlocking the Hidden Value of Patents*. Boston: Harvard Business Press, 2000.
50 Henry Chesbrough. "Graceful Exits and Missed Opportunities: Xerox's Management of Its Technology Spin-off Organizations." *Business History Review* 76.4 (2002), pp. 803–837; Henry Chesbrough. "The Governance and Performance of Xerox's Technology Spin-off Companies." *Research Policy* 32.3 (2003), pp. 403–421.
51 See Marshall Phelps and David Kline. *Burning the Ships: Transforming Your Company's Culture through Intellectual Property Strategy*. Hoboken, NJ: John Wiley & Sons, 2009.
52 Julia Love. "Google's Moonshot Factory Falls Back Down to Earth." *Bloomberg.com* (May 20, 2024). https://www.bloomberg.com/news/features/2024-05-20/googles-era-of-unrestrained-invention-is-coming-to-an-end (visited on January 22, 2025).

Chapter 12

1 Martin Kenney. "How Venture Capital Became a Component of the US National System of Innovation." *Industrial and Corporate Change* 20.6 (December 1, 2011), pp. 1677–1723.
2 David C. Mowery. "Plus ca Change: Industrial R&D in the 'Third Industrial Revolution.'" *Industrial and Corporate Change* 18.1 (2009), pp. 1–50.
3 Teresa C. Fort, Nathan Goldschlag, Jack Liang, Peter K. Schott, and Nikolas Zolas. *Growth Is Getting Harder to Find, Not Ideas*. CES Working Paper 25-21. U.S. Census Bureau, Center for Economic Studies, April 2025. https://www2.census.gov/library/workingpapers/2025/adrm/ces/CES-WP-25-21.pdf.
4 Interestingly, mega firms' share of breakthrough patents exhibits a U-shaped pattern over time: The share is larger in the 1970s and 2000s, but smaller in the 1980s and 1990s.
5 Fred Block and Matthew R. Keller. "Where Do Innovations Come from? Transformations in the US Economy, 1970–2006." *Socio-Economic Review* 7.3 (2009), pp. 459–483.
6 The concept of open innovation is frequently associated with seminal work by Henry Chesbrough: Henry William Chesbrough. *Open Innovation: The New Imperative for Creating and Profiting from Technology*. Cambridge, MA: Harvard Business Press, 2003. Other seminal contributions emphasising the importance of customers and lead-users to innovation include Eric

Von Hippel. See Eric Von Hippel. *Democratizing Innovation.* Cambridge, MA: MIT Press, 2006.

7 Ashish Arora, Wesley M. Cohen, and John P. Walsh. "The Acquisition and Commercialization of Invention in American Manufacturing: Incidence and Impact." *Research Policy* 45.6 (July 1, 2016), pp. 1113–1128.

8 Mark Dodgson, David Gann, and Ammon Salter. "The Role of Technology in the Shift towards Open Innovation: The Case of Procter & Gamble." *R&D Management* 36.3 (2006), pp. 333–346; Larry Huston and Nabil Sakkab. "Connect and Develop." *Harvard Business Review* 84.3 (2006), pp. 58–66.

9 The Census Enterprise Statistics Program (ESP), from which the 2011 figures are obtained, was discontinued after 2012.

10 Carol A. Robbins. "Measuring Payments for the Supply and Use of Intellectual Property." *International Trade in Services and Intangibles in the Era of Globalization.* University of Chicago Press, 2009, pp. 139–171.

11 The calculations are based on data from the USPTO Patent Assignment Dataset, replicating cleaning procedures in Serrano (2010) to identify patent reassignments that qualify as market transactions. See Stuart J. H. Graham, Alan C. Marco, and Amanda F. Myers. "Patent Transactions in the Marketplace: Lessons from the USPTO Patent Assignment Dataset." *Journal of Economics & Management Strategy* 27.3 (2018), pp. 343–371 and Carlos J Serrano. "The Dynamics of the Transfer and Renewal of Patents." *The RAND Journal of Economics* 41.4 (2010), pp. 686–708.

12 Robbins; see n. 10.

13 U.S. General Accounting Office. *Technology Transfer: Administration of the Bayh-dole Act by Research Universities.* GAO Report GAO/RCED-98-126. Washington, D.C.: United States General Accounting Office, May 7, 1998. https://www.gao.gov/assets/rced-98-126.pdf, p. 3.

14 Ashish Arora, Sharon Belenzon, and Jungkyu Suh. "Science and the Market for Technology." *Management Science* 68.10 (2022), pp. 7176–7201.

15 In current terms, AUTM data cited by the NSF's Science & Engineering Indicators from 2016 (Appendix Table 5–68) and 2000 (Text Table 6-11) reported university gross royalties at $130 million in 1991 and $1088.5 in 2004. The dollar values are deflated to 2017. See National Science Board. *Science and Engineering Indicators 2000.* NSB-00-1. Arlington, VA: National Science Foundation, 2000. https://www.nsf.gov/statistics/seind00/; National Science Board. *Science and Engineering Indicators 2016.* NSB-2016-1. Arlington, VA: National Science Foundation, 2016. https://www.nsf.gov/statistics/2016/nsb20161/.

16 David C. Mowery and Arvids A. Ziedonis. "Numbers, Quality, and Entry: How Has the Bayh–Dole Act Affected U.S. University Patenting and Licensing?": *Innovation Policy and the Economy, Volume 1.* Ed. by Adam B. Jaffe, Josh Lerner, and Scott Stern. Cambridge, MA: MIT Press, 2001, pp. 187–220.

17 Shira Boss-Bicak. "Moving Ideas off Campus." *The New York Times* (October 28, 2004). https://www.nytimes.com/2004/10/28/business/moving-ideas-off-campus.html.

18 Richard J. Green and Wil Lepkowski. "A Forgotten Model for Purposeful Science." *Issues in Science and Technology* 22.2 (Win. 2006).

19 Washington Correspondent. "RANN Cut down to Size." *Nature* 231 (May 1971), p. 8.

20 National Science Board. *A History in Highlights: 1950–2000.* NSB 00–215. Arlington, VA: National Science Foundation, 2000. https://www.nsf.gov/nsb/documents/2000/nsb00215/nsb50/1970/cmpt_priority.html, p. 18.

21 Jocelyn Kaiser. "NIH Budget Reaches Doubling Point." *Science* (Jan. 25, 2002). https://www.science.org/content/article/nih-budget-reaches-doubling-point.

22 Association of University Technology Managers (AUTM). *FY2018 U.S. Licensing Survey: Key Findings.* Press Release, 11 February 2020. https://autm.net/AUTM/media/About-AUTM/Documents/AUTM_FY2018_US_Licensing_Survey_PR_11FEB2020-FNL.pdf.

23 Charles E. Eesley and William F. Miller. *Impact: Stanford University's Economic Impact via Innovation and Entrepreneurship.* October 16, 2017. https://papers.ssrn.com/abstract=2227460 (visited on August 19, 2025). Pre-published, p. 6.

24 Walter D. Valdivia. *University Start-ups: Critical for Improving Technology Transfer.* Policy Brief. Brookings Institution, Center for Technology Innovation, November 2013. https://www.brookings.edu/wp-content/uploads/2016/06/Valdivia_Tech-Transfer_v29_No-Embargo.pdf.

25 University of California, Office of the President. *Annual Report FY 2011: Innovation and Accountability Series.* Annual Report. University of California, Office of the President, June 2011. https://www.ucop.edu/innovation-transfer-operations/_files/annualreports/

IASRptFY11.pdf; Harvard Office of Technology Development. *Driving Innovation toward Impact: Impact Report FY2024.* Impact Report. Harvard University, August 2024. https://otd.harvard.edu/uploads/Files/OTDImpactReport_081924.pdf; Duke Office for Translation and Commercialization. *Duke Inventions Returned $102 Million to Inventors and the University in FY23. Duke OTC News.* October 2024. https://otc.duke.edu/news/duke-inventions-returned-102-million-to-inventors-and-the-university-infy23/.

26 Sharon Belenzon and Mark Schankerman. "University Knowledge Transfer: Private Ownership, Incentives, and Local Development Objectives." *The Journal of Law and Economics* 52.1 (2009), pp. 111–144.

27 David L. Chandler. "*3 questions: Lita Nelsen and the Technology Licensing Office.*" *MIT News.* November 7, 2014. https://news.mit.edu/2014/3-questions-lita-nelsentechnology-licensing-office-1107.

28 Stanford Office of Technology Licensing. *Annual Report for Fiscal Year 2023–2024: Bridging to Impact.* Annual Report. Stanford University, June 2025. https://otl.stanford.edu/sites/g/files/sbiybj16766/files/media/file/stanford-otl-ar-fy2024_final.pdf.

29 Ross C. DeVol, Armen Bedroussian, Anna Babayan, Meggy Frye, et al. *Mind-to-market: A Global Analysis of University Biotechnology Transfer and Commercialization.* Research Report. Milken Institute, September 2006. https://thetechnocratictyranny.com/PDFS/Milken_Mind_to_Market_2006.pdf.

30 Israel Innovation Authority. *A Global Comparison: High-tech in Israel Relies Almost Entirely on the Private Sector, and Primarily on Foreign Investors. Israel Innovation Authority website.* 2023. https://innovationisrael.org.il/en/report/a-global-comparison/.

31 In Germany's case, this reform was accompanied with a federal subsidy for universities that did not have well-developed tech transfer offices. See p. 5. Dirk Czarnitzki, Thorsten Doherr, Katrin Hussinger, Paula Schliessler, and Andrew A. Toole. *Individual versus Institutional Ownership of University-Discovered Inventions.* Centre for European Economic Research (ZEW), December 2014. https://www.zew.de/en/publications/individual-versusinstitutional-ownership-of-university-discovered-inventions.

32 Hans K. Hvide and Benjamin F Jones. "University Innovation and the Professor"s Privilege." *American Economic Review* 108.7 (2018), pp. 1860–1898.

33 Sidonia von Ledebur, Guido Buenstorf, and Martin Hummel. *University Patenting in Germany before and after 2002: What Role Did the Professors' Privilege Play?* 2009–068. Jena Economics Research Papers, Friedrich-Schiller-University Jena, 2009. https://www.econstor.eu/bitstream/10419/32594/1/610738410.pdf.

34 L. L. Ouellette and A. Tutt. "How Do Patent Incentives Affect University Researchers?" Working Paper. 2019.

35 H. Sauermann and W. M. Cohen. "What Makes Them Tick? Employee Motives and Firm Innovation." *Management Science* 56.12 (2010), pp. 2134–2153.

36 Wesley Cohen, Richard Florida, Lucien Randazzese, and John Walsh. "Industry and the Academy: Uneasy Partners in the Cause of Technological Advance." *Challenges to Research Universities.* Ed. by Roger Noll. Washington, D.C.: Brookings Institution Press, 1998, pp. 171–199.

37 Cohen, Florida, Randazzese, and Walsh; see n. 36, p. 182.

38 MIT News Office. *IBM and MIT to Pursue Joint Research in Artificial Intelligence, Establish New MIT-IBM Watson AI Lab.* September 7, 2017. https://news.mit.edu/2017/ibmmit-joint-research-watson-artificial-intelligence-lab-0907.

39 MIT-IBM Watson AI Lab. *About – MIT-IBM Watson AI Lab.* https://mitibmwatsonailab.mit.edu/about/.

40 David Tennenhouse. "Intel's Open Collaborative Model of Industry-University Research." *Research-Technology Management* 47.4 (2004), pp. 19–26.

41 Wikipedia contributors. *Intel Research Lablets.* https://en.wikipedia.org/wiki/Intel_Research_Lablets.

42 Intel Corporation. *Intel Labs Programs and Partnerships.* 2025. https://www.intel.com/content/www/us/en/research/partnerships.html.

43 Kristen Bole. *UCSF Partners with Pfizer to Improve Drug Discovery, Development.* November 16, 2010. https://www.ucsf.edu/news/2010/11/98181/ucsf-partners-pfizer-improve-drug-discovery-development.

44 Google AI Blog. *Improving the Accuracy of Genomic Analysis with DeepVariant 1.0. Google AI Blog.* September 2020. https://research.google/blog/improving-the-accuracy-ofgenomic-analysis-with-deepvariant-10/.

45 Ashish Arora, Sharon Belenzon, Larisa Cioaca, Lia Sheer, Hyunmoh Shin, and Dror Shvadron. *DISCERN 2.0: Duke Innovation & Scientific Enterprises Research Network.* Zenodo, 2024. https://doi.org/10.5281/zenodo.3594642.

46 Dror Shvadron. Bread upon the Waters: Corporate Science and the Benefits from Follow-on Public Research. 2025. arXiv preprint arXiv:2512.04400.

47 See Josh Lerner and Ramana Nanda. "Venture Capital's Role in Financing Innovation: What We Know and How Much We Still Need to Learn." *Journal of Economic Perspectives* 34.3 (2020), pp. 237–261; Joshua Lerner. *The Architecture of Innovation : The Economics of Creative Organizations.* Oxford: Oxford University Press, 2012.

48 Daniel C. Fehder, Naomi Hausman, and Yael V. Hochberg. "Innovation and Capital." *Journal of Financial Economics* 169 (July 1, 2025), p. 104029.

49 Samuel Kortum and Josh Lerner. "Assessing the Contribution of Venture Capital to Innovation." *The RAND Journal of Economics* 31.4 (2000), pp. 674–692.

50 Lerner and Nanda; see n. 47.

51 Manju Puri and Rebecca Zarutskie. "On the Life Cycle Dynamics of Venture-Capital- and Non-Venture-Capital-Financed Firms." *The Journal of Finance* 67.6 (2012), pp. 2247–2293. https://onlinelibrary.wiley.com/doi/abs/10.1111/j.1540-6261.2012.01786.x.

52 Shai Bernstein, Xavier Giroud, and Richard R. Townsend. "The Impact of Venture Capital Monitoring." *The Journal of Finance* 71.4 (2016), pp. 1591–1622.

53 Roelof Botha. *The Sequoia Capital Fund: Patient Capital for Building Enduring Companies. Sequoia Capital website.* October 26, 2021. https://www.sequoiacap.com/article/the-sequoia-fund-patient-capital-for-building-enduring-companies/.

54 Lerner and Nanda; see n. 47.

55 Matt Marx, Lia Sheer, and Honggi Lee. "The Changing Role of Scientific Discovery in VC-backed Startups in the U.S. Innovation Ecosystem." 2025.

56 U.S. Small Business Administration, America's Seed Fund. *About SBIR and STTR.* 2025. https://www.sbir.gov/about.

57 Kyle R. Myers, Lauren Lanahan, and Evan E. Johnson. "Small Business Innovation Applied to National Needs." *Entrepreneurship and Innovation Policy and the Economy, Volume 5.* Chicago: University of Chicago Press, 2025.

58 Myers, Lanahan, and Johnson; see n. 57.

59 Sabrina T. Howell. "Financing Innovation: Evidence from R&D Grants." *American Economic Review* 107.4 (2017), pp. 1136–1164.

60 For comprehensive discussions of corporate venturing and its role in spurring innovation, see, for instance, Marco Ceccagnoli. "Corporate Venture Capital and the Markets for Technology." *The Palgrave Encyclopedia of Private Equity.* New York: Springer, 2025, pp. 233–238 and Lerner; see n. 47.

61 Gary Dushnitsky and Dovev Lavie. "How Alliance Formation Shapes Corporate Venture Capital Investment in the Software Industry: A Resource-based Perspective." *Strategic Entrepreneurship Journal* 4.1 (2010), pp. 22–48.

62 Arthur D. Little. *Unleashing the Power of Corporate Venture Capital. Viewpoint, Arthur D. Little.* February 2025. https://www.adlittle.com/en/insights/viewpoints/unleashing-power-corporate-venture-capital.

63 Ashish Arora and Alfonso Gambardella. "Evaluating Technological Information and Utilizing It: Scientific Knowledge, Technological Capability, and External Linkages in Biotechnology." *Journal of Economic Behavior and Organization* 24.1 (1994), pp. 91–114.

64 Thomas J. Chemmanur, Elena Loutskina, and Xuan Tian. "Corporate Venture Capital, Value Creation, and Innovation." *The Review of Financial Studies* 27.8 (2014), pp. 2434–2473. https://www.jstor.org/stable/24465662 (visited on August 19, 2025).

65 Michael Gofman and Zhao Jin. *Artificial Intelligence, Education, and Entrepreneurship.* July 31, 2022. https://papers.ssrn.com/abstract=3449440 (visited on August 19, 2025). Pre-published.

66 Ashish Arora, Sharon Belenzon, and Andrea Patacconi. "A Theory of the US Innovation Ecosystem: Evolution and the Social Value of Diversity." *Industrial and Corporate Change* 28.2 (2019), pp. 289–307.

Chapter 13

1 NASA purchased 60 per cent of America's entire output of integrated circuits in the early 1960s, according to Piers Bizony. "Apollo Technology: Back to the Future." *ASK Magazine* 36 (Aut. 2009). https://appel.nasa.gov/wp-content/uploads/2013/05/NASA_APPEL_ASK_36i_apollo_technology.pdf.

2 Data were collected using the Advanced Search feature on USAspending.gov. *Businesses* include recipient types "Small Business" and "Other Than Small Business." *R&D contracts* include product or service code "Research and development." *Production contracts* include product or service codes "Service" and "Product." *Grants* include award types "Project grants" and "Cooperative agreements."

3 Sharon Belenzon and Larisa Cioaca. "Guaranteed Demand and Corporate R&D." *Management Science* (August 6, 2025).

4 GlobalSecurity.org. *HAVE BLUE–Experimental Survivable Testbed (XST)*. July 7, 2011. https://www.globalsecurity.org/military/systems/aircraft/have-blue.htm (visited on September 20, 2025).

5 Anthropic PBC. *Offering Expanded Claude Access across All Three Branches of the U.S. Government*. August 12, 2025. https://www.anthropic.com/news/offering-expandedclaude-access-across-all-three-branches-of-government (visited on September 20, 2025).

6 Anthropic PBC. *Anthropic and the Department of Defense to Advance Responsible AI in Defense Operations*. July 14, 2025. https://www.anthropic.com/news/anthropicand-the-department-of-defense-to-advance-responsible-ai-in-defense-operations (visited on September 20, 2025).

7 Ashish Arora, Sharon Belenzon, Larisa Cioaca, and Elia Ferracuti. *The Private Value of Innovating for the Government*. Working Paper 33880. National Bureau of Economic Research, May 2025. https://www.nber.org/papers/w33880.

8 Larisa Cioaca. "Government R&D Contracts as Platforms for Experimentation." 2025.

9 https://en.wikipedia.org/wiki/High-electron-mobility_transistor.

10 Robert R. Hayes and Harry Wang. "A Subcompact Q Enhanced Active Hydrogen Maser." *Proceedings of the 18th Annual Precise Time and Time Interval Systems and Applications Meeting*, 1986, pp. 611–620.

11 Linda (Linda M.) Weiss. *America Inc.?: Innovation and Enterprise in the National Security State*. Cornell Studies in Political Economy. Ithaca, NY: Cornell University Press, 2014.

12 U.S. General Services Administration. *GSA FAS GWAC Sales Dashboard*. May 30, 2025. https://d2d.gsa.gov/report/gsa-fas-gwac-sales-dashboard (visited on May 30, 2025).

13 National Research Council. *Funding a Revolution: Government Support for Computing Research*. Washington, DC: National Academies Press, 1999. https://doi.org/10.17226/6323.

14 The Defense Science Board Task Force on Globalization and Security noted in their 1999 Final Report that the DoD was "relying increasingly on the U.S. commercial advanced technology sector to push the technological envelope and enable the Department to 'run faster' than its competitors" (p. 27). Defense Science Board. *Final Report of the Defense Science Board Task Force on Globalization and Security*. Washington, DC: Office of the Under Secretary of Defense for Acquisition and Technology, December 1999.

15 Ashish Arora, Sharon Belenzon, and Andrea Patacconi. "The Decline of Science in Corporate R&D." *Strategic Management Journal* 39.1 (2018), pp. 3–32.

16 Emily G. Blevins, Alice B. Grossman, and Karen M. Sutter. *Frequently Asked Questions: CHIPS Act of 2022 Provisions and Implementation*. CRS Report R47523. Washington, D.C.: Congressional Research Service, April 2023.

17 https://www.nasa.gov/artemis-partners/.

18 David C. Mowery, Richard R. Nelson, and Ben R. Martin. "Technology Policy and Global Warming: Why New Policy Models Are Needed (or Why Putting New Wine in Old Bottles Won't Work)." *Research Policy* 39.8 (October 1, 2010), pp. 1011–1023. https://www.sciencedirect.com/science/article/pii/S0048733310001320 (visited on September 21, 2025).

19 Mowery, Nelson, and Martin; see n. 18, p. 1091.

Chapter 14

1 Karl Marx. *Capital: A Critique of Political Economy. Volume I*. ed. by Friedrich Engels. Trans. by Samuel Moore and Edward Aveling. Moscow: Progress Publishers, 1867.

2 Joseph A. Schumpeter 1883–1950. *Capitalism, Socialism, and Democracy*. New York: Harper, 1950.

3 M. D. Fagen, ed. *A History of Engineering and Science in the Bell System, Volume 2: National Service in War and Peace (1925–1975)*. New York: Bell Telephone Laboratories, 1978.

4 Jon Gertner. *The Idea Factory: Bell Labs and the Great Age of American Innovation*. New York: Penguin, 2013.

5 Douglas Coupland. *The Ghost of Invention: A Visit to Bell Labs*. Wired. 2014-09-29, 2014. https://www.wired.com/2014/09/coupland-bell-labs/ (visited on August 7, 2025).

6 Martin Watzinger, Thomas A. Fackler, Markus Nagler, and Monika Schnitzer. "How Antitrust Enforcement Can Spur Innovation: Bell Labs and the 1956 Consent Decree." *American Economic Journal: Economic Policy* 12.4 (November 2020), pp. 328–359. https://www.aeaweb.org/articles?id=10.1257/pol.20190086 (visited on December 23, 2024).

7 Matt Marx and Aaron Fuegi. "Reliance on Science: Worldwide Front-Page Patent Citations to Scientific Articles." *Strategic Management Journal* 41.9 (2020), pp. 1572–1594.

8 Marx and Fuegi; see n. 7.

9 We focus on scientists with more than twenty publications with Bell Labs who worked for the lab for five years or more.

10 Felix Poege. "Competition and Innovation: The Breakup of Ig Farben." (2022). https://www.jstor.org/stable/pdf/resrep64963.pdf?acceptTC=true&coverpage=false&addFooter=false (visited on March 14, 2025).

11 Raymond G. Stokes. *Opting for Oil: The Political Economy of Technological Change in the West German Chemical Industry, 1945–1961*. New York: Cambridge University Press, 1994.

12 Ashish Arora and Alfonso Gambardella. "Implications for Energy Innovation from the Chemical Industry." *Accelerating Energy Innovation: Insights from Multiple Sectors*. Ed. by Arnulf Grubler and Charlie Wilson. Cambridge: Cambridge University Press, 2011, pp. 145–168.

13 Ajay Bhaskarabhatla and Deepak Hegde. "An Organizational Perspective on Patenting and Open Innovation." *Organization Science* 25.6 (2014), pp. 1744–1763.

14 R. J. Gilbert and A. D. Melamed. "Antitrust for Innovation: A Progress Report." *Antitrust Law Journal* 86.3 (2025).

15 Hyo Kang. "How Does Competition Affect Innovation? Evidence from U.S. Antitrust Cases." *Academy of Management Proceedings* 2019.1 (August 1, 2019), p. 13918.

16 Joshua Krieger, Danielle Li, and Dimitris Papanikolaou. "Missing Novelty in Drug Development." *The Review of Financial Studies* 35.2 (February 1, 2022), pp. 636–679.

17 Colleen Cunningham, Florian Ederer, and Song Ma. "Killer Acquisitions." *Journal of Political Economy* 129.3 (2021), pp. 649–702.

18 Sai Krishna Kamepalli, Raghuram Rajan, and Luigi Zingales. *Kill Zone*. National Bureau of Economic Research, 2020. https://www.nber.org/papers/w27146 (visited on March 14, 2025).

19 Ryan Decker, John Haltiwanger, Ron Jarmin, and Javier Miranda. "The Secular Decline in Business Dynamism in the US." Unpublished draft, University of Maryland 3.2 (2014). https://econweb.umd.edu/~haltiwan/DHJM_6_2_2014.pdf (visited on March 14, 2025).

20 Ryan A. Decker and John Haltiwanger. *High-Tech Business Entry in the Pandemic Era*. FEDS Notes. 2024-04-19, 2024. https://www.federalreserve.gov/econres/notes/feds-notes/high-tech-business-entry-in-the-pandemic-era-20240419.html (visited on August 7, 2025).

21 Korea offers a cautionary tale. The dominance of conglomerates, particularly Samsung, limits the pool of potential acquirers. A recent report indicates that fewer than half of VC-funded South Korean startups exited through acquisitions in the 2020s, and between a third and half of the exits were through an IPO. See Korea Economic Daily Global. *South Korea Aims to Become Asia's Top Startup Hub with $19 Billion Investment Plan*. Korea Economic Daily Global. 2025-05-30, 2025. https://www.kedglobal.com/venture-capital/newsView/ked202505300002 (visited on August 7, 2025). By comparison, in the United States., over two-thirds or more of such exits are through acquisition, and only 10 per cent or so are through IPOs. See PitchBook. *Early-Stage Acquisitions Powered VC Exits in Most Lucrative Quarter since 2021*. PitchBook News & Analysis. 2025-06, 2025. https://pitchbook.com/news/articles/earlystage-acquisitions-powered-vc-exits-most-lucrative-quarter-since-2021 (visited on August 7, 2025).

22 David Hounshell. "The Evolution of Industrial Research in the United States." Richard Rosenbloom and William Spencer. *Engines of Innovation: U.S. Industrial Research at the End of an Era*. Cambridge, MA: Harvard Business School Press, 1996; David C. Mowery. "The Boundaries of the U.S. Firm in R&D." *Coordination and Information: Historical Perspectives on the Organization of Enterprise*. Ed. by Naomi R. Lamoreaux and Daniel M. G. Raff. Chicago: University of Chicago Press, 1995, pp. 147–182.

[23] Eric Gilliam. *An Alternative Approach to Deep Tech VC.* FreakTakes. 2023. https://www.freaktakes.com/p/an-alternative-approach-to-deep-tech (visited on August 7, 2025).

[24] Mark McGranaghan. *Alt VC Math.* 2024. https://markmcgranaghan.com/altvc-math (visited on August 7, 2025).

[25] Calm Company Fund. *Calm Company Fund. Official Website.* 2025. https://calmfund.com/.

[26] Eric Gilliam. *An Alternative Approach to Deep Tech VC.* 2024. https://www.freaktakes.com/p/an-alternative-approach-to-deep-tech.

[27] Wikipedia contributors. *Harold McMaster.* In Wikipedia. May 4, 2025. https://en.wikipedia.org/wiki/Harold_McMaster?oldid=1288659098.

[28] Grand View Research. *Battery Contract Manufacturing Market Size & Outlook, 2030 (Global Horizon Outlook). Grand View Research website.* 2025. https://www.grandviewresearch.com/horizon/outlook/battery-contract-manufacturing-market-size/global.

[29] National Renewable Energy Laboratory. *Capabilities—ARIES: Advanced Research on Integrated Energy Systems.* National Renewable Energy Laboratory. 2025-06-24, 2025. https://www.nrel.gov/aries/capabilities (visited on August 7, 2025).

[30] Jeffrey Wolf. *How NREL Helps Startups from the Beginning.* January 18, 2024. https://www.nrel.gov/news/detail/features/2024/how-nrel-helps-startups-from-thebeginning (visited on September 20, 2025).

[31] University of Chicago. *AI-driven, Autonomous Lab at Argonne Transforms Materials Discovery.* University of Chicago News. 2025-03-05, 2025. https://news.uchicago.edu/story/ai-driven-autonomous-lab-argonne-transforms-materials-discovery (visited on August 7, 2025).

[32] National Science Foundation. *NSF Invests in Biofoundries to Drive Advances across Science and Engineering.* NSF News. 2024-08-28, 2024. https://www.nsf.gov/news/nsfinvests-biofoundries-drive-advances-across-science (visited on August 5, 2025); Hughes Marino PM. *Biosafety Laboratory Design and Construction: What to Know before You Begin.* Hughes Marino Blog. 2016-04-12, 2016. https://hughesmarino.com/san-diego/blog/2016/04/12/biosafety-laboratory-design-and-construction-what-toknow-before-you-begin/ (visited on August 5, 2025).

[33] GovCIO Media & Research. *NSF Funds 5 Centers to Expand Biotechnology Research.* GovCIO Media. 2024-08-29, 2024. https://govciomedia.com/nsf-funds-5-centersto-expand-biotechnology-research/ (visited on August 7, 2025).

[34] National Renewable Energy Laboratory. *NREL to Lead Grid-forming Inverter Consortium, Streamlining Renewable Integration at All Scales.* NREL Grid Modernization News. 2021-08-31, 2021. https://www.nrel.gov/grid/news/program/2021/nrel-tolead-grid-forming-inverter-consortium (visited on August 7, 2025); Microelectronics Commons. *Commercial Leap Ahead for Wide Bandgap Semiconductors (CLAWS) Hub.* Microelectronics Commons. 2025-06-09, 2025. https://microelectronicscommons.org/connect/commercial-leap-ahead-for-wide-bandgap-semiconductors-claws/ (visited on August 7, 2025).

[35] Chiara Franzoni, Paula Stephan, and Reinhilde Veugelers. "Funding Risky Research." *Entrepreneurship and Innovation Policy and the Economy* 1 (January 1, 2022), pp. 103–133.

[36] Mikko Packalen and Jay Bhattacharya. "NIH Funding and the Pursuit of Edge Science." *Proceedings of the National Academy of Sciences* 117.22 (June 2, 2020), pp. 12011–12016.

[37] Franzoni, Stephan, and Veugelers; see n. 35.

[38] Jacob G. Foster, Andrey Rzhetsky, and James A. Evans. "Tradition and Innovation in Scientists' Research Strategies." *American Sociological Review* 80.5 (October 2015), pp. 875–908.

[39] Jian Wang, Reinhilde Veugelers, and Paula Stephan. "Bias against Novelty in Science: A Cautionary Tale for Users of Bibliometric Indicators." *Research Policy* 46.8 (2017), pp. 1416–1436.

[40] Pierre Azoulay and Wesley H. Greenblatt. *Does Peer Review Penalize Scientific Risk Taking? Evidence from NIH Grant Renewals.* National Bureau of Economic Research, 2025. https://www.nber.org/papers/w33495 (visited on March 14, 2025).

[41] Danielle Li. "Expertise versus Bias in Evaluation: Evidence from the NIH." *American Economic Journal: Applied Economics* 9.2 (2017), pp. 60–92.

[42] Patrick Collison, Patrick Hsu, and Tyler Cowen. *What We Learned Doing Fast Grants.* Future. 2021-06-15, 2021. https://future.a16z.com/what-we-learned-doing-fastgrants (visited on February 7, 2022).

43 Pierre Azoulay, J. Graff Zivin, and Gustavo Manso. "Incentives and Creativity: Evidence from the Howard Hughes Medical Investigator Program." *The RAND Journal of Economics* 42 (2011), pp. 527–554.

44 Eric Gilliam. *A Report on Scientific Branch-creation: How the Rockefeller Foundation Helped Bootstrap the Field of Molecular Biology. FreakTakes [Substack].* January 12, 2023. https://www.freaktakes.com/p/a-report-on-scientific-branch-creation.

45 M. Mitchell Waldrop. *The Dream Machine.* San Francisco: Stripe Press, 2018.

46 Eric Gilliam. *A Category Theory–Inspired BBN. FreakTakes [Substack].* February 28, 2025. https://www.freaktakes.com/p/a-category-theory-inspired-bbn.

47 Ashish Arora, Sharon Belenzon, Larisa C. Cioaca, Lia Sheer, and Hansen Zhang. *The Effect of Public Science on Corporate R&D.* November 2023. https://www.nber.org/papers/w31899 (visited on August 19, 2024). Pre-published.

48 Wesley M. Cohen, Richard R. Nelson, and John P. Walsh. "Links and Impacts: The Influence of Public Research on Industrial R&D." *Management Science* 48.1 (2002), pp. 1–23.

49 National Academy of Inventors. *2024 Top 100 Worldwide Universities Announced by the National Academy of Inventors.* National Academy of Inventors. 2024-06-04, 2024. https://academyofinventors.org/2024-top-100-worldwide-universities-announcedby-the-national-academy-of-inventors/ (visited on August 7, 2025).

50 Association of University Technology Managers. *AUTM 2024 U.S. & Canadian Licensing Survey.* Association of University Technology Managers (AUTM), 2024. https://autm.net/surveys-and-tools/surveys/licensing-survey/2024licensingsurvey.

51 Matt Faherty. *New Science's Report on the NIH.* New Science. 2022. https://newscience.org/nih/ (visited on August 7, 2025).

52 Lasker Foundation. *DNA as the Chemical Substance of Heredity.* Lasker Foundation. 2021. https://laskerfoundation.org/winners/dna-as-the-chemical-substance-ofheredity/ (visited on August 7, 2025).

53 *The New York Times.* "Maclyn McCarty Dies at 93; Pioneer in DNA Research." *The New York Times* (January 6, 2005). https://www.nytimes.com/2005/01/06/obituaries/maclyn-mccarty-dies-at-93-pioneer-in-dna-research.html.

54 Matthew Rafferty. "The Bayh–Dole Act and University Research and Development." *Research Policy* 37.1 (February 1, 2008), pp. 29–40. https://www.sciencedirect.com/science/article/pii/S0048733307002107 (visited on September 15, 2025).

55 *The Economist.* "Innovation's Golden Goose." *The Economist* (December 14, 2002). https://www.economist.com/technology-quarterly/2002/12/14/innovations-goldengoose (visited on August 7, 2025).

56 David C. Mowery, Richard R. Nelson, Bhaven N. Sampat, and Arvids A. Ziedonis. "The Growth of Patenting and Licensing by US Universities: An Assessment of the Effects of the Bayh–Dole Act of 1980." *Research Policy* 30.1 (2001), pp. 99–119.

57 University of Waterloo. *Our IP Policy. Entrepreneurship, University of Waterloo website.* 2025. https://uwaterloo.ca/entrepreneurship/our-ip-policy, The University of Waterloo, well regarded for its engineering excellence, assigns the rights to the individual researchers.

58 Anne-Marie Mazza and Stephen A. Merrill. *Managing University Intellectual Property in the Public Interest.* National Academies Press, 2011, Chapter 4.

59 Erika Färnstrand Damsgaard and Marie C. Thursby. "University Entrepreneurship and Professor Privilege." *Industrial and Corporate Change* 22.1 (2013), pp. 183–218.

60 Cyclotron Road, Lawrence Berkeley National Laboratory. *About Us. Cyclotron Road website.* 2025. https://cyclotronroad.lbl.gov/about-us/.

61 Cyclotron Road, Lawrence Berkeley National Laboratory. *Cyclotron Road Companies Exceed $3 billion in Follow-on Funding. Cyclotron Road website.* December 2024. https://cyclotronroad.lbl.gov/2024/12/17/cyclotron-road-companies-exceed-3-billionin-follow-on-funding/.

62 J. S. Hallet. "The Uk's $1-Billion Bet to Create Technologies That Change the World." *Nature* 633 (2024), p. 19.

63 Ben Reinhardt. *Unbundling the University. Unbundling the University website.* February 2025. https://www.unbundle-the-university.com/#changes-to-the-researchecosystem-are-bottlenecked-by-where-the-work-is-done.

[64] Convergent Research. *FRO Portfolio. Convergent Research website.* 2025. https://www.convergentresearch.org/fro-portfolio.

[65] Caleb Watney. *Launching X-labs for Transformative Science Funding. Frontier Science & Technology, Techno-Industrial Policy Playbook, Rebuilding Tech.* May 2025. https://www.rebuilding.tech/posts/launching-x-labs-for-transformative-science-funding.

[66] Zvi Griliches. "Hybrid Corn: An Exploration in the Economics of Technological Change." *Econometrica, Journal of the Econometric Society* (1957), pp. 501–522.

[67] Cohen, Nelson, and Walsh; see n. 48.

[68] Bhaven N. Sampat and Frank R. Lichtenberg. "What Are the Respective Roles of the Public and Private Sectors In Pharmaceutical Innovation?": *Health Affairs* 30.2 (February 2011), pp. 332–339.

[69] Iain M. Cockburn and Rebecca M. Henderson. "Publicly Funded Science and the Productivity of the Pharmaceutical Industry." *Innovation Policy and the Economy* 1 (January 2000), pp. 1–34.

Index

Tables and figures are indicated by an italic *t* and *f* following the page number

E

Q